1 SAMUEL AS CHRISTIAN SCRIPTURE

A Theological Commentary

Stephen B. Chapman

WILLIAM B. EERDMANS PUBLISHING COMPANY

GRAND RAPIDS, MICHIGAN

41.85

OCLC# 921167314

Published 2016 by
Wm. B. Eerdmans Publishing Co.
2140 Oak Industrial Drive N.E., Grand Rapids, Michigan 49505

www.eerdmans.com

Printed in the United States of America

22 21 20 19 18 17 16   7 6 5 4 3 2 1

Library of Congress Cataloging-in-Publication Data

Names: Chapman, Stephen B., 1962- author.
Title: 1 Samuel as Christian scripture: a theological commentary /
Stephen B. Chapman.
Description: Grand Rapids, Michigan: Eerdmans Pub. Company, 2016. |
Includes bibliographical references and indexes.
Identifiers: LCCN 2015040450 | ISBN 9780802837455 (pbk.: alk. paper)
Subjects: LCSH: Bible. Samuel, 1st—Theology.
Classification: LCC BS1325.52 .C43 2016 | DDC 222/.4307—dc23
LC record available at http://lccn.loc.gov/2015040450

All abbreviations in this volume follow *The SBL Handbook of Style* (2nd ed.).

To Laceye, Gaston, and Clare

Contents

Acknowledgments

I am deeply grateful to Jon Pott and Eerdmans for their willingness to take on this project, especially as a stand-alone volume and not as a commentary in a series. Many people have contributed to the outcome, especially several colleagues at Duke and the students who gamely signed up for Hebrew and English exegesis classes on the book of 1 Samuel over the course of several years. In particular I would like to thank James Crenshaw, Ellen Davis, Curtis Freeman, Amy Laura Hall, Stanley Hauerwas, Richard Hays, Reinhard Hütter, Carol and Eric Meyers, Kavin Rowe, Allen Verhey, Lauren Winner, and Will Willimon for their conversations, questions and ideas. The staff members of the Duke Divinity Library were unfailingly helpful as I conducted my research.

Laceye and Gaston Warner deserve special acknowledgment for the generosity of their friendship to me. This book is dedicated to them and to their daughter, my miraculous godchild Clare.

Introduction

Soon it will have gone so far that people must make use of art in the most various ways to help get Christendom to show at least some sympathy with Christianity. But if art is going to help, be it the art of the sculptor, the art of the orator, the art of the poet, we will have at most admirers who, besides admiring the artist, are led by his presentations to admire what is Christian. But, strictly speaking, the admirer is indeed no true Christian; only the imitator is that.[1]

We do not need much more by way of prolegomena to exegesis; we do need more exegesis.[2]

Remember Jesus Christ, raised from the dead, a descendant of David — that is my gospel.[3]

This volume is a theological commentary, or even better a theological reading. My aim is to exposit the biblical book of 1 Samuel — not to comment on every aspect of this fascinating text, but to describe its center of gravity and its thrust, to make an argument about its narrative logic and focus.

Many fine commentaries on 1 Samuel already exist — quite a few of them appear in the notes and bibliography of this volume — and I am deeply indebted to them for all that I have learned in their pages. However, I have also become increasingly worried about the commentary format as it has evolved

---

1. Kierkegaard, *Practice in Christianity*, pp. 256-57.
2. Webster, *Domain of the Word*, p. 30.
3. 2 Tim 2:8.

within the discipline of biblical studies. What is a biblical commentary supposed to do? What is it for?[4] To borrow from A. E. Housman, the ground covered in a typical commentary often seems like "labour bestowed upon the circumference and not the centre of its subject."[5] Too many commentaries become preoccupied with preparatory matters and never proceed to the work at hand. The chief purpose of a commentary should instead be precisely to convey what a biblical book is centrally *about*.

Traditionally, a commentary has provided a fresh translation of a particular biblical text, treated text-critical and linguistic issues, established the historical background of the events to which the text refers, reconstructed the circumstances of the text's literary development, offered an explication of the text according to certain interpretive guidelines, and isolated particular themes or lessons that are said to represent the text's abiding meaning. Within Christian Old Testament scholarship additional challenges exist in the interpretive dimension to this work because of the historical and conceptual distance between Israelite religion and Christian doctrine. The commendable goal of honoring the historical situatedness of Old Testament texts, respecting Judaism's right to these scriptures as its own, has led to impressively "ecumenical" commentaries and commentary series. Yet these modern moves have also pushed Old Testament commentaries to venture far less in the way of concrete theological interpretation, to dwell on historical and linguistic minutiae, to deal in abstractions, and to say little that is specifically Christian.[6] Although

---

4. More and more scholars have been asking these questions. See Alter, "Literary Criticism"; Barr, "Exegesis as a Theological Discipline"; Barton, "On Biblical Commentaries"; Bruner, "How and Why of Commentary"; Childs, "Interpretation in Faith"; idem, "Genre of the Biblical Commentary"; Coggins, "A Future for the Commentary?"; Froehlich, "Bibelkommentar"; Gordis, "Observations on Problems and Methods"; Green, "Commentary"; Greenberg, "To Whom and for What"; Hagan, "What Did the Term *commentarius* Mean?"; Heringer, "Practice of Theological Commentary"; Koskie, "Seeking Comment"; Moberly, "On Theological Commentary"; Nolland, "The Purpose and Value of Commentaries"; Rowe and Hays, "What Is a Theological Commentary?"; Zenger, "Was sind Essentials?" See also the articles on this theme by Mordechai Cogan, Moshe Greenberg, Rolf Rendtorff, and Gordon J. Wenham in *Proceedings of the Tenth World Congress of Jewish Studies, Jerusalem 16-24, 1989* (Jerusalem: World Union of Jewish Studies, 1990).

5. As quoted in Naiditch, *A. E. Housman at University College London*, p. 206.

6. Another marker of the present dilemma is that some practitioners actually celebrate these aspects of modern commentaries. See, e.g., Carroll, *From Chaos to Covenant*, p. 273: "A straining after contemporary relevance in biblical studies seems to me to be a misguided way of handling the Bible." Contrast the more compelling view of Gorman, *Elements of Biblical Exegesis*, pp. 139-40: "Great works of art (including religious literature) inescapably invite engagement. They have an inherent capacity to inspire the imagination and to create new possibilities for thinking and living."

this range of problems has already spurred the creation of newer commentary series seeking a more robust theological alternative, as well as the inauguration of other series aiming to retrieve venerable theological interpretations from church tradition,[7] the success of these series is so far mixed.

A more subtle aspect of the present difficulty is that commentary series often stipulate a particular form of organization for their individual volumes. While the commentary format almost always reads "with" the biblical text literarily from beginning to end, it also typically divides the text into a series of manageable units, providing some type of "theological reflection" at the conclusion of each one. At its best, this manner of proceeding discloses the rich complexity of the biblical text and reminds readers that every portion of it has something meaningful to say. The smaller, individual units are also helpful for preachers and teachers within the church, where texts are often usefully explored in shorter sections.

Yet this format can ride roughshod over the literary presentation of a biblical book and what might be called its anticipated strategy for reading. That is, all writers assume — sometimes intentionally, sometimes unintentionally — that what they write will be read in a particular fashion. They write to communicate, so they want their readers to understand. Of course, an author's mind is inaccessible to us, especially the mind of an author who lived as long ago as the writer of a biblical text.[8] But authors, including the biblical writers, encode their expectations (intentionally and unintentionally) for how the work will be read into the work itself.[9] The point is that biblical writers often appear to have anticipated that their writings would be encountered differently from how modern commentaries present them. In narrative texts especially, the use of literary motifs, gaps, and echoes indicates not just the possibility of a more literary approach within contemporary biblical interpretation, but in fact the anticipated desirability of that interpretive approach on the part of those texts' ancient tradents. (By the term "tradents" I mean to include the later editors of the biblical literature as well as the texts' original, often multiple, authors.)

Indeed, the narrative texts of the Old Testament *rely* on a different form of

---

7. Examples of theologically oriented commentary series are, e.g., Belief: A Theological Commentary on the Bible (Westminster John Knox); Brazos Theological Commentary on the Bible (Brazos/Baker); Interpretation (Westminster John Knox); The Two Horizons Old Testament Commentary (Eerdmans). For series focusing on the history of interpretation, see Ancient Christian Commentary on Scripture (InterVarsity); Blackwell Bible Commentaries (Oxford); The Church's Bible (Eerdmans).

8. Watson, "Authorial Intention."

9. For another exploration of this dimension of the biblical literature, see Bockmuehl, *Seeing the Word*, pp. 68-69, 108.

reading and interpretation from that which has become customary in biblical commentaries. Of course, the past can never be recaptured. But the strength of newer literary approaches to the Old Testament appears more clearly when considered from the stance of the biblical text's implied reader.[10] By remaining relatively independent of the commentary format, literary approaches have had greater flexibility to explore certain features of biblical books, especially narrative texts, which had otherwise become attenuated or occluded. Yet although these approaches have in general been highly stimulating (usually resulting in much more interesting "reads" than the standard commentaries in the standard series), their advocates have also tended in turn to isolate individual books from their wider canonical context. Moreover, those advancing a literary approach have at times offered readings that depend upon suspect historical premises — although they typically deny any necessary historical basis to their interpretations — and they have regularly exhibited detachment from or antipathy toward theological concerns, especially in the ways those concerns assume a Christian form.

My goal in this volume is therefore to explore a substantially different approach to one particular narrative book of the Old Testament by offering a theological reading of it rather than a commentary per se. My reading is constructed upon the basis of the same careful historical and linguistic work found in biblical commentaries, but such work generally appears in the notes and is not always argued in the main text. In fact, one of the most challenging aspects of this project has been the pressing need to condense my own comments about the biblical text, so that the reading I offer possesses concrete shape, sustained engagement with identifiable themes, and rhetorical force. That has meant repeatedly deciding what *not* to write about. Because reading well means taking into full account the nature of the literature being read, I have also found it crucial not to begin with a number of working assumptions in biblical studies, but to probe anew into the nature of Old Testament literature and to explore the implications of my findings for the interpretive task at hand. Lastly, since the primary goal of this reading is theological, I have dared to pose explicitly Christian questions and consider explicitly Christian responses in my reflections on the biblical text. John Webster has trenchantly observed that Jesus has "virtually disappeared" in modern theological hermeneutics.[11] By contrast I have tried to proceed in a manner that does justice to the Christian belief that the books of the Old Testament were written also "for our instruction" (Rom 4:23-25; 15:4; 1 Cor 9:10), even as I have simultaneously

---

10. See further Briggs, *The Virtuous Reader*.
11. Webster, *Word and Church*, p. 48.

worked according to the conviction that one cannot move too quickly from the Old Testament to Christian language, concepts, and doctrine.[12]

There are crucial *theological* reasons not to move too quickly from the one to the other. First, although orthodox Christian tradition has always affirmed the identity between "God" in the Old Testament and "God" in the New, and thus the implicit presence of the Trinity in both Testaments, Christians have also always recognized the writings of the Old Testament as at the same time somehow "pre-Christian."[13] In other words, the Old Testament existed in a recognizable form (if not in an absolutely delimited canon) prior to the birth of Jesus, whose death and resurrection were viewed by his followers precisely as the Old Testament's fulfillment. Even while Christians have at times interpreted certain Old Testament passages as referring directly to Jesus or the Trinity, they have also perceived a shift over the course of the entire Christian Bible in the valence of these realities. Something *changes* with the birth of Christ. Even if the "economic" Trinity is judged to be identical with the "immanent" Trinity, following the influential "axiom" of Karl Rahner,[14] the economic aspect to the Trinity cannot be eliminated without doing violence to scripture's portrayal of God.[15] An unfolding of God's own nature is presented within the framework of the entire Christian Bible.[16] A powerful argument for this unfolding — not frequently enough acknowledged — comes from the

---

12. Cf. the similar judgment of Bonhoeffer, *Letters and Papers from Prison*, p. 79. For further discussion of Bonhoeffer's approach to the Old Testament, see Kuske, *The Old Testament as the Book of Christ*.

13. For this formulation in reference to the Old Testament, see Childs, *Old Testament Theology*, p. 9: "the Old Testament functions within Christian scripture as a witness to Jesus Christ precisely in its pre-Christian form. The task of Old Testament theology is, therefore, not to Christianize the Old Testament by identifying it with the New Testament witness, but to hear its own theological testimony to the God of Israel whom the church confesses also to worship."

14. Rahner, *The Trinity*, p. 22; cf. Barth, *Church Dogmatics I/1*, p. 333. For further theological evaluation, see Jüngel, "Das Verhältnis von 'ökonomischer' und 'immanenter' Theologie"; Holzer, "Karl Rahner, Hans Urs von Balthasar."

15. The economic dimension of the Trinity is real and critical to the witness of the New Testament as well as the Old: thus the Son lacks the eschatological knowledge of the Father (Mark 13:32); Jesus thought the end would occur within "this generation" (Mark 13:30).

16. For some hesitation with regard to Rahner's rule, see Placher, *The Triune God*, pp. 138-39: "we can neither infer back from what has been revealed of the economic Trinity to any detailed analysis of the immanent Trinity nor claim to have enough understanding of the immanent Trinity to infer from it the realities of the economic Trinity had we not encountered them." Placher also locates the ultimate grammar for immanent Trinitarian relations in the scriptural account of the economic Trinity. Thus the persons of the Trinity, although all coequal, have always been best identified by their place within the biblical story: God as uncreated Creator, the Son as born of the Father, the Spirit proceeding from the Father (and

side of christological doctrine: the earthly Jesus respected and did not efface the historical boundaries and limitations within which he lived and worked. In other words, Christ himself observed some sort of distinction between his divine nature and his own earthly existence (e.g., Mark 13:32). *God* does not change — that would be saying too much. God does not *become* triune in the process of revelation but is so "beforehand in Himself."[17] Nevertheless, in the incarnation of Christ something profound is nevertheless altered in the relation between God, on the one hand, and time, history, and the world, on the other. The ancient creeds of the church preserve and insist on this narrative shape to God's identity as well: God is what God does, just as God does what God is.

As with the Trinity specifically, so too Christian Old Testament interpretation more broadly possesses the characteristically double task of detailing theological continuity and discontinuity between the witness of the Old Testament and the substance of Christian faith. Specific elements of continuity and discontinuity are often not immediately plain but must be approached thoughtfully, patiently, and always in prayerful reflection upon the subject matter of scripture as a whole: what scripture, as the entire Christian Bible, is finally about.

The second reason not to move too quickly from the Old Testament to Christian theological description is related to the first. By establishing the canonical format of Christian scripture as one Bible in two testaments, the Church simultaneously proclaimed both that the Old Testament *had* a "Christian" witness *and* that its "pre-Christian" form had lasting theological significance. Of central importance, as Adolf von Harnack once observed, was that the Christian church recognized the authority of the Old Testament *as it was*, without the interpolation of Christian commentary into the biblical text, the interspersing of Old and New Testament books or some other editorial strategy.[18] To be sure, Gentile Christians overwhelmingly knew and used the Old Testament writings in Greek, and they read these writings through the light of their Christian experience. The writers of the New Testament heard the Old Testament as speaking directly of Christian realities. Yet, with some exceptions, even the Greek Old Testament (as the Septuagint or LXX) was

---

the Son). These descriptions are but shorthand expressions of scripture's full grammar and they preserve in brief the narrative shape of scripture in explicating the nature of the Trinity.

17. This felicitous phrase is used by Barth, *CD I/1*, pp. 390, 420, 467. But see also Jüngel, *God's Being Is in Becoming.* For a concise summary of Barth's position on the Trinity, see Busch, *Barth,* pp. 33-38.

18. Von Harnack, "Appendix 2." More recently, see Dohmen and Stemberger, *Hermeneutik der jüdischen Bibel.*

received as a preexistent authority by early Christians,[19] *not* subjected to significant editorial reworking,[20] and acknowledged — sometimes grudgingly — to have been Jewish scripture before it was Christian. That the Old Testament canon may still have been without hard and fixed boundaries into the early centuries of the church made little difference, if any, to its authority for most Christians.[21] From the very beginning of the Christian tradition, the Old Testament represented an identifiable corpus of sacred Jewish writings conveying holy truths of the faith.[22] One has only to register the force of the New Testament phrases "(as) it is written" (Matt 2:5; 4:4, and *passim*) and "in accordance with the scripture(s)" (1 Cor 15:3, 4; 2 Cor 4:13) to see how the Old Testament's religious authority was already firmly in place.

A third reason to linger with the Old Testament's pre-Christian form is that Christian approaches to it have always gone hand in hand with Christian attitudes toward Judaism. It is no accident that supersessionist theology (according to which the church decisively *replaced* the synagogue in God's affections), long prevalent within church history, has borne anti-Semitic fruit and made the church complicit in genocide.[23] Once there is no longer any rationale for Jewish *faith* within Christian theology, only a shockingly small step is necessary to conclude that there is no longer any rationale for Jewish *life*.[24] The

---

19. For a convenient description of notable exceptions (Marcion, etc.), see Ehrmann, *Lost Christianities*, pp. 103-9, 143-48.

20. Flint, "Noncanonical Writings," p. 83, notes that "virtually all" the books now known as Apocrypha and Pseudepigrapha, some of which were considered part of the Greek Old Testament by early Christians, exhibit Christian alteration and interpolation. However, this phenomenon is not evidence for the Old Testament's lack of authority, but of a distinction that has existed from the beginning between the deuterocanonical books and the books of the narrower canon, which overwhelmingly did *not* experience Christian editing.

21. See further McDonald, *The Biblical Canon*, pp. 208-9.

22. Von Campenhausen, *The Formation of the Christian Bible*; Chapman, "Old Testament Canon."

23. Sometimes the term "supersessionism" is used more broadly. Here I do not have in mind the basic Christian claim of being right that Jesus is the Messiah (which I do not view as necessarily "supersessionistic"), but the further claim that therefore Jewish believers have been rejected by God. For further discussion, see Soulen, *The God of Israel and Christian Theology*, pp. 1-18. Note, however, the judicious warning against drawing such a distinction too easily by Levenson, "Is There a Counterpart?" p. 244, "The distinction between anti-Judaism and Antisemitism is real, but so is the historical connection between them." On some forms of supersessionism as not necessarily objectionable from a Jewish perspective, see Novak, "What Does Edith Stein Mean for Jews?" p. 164; Pawlikowsky, *The Challenge of the Holocaust*.

24. Some may object that this attribution of Christian responsibility for the Holocaust is too strong. Much more could (and would need to) be said for a complete response, but consider this statement from Martin Niemöller's "Not und Aufgabe der Kirche in Deutschland," as cited

Shoah, that horrifying lesson from history, not only dictates an urgent need for increased Christian attention to Christian–Jewish dialogue, it also constitutes a dilemma internal to Christian theology. How could Christian theology, for centuries, have been so blind as to underwrite anti-Jewish prejudice, pogroms, and the Holocaust? One major reason for it, I am convinced, has to do with the treatment of Jews and Judaism in Christian biblical interpretation.[25]

Several long strides forward have been made of late in New Testament scholarship, with a reenvisioning of Paul,[26] a recognition that early Christianity functioned basically as a sect within Judaism for quite some time before "the parting of the ways,"[27] and a re-appraising exegesis of a number of specific texts that had traditionally been used to support the rejection of Israel "after the flesh."[28] Old Testament scholarship has responded to the same challenge by emphasizing how the Old Testament does not "lean" toward Christianity[29]

in Gutteridge, *Open Thy Mouth for the Dumb!* p. 304: "Christianity in Germany bears a greater responsibility before God than the National Socialists, the SS and the Gestapo. We ought to have recognized the Lord Jesus in the brother who suffered and was persecuted despite him being a communist or a Jew. Are not we Christians much more to blame, am I not much more guilty, than many who bathed their hands in blood?" Compare Elie Wiesel's reflections in Abrahamson, ed., *Against Silence*, p. 33: "All the killers were Christian . . . The Nazi system was the consequence of a movement of ideas and followed a strict logic; it did not arise in a void but had its roots deep in a tradition that prophesied it, prepared for it, and brought it to maturity. That tradition was inseparable from the past Christian civilized Europe." However, for Jewish resistance to any simplistic equation between Christianity and Nazism, see Novak, "What Does Edith Stein Mean for Jews?" pp. 148-50.

25. On the historical point, see Gerdmar, *Roots of Theological Anti-Semitism*; Manuel, *The Broken Staff*; Newman, "Death of Judaism in German Protestant Thought"; Siegele-Wenschkewitz, ed., *Christlicher Antijudaismus und Antisemitismus*. By contrast, a robust reading of the Old Testament as scripture within the French Protestant community at Le Chambon-sur-Lignon appears to have been one of the reasons for its willingness to harbor Jewish refugees during World War II; see Hallie, *Lest Innocent Blood Be Shed*. For a constructive theological proposal in the direction of a promising alternative, see the Pontifical Biblical Commission statement, *The Jewish People and Their Sacred Scriptures in the Christian Bible*. For analysis and criticism of this document, see Bockmuehl, "Jewish People and Their Sacred Scriptures"; Farkasfalvy, "Pontifical Biblical Commission's Document"; Hütter, "'In': Some Incipient Reflections"; Kereszty, "Jewish-Christian Dialogue"; Wansbrough, "Jewish People and Its Holy Scripture."

26. Sanders, *Paul and Palestinian Judaism*.

27. Dunn, ed., *Jews and Christians*.

28. See Levine, *The Misunderstood Jew*; Sanders, *Jesus and Judaism*.

29. Childs, "Interpretation in Faith," p. 448. With this stance Childs is arguing against the position of Gerhard von Rad, who supported the idea of such a "leaning" in his appeal to the history of tradition as linking both testaments. Childs did not reject the notion that both testaments were connected, but he emphasized more strongly than von Rad the radical newness of the gospel, which could not be construed merely as a "next logical step" within the

but rather opens out into the twin traditions of Christianity and Judaism, *both* of which discard certain aspects of Israelite religion and preserve others.[30] Indeed, when viewed from the vantage point of the history of biblical interpretation, Christians and Jews have always been interpretive partners, even when disagreeing with each other.[31]

So another reason to proceed slowly with the Old Testament text is to listen *with* Judaism as much as possible, to preserve our points of contact with each other for as long as possible before we must differ, to learn from the genuine insights into the biblical text and the nature of God offered by Jewish readers, and to move toward a Christian understanding of Old Testament texts that no longer contributes to the spiritual dispossession of Judaism or the killing of Jews. Although my book has an explicitly Christian goal, I therefore hope that it will have Jewish as well as Christian readers. Rather than offering a "lowest common denominator" account of theological interpretation that is perhaps initially more palatable to adherents of both faiths, I write here out of my own Christian particularity — also in contrast to other commentaries' frequent preference for religious abstractions — and I trust that the depth and complexity such particularity brings to the interpretive task will reach even readers whose specific religious commitments differ from my own. This hope is also true for non-religious readers, who of course possess their own commitments as well.

Finally, there is a theological concern underlying these others that also calls for critical attentiveness and the painstaking, judicious reading of the Old Testament text. This concern is simply to read *well*, but then again there is nothing "simple" about that. With the frenetic pace of modern life and the visual orientation of the communications media with which many people now predominantly interact, few things are more challenging — or more vital — than learning how to read slowly and *build* toward an interpretation, as it were, from the inside out.[32] I believe this challenge extends throughout modern society, especially in the United States, where the cultural impact of television, video games, movies, and the internet is surprising even to visiting citizens from other technologically advanced nations. I worry that such

biblical tradition. In other words, Childs's rejection of any "leaning" is actually made primarily on theological rather than historical grounds. For another rejection of von Rad's position and a different proposal regarding the way to move from the Old Testament to the New, see Janowski, "One God of the Two Testaments."

30. See further Dohmen and Mussner, *Nur die halbe Wahrheit?*; Koch, "Der doppelter Ausgang des Alten Testaments"; Zenger, *Das Erste Testament.*

31. Bockmuehl, *Seeing the Word*, p. 226.

32. Cf. Newkirk, *The Art of Slow Reading.*

visual media do not encourage complex interpretive skills but merely dispose viewers toward a basic choice between acceptance or rejection, watching or not watching.[33] When this posture is applied to reading, the response of the visually conditioned reader becomes similar: to agree or disagree, to approve or disapprove, to like or not like. The result is woodenly literal reading, in which nuance and irony often pass unnoticed and taste substitutes for imagination. By reducing the agency of the interpreter and impoverishing the interpretive dimension of culture, representative democracy is threatened and the potential for totalitarian political structures gravely enhanced.[34]

The alternative (and thank goodness some people still know how to do it) is to pay attention to *how* texts are written as well as to what they say — to notice in fact that the "how" contributes to the "what" of their saying. In this kind of interpretive practice, a reader will notice a rich word or turn of phrase from a poem or a novel, roll it around on the tongue several times, perhaps use it in conversation with others, and commit it to memory. The word or phrase then becomes part of the reader's lived reality. In fact, such a reader will progressively inhabit the world envisioned by the text, living into it, considering both its similarities to and differences from the world as the reader has previously known and experienced it. Such reading is not only a cultural desideratum but a theological imperative. In Jewish and Christian tradition, reading the Bible has always involved meditating on its words as if each and every one stood ready to disclose a divine message. The designation of a biblical canon established an identifiable literary space in which God's word for the present could be confidently expected and reliably sought. By not reading scripture at all, or by reading scripture without the attentiveness to individual words and phrases that so richly repaid former generations of the faithful, contemporary Christians shortchange their understanding of the gospel and hobble their effectiveness in the world. True of Bible reading generally, the need for loving attentiveness and humble, patient interrogation is especially

---

33. For other, more positive, thoughts about the impact of popular visual media on biblical interpretation, see Aichele, *The Control of Biblical Meaning*. I still have my doubts.

34. See Prothero, *Religious Literacy*, pp. 8-10. While Prothero also connects religious illiteracy to a lack of familiarity with key (scriptural) narratives (p. 14), he does not criticize the popular visual media of contemporary culture. However, he does note the ineffectiveness of "BibleZines" in increasing knowledge of the Bible (p. 36). Certainly there exist some hopeful aspects in popular visual media. At its best the internet represents a move in the direction of more inclusive social discussion (e.g., a global reach of news and information, decentralized and multiperspectival reporting, etc.); so, too, some television shows, movies, and even video games are better at inculcating critical discernment than others. For acute criticism of Prothero's conception of literacy and his presentation of the issues at stake, see Avalos, "Is Biblical Illiteracy a Bad Thing?"

true of the Old Testament, which continues to be overshadowed by the New in the lectionary readings and homiletical practice of Christian communities.[35]

I am persuaded that there are crucial theological resources in the books of the Old Testament that today's church badly needs but is not readily receiving, because the church does not attend to these texts as it could. I have therefore written this volume as a modest illustration of how one might approach a particular Old Testament book, lingering in its narrative world while at the same time peering in the direction of Christian theology. The volume can therefore also be considered a probe in the direction of what is variously termed "Old Testament theology," "biblical theology," or "theological interpretation."[36] My goal is not to offer the "correct" Christian interpretation of an Old Testament book; I do not think such a thing exists, although I do consider some interpretations better than others. Multiple readings are possible and faithful in their variety, so long as they lie within the parameters established by the narrative itself. (Yes, I do still think narratives provide interpretive parameters.) But rather than offering "the" Christian reading of 1 Samuel, I hope instead to provide only one way of reading this rich and subtle Old Testament book — a way of reading it that honors its historical integrity and literary complexity, while also listening expectantly for how it addresses, confronts, confirms, and deepens a Christian understanding of life before God. As will become evident, my approach characteristically treats biblical narrative as posing and negotiating what are essentially theological questions.

Why 1 Samuel? As I discuss in greater detail in the first chapter, I have selected this Old Testament book primarily because it offers a remarkably supple and sophisticated literary narrative. Older Romantic-era descriptions of Old Testament narrative as "primitive" and historical-critical claims of haphazard editing cannot be sustained when confronted with this particular narrative's intricate literary artistry. First Samuel also possesses a complicated history of literary development, which poses instructive textual problems and clarifies

---

35. While use of the Common Lectionary brought greater attention to the Old Testament in many churches, it still left out 80% of the Old Testament. See Olson, "Rediscovering Lost Treasure." An effort was made to adjust this percentage downward in the production of the Revised Common Lectionary, released in 1994, but great swaths of the Old Testament are still absent (now 70-75%?). Fortunately several Samuel texts are included, especially after Pentecost in Year B, which provides yet another reason for a theological commentary on this particular Old Testament book. Black church tradition has long been a noteworthy and inspiring exception to the neglect of the Old Testament in American church life, but I regularly hear now from students that the Old Testament no longer receives the attention it once did even in black churches.

36. On these terms and their implications in current debates, see Treier, "Biblical Theology and/or Theological Interpretation of Scripture?"

certain basic methodological choices. Indeed, modern translations of 1 Samuel have increasingly become composite or "eclectic" texts presenting novel "remixes" of ancient witnesses. There are good reasons for it: the Hebrew text of Samuel is of poorer quality than many other biblical texts,[37] and the Dead Sea Scrolls have confirmed that the Hebrew text (= 4QSam^a or 4Q51) behind one of the book's previously known Greek forms may well be older in some cases than the tradition represented by the Masoretic Text (MT).[38] But when ancient versions are thoroughly reconstructed or extensively mixed within a single translation, the end result is neither fish nor fowl. Assumptions about the text's meaning are already being used in translational decisions, muddying the book's theological profile.

This problem is compounded by a pervasive confusion between historical investigation and theological interpretation, so that "reading" 1 Samuel all too often becomes not reading 1 Samuel at all, but hypothetically reconstructing a "historical" story behind the biblical narrative. In what follows I want to show what it means to eschew such a mode of proceeding in order to read the received text of 1 Samuel *as scripture*. Literary texts are not only historical artifacts; they have their own logic and coherence as "works" and cannot adequately be described as simply the residue of cultural forces or the negotiated settlement of competing political factions. Although much intriguing study of 1 Samuel has been done along literary lines already, these previous investigations have not been much interested in Christian theology and their findings have remained largely separate from exegetical discussions. I want not only to engage this body of literary scholarship but to negotiate between its insights into 1 Samuel and historical-critical accounts of the book. In other words, I hope to explore how literary methods can assist in the retrieval of what might be termed a classical Christian hermeneutic.[39] Moreover, 1 Samuel in particular contains fundamental theological difficulties that compel a considered response — chiefly the problem of Saul and his rejection, but also the nationalistic elements of the royal Davidic tradition.

Another reason for choosing 1 Samuel is more personal but perhaps also instructive. In the spring of 1991, while I was a student at Yale, I took a course on 1 Samuel offered by Ellen Davis. That course fired my own readerly imagination

---

37. Barthélemy, "La qualité du Texte Masorétique de Samuel."

38. For an overview of the textual situation, see Aejmelaeus, "Septuagint of 1 Samuel"; Cross et al., eds., DJD 17; Hugo, "Text History of the Books of Samuel"; Parry, "Challenge of 4QSam^a and the Canon"; Pisano, *Additions or Omissions in the Books of Samuel*; Ulrich, "A Qualitative Assessment of the Textual Profile of 4QSam^a."

39. For a description of such a hermeneutic, see Lindbeck, "Scripture, Consensus and Community."

and gave me a glimmer of an approach to the book, one which I have pursued ever since. Interestingly enough, two other students in that course, Judy Fentress-Williams and Roy Heller, have already produced book-length treatments of 1 Samuel.[40] Clearly, the electricity in the air of that exegetical seminar was widely shared. I have continued to learn much from Judy and Roy, and from their fine work. Prof. Davis, now my esteemed colleague at Duke Divinity School, has good-naturedly threatened on occasion to retaliate with her own book on 1 Samuel, something that I am sure the rest of us would be only too glad to welcome. What is instructive in this regard is the deep connection between exegetical insights, communities of engaged readers and interpretive mentoring. I suspect that many of us in the academy pursue topics that skillful teachers first brought to our attention. In fact, many of us first consider going into our chosen fields of inquiry, I wager, because a cherished teacher inspired us to do so. The roots of this book ultimately lie in the stimulating conversations shared — and the friendly arguments exchanged — in that 1991 class at Yale under Ellen Davis's expert tutelage.

My book, like Caesar's Gaul, is divided into three parts. In the first section I ask questions about what kind of book 1 Samuel is, since the answers to such questions go a long way toward determining the best method to use in reading it. In this section I discuss the notion of a biblical "book" and the nature of the contributions that literary approaches can make to biblical exegesis generally. Throughout my exposition of 1 Samuel I use the present tense to indicate that I am primarily concerned with the story rather than historical reconstruction, a rhetorical practice I wish to model for other theological readers and preachers. Because 1 and 2 Samuel originally formed a single literary work, and because the nature of 1 Samuel involves a high level of ambiguity and "gapping"[41] (employing what I call a "retrospective" narrative technique), I further argue that it is first necessary to consider 2 Samuel, especially its conclusion in 2 Samuel

---

40. Fentress-Williams, *"What Has Happened to the Son of Kish?"*; Heller, *Power, Politics, and Prophecy.*

41. On narrative "gaps" generally, see Iser, *The Act of Reading*, pp. 164-70. Some narratives withhold or appear to withhold information that is needed by the reader in order to render judgments about its characters and their actions. For evaluation of Iser, see Schwáb, "Mind the Gap." For gaps as a characteristic feature of biblical narrative, see Berlin, "Point of View in Biblical Narrative." Meir Sternberg, *The Poetics of Biblical Narrative*, pp. 186-229, seems to want to restrict gaps to discontinuities in narrative order. However, Jerome T. Walsh argues for a wider application in his *Old Testament Narrative*, pp. 65-80, esp. p. 76: "Gaps and ambiguities require the reader to consider multiple possibilities for understanding a text." The nature of gaps is complicated — but also clarified — by the critical recognition of a distinction between "gaps" and "blanks." "Blanks" are "gaps" that are insignificant for interpretation; in other words, not all silences are as significant for interpreting the text in line with its own projected program of reading.

21–24, in order to adjudicate interpretive questions in 1 Samuel successfully. Only once this conclusion is in view and applied "backwards" can one return to 1 Samuel and read "forward" with insight and full comprehension. I refer to this hermeneutical procedure as "reading in two directions." As I discuss in my final chapter, this approach does not seem to be different in kind from a Christian reading of the Old Testament, which attempts to read both toward Christ and "back from" Christ simultaneously.

In the second part of this book I turn to 1 Samuel itself and offer an extended close reading of the narrative. In this reading I concentrate on working toward a literary sense of the text as a whole and largely postpone introducing specifically Christian questions and concerns. The focus is rather on developing the full meaning of the narrative and being as open as possible to the chance that what is said in this Old Testament book will prove continuous with Christian understanding. I have tried to offer an approachable reading that could in some sense stand apart from the methodological and historical concerns addressed in the first and third sections of this volume, so that, even in isolation, the second section in particular might be of practical use to pastors and teachers in the work of preaching and teaching within local church communities. I admit that I proceed at this point as most commentaries do — dividing up the text into broadly manageable units — but I do not attempt to synthesize Christian theological applications for each section of the book as it is treated. In my view that kind of sectional approach tends to become a series of repeatedly premature foreclosures of the narrative's overarching trajectory.

So I endeavor to read along the grain of the book in its received form, using the MT as my base text. This privileging of the MT constitutes an effort to interpret a text that exists as such, rather than a hypothetical text or a reconstructed history. I want to be clear that I do not necessarily presume the historical priority of the MT, and I do not shy away from adapting it at points. However, it should be noted how one major study has recently concluded that the textual tradition represented by the LXX and 4QSam[a] is expansionistic, indicating "further literary activity" *away* from that in the MT — at least when it comes to "a large plus or minus."[42] If this judgment is successfully sustained in subsequent scholarship, it may lend historical weight to interpretive approaches that continue to privilege the MT's large-scale literary presentation of Samuel.[43]

---

42. Pisano, *Additions or Omissions in the Books of Samuel*, p. 283. I try to avoid using the expression "the LXX" except in its very general sense of "Greek Bible." The term is imprecise and misleading. See Greenspoon, "Use and Abuse of the Term 'LXX.'"

43. See further Tov, "Nature of Large-Scale Differences."

Furthermore, even what are apparently later additions to or omissions from the MT often exhibit extensions of meaning that are visibly in line with what was presumably the earlier text. I try to deal with such issues on a case-by-case basis, but I still stay with the MT as much as possible without substantially rearranging the text based on text-critical factors or proposing diachronic reconstructions. Since many modern translations of Samuel now alter the MT to varying degrees, there may occasionally be differences between my translations of the text — which are my own unless otherwise noted — and what readers find in their own Bibles. Usually textual emendations will also be marked in readers' Bibles, with a footnote attributing the variant reading to an alternative manuscript tradition.

I have tried in this middle section to keep my own footnotes from burdening the text and inhibiting the reader. (I realize that I may have only been intermittently successful.) Readers with a knowledge of the field will observe my persistent indebtedness to those authors who have already done path-breaking literary work on 1 Samuel, in particular: Robert Alter, Lyle Eslinger, Jan Fokkelman, Moshe Garsiel, David Gunn, Philips Long, Peter Miscall, Robert Polzin, and Meir Sternberg. Their writings on 1 Samuel have contributed much to this volume and are cited in the annotations. Even where they are not cited, they have informed my own reading in fundamental respects. I gladly acknowledge my debt to these authors and my reliance on their work, even as I employ their insights and methods in the service of a new interpretation.

In the third and final part of this volume, I consider two further issues: whether there is a plausible historical context for the narrative as I have articulated it, and what the implications of that narrative are for Christian theology and the Christian life. In this section I conclude that the narrative of 1 Samuel, as often thought, fits well within the concerns of deuteronomistic theology,[44] the perspective of one stream of Israelite tradition commencing in the late seventh century BC. As the term "deuteronomistic" implies, this association indicates a closeness with the language and ideas found in the book of Deuteronomy. "Deuteronomism" is usually understood to have been a religious reform movement beginning during the reign of King Josiah (640–609 BC). I then take up the theological issues of personal piety and true worship that I locate at the center of 1 Samuel and bring them into conversation with Christian

---

44. Some scholars prefer the term "deuteronomic" or employ a distinction between an earlier stream of tradition (= "deuteronomic") and a later one (= "deuteronomistic"). But there is little consistency on this point within the field. I will generally use "deuteronomistic" unless I refer to the legal material within Deuteronomy, in which case I will use "deuteronomic." For further discussion, see Coggins, "What Does 'Deuteronomistic' Mean?"; Knight, "Deuteronomy and the Deuteronomists"; Ben Zvi, "On the Term Deuteronomistic."

theology. I maintain that 1 Samuel is not only about the rise of the monarchy; it is about the threat of civil religion. In 1 Samuel the formation of the Israelite state under a monarchy threatens to erode Israel's religious tradition, a heritage in which personal piety has a crucial place. Saul symbolizes this danger; David at his best sometimes manages to rise above it.

Worship-oriented material in 1 Samuel cannot be restricted to deuteronomistic influence or a deuteronomistic layer of redaction, as is quite often assumed in the secondary literature. A major reason for the more literary character of my approach is precisely to demonstrate how interest in worship is shot through the entirety of Samuel, binding its various figures and episodes together and animating the whole. I suspect that the "deuteronomists" may well have intensified this interest and shaped it in line with their own theological insights,[45] but I sincerely doubt that they initiated or invented it. It is vexing to me to see how often critical scholars not only want to restrict "theology" to the status of a "late" concern in Israel but also imagine "early" Israel as blithely secular. Surely this move says more about such scholars and their modern anxieties than it does about ancient Israel — as if an ancient culture could have really been non-religious![46]

At the heart of the Samuel narrative is then this question: With the rise of the monarchy, will Israel develop a "civil religion"?[47] Both David and Saul participate in such a project, but Saul does so *without* evident personal piety, while David does so *with* personal piety. The contrast highlights the priority of piety above and beyond political constructions of the religious and points to something uncivil at the heart of Israel's vision of life before God. By the term "uncivil" I do not mean to suggest that such a vision is essentially intolerant (= "*in*civil"),[48] but rather that it cannot be captured or harnessed by the reli-

---

45. Note the judgment of Carroll, *From Chaos to Covenant*, p. 90, that the deuteronomists were "obsessed" with right worship.

46. Cf. the refreshing judgment of Dietrich, "König David," p. 10: "Alle Menschen waren damals fromm, auch und erst recht die Könige" (= "All people at that time were pious, also and especially the kings").

47. Cf. Polzin, *Samuel and the Deuteronomist*, p. 47: "How can Israel honor its king and still honor God?"

48. For historical investigations of civility and incivility, see Bryson, *From Courtesy to Civility*; Davetian, *Civility*. For contemporary reflection on civility/incivility and religion, see Clayton and Elgar, *Civility and Democracy in America*; Davis, *In Defense of Civility*; Hall, *The Importance of Being Civil*; Harden, *Professional Civility*; Herbst, *Rude Democracy*; Mower and Robison, eds., *Civility in Politics and Education*. It is noteworthy that several prominent Christian writers have called for renewed attention to civility in contemporary American society: Guinness, *The Case for Civility*; Carter, *Civility*; Mouw, *Uncommon Decency*; Wallis, *Who Speaks for God?*

gious apparatus of the state (= "civil religion").[49] I believe in civility within our common political life, but I also recognize the deficiencies of a "naked public square" in which the particular commitments of various constituencies within society are trivialized or barred.[50] I concede a degree of anachronism by using the notion of "civil religion" with reference to ancient Israel, yet I do seek to ground the basis of my position historically within deuteronomistic theology.

By adopting the category of tragic "overliving," first proposed by the literary scholar Emily Wilson,[51] I attempt to reconcile the resultant tensions in 1 Samuel's portrait of Saul. I argue that the narrative never blames Saul entirely for his shortcomings, which are depicted as innate as well as behavioral, and yet never excuses him from responsibility for his actions either. His tragedy is not the tragedy of his dying but the tragedy of living too long, of being in the impossible position of being rejected by God as king but still inhabiting the kingship. This situation brings about a shocking disintegration of Saul's character, which the narrative explores with tropes common to the tragic tradition that Wilson has identified: madness, darkness, blindness, confusion about time, and suicide. The impact of this tragic tradition, especially in its later Christian form (as exemplified above all by John Milton's work), is to compel the reader or audience to confront how the suffering of "overliving" is an inevitable part of every human life, even when viewed against the horizon of the ultimate victory over sin and death represented by the resurrection of Jesus Christ.

In this way "overliving" becomes a trope for the experience of death in life or, in Christian language, "crucifixion." The character of Saul may therefore be, and I argue must ultimately be, viewed christologically within the context of Christian biblical theology. In his struggle to die, Saul adumbrates Christ. Yet recognizing that Saul, as well as David, can function as a "type" for Christ does not necessarily impose an unfairly Christian meaning on the narrative of Samuel. Instead, as the theologian Karl Barth brilliantly perceived, the typology

---

49. For the notion of "civil religion," see Bellah, "Civil Religion in America"; cf. idem, *Broken Covenant*, esp. pp. 164-88. Bellah lately appears to have distanced himself from the term. For the history of the early discussion and further analysis, see Gehrig, *American Civil Religion*; Mathisen, "Twenty Years after Bellah." For a critique of Bellah's notion, see Kelly, *Politics and Religious Consciousness in America*. For theological criticism of America's civil religion, see Marvin and Ingle, *Blood Sacrifice and the Nation*; Noll, Hatch, and Marsden, *Search for Christian America*. For an international perspective, see Gentile, *Politics as Religion*. Gentile traces the concept of a "civil religion" back to Rousseau.

50. Neuhaus, *Naked Public Square*; Carter, *Culture of Disbelief*; Wolfe, ed., *Naked Public Square Reconsidered*.

51. Wilson, *Mocked with Death*.

can actually reinforce the plain sense of the Old Testament narrative, which itself never demonizes Saul and registers persistent anxiety about David.[52] Unfortunately, however, Christian interpretation of 1 Samuel has usually demonized Saul and interpreted David triumphalistically.[53]

On this basis I further maintain — building on the presentation of these themes in the Samuel narrative — that the idolatry of empty ritual continues to be a danger for Christians in the present, both within the church and in wider society.[54] Although certainly no conception of "separation of church and state" existed in ancient Israel, such a political principle finds its most persuasive justification in the need to protect genuine piety from the threat of civil religion. Just as the Israelite union of the sacred and the mundane under a monarchic form of government precipitates a theological crisis in the Samuel account, so civil religion today threatens to evacuate the vitality of particular religious traditions. Government in its will to power inevitably seeks to leach out the substance of faith in God and domesticate religion by placing it at the state's service.[55]

Because the history of biblical interpretation demonstrates how the Samuel narrative was usually heard by Christians as speaking above all of David's legacy as it came to fruition in Jesus, "David's royal son,"[56] I also ask to what extent the Davidic legacy amplifies the church's testimony about Jesus, or whether it might erode or corrupt that testimony. Both the Samuel narrative's celebration of David *and* its admission of his ambiguity finally warrant — from different directions — a crucial discontinuity between the Old Testament and the gospel, a discontinuity that can be identified as the imperialistic dimension of David's legacy.

However, the needed contemporary counter-response to this danger is also drawn from Samuel: namely, institutional and personal modesty, the relinquishment of imperial ambitions in favor of *meekness*, a spiritual dependence upon God. Hence I ultimately argue that the "little way" of Thérèse of Lisieux can express for our time something similar to what the Samuel narrative wanted to communicate on its own terms, and continues so artfully to convey.

52. Barth, *Church Dogmatics II/2*, pp. 390-92.

53. For examples, see Gunn, *Fate of King Saul*, pp. 23-31.

54. Barton, ed., *Idolatry*; Beale, *We Become What We Worship*; Dawn, *A Royal "Waste" of Time*; Kinneson, *Selling Out the Church*.

55. I am also aware that this focus on the problem of civil religion, as well as the emphasis on a need for genuine piety, may arise in part out of my own Baptist heritage and convictions. For reflection on what makes Baptist Old Testament scholarship "Baptist," see Chapman, "Interpreting the Old Testament in Baptist Life"; Fiddes, "Prophecy, Corporate Personality, and Suffering."

56. The familiarity of this phrase in Christian circles comes from its appearance in the well-known hymn "All Glory, Laud, and Honor" (text by Theodulph of Orléans, as translated by John Mason Neale), often sung for Palm Sunday.

PART ONE

Taking Up the Task

CHAPTER 1

Reading 1 Samuel as a Book

An oblivion to the text itself seems to me the greatest defect in present-day biblical scholarship.[1]

Those who talk of the Bible 'as literature' sometimes mean, I think, reading it without attending to the main thing it is about.[2]

The time is out of joint.[3]

What does it mean to interpret the Bible as *scripture*? Does it mean to read the Bible "like any other book"?[4] If so, then why is its historical and religious particularity thought to be relatively unimportant? And if reading scripture

---

1. Sandmel, "Haggadah within Scripture," p. 108.

2. Lewis, *Reflections on the Psalms*, p. 10. However, Lewis goes on to add: "But there is a . . . sense in which the Bible, since it is after all literature, cannot properly be read except as literature; and the different parts of it as the different sorts of literature they are."

3. Shakespeare, *Hamlet*, Act 1, Scene 5, line 190.

4. The prospect of reading the Bible "like any other book" tends to be dismissed by theologically oriented interpreters who worry that such an approach will pay insufficient attention to the Bible's religious truth. For this reason, it bears remembering that in contrast to a dreary moralistic use of scripture in church, reading the Bible "like any other book" can sometimes be an exciting improvement. Robert Louis Stevenson found it so: "The next book, in order of time, to influence me was the New Testament, and in particular the Gospel according to St. Matthew. I believe it would startle and move anyone if they could make a certain effort of imagination and read it freshly like a book, not droningly and chillily like a portion of the Bible. Anyone would then be able to see in it those truths which we are all courteously supposed to know and all modestly refrain from applying." See his "Books which have influenced me," in *The Works of Robert Louis Stevenson*, 16:274, cited in Norton, *A History of the Bible as Literature*, 1:297-98.

is not like reading any other book, then in what way does one read scripture differently?[5]

Christian communities presently experience great uncertainty about interpreting the Bible theologically. The confusion stems in large part from an erosion of traditional reading practices within those Christian communities themselves. It is difficult to know how to read scripture well in the absence of models and experiences of doing so. Additional difficulty arises from the challenges these communities face in maintaining their particular manner of life as they are increasingly confronted by a global capitalism deeply antagonistic to social difference and non-commercial value. Yet a third factor consists of ongoing theological disputes about the nature of scripture and the proper method for scriptural interpretation.[6]

What is the appropriate focus for a theological reading of scripture? Is it the events that scripture reports, the characters it depicts, the themes it illustrates, or the doctrines it upholds? Theological readings continue to center on one or more of these possibilities without necessarily differentiating or adjudicating among them. Further challenges surface when the scriptural book being interpreted comes from the Old Testament. How can the Christian community do justice to the Old Testament's pre-Christian form but at the same time interpret the Old Testament as a truthful witness to the One it calls Lord? An even more basic problem has to do with the relationship between history and text. Is the proper subject matter of a theological reading of scripture the *historical* events to which the biblical text refers? Or is it the text itself as a literary work? Put more provocatively, is even the history unreported by the biblical text theologically significant? In what way? Or, conversely, can a text that is unsubstantiated or even apparently contradicted by historical research still ground an authoritative theological point? How and why?

Precisely because the findings of historical-critical research on the Bible

5. For the history of this expression, see Rogerson, "Die Bibel lesen wie jedes andere Buch?" For contemporary reflection on the phrase's continued applicability, see Moberly, "Interpret the Bible like Any Other Book?"

6. For differing perspectives on the current theological discussion and a variety of constructive proposals, see Adam et al., *Reading Scripture with the Church*; Barton, *Nature of Biblical Criticism*; Collins, *Bible after Babel*; Davis and Hays, eds., *Art of Reading Scripture*; Ford and Stanton, eds., *Reading Texts, Seeking Wisdom*; Fowl, *Engaging Scripture*; Green, *Practicing Theological Interpretation*; Harrington, *How Do Catholics Read the Bible?*; Holcomb, *Christian Theologies of Scripture*; Treier, *Introducing Theological Interpretation of Scripture*; Williams, *Receiving the Bible in Faith*. For sustained engagement with the topic, see the various volumes of the Scripture and Hermeneutics Seminar series, especially Bartholomew, Greene, and Möller, eds., *Renewing Biblical Interpretation* (SHS 1); and Bartholomew et al., eds., *Out of Egypt* (SHS 5).

have consistently pointed out qualitative distinctions between historical event and textual depiction, modern Christian scholars have perceived themselves as faced with a fundamental choice between the two. At the risk of painting with too broad a brush, evangelicals and liberals have both tended to respond to that sense of a choice by privileging history, resulting in an ironic pairing of otherwise strange bedfellows.[7] The now "traditional" disagreement between these two camps exists because evangelicals typically refuse on principle to allow any biblical text to be considered unhistorical,[8] while liberals largely insist, also on principle, that some biblical texts must be judged historically inaccurate in order to be interpreted correctly. But in this way historical issues dominate the readings of both camps. Ultimately they each view the religious truth they seek as having been revealed in the history *behind* the biblical text. For both, reading the Bible theologically means reading it in order to reconstruct and illuminate a religious history to which the Bible, more or less reliably, gestures.

It is important to emphasize, however, that for both groups the position taken on the historicity of the biblical traditions is ultimately theological in nature. For liberals, the ability to root biblical theology in history provides a means of reconciling the Bible with modernity and discriminating within the canon, of subordinating certain texts to others. This hermeneutical move has allowed for the depreciation or dismissal of morally troublesome texts as being of dubious historicity (e.g., Joshua, Jonah, Esther)[9] or as representing an earlier stage of "progressive revelation."[10]

7. I use the broad term "liberal" rather than "liberal Protestant" in order to include liberal Catholic scholars in the designation. The term is also used theologically rather than politically.

8. For a searching exposition of this tendency, often unacknowledged but clearly operative in practice, see Grabbe, "Comfortable Theory"; Sparks, *God's Word in Human Words*, pp. 133-70.

9. The moral grievance fueling historical criticism from its beginning is ably described in Moore and Sherwood, *Invention of a Biblical Scholar*, pp. 46-81.

10. Classically within the American context, see Fosdick, *A Guide to Understanding the Bible*, e.g., p. 50: "the idea of God had been progressively formulated." This move has recently been given a sociological twist in Oakman, "Biblical Hermeneutics — Marcion's Truth and a Developmental Perspective." Evangelicals now routinely also embrace the idea of progressive revelation: e.g., Bartholomew and Goheen, "Story and Biblical Theology," p. 149; Carson, "Unity and Diversity in the New Testament"; Klein, Blomberg, and Hubbard, *Introduction to Biblical Interpretation*, p. 112; Packer, "An Evangelical View of Progressive Revelation." For a fully articulated example, see VanGemeren, *Progress of Redemption*. In British scholarship this theme was famously emphasized in the Lux Mundi essays of 1889; see Lampe, "Bible since the Rise of Critical Study," p. 138. C. H. Dodd is often credited with popularizing the idea. In his *The Authority of the Bible* (first published 1928), pp. 248-63, he prefers the term "progressive discovery." In his later work *The Bible Today* (1956), p. 98, he appears to have made his peace

Once the nineteenth century had given birth to the conception of history as developing, not static, it was no longer necessary to believe that the divine command to Saul to slaughter the women and children of the Amalekites was as adequately revelatory of the character and purpose of God as the love-commandment of the Sermon on the Mount.[11]

By proceeding along these lines, liberalism's weak flank has always been viewed by religious conservatives as its inability to sustain a fully robust doctrine of scripture, seen above all in the usually otiose character of the Old Testament within liberal theologies.[12]

By contrast, conservative evangelicals have sought ever since the intensification of such debates in the nineteenth century to insist upon a high view of scripture, even as they, too, rooted revelation in history. Yet, as liberals were quick to point out, the inconsistent result was a standing evangelical appeal to history, combined with persistent special pleading (i.e., certain historical claims were actually invoked for theological rather than historical reasons). Examples of the phenomenon are quite numerous, but in keeping with the theme of this book, a particularly relevant instance is provided by the volume on Samuel by Robert Bergen in the New American Commentary series.[13] In his introductory remarks Bergen discusses "1, 2 Samuel as History," acknowledging that there are valid questions about various aspects of the book's historicity and that "the canonical writer had a larger agenda than mere historical reportage."[14] However, in the subsection "1, 2 Samuel as Theology," Bergen

---

with the expression "progressive revelation." For another view of the pedigree of this notion within British biblical studies, see Rogerson, "Progressive Revelation." Cf. the criticisms of the view in Barr, *Old and New in Interpretation*, pp. 65-102; idem, *Bible in the Modern World*, pp. 144-46; Davies, "Morally Dubious Passages of the Hebrew Bible"; Reid, *Authority of Scripture*, pp. 177-93.

11. Alan Richardson, "Rise of Modern Biblical Scholarship," p. 302.

12. E.g., von Harnack, *Marcion*; Bultmann, "Significance of the Old Testament." Bultmann allowed the Old Testament to have only an indirect "pedagogical" purpose within Christian theology; namely, to illuminate by its difference from the New Testament what the gospel is genuinely about (pp. 21, 34). However, as Bultmann famously went on to assert, "to the Christian faith the Old Testament is not in the true sense God's Word. So far as the Church proclaims the Old Testament as God's Word, it just finds in it again what is already known from the revelation in Jesus Christ" (p. 32). Interestingly, the oblique witness of the text is further distinguished by Bultmann from the history of Israel, which for him has no unique revelatory value to Christian theology at all (pp. 31-32). With this stance, Bultmann exhibited both his independence from liberal Protestantism and also one of the ways in which his theology remained broadly neo-orthodox in inclination.

13. Bergen, *1, 2 Samuel*.

14. Bergen, *1, 2 Samuel*, pp. 28-32; esp. p. 32.

argues that the books of Samuel provide "an accurate historical record," now basing this judgment on the acceptance of Samuel as having "full scriptural authority" by Jesus (Bergen cites Mark 2:26 as evidence) and Paul (here Bergen refers to Acts 13:20-21).[15] He further asserts that the genealogies of Jesus found in the New Testament must be considered historically accurate so as to avoid "error or myth," and that both the Matthean (Matt 1:6) and the Lukan (Luke 3:31-32) genealogies make reference to figures found in the books of Samuel.[16] To make the critical point, here a dogmatic theological position is offered not so much in combination with, or even in lieu of, but in the guise of historical investigation.[17]

Common to both theological views — the evangelical and the liberal — is thus the idea that scriptural authority is primarily, if not exclusively, determined by scripture's ability to provide access to history. The tenacity of this historical appeal must be judged respectfully as reflecting a theological commitment on the part of these biblical interpreters to the historical nature of revelation.[18] Yet to make scriptural authority primarily about history also involves a reductionistic move in which truth is ultimately *equated* with historicity.[19] It is precisely the effort within more recent biblical interpretation to explore other dimensions of meaning and truth which has led to the remarkable surge of interest in literary readings of the Bible, as well as to a widening awareness that the old liberal–conservative debate cannot, on its own terms, overcome the impasse it now both reflects and, sadly, continues to reinforce.

Considered as a group, literary approaches have therefore not infrequently been described by their proponents (as well as their opponents) as different in kind from historical scholarship:

15. Bergen, *1, 2 Samuel*, pp. 45-55; esp. p. 54. The historical distance between the Gospel of Mark and the historical Jesus, and between the book of Acts and the historical Paul, is not raised as problematic in any way. Also unmentioned is the apparent "accommodation" of Jesus to his cultural and historical context. Otherwise, for example, when the figure of Jesus refers to the "rising" of the sun (Matt 5:45), his comment might be used, according to the same logic, as a theological warrant for a geocentric cosmology.

16. Bergen, *1, 2 Samuel*, pp. 54-55. The possibility that such figures might have been known apart from scripture, and thus that tradition rather than scripture could be functioning authoritatively in this case, similarly goes unmentioned.

17. For additional examples of this kind of methodological move and further criticism, see Ramsey, *Quest for the Historical Israel*, pp. 107-15.

18. For a defense of history as a theologically significant category, see Barr, *History and Ideology in the Old Testament*, pp. 1-15, 59-101.

19. The story of how this modern equation arose is told with subtlety and insight by Frei, *Eclipse of Biblical Narrative*.

The text to us is not sacred and whether the events it describes are historical is not relevant to our purposes . . . Our approach is essentially ahistorical; the text is taken as received, and the truth of an action or an idea of a motive, for literary criticism, depends on its rightness or appropriateness in context. Is it true, we ask, not in the real world but within the fictive world that has been created by the narrative?[20]

Yet despite its seemingly extreme conclusion, this statement's judgments regarding the text's sacredness and historicity are simply framed in explicit relation to the methodology being advocated. Rather than rejected absolutely, historical questions are "bracketed" as irrelevant to the methodology (note the term "ahistorical" rather than "antihistorical"). The pragmatic nature of this bracketing suggests that the difference between a literary approach to scripture and historical-critical scholarship of the Bible may not, in the end, be insuperable.[21] Such a possibility informs the trajectory of this volume.

That kind of possibility has become a crucially needed venture not only as a means of avoiding the critical impasse just described, but also as a way to resuscitate a non-reductionistic view of truth in which the aesthetic dimension of scripture can also be viewed as theologically meaningful.[22] From a theological perspective, the most suggestive and intriguing aspect of literary treatments of the Bible is to be found in their description of the aesthetic "surplus" of the text. This term is used here to refer to those qualities of the biblical text that exceed, or are even apparently superfluous to, its historical witness. Robert Alter puts the point quite strongly: "I do not think . . . that every nuance of characterization and every turning of the plot in these stories can be justified in either moral-theological or national-historical terms."[23] In the Bible, one also encounters "the most serious playfulness," so that one is:

endlessly discovering how the permutations of narrative conventions, linguistic properties, and imaginatively constructed personages and circumstances can crystallize subtle and abiding truths of experience in amusing or arresting or gratifying ways.[24]

20. Gros Louis, ed., *Literary Interpretations of Biblical Narratives*, 2:14. This passage is also cited as an example of the problematic nature of literary approaches by Bergen, *1, 2 Samuel*, p. 33.

21. Historical approaches characteristically rely on their own "bracketing" of truth claims; see Barton, *Nature of Biblical Criticism*, pp. 171-72.

22. Clines, "Story and Poem."

23. Alter, *Art of Biblical Narrative*, p. 53.

24. Alter, *Art of Biblical Narrative*, p. 54.

Even if some of the examples that Alter and others have cited occasionally strain credulity, it is nevertheless impossible to read the biblical Hebrew text closely without recognizing throughout it the presence of wordplay and a most careful use of language.[25] The sheer existence of such features provides a highly compelling reason to develop a theological perspective capable of appreciating their presence in the text.

Aesthetic approaches to biblical interpretation have been critiqued on historical grounds.[26] Yet the stronger objection to a literary approach appeals to the nature of the biblical literature itself. C. S. Lewis expresses such an objection in these terms:

> Most of [the Bible's] component parts were written, and all of them brought together, for a purely religious purpose. It contains good literature and bad literature. But even the good literature is so written that we can seldom disregard its sacred character. It is . . . not merely a sacred book but a book so remorselessly and continuously sacred that it does not invite, it excludes or repels, the merely aesthetic approach. You can read it as literature only by a *tour de force*. You are cutting the wood against the grain, using the tool for a purpose it was not intended to serve.[27]

Lewis's primary concern thus has to do with the way that literary approaches read "against the grain" of what scripture really is.

George Steiner has made the similar objection that the literary dimension of scripture cannot in fact be separated from the theological:

> The author of Job — and there is a poet's voice and transcendent genius in almost every line — was not producing "literature." Nor were those who

25. Such usage is most obvious in poetry; for a concise and readable overview of instances and techniques, see Watson, "Hebrew Poetry." For investigations into the poetics of biblical prose, in addition to Alter, *Art of Biblical Narrative*; see Amit, *Reading Biblical Narratives*; Bar-Efrat, *Narrative Art in the Bible*; Berlin, *Poetics and Interpretation of Biblical Narrative*; Exum and Clines, *New Literary Criticism and the Hebrew Bible*; Fokkelman, *Reading Biblical Narrative*; Sternberg, *Poetics of Biblical Narrative*; Walsh, *Style and Structure in Biblical Hebrew Narrative*; idem, *Old Testament Narrative*.

26. Barr, *Bible in the Modern World*, pp. 10-33, 55. For an account of how an older style of literary approach to the Bible became popular in the late nineteenth and early twentieth centuries, see Norton, *A History of the English Bible as Literature*, pp. 358-86.

27. Lewis, *Literary Impact of the Authorized Version*, pp. 32-33. Cf. the earlier statement of T. S. Eliot, "Religion and Literature," p. 33: "the Bible has had a *literary* influence upon English literature *not* because it has been considered as literature, but because it has been considered as the report of the Word of God" (emphases original).

bore witness to the "darkness upon the earth" the evening of Good Friday. A literary elucidation of such texts is legitimate and can be helpful, but only if it acknowledges, in however polemic a vein, its own principles of exclusion — only if it tells us that that which it omits is the essential.[28]

The truly grave danger of a literary approach reveals itself most fully when biblical interpretation becomes a way of talking about texts rather than talking about God.[29] The proper challenge is therefore how to work exegetically with a sensitive appreciation for the literary features of the biblical text, while at the same time engaging its actual subject matter, what the biblical text is about.[30] The need, as Alter has again helpfully insisted, is not so much for "a more 'imaginative' reading of biblical narrative but . . . a more precise one." By focusing on "discernible details in the Hebrew text, the literary approach is actually a good deal less conjectural than the historical scholarship that asks of a verse whether it contains possible Akkadian loanwords, whether it reflects Sumerian kingship practices, whether it may have been corrupted by scribal error."[31]

Thus *how* a biblical text tells its subject matter is itself part of that subject matter. This is the truth once emphasized especially by form criticism in biblical studies, but applied now in new ways by literary approaches to biblical interpretation. Gerhard von Rad, for example, saw less difference between poetry and history than some do today:

> . . . a great part of even the historical traditions of Israel has to be regarded as poetry, that is, as the product of explicit artistic intentions. But poetry — especially with the people of antiquity — is much more than an aesthetic pastime: rather is there in it a penetrating desire for knowledge directed towards the data presented by the historical and natural environment.[32]

28. Steiner, "Good Books," p. 16.

29. Just this concern is raised by Thiemann, "Response to George Lindbeck." Also apropos in this regard are Kierkegaard's comments on the "new paganism" of Christian art, which results in admiration but not imitation; see Kierkegaard, *Practice in Christianity.*

30. See Wilder, "Holy Writ and Lit Crit."

31. Alter, *Art of Biblical Narrative,* p. 22.

32. Von Rad, *Old Testament Theology,* 1:109. Von Rad thought that with the Deuteronomistic History Israel had finally developed a "prosaic and scientific presentation of her history." Yet there are also plenty of literary techniques in evidence in these books, as much recent scholarship has shown; see Eslinger, *Kingship of God in Crisis;* Fokkelman, *Narrative Art and Poetry in the Books of Samuel;* Garsiel, *First Book of Samuel;* Gunn, *Fate of King Saul;* Long, *Reign and Rejection of King Saul;* Miscall, *1 Samuel;* Polzin, *Samuel and the Deuteronomist.*

In other words, there are good historical grounds for responding to the question of history *versus* literature by working toward a "both/and" rather than an "either/or" solution.

The position adopted in this book is that biblical theology, or something like it by another name,[33] has as its primary task to reflect upon the literary presentation of the biblical text, not to the exclusion of historical concerns (or, for that matter, the elimination of any other kinds of concerns or criticism), but still in such a way that as much justice as possible is done to the written character of the text and its literary features. By proceeding in this fashion, the text remains the ultimate criterion for the methodology applied to it and the interpretive use made of it, a hermeneutical stance that has been a traditional touchstone for Christian theology. This variety of biblical theology entails the interpretation of the Bible as fully as possible as a *text*, and is therefore properly hermeneutical in intention, method, and purpose.[34]

In sum, the Bible *as text* projects a narrative world for consideration and engagement.[35] Literary theorist Boris Uspensky usefully describes the process of this type of engagement:

> In a work of art, whether it be a work of literature, a painting, or a work of some other art form, there is presented to us a special world, with its own space and time, its own ideological system, and it own standards of behavior. In relation to that world, we assume (at least in our first perceptions of it) the position of an alien spectator, which is necessarily external. Gradually, we enter into it, becoming more familiar with its standards,

33. The term "biblical theology" has been tainted by its use as a title for an influential but ultimately unsuccessful movement within English-language biblical scholarship in the 1950s and 1960s. For this reason, alternatives such as "theological interpretation" or "theological reflection" have gained in popularity. A classic discussion of the Biblical Theology movement and its shortcomings can be found in Childs, *Biblical Theology in Crisis*. For more recent criticism of the term, see Johnson, "Imagining the World Scripture Imagines," pp. 8-9. For an alternative proposal, see Fowl, *Engaging Scripture*, pp. 13-21. While not opposed to other terminological alternatives, I retain "biblical theology" in order to situate theological work in a particular way within the discipline of biblical studies. For a description of such situating with which I am in substantial agreement, see Welker, "Sola Scriptura?" pp. 384-86.

34. Rather than distinguishing "biblical theology" from the rest of theology, as is sometimes implied, this description may prove to apply just as much to theology in general. For a powerful explication of all theology as "the grammar of the language of the Scriptures," see Bayer, "Hermeneutical Theology."

35. Clines, "Story and Poem." Cf. Ricoeur, *Essays in Biblical Interpretation*, pp. 100-104. For further discussion of a narrative's "worldview" and how to discern it, see Ryken, *Windows to the World*, pp. 131-51.

accustoming ourselves to it, until we begin to perceive this world as if from within, rather than from without.[36]

The task of theological interpretation is therefore to describe the narrative world of the biblical story and to detect what it offers the world of the reader — a hermeneutical project involving comparison and differentiation as well as observation and restatement. But it all needs to grow out of attentive, loving engagement with the biblical text as *text*. God gave us stories.

1 Samuel as a Book?

If it is at least possible that the biblical text can provide literary criteria or rules for its own right reading — an admittedly controversial claim — then what criteria or rules for such reading may be identified?

In what follows, the theological implications of one particular major literary feature of the biblical text will be discussed. The intention is to be illustrative rather than exhaustive. Other textual features can and certainly would need to be explored in order to develop a full theological treatment. The further argument presented here, however, is that no adequate theological interpretation of 1 Samuel can overlook its received literary character as a *book*. Even though the hermeneutical implications of the biblical "book" have only rarely been examined as such, one of the most notable large-scale features of biblical texts generally is their historical transmission as discrete book-units. In what follows, therefore, an effort will be made to answer a more specific question: What theological difference does it make that biblical texts have been transmitted in "booked" literary form?

The biblical book of 1 Samuel provides an especially illuminating example of what is at stake in this question, both because its status as a book involves more complicated historical issues and because the significance of its character as a book has recently been explicitly called into question. In an essay entitled "What, if Anything, is 1 Samuel?" David Jobling insists more sharply than any other previous interpreter on the artificiality of the present literary boundaries of this book.[37] Central to his argument is that "the canonical division [of the present book] exerts a tremendous pressure on scholars to read the beginning

---

36. Uspensky, *Poetics of Composition*, p. 137; also cited in Ryken, *Windows to the World*, p. 138.

37. Jobling, "What, If Anything, Is 1 Samuel?" This essay can now also be found as a chapter in his commentary, *1 Samuel*, pp. 28-37. I cite from the latter text.

of 1 Samuel as a new beginning — to read it *forward* rather than *backward*."[38] Jobling wants to problematize this kind of reading in order to "exploit the tension between reading 1 Samuel in itself and reading it as part of something larger."[39] This "something larger" includes for him not only 2 Samuel and the rest of the Deuteronomistic History (i.e., Deuteronomy, Joshua, Judges, 1–2 Samuel, 1–2 Kings) but also contemporary concerns like gender, class, and race, which Jobling indeed brings into relation with the content of 1 Samuel in fresh and often illuminating ways.

Using the results of prior historical-critical investigation into the larger structure of the Deuteronomistic History, Jobling proposes a reading of 1 Samuel corresponding to other critically reconstructed narrative units: namely, Judges 2 to 1 Samuel 12 and 1 Samuel 13 to 2 Samuel 7.[40] If historical scholarship is to be taken seriously, he suggests, then these primary, possibly original, literary boundaries should shape the interpretation of 1 Samuel decisively — more in fact than its present canonical format. Jobling says at first that he adopted this interpretive strategy heuristically in order to undermine customary approaches to the book of 1 Samuel and to explore an alternative book-shape with equal claim to validity.[41] No valid reason exists, he asserts, for the reconstructed divisions of critical scholarship to be dismissed as an inadequate basis for the literary interpretation of 1 Samuel.[42] Thus Jobling initially intends his procedure to function only as a type of thought experiment, designed precisely to call attention to the way in which an uncritical adoption of the standard canonical boundaries of 1 Samuel shifts the course of interpretation from the outset.

In pursuing that experiment, however, Jobling gradually seems to become convinced of the literary superiority and historical accuracy of the reconstructed earlier divisions, largely because they turn out to match and reinforce his own reading so well.[43] Jobling further claims on the basis of this conviction that the present literary boundaries of Samuel can only be viewed as a tendentious revision of the former deuteronomistic version, a revision conditioned by a new understanding of Israel's past as well as by a transformed hope for Israel's

---

38. Jobling, *1 Samuel*, p. 33. His italics.

39. Jobling, *1 Samuel*, p. 3.

40. For these alternative literary divisions Jobling relies upon the influential work of Noth, *Deuteronomistic History*, especially as revised by McCarthy, "II Samuel 7 and the Structure of the Deuteronomistic History."

41. Jobling, *1 Samuel*, p. 36.

42. Jobling, *1 Samuel*, p. 29.

43. Jobling, *1 Samuel*, p. 36: "So I take seriously the possibility they did serve as working divisions in a pre-canonical (Deuteronomic) but otherwise essentially identical text."

future (on the part of those responsible for the canonical restructuring of the book).[44] Less carefully, Jobling then also polemically describes the critically reconstructed divisions of the "original" Samuel as "natural"[45] and refers to the canonical arrangement of the text as a distortion.[46]

Central to Jobling's reading is an effort to read the beginning of 1 Samuel "backward" — that is, as more of a continuation of the events and themes within the book of Judges than is normally done. Rather than viewing 1 Samuel as a new narrative departure, he wants to read the first seven chapters of the book as the "triumphant" conclusion to a narrative depiction of government by judgeship, a culmination that embodies what Jobling also terms a "lost ideal."[47] Even though often depicted by its failings, this wisp of an ideal serves to perpetuate a perished alternative to monarchy, one that "haunts" the later stories of the monarchy's rise and fall.[48] Accordingly, those later narratives of 1 Samuel are read by Jobling as more consistently negative with regard to the kingship than most critics have maintained.[49] By his approach, Jobling thus reverses the standard interpretation of the relationship between both of these two periods within the received form of the Deuteronomistic History, in which the chaotic and wicked events detailed in Judges provide the main justification for the ultimately positive, if also nuanced, view of kingship emerging in the course of 1 Samuel.[50] For Jobling, it

---

44. Jobling, *1 Samuel*, pp. 105-11.

45. Jobling, *1 Samuel*, p. 105.

46. Jobling, *1 Samuel*, p. 42. A major difficulty for Jobling's thesis, however, is that the reconstruction on which he relies is not the only one on offer. Thus Frolov, *Turn of the Cycle*, argues that 1 Samuel 1–8 may well be a secondary "anti-Deuteronomistic" addition to Samuel–Kings, and Janet Tollington, "Ethics of Warfare," entertains the possibility that Judges, especially Judges 19–21, may be a secondary interpolation into the Deuteronomistic History. On this latter possibility, see further Provan, *Hezekiah and the Book of Kings*, p. 168. The plurality of conflicting critical theories seriously undercuts Jobling's argument for reading 1 Samuel 1–8 as a simple continuation of Judges.

47. Jobling, *1 Samuel*, pp. 34, 70.

48. Jobling, *1 Samuel*, p. 75.

49. Jobling, *1 Samuel*, pp. 110-11.

50. The phrase "In those days there was no king in Israel" begins narrative sections in Judg 18:1 and 19:1. It is echoed in the larger surrounding frame and combined with the phrase "all the people did what was right in their own eyes" in Judg 17:6 and 21:25. While it has long been debated whether this latter phrase is used positively or negatively, the implicit contrast with Deut 12:25, 28; 13:19 suggests that, at least for the deuteronomistic tradents of Judges, the phrase was viewed negatively. In deuteronomistic tradition, what Israel is to do is precisely "what is right in the sight of the Lord" (cf. Judg 2:11; 3:7, 12; 4:1; 6:1; 10:6; 13:1). See Satterthwaite, "No King in Israel." For a more positive interpretation of the phrase and the situation in Judges, see Dumbrell, "'In Those Days There Was No King in Israel'"; Shapira, "'In Those Days There Was No King in Israel'; Olson, "Buber, Kingship, and the Book of Judges," understands the

is those responsible for the History's *present* literary divisions who created the possibility of that (re-)interpretation.[51]

Ironically, the more Jobling attempts to undermine what he considers to be the standard interpretation of Judges and 1 Samuel, the more he persuades that the received book divisions really do shape, even determine, a reading of the Deuteronomistic History in its present form. With his stance, Jobling is in fact closer to exponents of "foolproof" reading than he would likely care to admit. He polemicizes against interpreters like Meir Sternberg,[52] who claims that biblical literature has been composed in such a way as to ensure a single, normative interpretation for the attentive reader.[53] In the course of his own critique, however, Jobling credits the canonical literary divisions with precisely this same capability! In fact the "power of the book" is so much a force to be reckoned with[54] that the only way for Jobling to develop an alternative interpretation of 1 Samuel is apparently to readjust the canonical boundaries of the book, employing the fragile implement of a reconstructed, and therefore speculative and unprovable, historical claim.[55]

However, Jobling's suspicion of 1 Samuel's inherited literary shape nevertheless merits close attention, not because that shape is somehow defective or misleading but because his suspicion causes him to be attentive to a feature of 1 Samuel that most other critics have largely taken for granted: its shape as a "book." Thus in the received form of 1 Samuel, for example, the first chapter *does* mark a fresh narrative departure, encouraging the reader to connect the events of that chapter with what follows rather than what precedes.[56] Similarly, the effect of concluding the present book of 1 Samuel at the end of what is now chapter 31 must also be considered thoughtfully, since the status of that chapter as an *ending* inclines the reader to interpret it more in line with what has come before it than with what continues after. Notwithstanding his critical suspicion,

---

phrase negatively but makes a compelling case for greater ambiguity in Judges — as opposed to a reading in which the phrase is heard instead as straightforward royalist propaganda.

51. Jobling, *1 Samuel*, pp. 33-34.

52. Jobling, *1 Samuel*, pp. 29-31. For additional criticism of Sternberg in the same vein, see Gunn, "Reading Right."

53. Sternberg, *Poetics*, pp. 48-56.

54. Jobling, *1 Samuel*, p. 31.

55. By arguing for an original work in which the literary divisions were alternatively placed as some historical-critical scholars have suggested, but with the text itself remaining "otherwise essentially identical" (*1 Samuel*, p. 36), Jobling seems to want to retain those aspects of both arguments that are congenial to him without acknowledging the significant tension they also generate with respect to each other: in other words, to have his cake and eat it, too.

56. See Brueggemann, "1 Samuel 1." His reading is in this regard precisely the inverse of Jobling's argument (*1 Samuel*, p. 33).

therefore, Jobling actually understands the prominence of certain features of 1 Samuel more clearly than some theologically oriented readers who are in such a hurry to justify the text's every aspect that they are not always able to differentiate between what is more and less noteworthy.

Perhaps a certain nervousness accounts for the way in which the text's rapid justifiers still resist the full implications of 1 Samuel's received form. The phenomenon is particularly apparent in discussions of 1 Samuel 31, which now exists as a "concluding" chapter because the single book of Samuel first known in Hebrew (as confirmed by 4QSam[a] at Qumran) was only later divided into two in Greek Bibles, presumably for pragmatic reasons (i.e., it would have been too long in Greek to be included on a single scroll).[57] Not until the late Middle Ages did a similar division occur in Hebrew Bibles.[58] Treating 1 Samuel 31 as an intentional literary conclusion surely seems to put too much weight on the received form of the text when that form is apparently the result of contingent historical circumstances, although the difficulty has not stopped some interpreters from trying:

> I recognize . . . that the division of the text into books is itself artificial and must have taken place much later than the composition of the History. Nevertheless, by whatever process this division took place . . . this process, by and large, has recognized and remained faithful to the structural plan of the History that I assume existed in the original composition.[59]

With such a statement Robert Polzin exemplifies the bind in which contemporary literary scholars frequently find themselves: they attempt to unloosen the historical knots that constrain them but are also often unwilling in the end to abandon history altogether.

Rather than simply accepting tradition and working with a received text, Polzin makes a history-like counterclaim that in actuality represents another version of special pleading: that this particular literary tradition has somehow been mysteriously immune to accident, deterioration, or corruption over time.

---

57. For additional reasons for this judgment, see especially Bergen, *1, 2 Samuel*, pp. 17-18; McCarter, *I Samuel*, p. 3. Cf. Williams, "Writing and Writing Materials," p. 920: "Since *ca.* thirty feet was the normal length of a scroll, it was just sufficient for a book like Isaiah, but necessitated the division of the Pentateuch into two sections. Samuel, Kings, and Chronicles would each fill one scroll in the unvocalized Hebrew scripture; but when these were rendered into Greek, each book required two scrolls, because the use of vowels in the Greek script doubled the length of the text — hence our division into I and II Samuel, etc."

58. McCarter, *I Samuel*, p. 3, dates this development to the sixteenth century.

59. Polzin, *Samuel and the Deuteronomist*, p. 230 n. 2.

So even Polzin, who is otherwise fond of polemicizing against historical-critical scholarship on the Bible, appears unable to say that he is working with this text just as it is, just because it is there. Once again, Jobling is right to argue that there are alternative possibilities for determining a book's literary shape — that the rightness of an interpretation of 1 Samuel need not, in fact cannot, preclude the rightness of another interpretation of a differently divided text, because the particular book-shape of the text makes a crucial difference to the reading of it.

The realization of the crucial nature of the text's book-shape in turn means that the determination of how one text is "more right" than another is not a literary question but a theological one — and it is exactly Polzin's unwillingness to express a theological justification for his claim that leads him to mask it as a historical phenomenon. In similar fashion historical-critical scholars also often display anxiety about the biblical text's received form because they realize at some level that their acceptance of that form, especially when confronted with other historical or even contemporary possibilities, involves a theological and not only a historical or literary stance. For example, the books of the Bible are in fact being read "canonically" simply when they are read together, either in exclusion from or with priority over other "extra-biblical" texts (both ancient and modern), for there can be no purely historical reason for doing so.[60]

A more difficult theological aspect of the question of 1 Samuel's literary shape is posed by the difference between textual forms of Samuel in the Jewish and Christian traditions. As mentioned, Samuel exists in two parts within modern Jewish and Christian Bibles but constituted a single book in early Judaism. If a Christian interpreter works with the received bipartite text of Samuel, is Greek tradition then appropriately trumping the Hebrew, even when it seems that the division between the books of Samuel in Greek Bibles was made more for pragmatic than for theological considerations? Or should early Hebrew tradition, as the more "original," instead trump the Greek? Why in the end read "books" of Scripture at all? Why not read at the level of larger literary units, like the entire Pentateuch or Deuteronomistic History? Or why not read snippets of chapters or single verses in "oracular" fashion, as Christian preaching throughout the centuries has often done?[61]

---

60. This point is made strongly by Jenson, "Scripture's Authority in the Church." To read a biblical book as part of the "Hebrew Bible" or "Old Testament," as opposed to its simply being an isolated specimen of ancient Near Eastern literature, makes an implicit theological claim, whether that claim is recognized as such or not.

61. As argued by Barr, *Holy Scripture*, pp. 80-81, 91-92; cf. Barton, *Oracles of God*, pp. 149-50.

Did Jews in Antiquity Read Books?

Benjamin Sommer has mounted a thoroughgoing critique of the whole idea of the "book" as a theologically significant literary unit within Judaism.[62] He writes,

> In Jewish scripturality the literary unit of "book" is insignificant. For the midrashic exegete, the next unit after the verse that matters is the Bible as a whole, or perhaps the section . . . but certainly not the book.[63]

This judgment is made by Sommer as part of an effort to develop a modern Jewish approach to the Bible that is nevertheless still "sensitive to the emphases of older Jewish biblical exegesis."[64] Contemporary Judaism can therefore be said to have no real use for the kind of book-oriented approaches to scripture that have emerged within Christian scholarship because such a way of reading is foreign to "classical Jewish exegesis."[65] Sommer concludes, "For the rabbinic exegete (and hence . . . for the modern Jew attempting to create a specifically *Jewish* mode of relating to the Bible as scripture), Isaiah does not function as a book but as a collection of verses and pericopes."[66] It may be significant that Sommer's position grows out of his work on Isaiah, a largely non-narrative text. Still, for Sommer, there is no genre of the "book" to be discovered in history or functioning consequentially in Jewish interpretation at all. Scriptural "books" are really anthological scrolls and are best read without regard to any sense of a literary macro-structure.

Sommer is likely correct that midrashic exegesis primarily works with particular words and verses "independently of their context in a given biblical book,"[67] seeking rather to relate them to the framework of the canon as a whole.[68] He may also very well be correct in viewing this type of interpretive

---

62. Sommer, "Scroll of Isaiah as Jewish Scripture."

63. Sommer, "Scroll of Isaiah as Jewish Scripture," p. 230.

64. Sommer, "Scroll of Isaiah as Jewish Scripture," p. 227.

65. I believe Sommer overestimates the extent to which Christian biblical scholarship is guilty of making anachronistic, codex-type assumptions about the biblical books, although instances can certainly be found. For examples of Christian scholars who were already aware of this danger prior to Sommer's paper, see Barr, *Holy Scripture*, p. 8 n. 4; Conrad, "Heard but Not Seen." Now also see Barton, "What Is a Book?"; Blenkinsopp, "What Is a Book?" in his *Opening the Sealed Book*, pp. 1-8; Brueggemann, "On Scroll-Making in Ancient Jerusalem"; Finsterbusch and Lange, eds., *What Is Bible?*

66. Sommer, "Scroll of Isaiah as Jewish Scripture," p. 231 (his italics).

67. Sommer, "Scroll of Isaiah as Jewish Scripture," p. 230.

68. This is also the assessment of Alter, *Art of Biblical Narrative*, p. 11.

practice and its presuppositions as still authoritative, or at least exemplary, for contemporary Jewish biblical interpretation. However, Sommer elides a crucial point of distinction when, without acknowledgement of the shift, he extends his claims on behalf of "classical" Jewish interpretation to cover the entirety of Judaism's "ancient" hermeneutical practice.[69] In fact, by equating rabbinic exegesis and "all ancient Jewish hermeneutics" Sommer engages in precisely the kind of anachronism he attributes to the Christian scholars of whom he is critical.[70]

Sommer advances three arguments for including ancient Judaism within the scope of his claims: (1) ancient Jews read *scrolls* rather than codices, which means that they could not read by flipping pages back and forth in order to gain a sense of the whole;[71] (2) because ancient Jews are not likely to have had their own scrolls, they would only have heard and remembered shorter biblical passages (as those passages had been read out loud to them);[72] and (3) the later midrashic practices of rabbinic exegesis can already be seen at work in pre-rabbinic exegesis (e.g., at Qumran), with the implication that rabbinic exegesis involved no significant development or change from the basic hermeneutical methods of ancient Judaism.[73] Sommer makes the further related

---

69. Sommer, "Scroll of Isaiah as Jewish Scripture," p. 232. As Sommer remarks in a footnote, certain rabbinic rulings do in fact indicate an awareness of the distinction between discrete books (e.g., m. Meg. 4:4), so to this extent the booked shape of the biblical literature *did* hold some significance for rabbinic interpretation. Sommer counters, however, that the idea of a book was basically that of a collection of individual units and therefore without any controlling hermeneutical significance in and of itself: "for [the rabbis] these units did not relate to other units within the same book in any meaningful or unique way" (n. 20). It should be observed that here again Sommer has the prophetic books of scripture foremost in mind. It is not really clear if he would attempt to argue the same case for other biblical books (e.g., the books of the Pentateuch).

70. Sommer, "Scroll of Isaiah as Jewish Scripture," 233. Sommer attributes codex-type anachronisms to a Protestant impulse, filtered through a "New Critical" literary lens. For a similar critique, see Barton, *Reading the Old Testament*, pp. 140-67, on New Criticism and Brevard Childs. Sommer is also especially critical of Childs (p. 233 n. 24), who, so he charges, claims to be working with the intrinsic structure of scripture and yet imports the extrinsic category of "book" in doing so. Childs, however, understood the charge of "text-immanent" interpretation to be a basic misperception of his approach; see Childs, *Struggle to Understand Isaiah as Christian Scripture*, pp. 320-21. It is also necessary to question the tight relationship between "codex" and "book" that Sommer has asserted for the Christian tradition. "Book" can and does refer to a variety of literary formats within the history of Christianity; see Swanson, ed., *Church and the Book*.

71. Sommer, "Scroll of Isaiah as Jewish Scripture," p. 233 n. 22.

72. Sommer, "Scroll of Isaiah as Jewish Scripture," p. 233.

73. Sommer, "Scroll of Isaiah as Jewish Scripture," p. 233 n. 24.

observation that the Jewish synagogue liturgy includes only excerpts from the prophetic books (*haftarah*), and not generally in any particular literary order (i.e., only the Pentateuch is read as *lectio continua*).[74]

What Sommer neglects to mention, however, is that the "book" divisions of the Jewish canon exist today precisely because they themselves have been carefully preserved from antiquity. Rabbinic copying rules explicitly dictate:

> ... between one of the five books of the Torah and another book of the Torah, four lines [should be left blank], and similarly between one Prophet [i.e., one book included among 'the Prophets'] and another Prophet [i.e., four lines are to be left blank], but concerning one Prophet [i.e., a prophetic book] of the Twelve [and another] three lines [should be left blank].[75]

As Ehud Ben Zvi has rightly seen, such rules provide strong evidence that the individual books of the Minor Prophets were considered by the rabbis to be independent literary works, despite their all being contained on a single scroll and transmitted in that form.[76] Even more, these rules indicate an awareness in which the literary unity of biblical compositions was not viewed as identical with the manner of their material presentation. Copy spaces between the books usually appear already at Qumran, and not only within the book of The Twelve; the books of the Pentateuch also sometimes display a similar spacing and separation (e.g., 4QpaleoGen–Exod[1]).[77]

Frank Moore Cross helpfully summarizes the situation at Qumran:

> At Qumran we have Pentateuchal books written on single scrolls, in three instances two Pentateuchal books on a single scroll (Genesis–Exodus, Exodus–Leviticus, Leviticus–Numbers), but in no case more than two on a single scroll. The Twelve are inscribed usually on one scroll and in all but

74. Sommer, "Scroll of Isaiah as Jewish Scripture," p. 233. See further, Fishbane, *Haftarot*.

75. b. Baba Batra 13b (cf. *Soferim* 2.4). This is the translation as it appears in Ben Zvi, "Twelve Prophetic Books," p. 132 n. 22.

76. Ben Zvi, "Twelve Prophetic Books," p. 132. The opposite conclusion — that these rules imply how all of the individual books of the The Twelve were treated as a single literary unit — has more usually been claimed in recent scholarship, as Ben Zvi notes. A distinction must be observed, however, between writing conventions and genre, as the following discussion attempts to make clear.

77. Tov, "Scribal Practices." Tov examines a wide variety of scribal practices, concluding that both continuities and discontinuities may be found between the scribal techniques observable in the Dead Sea Scrolls and those later in evidence on the part of the rabbis. The matter of line spacing, with its implication for how literary units of Scripture were perceived, is identified by Tov as an area of continuity or agreement.

one instance in their traditional order. In the case of the *Five Megillot*, extant Qumran manuscripts contain but a single book on each scroll extant.[78]

In other words, while the biblical books customarily do appear one-to-a-scroll, regardless of their length, they can also be combined sequentially in a manner that nevertheless preserves their individual literary integrity.

The relative independence of the individual books within the Minor Prophets is also shown by the existence at Qumran of interpretive texts or *pesharim* on particular books of The Twelve.[79] Their continued literary independence is further indicated by the way in which the Masoretic practice of counting the total number of verses in a book is applied to each book of The Twelve.[80] It is surely extraordinary that despite being copied routinely on a single scroll, the individual books of The Twelve retained discrete literary identities. Contrary to Sommer's claim that in Judaism "book" always meant "scroll," significant historical evidence thus indicates that in ancient Judaism "book" (in the sense of a "literary work" or "composition") and "scroll" were once two separate, although related, phenomena. In the case of the Minor Prophets, for example, an idea of a book-unit existed that was different from (and smaller than) the scroll containing all twelve of them.

However, the reverse is the case, too. With respect to both the Pentateuch and the Deuteronomistic History, one encounters the idea of a literary work that was larger than a single scroll. Emanuel Tov is persuaded that larger books such as Samuel would have been written on multiple scrolls, as was also the case with the literature of ancient Greece and Rome.[81] Menahem Haran has determined through extensive study of the material aspects of ancient bookmaking that each of the reconstructed pentateuchal sources (J, E, or P) would have contained too much material to fit onto a single scroll.[82] To the extent that historical-critical scholars want to continue to

---

78. Cross, *From Epic to Canon*, p. 229 n. 24. His italics.

79. Ben Zvi, "Twelve Prophetic Books," p. 131 and n. 21. E.g., 1QpHab and 4QpNah (= 4Q169).

80. Ben Zvi, "Twelve Prophetic Books," p. 133 n. 22. As Ben Zvi concedes, however, there also exists a final tally of verses for the entire book of The Twelve. Similarly, the individual books of The Twelve do not each contain a marked middle verse in the Masoretic text (as appears in other prophetic books), but Mic 3:12 is marked as the middle verse of the book of The Twelve as a whole.

81. Tov, "Scribal Practices," p. 18. For the classical world, Tov cites (among others): Gamble, *Books and Readers in the Early Church*; Kenyon, *Books and Readers in Ancient Greece and Rome*; Van Sickle, "Book-Roll and Some Conventions of the Poetic Books."

82. Haran, "Book-Scrolls at the Beginning of the Second Temple Period," p. 114. This conclusion appears to be accurate even if one does not accept Haran's further judgment that

work with a notion of discrete longitudinal sources behind the Pentateuch (to my mind an increasingly doubtful idea), then they also have to accommodate a notion of multiple scrolls for each of the sources from the beginning of the process of literary composition — a complicating factor still not widely enough recognized.[83]

For Haran, the deuteronomic source ("D") was the first literary work to be fitted onto a single scroll, an outcome acknowledged rhetorically in Deuteronomy's repetitive self-referential language of "this torah" (Deut 1:5; 27:3, 26; etc.), "this book [*sēpher*]" (Deut 28:58; 29:19, 26) and "this book of the *torah*" (Deut 29:20; 30:10; 31:26).[84] According to Haran, the noun *sēpher* always means a particular written scroll in biblical Hebrew, not the literary work itself.[85] To this extent, Haran and Sommer are in agreement. However, the reason for this usage, Haran insists, is that as much as possible it was the practice of the scribes to write each literary composition on its own scroll.[86] The close relationship between the two is also seen in the fact that in post-biblical Hebrew the substantive *sēpher* does come to refer to the literary work itself, a "broadening of meaning," Haran remarks, that "would have been impossible if, originally, there was no full correlation between the work and the *sēpher* ['book'] containing it."[87] Haran thus perceives a shift between biblical and rabbinic understandings and practices where Sommer sees only continuity.

With the literary construction of larger compositions such as the Pentateuch and the Deuteronomistic History, more extensive narratives were subdivided so as to fit onto a standard number of scrolls. Haran observes, however, that the subdivision of the Pentateuch into five parts was by no means a given.[88] On strictly material grounds, a subdivision into four parts, or more than five parts, was fully possible. It follows quite logically, Haran concludes, that the Pentateuch's "division precisely into five parts can only

---

the sources continue on into the books of the Former Prophets. Cf. Haran, "Books of the Chronicles," p. 160; Meyers, "Torah Shrine in the Ancient Synagogue," pp. 309-10.

83. A parallel exists here with some Mesopotamian works, such as the epics of Gilgamesh and Atraḥasis, which were written on multiple tablets due to their length. The tablets were then numbered and filed for storage and consultation. See Millard, "Authors, Books, and Readers in the Ancient World," p. 547.

84. Haran, "Book-Scrolls at the Beginning of the Second Temple Period," p. 116.

85. Haran, "Book-Size and the Thematic Cycles," p. 166 n. 3. Cf. Haran, "Books of the Chronicles," p. 159.

86. Haran, "Book-Size and the Thematic Cycles," p. 165.

87. Haran, "Book-Size and the Thematic Cycles," p. 166 n. 3. One does not necessarily have to consider other scenarios "impossible" to find Haran's reconstruction convincing.

88. Haran, "Book-Size and the Thematic Cycles," pp. 172-73.

be explained by assuming that, beyond mere technical necessity, this division also bears a thematic significance and was premeditated from the outset."[89] Quite strikingly, Haran then goes on to refer to the five pentateuchal "books" as both "parts of a large cyclical composition and, at the same time, quasi-independent units in themselves."[90] Here again, a historically based distinction emerges between the physical "scroll" and the literary unit or "book." To the extent that Judaism has elevated the entire Pentateuch as Torah over the other biblical writings, while at the same time resisting any gradations of authority or significance within that Torah, it is all the more striking that the Torah's fivefold "booked" shape has been preserved so consistently by Jewish tradition.

Nor is that preservation simply a function of content, an idea Haran also explores, although each of the five books of the Pentateuch can readily be viewed as detailing a crucial act in a five-part drama.[91] As Ben Zvi has perceived, formal literary markers exist at the seams of the pentateuchal books in order to bind them together, even while also distinguishing them from each other.[92] The same sort of formal markers exist within the Deuteronomistic History. In that connection, Ben Zvi notes how the end of Deuteronomy (Deut 34:5-8, 9) and the beginning of Joshua (Josh 1:1-2) both refer to the death of Moses and to Joshua as his successor.[93] Ben Zvi neglects to mention as well the matching introductory phrases in all of the books in the Deuteronomistic History (except for 1 Samuel and 1 Kings), a literary phenomenon that additionally strengthens his point.[94] In particular, the common phrase "after the death of . . ." gives the appearance of having been used redactionally to mark literary boundaries at the time when the present structure of the Deuteronomistic History was determined. One can speculate that this phrase may not have been needed at the beginning of Samuel or Kings because those boundaries were already sufficiently clear. At any rate, as Ben Zvi has carefully reasoned,

89. Haran, "Book-Size and the Thematic Cycles," p. 173. Haran's ascription of intentionality to the fivefold form of the Pentateuch is still valid without necessarily assuming, as he does, that this situation was the case "from the outset." Theoretically, the subdivision into five "books" could have been introduced at some later point in the history of the Pentateuch's transmission, although there exists no dispositive historical evidence for such a speculation. Haran himself does not mean to suggest that a fivefold division already existed at the level of the pentateuchal sources, for he explicitly rejects this idea.

90. Haran, "Book-Size and the Thematic Cycles," p. 173.

91. Haran, "Book-Size and the Thematic Cycles," pp. 174-76.

92. Ben Zvi, "Closing Words." Compare Exod 40:38 (LXX) with Deut 34:12, and Lev 27:34 with Num 36:13. As Ben Zvi points out, Gen 50:26 is conspicuously different.

93. Ben Zvi, "Looking at the Primary (Hi)story," p. 37.

94. Compare Josh 1:1; Judg 1:1; 2 Sam 1:1; 2 Kgs 1:1.

such redactional devices not only bridge literary gaps, they also presuppose their existence.[95]

In other words, had there not been a strong preexistent sense of discrete literary units, presumably such redactional "bridging" would not have been necessary. Evident in this phenomenon, therefore, is an ancient awareness within the Deuteronomistic History that discrete literary units did exist. The process responsible for the later shape of the biblical canon has preserved this awareness by transmitting both the Pentateuch and the Deuteronomistic History primarily as collections of such literary units or "books" and only secondarily as composite works. Or, to put it differently, "books" of the Pentateuch and the Deuteronomistic History were not construed merely as "chapters" within larger literary works.[96] They were discrete, coherent literary works in their own right that nevertheless were eventually gathered into larger composite literary wholes.[97]

In sum, modern Jews may certainly choose not to engage in book-oriented readings of the Bible and medieval rabbis may well have been uninterested in the "book" as a theologically meaningful horizon for interpretation.[98] Ancient Judaism, however, recognized discrete literary units that were not simply congruent with the scrolls on which they were written, and these units can fairly be designated literary "works" or "books."[99] Moreover, the process of scriptural can-

95. Ben Zvi, "Looking at the Primary (Hi)story," p. 37 n. 18.

96. Cf. Ben Zvi, "Twelve Prophetic Books," p. 132 n. 22. This conclusion also provides one way to answer the kind of literary question posed by Gunn, "Hebrew Narrative," p. 226: "For example, what if my interest is in the story of David and Goliath? As I seek to read this text in context, this episode within its larger story, what is the larger story? Is Cain's killing of Abel an episode in my story? That inclusion would make a difference to how I read David's killing of Goliath." Based on the booked shape of the biblical literature, the answer in the first instance would be no; Cain and Abel are not part of the immediate story of David and Goliath. However, the story of Cain and Abel might still function as a distinct, but more distant, intertextual echo between books. The heuristic notion of concentric circles as demarcating zones of more and less proximate literary relationships could prove helpful at this point. But on the theory outlined above, each book is its own *primary* interpretive horizon.

97. Schiffman, "Memory and Manuscript," identifies the basic biblical meaning of *sēpher* as "document" rather than "book," but he similarly argues that "scroll" (*megillah*) "refers only to the physical form of the material, not to its status, canonicity, or contents" (p. 150). He also interestingly observes that almost all of the uses of *sēpher* at Qumran refer to biblical books, while sectarian texts are mostly called *serekh/serakhim* ("rule collection[s]"). Schiffman believes that the wider range of meaning of biblical *sēpher* "atrophied in postbiblical Hebrew" (p. 136).

98. For further exploration of "scripture" within Jewish tradition, now see Sommer, ed., *Jewish Concepts of Scripture*.

99. For additional reflection on the nature of "texts" in antiquity, see Morenz and Schorch,

onization established those discrete book-units as the primary contours within the biblical canon.[100] That is not to say larger canonical designations like "Torah" or "Prophets" should have no weight for contemporary biblical interpretation. To the contrary, much important work remains to be done on the relationship between "books" and the larger literary-canonical structures in which they are now found.[101] But it is to affirm that both historical and literary approaches to biblical interpretation can and should find common ground in affirming the primacy of the biblical book in setting the main horizon for the interpretive task.[102]

Reading 1 Samuel as if a Book

In returning to the particular problem of reading 1 Samuel, two methodological conclusions should be drawn from the preceding discussion. First, to the extent that Christian theological interpretation of the Bible wishes to be historically grounded, literarily sensitive, and canonically faithful, it will chiefly

---

eds., *Was ist ein Text?* For an exploration of how an artistic "work" may be said to exceed a given format, see Genette, *Work of Art*; Ricoeur, "What Is a Text?"

100. Trebolle Barrera, "Origins of a Tripartite Old Testament Canon," p. 135: ". . . a method of study which starts with the biblical manuscripts from Qumran favors the study of each book of the Pentateuch separately, or at most in pairs such as Genesis–Exodus (4Q1), Exodus–Leviticus (4Q17), or Leviticus–Numbers (4Q23)." Trebolle Barrera thinks there were shorter compositions in the pre-exilic period corresponding to various sections of the Pentateuch. In this view, he draws on the work of Rendtorff, *Problem of the Process of Transmission*; and Albertz, *A History of Israelite Religion*, pp. 464-93. Trebolle Barrera also sees shorter compositions from various sources as lying behind the Deuteronomistic History, subsequently redacted into the larger structure.

101. See especially the pioneering work of Sheppard, *Wisdom as a Hermeneutical Construct*; idem, "Book of Isaiah." For other examples of how the literary placement of biblical books within a particular canonical division contributed to their usage within early Judaism and Christianity, see Chapman, "A Threefold Cord."

102. Relevant here are the theoretical reflections of Paul Ricoeur regarding what constitutes a literary "work"; see his *Essays on Biblical Interpretation*, pp. 99-100. Wolterstorff, "Unity behind the Canon," argues that "work" status is a reader-oriented claim rather than a textual property, and that its probity ultimately lies in whether the reader gets something out of reading a text as a whole. The historical reality of the canon can thus be viewed as a prior authorizing act, which instructs contemporary Christian readers to approach the entire Bible as a single "work" and individual books as "chapters" within the larger unity. Cf. Ricoeur, "Canon between the Text and the Community." In a stimulating discussion, Gerd Theobald has called for "biblical theology" to be replaced with a "book theology" in which the entire Bible is treated as a single work, but also an internally differentiated one in which earlier portions have given rise to later additions and reinterpretations; see his "Von der Biblischen Theologie zur Buch-Theologie."

take the form of book-oriented interpretation — focusing, that is, on the theological witness of individual biblical books. Second, the question of treating 1 Samuel apart from 2 Samuel calls for hermeneutical agility and an avoidance of hard and fast methodological judgments. On the one hand, Christian interpreters can certainly point to the subdivision of Samuel in septuagintal tradition as providing a warrant for the interpretation of 1 Samuel on its own. On the other hand, however, the Masoretic text (MT) of Samuel should remain the primary text for Christian interpretation, and for a profoundly theological reason. The importance of retaining a common scriptural text with Judaism is paramount for Christians. It has not yet been sufficiently appreciated how deeply intertwined were Christianity's use of the Septuagint and its tragic tradition of supersessionistic theology.[103] As divinely appointed interpretive partners, Christians and Jews should, as much as possible, struggle over the same scriptural text together.[104] Especially in view of the Holocaust, it is crucial for Christianity to affirm its willingness to meet Judaism at the Hebrew text.[105]

Yet while Western Christianity has generally affirmed the priority of the Hebrew text, it has at the same time retained the book order it inherited largely from septuagintal tradition. Septuagintal Bibles sometimes — but not always![106] — exhibit a fourfold organization of Law, Histories, Poetry, and Prophets in contrast to the traditional threefold Hebrew order of Torah, Prophets, and Writings. Modern English Bibles, especially those with Protestant sponsor-

103. *Contra* Müller, *First Bible of the Church.* Again, by "supersessionistic" I do not mean simply Christianity's claim to religious truth but historical expressions of that claim in which Judaism is viewed as rejected or replaced by God, and therefore no longer capable of receiving divine favor or guidance.

104. This normative judgment is made from a Christian point of view; it is for Jews themselves to decide to what extent having a common biblical text with Christians is theologically desirable within their own tradition. But for a similar Jewish view, see Novak, "What Does Edith Stein Mean for Jews?" p. 161: "Because of our historical connections, most importantly our agreement on the exact text of the Hebrew Bible and that it is the intact word of God for both us, Christians are for Jews different from all other non-Jews, and Jews are for Christians different from all other non-Christians."

105. The adoption of this position should not be thought to entail a total objection to the use of septuagintal evidence in determining the best Hebrew text. The MT must certainly not be adopted uncritically. Deep theological concern should arise, however, when septuagintal traditions are used so heavily to revise the MT that the resultant eclectic text is in fact one that has never been used by any worshiping community within Judaism or Christianity.

106. The early LXX codices do not agree on either the scope (i.e., the number) or the order of the Old Testament books. For example, both Alexandrinus and Sinaiticus have the poetical books at the end of the collection and the prophetic corpus in the middle, as the Hebrew Bible does. Only Vaticanus exhibits the fourfold format usually claimed for "the LXX." For further details, see Chapman, "Canon: OT"; Elliott, "Manuscripts, the Codex and the Canon."

ship, have thus tended to retain the same books as in the narrower Jewish canon but in their so-called "Christian" order.[107] This mixed legacy means that ultimately a Christian argument from tradition must retain flexibility with respect to text type and canonical order. Modern Christian Bibles are canonical compromises; theological arguments appealing to tradition can be ranged on either side of the question about reading 1 Samuel apart from 2 Samuel. The arguments regarding the scope of the canon (i.e., which books it contains) are also compromises between ecclesial usage and Jewish origins. The most compelling theological argument for the narrower canon, at least to my mind — and one affirmed within Protestantism — is also to retain a common scripture with Jews.

The ancient manuscript evidence regarding the division of Samuel is in fact ambiguous as well. It appears that Hebrew Samuel did exist as a single work before its subdivision in Greek, since the large Samuel scroll found at Qumran (4QSam^a) continues from what is now 1 Sam 31:13 to 2 Sam 1:1 without a major break.[108] On the other hand, there seems to be no absolute reason why the Hebrew *Vorlage* behind the earliest septuagintal tradition might not have existed at some earlier point in time on two or more separate scrolls. It remains intriguing that 2 Sam 1:1 echoes the introductions in Josh 1:1 and Judg 1:1.

These findings mean that the best line of approach must be both more pragmatic and more tentative. Rather than deciding the issue in advance, an interpretive approach will need to remain relatively open. The better question will then be: What kind of literary reading can one develop if one interprets 1 Samuel *as if* it were its own book? Will the reading make sense? Will the interpretation be persuasive? How does what is now 1 Samuel relate to what is now 2 Samuel? Even at the end of such an interpretative exploration, a strong claim of intentionality for 1 Samuel as a discrete literary composition will probably not be possible, but through careful interpretive work one may be able to show how a narrative with such boundaries can be read in a coherent and illuminating fashion.

---

107. I say "so-called" because in reality there were likely multiple orders within ancient Judaism, one of which is now associated with the LXX and another with the MT. We should therefore not assume that the LXX order is of Christian origin. Neither should we assume that because there were different orders in circulation no canon existed at all.

108. See A. Fincke, *Samuel Scroll from Qumran*. Plate XIII contains a hand copy of the column of the text in question. Line 31 consists of what is now regarded as 2 Sam 1:1. It is begun on a new line, leaving an open line above it. This feature corresponds to the later Masoretic device of *petuchah*, which was used to organize sections of the text into discrete lectionary readings. The line breaks in 4QSam^a do not always appear where they do in the MT; Fincke estimates the percentage of agreement at only 36% (p. 272).

In interpreting 1 Samuel, therefore, one must maintain an awareness of the provisionality of the view that 1 Samuel is a literary whole. This caveat comes not only from uncertainties in the historical evidence pertaining to the issue but again from the work itself. As Jobling has also pointed out forcefully, 2 Sam 21:1-14 conveys a story about Saul's second wife Rizpah, a story that relies upon a previous event unreported in the book of 1 Samuel. Has this information been added almost randomly to the end of what is now 2 Samuel simply in order to preserve a tradition that might otherwise have been lost? Or is a more sophisticated literary effect intended by such narrative displacement? These questions should give one pause and prevent the attribution of too much intentionality or literary coherence to the book of 1 Samuel as a discrete composition apart from 2 Samuel.

On the other hand, a reading of 1 Samuel on its own will inevitably emphasize the figure of Saul, doomed but noble in tragedy, because the ending of 1 Samuel now coincides with his death and an accompanying reference to the village of Jabesh-gilead (31:11-13), which literarily ties together both the beginning and the ending of the entire Saul account (cf. 1 Samuel 11). Thus those readers are not wrong who see heroic dimensions to the account of Saul, especially when they restrict the scope of their reading to 1 Samuel.[109] Yet in the end I will argue that this kind of interpretation is subverted by other features of 1 Samuel and mitigated by consideration of 2 Samuel, which — by further developing David's portrait as a pious and just king without peer — increasingly diminishes Saul's heroism. To be sure, David has failings of his own, and these disappointments ironically preserve sympathy for Saul at the same time.

So 1 Samuel certainly contains tragic elements, but when read together with 2 Samuel these elements increasingly appear in retrospect to have been a tragic episode en route to something else. In fact, the position taken here is that a reading of 1 Samuel as part of a single literary composition, including 2 Samuel, will ultimately take its most important interpretive cues from 2 Samuel 21–24 as that entire composition's conclusion.[110] Precisely in this manner will an effort be made to negotiate between 1 Samuel as a coherent literary narrative and 1 Samuel as part of the larger composition of 1–2 Samuel. As will become

---

109. E.g., Isser, *Sword of Goliath*; Mobley, "Glimpses of the Heroic Saul"; Preston, "Heroism of Saul." But note that Isser has to appeal to a prior "heroic narrative" (p. 138) of Saul's story rather than the one now represented by the text's final form, and that for Mobley the "heroic" reading of Saul emerges from reading against the received text. Only Preston argues that the *present* form of the text depicts Saul in an essentially "heroic" light.

110. This fundamental point has been increasingly argued in other detailed studies; see Klement, *II Samuel 21–24*; Simon, *Identity and Identification*. But cf. Campbell, "2 Samuel 21–24."

evident in due course, the tension between reading 1 Samuel on its own and 1 Samuel together with 2 Samuel inevitably centers on how best to handle the narrative's extended comparison of Saul and David.

The Further Horizon: 2 Samuel 21–24

In addition to the Rizpah episode (2 Samuel 21), to which Jobling has helpfully called attention, there are other significant elements for the interpretation of 1 Samuel to be found in 2 Samuel 21–24.

The Rizpah narrative concerns a famine later in David's reign that is explicitly said to be the result of bloodguilt on Saul and his house because of Saul's killing of the Gibeonites. Yet this aspect of Saul's reign is not presented anywhere in 1 Samuel, apparently causing the narrator of 2 Samuel 21 to offer a word of retrospective background (2 Sam 21:2). The difficulty of the bloodguilt is resolved through the impaling of seven of Saul's male descendants, two sons of Rizpah and five sons of Merab. Out of loyalty to Jonathan, David spares Mephibosheth, Jonathan's son and Saul's grandson (2 Sam 21:3-9). Rizpah then protects the bodies of her two sons from the predations of wild animals until David is moved by her example to gather up the bodies of all seven sons, together with the bones of Saul and Jonathan from Jabesh, and bury them in the tomb of Saul's father, Kish (2 Sam 21:10-14).[111]

Here it is also of interest that the impaling of Saul and Jonathan is briefly recapitulated from 1 Samuel 31 in 2 Samuel 21, with the difference that in 2 Sam 21:12 Saul and Jonathan are said to have been "hung up" ($\sqrt{tl'}$) in the "public square" (*rĕḥôb*) in Beth Shean, whereas in 1 Sam 31:10 Saul is described as having been "fastened" ($\sqrt{tq'}$) to Beth Shean's "wall" (*ḥômâ*), along with his three sons, Jonathan, Abinadab and Malchishuah. Neither is there any mention in 2 Samuel 21 of Saul's sons Abinadab and Malchishuah. These differences in detail might suggest slightly divergent traditions of Saul's defeat;[112] yet the narrator in 2 Samuel 21 appears to exhibit an awareness of what has not been previously told in the narrative (e.g., Saul's killing of the Gibeonites).

Jobling offers the Rizpah example as proof that the literary organization of the books of Samuel is not strictly chronological. The story of Rizpah in 2 Samuel 21 relies upon an earlier event that the narrative has left untold until now. Yet what is truly unusual about this retrospective addition is not so much

111. On the remarkably robust afterlife of Rizpah in biblical reception history, see Brenner, "Rizpah [Re]Membered."
112. Hentschel, "Hinrichtung der Nachkommen Sauls."

that it has been made but that the earlier narrative has been left unaltered in the literary transmission of the book. Also interesting is the fact that this retrospective gesture appears in 2 Samuel 21, the first chapter in a group of four chapters routinely treated by historical-critical interpreters as an "appendix" or later addendum to 1–2 Samuel as a whole.[113]

That these chapters focus on David as an ideal ruler is hardly in dispute. In addition to detailing his efforts to counter divine displeasure and bloodguilt in 2 Samuel 21, the four chapters also feature: (1) an account of how four giants were slain in battles between David and the Philistines (2 Sam 21:15-22), including one called Goliath (v. 19); (2) a song of David (paralleling Psalm 18), which he is said to have declaimed "on the day when the Lord delivered him from the hand of all his enemies and from the hand of Saul" (2 Sam 22:1// Psalm 18 superscription); (3) the "last words" of David (2 Sam 23:1-7); (4) lists of David's warriors (2 Sam 23:8-38); and (5) another account of divine anger, which David averts by interceding with God on behalf of the people and then buying the threshing floor of Araunah (2 Samuel 24). With respect to the literary organization of this material, the "again" ($\sqrt{ysp}$ Hiph.) of 2 Sam 24:1 indicates an awareness of the collective unity of the four chapters by explicitly referring back to the earlier account of divine displeasure in 2 Samuel 21.

In this way *all* of the "appendix" material exhibits a chronological displacement from the larger narrative as it continues from 2 Samuel 20 into the book of 1 Kings, which begins in jarring fashion with a suddenly senile David. This displacement is not only indicated by the fact that the Rizpah episode gestures to an untold past but also by the non-narrative quality of much of 2 Samuel 21–24, which as a compound literary unit contains primarily poetry and brief notices (or expanded lists). The two main narrative sections, one at the beginning and one at the end of the unit (2 Sam 21:1-14; 24), both concern David's successful efforts to intercede with God in order to prevent misfortune coming upon the entire people, and thus these narratives function as literary bookends for the whole. Their double emphasis suggests that the main point of this material is not only to offer a positive, even idealized, portrait of David as king, but to underscore the sacral dimension of his kingship. Thus this final section of the larger composition of Samuel can be read as David's symbolic revival following Sheba's rebellion (2 Sam 20).[114] Furthermore, the notion of intercession plays a key role in 2 Samuel 24, and in both chapters 21

---

113. E.g., Wellhausen, *Prolegomena to the History of Israel*, p. 178: "an appendix of a very peculiar structure"; Smith, *Books of Samuel*, p. 373: "it seems as if the compiler threw together the fragments which were left . . . and he did not know where else to put them."

114. Carlson, *David, the Chosen King*.

and 24 David is depicted as interacting responsively with various individuals and groups within his kingdom. Accordingly, these two narratives present an understanding of his kingship as active, responsible, concerned for the social fabric of society, and religiously representative.

It has been forcefully argued by Walter Brueggemann that these concluding chapters comprise a subversive appendix with the goal of "deconstructing" royal ideology.[115] There can be no denying how several features of this material can be viewed as portraying David in an ambiguous or negative light, especially in the puzzling final chapter (2 Sam 24). What is being critiqued, however, is not David or even the monarchy per se, but any ruler or reign that ignores or diminishes God's overlordship. David's mishandling of the census appears to do just that.[116] Yet this concluding admonition has to be held together with the fundamentally positive treatment of David in the rest of these chapters. In context, 2 Samuel 24 does function as a final caution, but it does not negate or replace the narrative's celebration of David as God's paradigmatic ruler. At stake instead is whether even under David Israel's ritual and cult will become subsumed into the initiatives and machinery of the state (= civil religion) — or whether worship in Israel will maintain its own integrity and openness to God.

That perspective is shared by the other non-narrative material in 2 Samuel 21–24. The account of the four giants (2 Sam 21:15-22), whatever its historical origins may have been, is not in its present context simply an assortment of misplaced doublets with respect to the Goliath episode in 1 Samuel 17. Instead, there is a purposeful evocation of earlier tradition. The entire section now functions together as a sign of David's symbolic return to power and vitality. The same spirit he had once exemplified in 1 Samuel 17 returns upon his soldiers. David's youthful vigor had seemed almost completely lost in the narratives of Absalom's and Sheba's rebellions, but the description of additional giant-killing on the part of his men contributes to the picture of a timeless Davidic Camelot in 2 Samuel 21–24, in which the king is eternally young, strong, and full of promise.

Similarly, the poem in 2 Samuel 22 appears to look backward to "the day God delivered [David] from the hand of all his enemies and from the hand of Saul" (2 Sam 22:1), but the precise day of that deliverance is not named nor is it obvious from the context which day is meant. The most likely candidate for a particular "day" within the narrative is perhaps the day of Saul's death, as narrated in 1 Sam 31:6. Yet in its present context the "deliverance" ($\sqrt{nṣl}$, Hiph.) of

115. Brueggemann, "2 Sam 21–24."
116. See Klement, *II Samuel 21–24*, pp. 174-78.

David also seems to possess broader significance. Is it stretching the semantic range of *nṣl* too far to entertain the idea that here a *cumulative* deliverance is in view, one that has finally become complete and actual because of the final subjection of Israel's primordial enemies — the "descendants of the giants" (2 Sam 21:18) — and the final resolution of Saul's troublesome legacy (2 Sam 21:14)? The poem in 2 Samuel 22 additionally contains echoes of Hannah's Song in 1 Samuel 2, thus rounding out the narrative of the entire work.[117]

Use of the "lamp" (*nēr*/*nîr*) image for God in 2 Sam 22:29 is not only an oblique reference to David's royal status[118] but also contributes to a persistent contrast between David as a figure of light[119] and Saul as a person of darkness. Saul has trouble seeing and locating things: he is introduced by a search for his father's lost asses (1 Sam 9) and he spends much of the narrative trying to find David.[120] Throughout the book, Saul is placed in narrative settings in which darkness and nighttime are conspicuous features.[121] His lack of vision is subtly reinforced by his lack of information. He characteristically asks questions.[122] For example, his repeated question to David, "Is that your voice, my son David?" (1 Sam 24:17; 26:17), makes it sound as if he cannot quite see who is speaking to him. He certainly has difficulty recognizing David on more than one occasion, most notably just after David has killed Goliath (1 Sam 17:55-58)! Even at the very outset of Saul's story, Saul seems not to know there is a prophet in the area, although his own servant does — Saul only knows that one should give a prophet payment (1 Sam 9:7). Saul's *senses* are therefore portrayed as unreliable, subject to disruption and misperception (e.g., 1 Sam 10:10) and a topic of public discussion (e.g., 1 Sam 10:11-12). His judgments are weak and suspect.

117. For the literary relation between 2 Samuel 22 and 1 Samuel 2, see Mathys, *Dichter und Beter*, pp. 126-57; Polzin, *Samuel and the Deuteronomist*, pp. 30-36. Mathys views the two poetic compositions as late interpolations from the same redactional hand.

118. Cf. 2 Sam 21:17; 1 Kgs 11:36; 15:4; 2 Kgs 8:19. See further Firth, "Shining the Lamp." On the possibility that *nir* can mean "(territorial) dominion" or "fief," see Ben Zvi, "Once the Lamp Has Been Kindled"; Hanson, "Song of Heshbon and David's *Nîr*."

119. E.g., David's "bright eyes" in 1 Sam 16:2; cf. 2 Sam 23:4. In 1 Sam 29:9-10 David is described as an angelic figure and associated with the morning light.

120. E.g., 1 Sam 19:8-10; 20:27; 23:14; 26:1-5.

121. For this insight and a few examples, see Polzin, *Samuel and the Deuteronomist*, p. 146. E.g., Saul fights by night in 1 Sam 14:34, 36; he tries to kill David during the night in 1 Sam 19:10-11; he is found by David in the darkness of a cave in 1 Samuel 24; he is asleep in his camp when found again by David in 1 Sam 26:5, 7, 12 ("no one *saw* because they were asleep"); Saul visits the medium in Endor by night in 1 Samuel 28 ("What do you *see*?" Saul asks the medium).

122. Polzin, *Samuel and the Deuteronomist*, p. 103. As Polzin notes, Saul is not the only character in the narrative who asks questions, but his characterization conveys a more uncertain and interrogative nature than any of the narrative's other characters.

Saul's lack of vision is also supported in the narrative by the motifs of David's hiding (e.g., 1 Sam 23:19-23; 26:1) and pretending or play-acting (e.g., 1 Sam 21:13-16; 27:8-12). David is thus depicted as one who has the *ability* to hide and dissemble (also a type of hiding); Saul is instead the one who attempts to "look for" things, who literally becomes mad — not by pretending (as David does) but by sustaining seizures over which he has no control.[123] Indeed, Saul is the one who *cannot* control himself or hide successfully, because his physical stature and social position make him obvious and unable to escape the expectations of those around him (e.g., 1 Sam 10:22-24; 28:8, 12).

The poem in 2 Sam 23:1-7 also implicitly stands out of time from the wider narrative of Samuel.[124] It is presented as constituting David's "last words," but his actual death is not narrated until 1 Kgs 2:10.[125] Moreover, in 1 Kgs 2:1-9 there exists another version of David's final speech, this time in the form of an address to Solomon. Thus 2 Samuel 23:1-7 is styled as a prophetic oracle in which David utters the word of God. Use of the particle *ně'ûm* not only underscores the prophetic quality of David's speech, it provides a pointed contrast to Saul, whose own prophetic activity is non-verbal, unbalanced, and embarrassing.[126] As Herbert Klement observes, this oracular particle also forms a literary bookend with the *ně'ûm* prefacing the speech of the shadowy "man of God" in 1 Sam 2:30: "While the first *ne'um* of Jahweh in the book of Samuel concerned the rejection of Eli's dynasty, here the import of the second and last *ne'um* of Jahweh is the choosing of David's dynasty."[127] Significantly, these are the only two instances of this particle in 1–2 Samuel.

Likewise, the honor roll of warriors (2 Sam 23:8-39) following the poem in 2 Samuel 23 emphasizes the vigor and righteousness of David's kingship (cf. 2 Sam 8:15).[128] It is a summarizing statement or list — in other words, an *atemporal* literary unit — offering a characterization of David's reign as a whole. As a list, it stands apart from the larger narrative sequence. Its present literary purpose, beyond the merely informational goal of relating names and brief historical traditions, is to depict David as appreciative of his men and unwilling to stand on privilege: he is an admirable leader. He will not drink water from the well of Bethlehem, which has been gained for him by his men

---

123. Saul is described as becoming "another man" when he is gripped by the spirit of the LORD in ecstasy in 1 Sam 10:6; an "evil spirit" comes over him in 1 Sam 16:15-16; 19:9-10; he "raves" (√*nb'* Hithp.) ecstatically in 1 Sam 10:10; 19:23-24.

124. See further del Olmo Lete, "David's Farewell Oracle."

125. McCarter, "Apology of David."

126. For further background, see Levenson, "Technical Meaning for *n'm*."

127. Klement, *II Samuel 21–24*, pp. 215-16.

128. See further Dietrich, "König David," p. 15.

at the risk of their lives (2 Sam 23:14-17) — not when he did not risk his life in the same way (cf. 1 Sam 30:9-12). Accordingly, 2 Sam 23:13-17 exhibits both the warriors' willingness to risk injury for David and David's noble generosity in honoring that risk.[129] The motif of David's generosity again provides an implicit contrast with Saul, who, by contrast, is depicted in 1 Samuel as prickly, suspicious, and hypercritical in his personal interactions, with a tendency to engage in intrigue and then to blame his men and members of his family for his own miscalculations and errors in judgment.[130] Saul seems to have the support of Israelite warriors early on (1 Sam 10:26), but he appears oddly isolated at his death on Mount Gilboa (1 Sam 31:1-7).

The "appendix" concludes with 2 Samuel 24, a complex and challenging chapter. Interpreters have often struggled with how God, without giving a reason, apparently incites David to take a census and then proceeds to punish him for it.[131] God's role in the story is further problematized by the apparent substitution of "Satan" for God in the parallel account found in 1 Chronicles 21.[132] But Sara Japhet has mounted a compelling case that *śāṭān* is used in 1 Chronicles 21 as a common noun (= "accuser, tempter") rather than a personal name.[133] If so, then 2 Samuel 24 turns, not on the issue of theodicy (as the preoccupation of many interpreters might suggest, whatever their intentions), but on the link between numbering and the existence of a standing army, which

129. Cf. 1 Sam 22:1-2; 29:6; 30:21-31. Brueggemann, *David's Truth in Israel's Imagination and Memory*, p. 106, observes how this motif contrasts sharply with David's treatment of Uriah in 2 Samuel 11. Rather than using 2 Samuel 11 to subvert the claim of 2 Samuel 23, I view 2 Samuel 23 as retrospectively illuminating one of the several tragic failings of David in the Bathsheba episode: his betrayal of a man under his own command.

130. E.g., 1 Sam 14:24-30, 36-45; 18:17-29; 19:1, 11-17; 20:30-34; 22:6-19; 23:19-28. The two seeming exceptions (that prove the rule) are Saul's statements in 1 Sam 15:24-25 and 26:21. In 1 Sam 15:24-25 Saul seeks Samuel's forgiveness by saying, "I did wrong to transgress the Lord's commandment and your instructions; but I was afraid of the troops and I yielded to them. Please, forgive my offense and come back with me, and I will bow low to the Lord." With these words, Saul not only continues to offer excuses for his disobedience, he also addresses himself to Samuel rather than directly to God (cf. 1 Sam 15:30). In 1 Sam 26:21 Saul tells David, "I am in the wrong." Yet there are good reasons to doubt the sincerity of Saul's words at this point, not the least of which is that David continues to flee from him (1 Sam 26:25) and then explicitly expresses his own doubt about Saul's intentions (1 Sam 27:1).

131. Andrew of St. Victor instead reads canonically here, suggesting that David is in violation of the law set forth in Exod 30:12; see his *Commentary on Samuel and Kings, ad loc.*

132. For a typical "substitutionary" approach to this phenomenon, see Fokkelman, *Reading Biblical Narrative*, pp. 57-58.

133. "The satan" was conceived as something like the prosecuting attorney within God's heavenly court. See Japhet, *1 & 2 Chronicles*, pp. 370-75. For an alternative interpretation, based on *śāṭān* as a proper name, see Hahn, *Kingdom of God as Liturgical Empire*, pp. 86-90.

is treated as a mark of unfaith in God, and one for which atonement must be made (cf. Exod 30:11-16).[134] Here the "census" might in fact be better translated as a military "draft," since it places control of the army into the hands of the nation-state instead of maintaining the "charismatic" dimension of traditional warfare.[135] This motif would then go hand in hand with the great number of other motifs in Samuel aimed at subverting militarism, as well as the considerable number of other Old Testament texts warning against a reliance on purely pragmatic approaches to war.[136] Another possibility — which does not rule out the previous one — is that this census represented preparatory work for the building of the Jerusalem temple, which later tradition reports was built on the site where David interceded with God to stem the ensuing plague.[137] The task of building the temple was reserved for Solomon and forbidden to David because David was a "man of blood."[138]

Moreover, the "again" in 2 Sam 24:1 actually forecloses the possibility that God's anger at this juncture is capricious by directing the reader to the prior actions recounted in 2 Samuel 21. God's anger has a history. The exact relation between census, sanctuary, and plague is difficult to discern, as it is apparently rooted in a worldview no longer our own. Yet other Old Testament texts also testify to a conventional association between census and plague (e.g., Exod 30:12), and between plague and sanctuary (e.g., Num 8:19). David Penchansky has insightfully pointed out the central irony of the chapter: that David's effort to use numbers for Israel's defense results in Israel's loss of numbers.[139] The chapter is structured according to three sets of three: David is to pick his own punishment of either three years, three months, or three days. Tellingly, he selects the alternative that will produce the greatest dependency on

---

134. In a fascinating exploration of global biblical interpretation, Jenkins, *New Faces of Christianity*, p. 46, notes how the African Gikuyu share this taboo against enumeration. This example and others support Jenkins's contention that readers from the Two-Thirds World often have a striking closeness to the world of the Bible, a shared perspective that frequently reduces or eliminates the "obvious" tensions noted by First World readers.

135. Yoder, *Original Revolution*, p. 105.

136. Working text-critically, and thus not presuming an originally unified text, William Yarchin comes to a similar conclusion about the logic of 2 Samuel 21–24 as a section; see his "Text Criticism, Text Composition, and Text Concept," pp. 328-29: "The present juxtaposition of these two pericopes [i.e., 2 Sam 23:8-39 and 2 Samuel 24] moves the reader from the honorable development of David's military force that yields salvation for Israel to the excessive development of his forces that proves catastrophic for Israel."

137. There is, however, no hint of this connection in 2 Samuel. See Amit, "Araunah's Threshing-Floor." The link is made in 1 Chronicles 21–22.

138. See Greenwood, "Labor Pains," pp. 467-78; Meyers, "David as Temple Builder."

139. Penchansky, *What Rough Beast?* pp. 44-47.

God. Here again a striking contrast is evident between David's costly sacrifice (2 Sam 24:24) and Saul's earlier "worthless" one (1 Sam 15:9).[140] It is also David's "heart" that strikes him, a motif echoing earlier "heart" language in Samuel and reminding the reader of the tension between "heart" piety and state religion, a tension that animates the entire Samuel narrative. Rather than criticizing God or David, 2 Samuel 24 instead provides a final warning against empty ritualism, especially when used in the service of military power. The passage turns in fact on the need for a distinction between what might be called "church" and "state" (cf. 2 Chr 26:18).

Ultimately, the effect of all of the material in 2 Samuel 21–24 is to make explicit what has previously been a series of implicit contrasts between David and Saul. Especially in retrospect, Saul appears high-handed and isolated in comparison with David. Saul's characteristic weapon is the "spear" (*ḥănît*),[141] which he hurls at people. David, by contrast, knows that neither "sword nor spear" (*ḥănît*) brings victory (1 Sam 17:47). David even purloins Saul's spear later in the narrative (1 Sam 26). The spear is a suspect weapon, tainted with Canaanite associations.[142] In retrospect, 1 Samuel appears noticeably reticent regarding the sociability of Saul.[143] Did Saul ever gather to himself the loyal warriors that David did? Saul does seek physically imposing warriors (e.g., 1 Sam 14:52), but stories of their loyalty to him seem absent from the narrative — a conspicuous absence. Indeed, the narrative in 1 Samuel depicts Saul as increasingly isolated and alone. In the account of his death he is curiously removed from the fighting of his army. Although the battle rages around him, he appears cut off from human support — he is forced to beg a lowly servant to help him end his life (1 Sam 31:4).

Finally, the theme of intercession in 2 Samuel 24 also establishes a contrast with Saul, a king who repeatedly attempts to perform sacral functions but each time is unsuccessful. The chapter thus provokes retrospective questions (without explicitly answering them) about the precise nature of Saul's reli-

---

140. On the syntactical difficulty with the phrase in 15:9, see McCarter, *I Samuel*, p. 262. Its general sense is nevertheless clear.

141. See 1 Sam 13:22; 18:10; 19:9; 20:33; 22:6; 26:6-22; 2 Sam 1:6. On the spear motif, see Mobley, "Glimpses of the Heroic Saul," pp. 83-84.

142. Hoyle, "Weapons of God." Hamilton, *Body Royal*, p. 159, notes further that no other Israelite king, with the exception of Joash (2 Kgs 11:10) bears a spear. Saul's spear thus sets him apart and serves as a distinctive symbol for his character (1 Sam 8:10-11; 9:9-10; 20:33; 21:9; 26:7, 11-12, 16, 22). Joshua wields a short spear or javelin (*kîdôn*, e.g., Josh 8:18, 26) — as does Goliath (1 Sam 17:6), in addition to his own spear (*ḥănît*, 1 Sam 17:7).

143. Thus Saul is attributed with a "rash" act only in the LXX of 1 Sam 14:24. In the MT of 1 Samuel 14 his interactions with his servants and soldiers are narrated without explicit evaluations on the part of the narrator.

gious deficiency. What is it about Saul that fails to win the reader's approval? Perhaps his docility?[144] Yet the distinction between David and Saul is not that Saul engages in sacral functions whereas David does not. Both kings perform official religious acts, yet only David does so successfully.[145] However, "[David] never undertook a war without consulting the Lord first," observed Ambrose.[146] Saul can refer to God, even speak for him,[147] but he is only once (1 Sam 14:41) depicted as speaking to God directly (i.e., in second-person discourse). Even here, however, his address to God sounds formulaic, and occurs in a highly ritualized context.[148] Some of his references to God are found in the context of ritual greetings (e.g., 1 Sam 15:13; 23:21). Oaths also accordingly play a prominent role in the narratives about Saul and are used to illustrate his progressive deterioration (1 Sam 11:7; 14:24, 39, 44; 17:55; 19:6; 24:21; 28:10).[149]

In fact, whenever Saul uses pious language it seems as if "God" does not

---

144. Alter, *Art of Biblical Narrative*, p. 104.

145. David is depicted as seeking oracles from God, especially prior to initiating battle, in 1 Sam 22:5, 10, 13, 15; 23:1-5, 12; 30:7-8; 2 Sam 2:1; 5:17-25 (= 1 Chr 14:8-17); 21:1. He is shown praying in 1 Sam 23:10-11; 25:32, 39; 2 Sam 7:18-29; 12:13; 24:10, 17; 1 Kgs 1:47-48. Like a priest, he wears the ephod, dances before the ark and blesses the people in 2 Sam 6:12-19. He even offers sacrifices (2 Sam 6:13, 17). David also conducts offerings in 2 Sam 24:25 at the conclusion of the entire Samuel narrative. Second Samuel 8:18 reports that his "sons" (appointees?) were priests (cf. 2 Sam 20:23-26; 1 Kgs 4:1-6). On the historical likelihood of this possibility, see Armerding, "Were David's Sons Really Priests?"; Wenham, "Were David's Sons Priests?" On sacral aspects of the monarchy more generally, see Boccaccini, *Roots of Judaism*, p. 45.

146. Ambrose, *De officiis*, 1:177.

147. E.g., 1 Sam 11:13; 14:34, 39; 15:13, 20-21, 24, 30; 17:37; 23:7, 21; 24:19-22; 28:10.

148. Note that 1 Sam 14:41 (MT) reads only: "And Saul said to the Lord, the God of Israel, 'Give Tammim.'" The NRSV takes the divine name as a vocative (2×), reproducing an emotional speech by Saul found in the LXX: "Then Saul said, 'O Lord God of Israel, why have you not answered your servant today? If this guilt is in me or in my son Jonathan, O Lord God of Israel, give Urim; but if this guilt is in your people Israel, give Thummim.'" This speech is not at all in keeping with the rest of Saul's portrait in the MT. Speaking to God in such a personal manner is precisely what Saul does *not* do. By contrast David does so on numerous occasions. He can even invoke God against Saul (1 Sam 23:9-13). One of the clearest examples of the difference between David and Saul in this regard is provided by 1 Samuel 30, in which David successfully battles the Amalekites by seeking God's direction through divination. With this later account the reader can retrospectively identify what was missing from Saul's attempt to fight the Amalekites in 1 Samuel 15: namely, any attempt on Saul's part to seek divine instruction as he performed Samuel's prophetic instructions. One can argue that such divine instruction was unnecessary, given the specificity of the prophet's command. Yet from the perspective of 1 Samuel 30, Saul appears all the more distant from God in the performance of his duty. Note his odd use of the expression "the LORD *your* God" three times when speaking to Samuel (1 Sam 15:15, 21, 30; my emphasis). For the significance of this phrase, see Davidson, "Saul's Reprobation," p. 154.

149. See further Ziegler, *Promises to Keep*, pp. 153-83.

refer to a personal being but rather to something more like an institution, cause, or idea. When Saul does "inquire" (√š'l) of God, an action that only happens twice in the narrative (1 Sam 14:37; 28:6), God does not answer.[150] These two passages do convey the view that God *no longer* answered Saul after his rejection in 1 Samuel 13 and 15 (e.g., 1 Sam 14:37; 28:15), but curiously there is no explicit report of successful divination by Saul even before these rejections. Earlier in 1 Samuel 14 he breaks off his attempt to engage in divination with the help of the priest Ahijah (1 Sam 14:18-19). Later in 1 Samuel 14 he tries to use the sacred lots, but that narrative also suggests problems with Saul's use of divination.[151]

There is finally a world of difference between Saul's interaction with the deity in 1 Samuel 14 and David's keen sense of God as a dynamic presence with personality and purpose.[152] David's animated apprehension of God comes strongly to the fore in his frequent descriptive references to God.[153] For Saul, "God" seems more like a conventional form to be followed, a religious custom to be observed — if done correctly, blessing will inevitably follow; if done incorrectly, disaster will invariably strike.[154] Saul therefore relies on ritual, over and over again, but his ritual practices do not work as he expects them to because a certain religious awareness or sensibility appears to be lacking. That is precisely what Samuel pinpoints as Saul's failing in 1 Samuel 15: substituting inauthentic "divination" (*qesem*) for genuine religious faith or "obedience" (lit., "listening" [√šmʿ]; 1 Sam 15:22-23) to "the word of the Lord" (*děbar yhwh*). It is also how Saul is remembered in the biblical tradition outside of the Samuel

150. Craig, "Rhetorical Aspects of Questions."

151. Polzin, *Samuel and the Deuteronomist*, pp. 135-37. I am using the term "divination" neutrally and broadly to mean any type of communication between human beings and the divine. See further Ciraolo and Seidel, eds., *Magic and Divination in the Ancient World*; Cryer, *Divination in Ancient Israel*, esp. 263-312; Huffmon, "Priestly Divination in Israel"; Jeffers, *Magic and Divination*; Long, "Effect of Divination upon Israelite Literature"; Nigosian, *Magic and Divination in the Old Testament*.

152. Cf. Levinson, "Psychopathology of King Saul," p. 135: "Saul, apart from the two occasions when God's spirit alights on him uninvited, has no experience of God, no relationship with him; God never speaks to him directly. His idea of God is an abstraction exploited by Samuel to thwart and ruin him. But David's buoyant self-confidence, his mobility, freedom, and joyousness, his prudence and wisdom . . . proclaims his harmony with God, his perfect trust, his ardent delight in him."

153. E.g., 1 Sam 17:37, 45-47; 24:9-16; 25:32-34, 39; 26:10-11.

154. See the discussion of Saul's "rituals of certainty" in Polzin, *Samuel and the Deuteronomist*, p. 145. The Deuteronomists are often caricatured as holding to this kind of strict retributional understanding. I am suggesting instead that they opposed an automatic or mechanistic version of it (as exemplified by Saul). They were nevertheless still committed to the fundamental conviction that God punishes sin and blesses faithfulness.

narrative: "So Saul died for his rebellion; he rebelled against the Lord by not keeping (√*šmr*) the word of the Lord (*dĕbar yhwh*); moreover, he had consulted (√*š'l*) a medium, seeking guidance (√*drš*), and did not seek guidance (√*drš*) from the Lord" (1 Chr 10:13-14a).[155]

For David, by contrast, God is ultimately a living presence who remains unpredictable (even if one has been obedient) and is characteristically merciful in spite of one's disobedience (e.g., 2 Sam 12:22-23: "Who knows? The Lord may have pity on me."). Is there not something much more profound about David's impression of God than Saul's in this respect?[156] Yet the most striking feature of David's portrait is his tendency to approach God directly for forgiveness (e.g., 2 Sam 12:13, 30; 24:10).[157] Saul never does.[158] The closest candidate for such repentance on Saul's part occurs when the narrator reports that Saul says "I have sinned" and engages in worship, together with Samuel, after his final rejection by God (1 Sam 15:30-31). Yet again there is no direct appeal from Saul to God for forgiveness, no direct discourse between Saul and God at all. Saul seems more concerned about his social standing than his standing before God. Thus 2 Samuel 24 once more presents an ideal of kingship that has strong retrospective implications for how 1 Samuel, and especially the figure of Saul, should be read.

Nowhere in 2 Samuel 21-24 does the portrait of David become idealized to the point of propaganda, so that David is depicted without weaknesses, shortcomings, and personal ambiguities. To the contrary, David is portrayed realistically, with full attention to his own moral struggles and ethical lapses, precisely to make the point that the difference between Saul and David is not a *moral* one. Indeed, the narrative appears at times almost to go out of its way to preclude such an interpretive conclusion. David can be merciless in battle (2 Sam 5:7-8; 8:2; 12:31; 20:3). He remains the "man of blood," disqualified from building the temple (2 Sam 16:8; cf. 1 Chr 22:8; 28:3). What increasingly distinguishes David

---

155. Use of the verb √*š'l* for "consult" is a pointed play on Saul's own name, suggesting that the need for this kind of action was essential to his character. On *lš'l byhwh* as a technical term for oracular inquiry, see Van Dam, *Urim and Thummim*, pp. 182-90. See also 1 Chr 13:3, "we did not consult (√*drš*) [the ark] in the days of Saul." Saul's deficiency in worship is understood here to have misled the entire community.

156. The dynamic dimension of God's identity is also underscored by Jonathan in 1 Sam 14:6. His bold statement creates early doubt for the reader about Saul's sense of God and prefigures David's impressive awareness of God's capacity for reversal, to bring defeat to the seemingly mighty and success to the apparently weak (e.g., 1 Sam 17:31-40).

157. Barth, *Church Dogmatics IV/2*, p. 465, points to David's confession in 2 Sam 12:13 as representing his chief distinction from Saul.

158. Cf. Dietrich, "König David," p. 16. Exum, *Tragedy and Biblical Narrative*, p. 81, thus considers Saul's suicide "his last desperate attempt to control his destiny."

throughout 1–2 Samuel instead, especially in the concluding literary portrait found in 2 Samuel 21–24, is his own awareness of those shortcomings and his intimate "feel" for God, particularly when he has done something wrong. Thomas Carlyle got this central aspect of the Samuel narrative exactly right:

> David, the Hebrew king had fallen into sins enough; blackest crimes; there was no want of sins. And therefore the unbelievers sneer and ask, Is this your man according to God's heart? The sneer, I must say, seems to me but a shallow one. What are faults, what are the outward details of a life; if the inner secret of it, the remorse, the temptations, true, often-baffled, never-ended struggle of it, be forgotten? "It is not in man that walketh to direct his steps." Of all acts is not, for a man, *repentance* the most divine? The deadliest sin, I say, were that same supercilious consciousness of no sin; — that is death; the heart so conscious is divorced from sincerity, humility and fact; is dead: it is "pure" as dead dry sand is pure.[159]

In the aftermath of his sins David is strikingly depicted as praying to God directly, without an intermediary or an official religious context for such prayer. David's sin is also explicitly forgiven (2 Sam 12:13), whereas Saul's is not (1 Sam 15:30).

David's personal growth appears to lie in his understanding of the public dimension of kingship rather than its inner faith dimension — which in retrospect he always seems to have possessed to a large degree. Strikingly, Saul sins publicly (1 Sam 13; 15) and attempts to hide his sin, while David sins privately and is therefore punished precisely by having his sin revealed to everyone (2 Sam 11–12).[160] By the end of the book David arrives at a notion of representative, even vicarious, kingship — a sense that the role of the king is to represent the people in religious terms, as well as in other respects, interceding on their behalf with God (2 Sam 24:21). David, if necessary, will pay the cost of his people's right relation to God (2 Sam 24:24). It is finally quite remarkable that 2 Samuel ends with a vision of David "making supplication for the land" and performing priestly offerings (2 Sam 24:25).

159. Carlyle, *On Heroes*, p. 41 (his emphasis). In its immediate context Carlyle's interpretive summary relates to the portrait of David in the Psalms, but his point about the religious value of repentance is just as valid for the portrait of David in Samuel. Note also the Talmudic dictum that "David sins only in order to teach us how to repent" (b. 'Abodah Zarah 4b, with Rashi's interpretation). For additional rabbinic observations in his vein, see Elitzur, "David Son of Jesse," pp. 144-49.

160. For this central juxtaposition, see Herzfeld, "David and Batsheva," pp. 250-52. Herzfeld also locates David's ultimate significance in his modeling of repentance.

As well as providing an insight into the narrator's conception of David, this literary conclusion in 2 Samuel 24 thus confirms a worrying suspicion about Saul that has lingered since the account of his death in 1 Samuel 31, namely that he was in some way religiously deficient. Yet the narrative never blames Saul for this deficiency in any facile, moralistic manner.[161] His failure is instead portrayed as something innate to his person and providentially used by God, as well as the consequence of his own choices and actions. The narrative's dual commitments to both divine will and human freedom are never simply harmonized but allowed to stand in tension. That tension *produces* the exemplary character of David, but it also *requires* the existential possibility of Saul.

The concluding material in 2 Samuel 21–24 therefore provides a series of contrasts between David and Saul that in retrospect can be seen to have structured the entire composition of Samuel from its beginning. The introductory portrait of Hannah had already set forth the crucial terms of the narrative's furthest unfolding: personal religious conviction is more important than conventional religious practices and forms (1 Sam 1:9-19).[162] Or: to "listen up" is better than to sacrifice (1 Sam 15:22).

Rhetorically, the final chapters of 2 Samuel display an astonishing rush of emotion, an almost explosive outpouring of feeling. David's interior life, which up to now has been largely withheld, is at last brought into full view.[163] The exception proving the rule occurs in David's lament for Saul and Jonathan in 2 Samuel 1.[164] As Tod Linafelt has shown, this lament represents both an intensely personal expression of David's sense of loss *and* a calculated effort to employ politically useful rhetoric. Linafelt further suggests that 2 Samuel 22 and 2 Sam 1:19-27 share verbal links, primarily martial terms, which are used of Saul and Jonathan in the the lament but of David and God in 2 Samuel 22. Furthermore, David's confession that "I pursued my enemies and destroyed

---

161. Part of the way that the narrative does this is to insist that David possessed failings, too. His habit of deception is particularly worrisome. Indeed, in retrospect one of his chief failings consists of the later violation of his oath in 1 Samuel not to kill Saul's descendants (1 Sam 24:21-22; Heb. 1 Sam. 24:22-23). The other way the narrative avoids a simple binary opposition between Saul and David is by including positive actions and commendable characteristics on the part of Saul.

162. Magonet, *Rabbi Reads the Bible*, p. 137, points out the introduction of the dual themes of providence and human responsibility in the account of Hannah (1 Samuel 1–2).

163. Alter, *Art of Biblical Narrative*, p. 149: "Indeed, one of the most striking aspects of the entire David story is that until his career reaches its crucial breaking point with his murder-by-proxy of Uriah after his adultery with Bathsheba, almost all his speeches are in public situations and can be read as politically motivated. It is only after the death of the child born of his union with Bathsheba that the personal voice of a shaken David begins to emerge."

164. E.g., Linafelt, "Private Poetry and Public Eloquence."

them, and did not turn back [√*šwb*] until they were consumed ['*ad-kallôtām*]"
(2 Sam 22:38) is taken by Linafelt to be a "pointed allusion" to 2 Sam 1:22, in
which David said of Saul's sword that it did not "return [√*šwb*] empty." The
link, however, is ironic: Saul was in fact divinely deposed precisely because
he did not slaughter the Amalekites "until they were consumed ['*ad kallôtām*
'*ōtām*]" (1 Sam 15:18). So David's lament in 2 Samuel 1 represents both a veiling
and an unveiling of his internal life.[165] Even David's outpouring of emotion in
2 Samuel 1 is more about his grief than his piety, which is only fully revealed
in 2 Samuel 22–23.

There are earlier, tantalizing clues to the vitality of David's emotional life
scattered throughout the Samuel narrative (1 Sam 26:19-20; 2 Sam 16:11-12),
but it is difficult to make much of them when they initially appear. A further
intimation of David's inner exuberance can be glimpsed along the way in
David's sexuality and apparent sex appeal.[166] He *desires*, which indicates that
there are strong passions flowing beneath the surface of his words and actions.
Yet we are *shown* his desire rather than informed of it; the narrative repeatedly
reports how others "love" David, but about his love for others the narrative is
mum.[167] David is thus desirable and desired,[168] which in fact contributes to
the sense that he is God's chosen one. To be sure, David shockingly misuses
his desirability (e.g., 2 Sam 11), but even his misuse underscores how sexuality
is powerfully part of his personal makeup. By contrast Saul, with his single
wife Ahinoam (1 Sam 14:50) and lone concubine Rizpah (2 Sam 3:7; 21:8, 11),
seems comparatively sexless and undesirable, despite his physical stature and
strength.[169]

165. Linafelt, "Private Poetry and Public Eloquence," p. 507: "[E]very bit of dialogue that
David has spoken up to . . . 2 Samuel 1 is spoken publicly and guardedly, so that we are always
left uncertain how much, if any, of the 'real' David is being revealed."

166. Wootton, "Monstrosity of David," p. 114, also emphasizes David's attractiveness to
men and women, but she instead treats this aspect of the narrative as evidence of David's
bisexuality.

167. Fewell and Gunn, *Gender, Power, and Promise*, pp. 148-51. See further Naumann,
"David und die Liebe."

168. David's wives apparently number six in 2 Sam 3:2-5. More wives and concubines are
mentioned in 2 Sam 5:13. Michal resents precisely this appeal that David possesses for young
women (2 Sam 6:20), and it is hard to blame her for that. Nevertheless, the narrative responds
to her critique of David's sex appeal with a notice regarding her own childlessness (2 Sam
6:23). Physical and spiritual vitality coexist in some kind of relationship within this narrative,
although it is challenging to say for sure what that relationship is.

169. Cook, "'Fiction' and History," p. 35: "[W]hereas sexual relations punctuate David's
career at several key points . . . they are virtually absent from Saul's." Cf. Măcelaru, "Saul in the
Company of Men," p. 61: "There is no romance or anything of the sort in Saul's life." It bears
remembering that David took Ahinoam as his own wife even before Saul's death (1 Sam 25:43;

At the end of 2 Samuel, therefore, the effect is not exclusively one of temporal culmination, as if only here at the end has David learned a certain manner of approaching God and can describe his life in such terms. These chapters possess additionally the force of a revelation of what has been the case all along (as is also implied by the ambiguity of the timeline they reflect). The literary "reveal" is similar to the final chapter of James Clavell's novel *Shōgun*, in which Toranaga, the central character, finally admits to the reader in soliloquy fashion what has been driving him throughout the entirety of the novel — the one thing in fact that he has repeatedly concealed or denied.[170] This literary comparison with the Samuel narrative is instructive because 2 Samuel 21–24 offers an analogous revelation by the central character, one that compels a reconsideration of all that the narrative has previously reported.

In this instance, however, David has not denied either his ambition to rule or his personal convictions. Both have figured in the narrative and been noted. But David has also been depicted as possessing moral failings. Moreover, his interior thoughts and motivations have mostly been obscured or withheld by the narrative. So the "somersaulting, cartwheeling exuberance"[171] of David's song (2 Samuel 22) and "last words" (2 Samuel 23) abruptly crash into the narrative like a meteor.[172] So this has been what David has been thinking the whole time! His language is massively theocentric, florid, and personal.[173] God is his rock, a shelter, a refuge, a fortress.[174] God brings down the arrogant (1 Sam 22:28); God is his shining lamp (1 Sam 22:29).

David's power derives from God's. His almost boyish pleasure in God's strength is both charming and infectious: "By you I can crush a troop, and by

---

27:3; 30:5; 2 Sam 2:2; 3:2), so that a cuckolding motif also underscores the difference between the two characters.

170. Clavell, *Shōgun*.

171. Peterson, *Leap Over a Wall*, p. 212.

172. Not everyone agrees. For a contrary interpretation, see Gros Louis, "Difficulty of Ruling Well," p. 32: "With Saul, Bathsheba, Absalom behind him, [David] speaks in a voice so public that it has no personal tone or emotion at all."

173. Compare Ambrose, *De officiis*, 1:114: "[David] kept due measure in all his affairs and watched his timing carefully so that he always struck the right note for each particular stage of his life. In fact, it seems to me that he poured forth a great immortal melody of his worth just as much in the way he lived as he did in the wonderful sweetness of his singing: it was all one great hymn of praise to God."

174. Brettler, *God Is King*, pp. 57-68, notes that these terms are often used in relation to human kings in Mesopotamia but "nowhere applied to reigning or dead Israelite kings in the Bible." In other words, biblical tradition reserves this kind of rhetoric for God. By employing it here, David models how a human monarch is rightly — and happily — subordinate to God's sovereignty.

my God I can leap over a wall" (1 Sam 22:30). What a sense of confidence in God! David's "last words" in 1 Samuel 23 are only slightly more subdued, with an emphasis on ruling justly before God. Yet even here the strong sense of intimate connection between David and God is palpable. David speaks using a prophetic formula (*nĕ'ûm*) and explicitly claims to speak on behalf of God (1 Sam 23:2). As both of these poetic compositions imply, coming at the end of the Samuel narrative as they do, David's "prophecies" take the form of religious compositions like the Psalms, a connection also made by the superscriptions of the Psalter.[175]

As we have seen, this culminating revelation of the full scope of David's piety has been framed literarily by two problematic accounts of bloodguilt and census taking (2 Samuel 21; 24). The effect is to suggest a distinction between David's personal piety and his activity as king. In other words, rather than simply celebrating David as a believing king, who can therefore rule without religious error or moral lapses, the narrative implies that even such a devout king as David cannot escape the pressures of power and the structural limitations inherent to the monarchy. His piety is genuine and strong, but even his exemplary piety cannot prevent violence, bloodguilt, and the threat of divine chastisement, not only directed toward him but also toward his people. Rather than presenting a vision of the complementarity of piety and power, as if that is the ideal for which to strive, 2 Samuel 21–24 insists on their disjuncture. David's intense religious conviction is primarily his own, just as all faith must finally be individual faith in order to be genuine and vital. But as these chapters also demonstrate, especially with 2 Samuel 22 as a psalm that may be sung by all (as Psalm 18) and concludes with a reference to David in the third person (2 Sam 22:51), David's faith does make a difference. His reign is better able to model justice and mediate divine blessing because of his personal convictions, and the choices that he is sometimes able to make on the basis of those convictions.

Yet faith is no guarantee for problem-free rule, even though the absence of such faith (as with Saul) is worse. The deeper problem is that structures and institutions, while they can at times mediate God's will and blessing, can never do so with complete consistency and full reliability, no matter how "believing" their leadership is. In this way, the Samuel narrative points beyond itself to a radically different kind of politics in which a communitarian ethic takes an altered shape, in which hierarchy and violence are transposed into egalitari-

---

175. On the Davidic portrait in the Psalms, see Anderson, "King David and the Psalms of Imprecation"; Childs, "Psalm Titles and Midrashic Exegesis"; Cooper, "Life and Times of King David"; Johnson, *David in Distress*; Kleer, *Der liebliche Sänger der Psalmen Israels*.

anism and reconciliation. Christians call this vision the "church," even though their churches retain all the same temptations toward hierarchy and violence, and must constantly be on guard in order to resist becoming merely one more worldly power. At its best, however, the church — like David — serves as a reservoir, host, and embodiment of an alternative political vision, which is occasionally, if only partially, borne out. In the Samuel narrative this vision is oriented toward the future and goes by the name "anointed one" or *měšîaḥ* (1 Sam 2:10; 2 Sam 23:1). The church's vision, too, focuses on a messiah who has already come, is now present, and will yet be.[176]

Because of this volume's concentration on 1 Samuel, it may be objected that my neglect of 2 Samuel 1–20 leads to an over-estimation of David's good qualities and a corresponding minimization of his flaws. There is fairly wide agreement among interpreters, after all, that the David traditions now found in 1 Samuel present David in a mostly positive manner, and the more negative episodes in 2 Samuel are therefore difficult to square with the earlier portrayal. David performs some truly appalling acts in 2 Samuel, and nothing that I have stated up to this point is intended in any way to whitewash or excuse them. I do, however, want to view those acts within the wider context of Samuel as a whole composition. While I cannot engage in a close reading of 2 Samuel 1–20 within this study, I would nevertheless offer two further observations about the relation between this part of the Samuel narrative and the rest of the work.

First, I agree with an increasing number of exegetes who are more inclined to read 2 Samuel 1–20 as an integral portion of the final composition of the entire book — as opposed to earlier historical-critical scholarship that tended to view 2 Samuel 9–20 as a distinct, perhaps preexistent narrative unit (= the "Succession Narrative") that had been incorporated into the Deuteronomistic History en bloc and therefore possessed its own individual literary characteristics and point of view.[177] In my judgment the postulation of a separate origin for this material largely arose from critics' inability to imagine how such negative stories about David could coexist with the earlier, more

---

176. Childs, *Introduction to the Old Testament as Scripture*, p. 275: "In sum, the final four chapters [of Samuel], far from being a clumsy appendix, offer a highly reflective, theological interpretation of David's whole career adumbrating the messianic hope, which provides a clear hermeneutical guide for its use as sacred scripture."

177. For critical discussion of the Succession Narrative and 2 Samuel, see Ackroyd, "Succession Narrative (So-Called)"; Barton, "Dating the Succession Narrative"; Blenkinsopp, "Another Contribution to the Succession Narrative Debate"; Fischer, *Von Hebron nach Jerusalem*; Gordon, "In Search of David"; Gunn, *Story of King David*; Keys, *Wages of Sin*; de Pury and Römer, eds., *Die sogenannte Thronfolgegeschichte Davids*; Rudnig, *Davids Thron*; Whybray, *Succession Narrative*.

positive, ones. A central flaw of much historical-critical work, in fact, is its tendency to think that everyone at a certain period of time felt the same way — or, if pushed, at least everyone within a certain group. Another way to point out this same flaw is to ask about the nature of perceived similarity or contradiction that historical critics have registered in their exegetical comparisons. What are the precise criteria for judgments about whether two different writings should be, or should not be, construed as coming from the same stream of tradition? We should know better than to make simple judgments about what constitutes "consistency." The literary artistry evident throughout Samuel indicates sophistication, ambiguity, and profundity — the very *opposite* of propagandistic groupthink. So the failures of David need not, and in fact do not, flatly "contradict" the earlier, more positive assessments about him.

Second, it seems crucial to me that in the particular combination of the literary materials now before us the more positive traditions do appear first, thus providing a larger context for David's later sins and the misfortunes of his house. The concluding chapters of 2 Samuel remain somewhat ambiguous precisely because they seek to "conclude" David's story with a theological portrayal of his personal strengths and his paradigmatic significance as a ruler, even while acknowledging his flaws — thereby negotiating the presence of the good and the bad in a dialectical synthesis.[178] In this synthesis the good and the bad are not "harmonized" (this is again a category often employed by historical-critical scholars, who tend to want narratives to mean just one thing), but intentionally put side by side in tension.

Retrospective Reading

To read 1 Samuel theologically thus means to interpret literarily its theological themes, insights, and questions primarily against the horizon of the entire "book." In the case of Samuel, historical factors serve as crucial reminders that this particular work once comprised what is now 1 and 2 Samuel. Reading both halves together heightens the contrast between David and Saul, and emphasizes the tragic, rather than heroic, portrait of Saul as Israel's first king. Interestingly, the style of the Samuel narrative typically involves spare storytelling without much explicit editorial intervention. Yet as the story continues, additional details and episodes play a retrospective role, compelling the reader to revisit earlier portions of the narrative and to pose new questions. This

---

178. See further Whedbee, "On Divine and Human Bonds."

peculiar art of the storytelling leads readers to construct provisional reading strategies (or interpretations), which are then either sustained or rejected, confirmed or disconfirmed by the subsequent narrative.[179] Alter puts the point like this:

> Indeed, an essential aim of the innovative technique of fiction worked out by the ancient Hebrew writers was to produce a certain indeterminacy of meaning, especially in regard to motive, moral character, and psychology ... Meaning, perhaps for the first time in narrative literature, was conceived as a *process*, requiring continual revision — both in the ordinary sense and in the etymological sense of seeing-again — continual suspension of judgment, weighing of multiple possibilities, brooding over gaps in the information provided.[180]

In this way the narrative functions prospectively, too, by laying the groundwork for future developments in the story.

Thus considerable skill is required for a sensitive reading of any particular passage in 1 Samuel because in a real sense one cannot interpret a single passage adequately without having a provisional understanding of the entire book. Reading this wider narrative as a whole will additionally mean a much fuller reliance upon 2 Samuel 21–24 as the material that contributes finally, and therefore most decisively, to the retrospective rereading of all the prior narrative. By the terms of 2 Samuel 21–24, Saul's deficiency as king is confirmed as his lack of spiritual conviction. Such a judgment may at first glance appear anachronistic: too much beholden to the Enlightenment's legacy of religion as an interior and private disposition, much too Protestant in its suspicion of religious formalism and its individualistic emphasis. After all, Saul is clearly "religious" in terms of seeing the importance of sacral acts and his willingness

179. A historical possibility exists that the Samuel narrative now functions literarily in this way because it was actually composed in reverse. Thus Albertz, *A History of Israelite Religion*, p. 124 n. 78 maintains that the History of David's Rise (1 Sam 16:14–2 Sam 5:12) refers to the Succession Narrative (2 Samuel 9–1 Kings 2) because the Succession Narrative preceded it in the history of the book's formation. Albertz points to how 1 Samuel 20:16, 46; 23:17; and 24:22 look ahead to the sparing of Saul's sons in 2 Samuel 9; 16:3; and 19:25-31, how 2 Sam 3:39 apparently refers to 1 Kgs 2:32-34, and 2 Sam 4:4 refers to 2 Samuel 9. But, even if accurate, this analysis would seemingly incline the narrative toward a more "prospective" emphasis and lead it to stress fulfillment rather than disambiguation.

180. Alter, *Art of Biblical Narrative*, p. 12 (his emphasis). Cf. McGinnis, "Swimming with the Divine Tide," p. 269: "Literary characterization is indeterminate in that a reader's perception shifts as he or she moves through the text and weighs present information with what came previously, reassessing earlier understandings on the basis of new information."

as king to administer them. But it is still the case that he is never depicted as praying to God in the manner of David, nor does he ever ask God directly for forgiveness. In fact, Saul never addresses God directly by name (i.e., in the second person) at all.[181]

First Samuel can therefore be read on its own as a book only in provisional terms. Yet it is still more of a "book" than any reconstructed stage of a reconstructed Deuteronomistic History. Jobling has performed a useful service by calling attention to wider narrative linkages between Judges and Samuel. There are echoes between 1 Samuel and the rest of the Deuteronomistic History certainly worth further exploration.[182] Judging by the reference to Jabesh-gilead in 1 Samuel 31, however, the present break between 1 and 2 Samuel is hardly random in nature, even if it was made for the very practical reason of dividing the literary composition of Samuel roughly in two. The issue of the "two anointeds" on which the second half of 1 Samuel turns is resolved in 1 Samuel 31. So the present divide between 1 Samuel 31 and 2 Samuel 2 makes compelling narrative sense.

I have therefore attempted to argue that what is now the book of 1 Samuel can certainly be the focus of a detailed reading apart from 2 Samuel. Why not? However, if 1 Samuel is to be read theologically, and read well, it must ultimately be interpreted within the horizon of both books of Samuel, which together constitute a single, coherent literary composition. In such a reading the retrospective implications of 2 Samuel will need to be brought to bear upon the storytelling possibilities of 1 Samuel. My contention is not that the conclusion of every biblical narrative should be regarded as interpretively determinative to this same degree — although endings certainly are important in the Bible and in literature broadly[183] — just that the conclusion to the Samuel narrative functions in this manner because the Samuel narrative has been composed throughout with techniques of narrative postponement, skillful misdirection, and retrospective disambiguation.[184] Even if the latter chapters

181. As we have seen, the MT of 1 Sam 14:41 is not an exception.

182. E.g., on significant semantic links among Judg 13:2; 17:1, 7; 19:1; 1 Sam 1:1; 9:1, see Chisholm, "Role of Women"; Frolov, "Certain Men"; Leuchter, "Now There Was a Certain Man."

183. See Benjamin, "Storyteller"; Gottlieb, "Sof Davar"; Kermode, Sense of an Ending; Rabinowitz, "Reading Beginnings and Endings," esp. pp. 300-313 on their "privileged position"; Smith, Poetic Closure, p. 10 on "retrospective patterning"; Zeelander, Closure in Biblical Narrative. Even the identification of basic narrative units has a strongly retrospective character, according to Culler, "Defining Narrative Units."

184. Interestingly, one recent exploration of closure in the Bible has stressed how rituals often appear in the end-section, just as in 2 Samuel 24; see Zeelander, Closure in Biblical Narrative, pp. 8-9.

of 2 Samuel were added to the Samuel narrative secondarily, the revelation they offer regarding David's character is entirely in keeping with the overall strategy of the narrative.

Reading in Two Directions

Now that 2 Samuel 21–24 has been identified as the literary horizon against which individual interpretive choices in 1 Samuel must ultimately be adjudicated, it is necessary to turn to the start of 1 Samuel and read the narrative from beginning to end. Even with what I have identified as the retrospective strategy of the narrative, 1 Samuel has been crafted as a sequentially unfolding story. The challenge is now to read forward, at the same time exercising sensitivity with respect to the story as a whole.[185] How will the narrative withhold information, thereby creating multiple interpretive possibilities? How does the narrative only gradually shape such possibilities in a particular direction? How will the difference in spiritual disposition between Saul and David, which becomes so apparent later in the narrative, be prepared in advance by the earlier narrative? Will the concern about genuine worship be taken up in the narrative even prior to the introduction of Saul and David as characters? My interpretive goal from the outset is to let the narrative lead without assuming in advance where it will go, but then also to use knowledge of the narrative's ultimate conclusion in consideration of interpretive possibilities along the way. One of the most important reasons to read 1 Samuel in its narrative order is to track the predominantly retrospective style of the narrative.

In my close reading I will pay particular attention to aspects of character and characterization because in 1 Samuel that is where the narrative expends most of its energy.[186] It is with David's character that the narrative engages in the greatest degree of withholding, and where in time the most surprising revelation occurs.

---

185. I do not believe that this way of reading "backward" and "forward" is exclusively Christian, although it may well take on a distinctively Christian style. The distinction between *peshat* and *derash* in traditional Jewish interpretation exhibits some similarities at this point; see Elman, "Progressive *Derash* and Retrospective *Peshat*."

186. *Contra* Ska, *"Our Fathers Have Told Us"*, p. 94, "Biblical narratives are not really interested in the study of characters as such."

PART TWO

Reading 1 Samuel Closely

CHAPTER 2

1 Samuel 1–12

Not by might, not by power, but by my spirit, says the Lord of hosts.[1]

[YHWH] is not content to be "God" in the religious sense. He does not want to surrender to a man that which is not "God's," the rule over the entire actuality of worldly life: this very rule He lays claim to and enters upon it; for there is nothing which is not God's. He will apportion to the one, for ever and ever chosen by Him, his tasks, but naked power without a situationally related task He does not wish to bestow.[2]

I gave you a king in my anger and I took him away in my wrath.[3]

To read 1 Samuel 1 is to consider its nature as a *beginning* within a larger narrative context. To what extent does this book represent a continuation of Judges or Ruth and in what ways does it mark a fresh departure? What new information does it provide? How much of that information is *told* by the narrator? What is left to the unfolding of the narrative to *show*? Does the beginning of 1 Samuel present new characters facing a changed situation? What is the focus of this narrative? Where is God in this story? For Christian communities, how does this narrative evoke the words and actions of Jesus?

As David Jobling has pointed out, certain formulaic expressions within

1. Zech 4:6.
2. Buber, *Kingship of God*, p. 119.
3. Hos 13:11.

the books of Samuel and Judges suggest an earlier organization of the narrative in which what is now 1 Samuel 1 would have constituted more of a continuation than a genuinely new start — thus the phrase "And the Philistines were brought low [√knʻ]" in 1 Sam 7:13 echoes Judg 3:30; 4:23; 8:28; and 11:33.[4] On this reading the first seven chapters of 1 Samuel emerge as the culmination of a conquest begun in Joshua–Judges. An alternate attempt to find connections between Samuel and preceding narratives, one depending on the canonical arrangement of the books now in the English Bible, might also point to use of the verb "to be" (√hyh) and the introduction of a particular "man" (ʼîš) in the first verse of Ruth and the first verse of 1 Samuel — two narratives that focus on the efforts of women to preserve their families.[5]

Opposing such readings is first of all the tradition's shaping of the Samuel material into its own book. The scholarly reconstruction of a Deuteronomistic History antecedent to the present books of Joshua, Judges, Samuel, and Kings continues to possess compelling explanatory power for many scholars, but it remains a reconstruction. Even beyond this fundamental point, however, is the pronounced presence of introductory information in 1 Sam 1:1-7. While the introductory character of that narrative information can certainly be debated on the basis of its content, these seven verses also employ a special verbal syntax to indicate that they are setting the scene for the action to follow. No narrative introduction within Judges approaches the length of the Samuel introductory material, which delays the onset of narrative action in order to provide prior background essential to the plot. For this reason the beginning of 1 Samuel can legitimately be said to present itself as a fresh narrative start.

To be sure, this beginning is not absolute and to an extent relies upon the reader's awareness of certain narrative constants from Judges. God is not reintroduced in 1 Samuel, for example; neither is the presence of the Israelites in the land of Canaan explained.[6] Moreover, Saul's depiction seems at points to have been shaped with the figure of Joshua in mind, especially Saul's lack of faith with regard to the Gibeonites (2 Sam 21:1-9), with whom Joshua made a covenant (Josh 9:18-27; 10:6-7).[7] In other words, some items of readerly knowledge are simply assumed by the Samuel narrative, a phenomenon suggesting

4. Jobling, "What, If Anything, Is 1 Samuel?" p. 31. The same verb is used in each reference but with a different nation as the subject.

5. Jobling, "What, If Anything Is 1 Samuel?" p. 35. Such links are even stronger between 1 Samuel 1 and Judges 13.

6. Only scattered references to Israel's history are made later in the narrative (e.g., 1 Sam 8:8), but in 1 Samuel 1 not even that kind of information is available.

7. For this and other contrasts between the two figures, see Hall, *Conquering Character*, p. 201.

that it was likely always read within the context of a wider story.[8] Thus it is crucial that 1 Samuel 1 be read as a new narrative departure but not an absolutely new beginning. The book of 1 Samuel also continues a broader narrative about God's interaction with Israel. That continuity in turn lends a sense of suspense to the apparently mundane, repetitive details of 1 Samuel 1: how will God break into this set pattern of daily life, family conflict, and ritual activity in order to maintain a divine purpose already extending over generations?

Hebrew prose narrative in the Bible generally favors showing rather than telling,[9] advancing characterization primarily through plot sequencing and engaging only sparingly in physical description — whether of persons, locations, or situations.[10] The result is not only a concise narrative style, in which descriptive words appear carefully selected and freighted with meaning, but also a narrative in which the narrator's own voice is often not explicitly articulated, and unreported aspects of the story are pregnant with significance.[11] Because of the relative absence of description, direct discourse also assumes heightened importance as a main device for characterization and plot development.[12]

A Broken Family (1 Sam 1:1-8)

The fundamental oddity of 1 Samuel's opening should not be overlooked. This biblical story, which is to relate the deeds of kings and nobles, begins with a socially marginal woman in an obscure Israelite village.[13] The sheer fact of her narrative appearance introduces a note of theological drama: how will these mundane affairs turn out to be significant within the providential purposes of God? What sort of God is this, who implements far-reaching social change through an ordinary interpersonal conflict within an average household? Why does God choose to act in this instance and in this fashion? If God wants to help Hannah, why does God not simply perform a big miracle, with all the heavenly bells and whistles?[14]

---

8. An analogous argument has been made about the absence of the major (writing) prophets from the Deuteronomistic History; see Clements, *Prophecy and Tradition*, pp. 47-48.

9. For the basic distinction, see Booth, *Rhetoric of Fiction*, pp. 3-20.

10. Alter, *Art of Biblical Narrative*, pp. 143-62; Amit, *Reading Biblical Narratives*, pp. 69-92; Bar-Efrat, *Narrative Art in the Bible*, pp. 47-92.

11. Auerbach, *Mimesis*, pp. 3-23.

12. Alter, *Art of Biblical Narrative*, pp. 79-110.

13. For a historical-critical treatment of 1 Samuel's introduction, see Hutzli, *Erzählung von Hanna und Samuel*.

14. Cf. Magonet, *Rabbi Reads the Bible*, p. 137.

The repetitive nature of the actions described in 1 Sam 1:1-7 effectively postpones the inception of new narrative action, even as it portrays that action as emerging ineluctably from a repeated pattern of cyclical behaviors. The narrative achieves this effect by using *wqtl* verb forms in Hebrew rather than the *wayyqtl* form regularly used for the sequential narration of past events. This narrative strategy can be difficult to reproduce in English, although both the NRSV and the NJPS translations make a valiant effort by rendering most of the verbs in vv. 3-7 as past repetitives (e.g., v. 3, "this man *used to go up . . .*").

So where does the action of the story in fact begin? The first two verses of the chapter introduce names and basic relationships: Elkanah the Ephraimite has two wives, Hannah and Peninnah; Peninnah has children but Hannah does not.[15] It is worth noting that by highlighting the two wives the narrative also introduces a notion of doubleness. There is an accompanying implication of chosenness and rejection, of blessing and curse.[16] These names and relations are reported in nominal sentences without the inception of any kind of action. In v. 3 further background is specified but still without the action of the narrative beginning in earnest. Elkanah *used to go* every year to sacrifice at Shiloh.

The action of the plot seems to begin in v. 4: "then one day Elkanah offered a sacrifice." The transition introduced by this verse is disguised somewhat because the narrative immediately reverts to further scene painting with more habitual verb forms: Elkanah *used to give* portions to Peninnah. Peninnah *would receive* more portions from Elkanah's sacrificial offerings because of her children, and she *would taunt* Hannah for being childless. Every year it *would happen* the same.[17] The forward movement of the plot only resumes with Hannah's weeping in v. 7, thus forming the conclusion of a parenthesis begun in v. 4.[18] In the beginning of v. 8 the Hebrew verb form "and he said"

15. The names of these two wives are charmingly translated as "Pearl" (Peninnah) and "Grace" (Hannah) in van Wijk-Bos, *Reading Samuel*, p. 25.

16. Note that the text does not say Hannah was barren but that she had no children; for discussion of this distinction, see Cook, *Hannah's Desire, God's Design*, pp. 10-12. Rather than designating a biological condition, the narrative makes explicit how Hannah's childlessness is the consequence of divine action (v. 5, "the Lord had closed her womb"). However, the difference between barrenness and childlessness has been blurred by later tradition: the reference in Hannah's song (1 Sam 2:5) to "a barren woman ['*āqārâ*] who bears seven" appears to draw upon, and perhaps comment on, Hannah's own situation.

17. This is why Joosten, "Workshop," characterizes v. 4a as a "false start" by the narrator.

18. Verse 7 is pointed as a waw-consecutive verb form by the Masoretes and should therefore be taken as a simple past tense reference. Thus Driver, *Notes on the Hebrew Text*, p. 11. However, the long form of the imperfect is also used, *wattibkê* rather than *wattēbk*. *Wattēbk*

(*wayyō'mer*) continues the main temporal thread and bridges to the start of a new scene: "now Hannah rose."[19]

Of special interest in Elkanah's comments in v. 8 is his mention of Hannah's "heart" (*lĕbābēk*). The particular expression "sad at heart" (*yēraʿ lĕbāb*) is also found in Deut 15:10, a passage about the needy in which, however, it describes grudging assistance by those with financial means. There is no little irony, therefore, in Elkanah's implication of ingratitude on Hannah's part, considering that she, rather than Elkanah, is the one at a cruel disadvantage. But even beyond the particular expression, use of the word "heart" immediately suggests a verbal connection with the book of Deuteronomy, in which this word is prominent. The word appears, for example, in that book's well-known and regularly repeated formula "with all the heart and all the soul."[20] For the book of Deuteronomy, a truly undivided commitment of the human heart is both the condition for and consequence of belief in God. By referring to Hannah's *heart* as well as her actions, Elkanah acknowledges both the reality of Hannah's interior distress and the inability of their annual sacrificial routine to provide relief for her.

The entire story of Samuel rests tensively in this acknowledgment. The stage is now set and the actors are ready.

Worship as a Problem (1 Sam 1:9-28)

By beginning as it does, 1 Samuel describes a prior background of stable ritual activity.[21] Against the structured life of pilgrimage and sacrifice, one family's conflict is also introduced. However, the resulting narrative tension does not simply relate to the need for a resolution within this one particular family; a deeper theological problem is being dramatized. As worshipers of God, Elkanah and his family are entitled to the expectation that God will assist them in their difficulties. Yet the ongoing cycle of sacrifice appears only to increase Hannah's distress, since it emphasizes her misfortune in concrete terms and provides regular opportunities for Peninnah to bait her. Instead of helping, the worship of God thus reinforces social inequality and deepens Hannah's distress. The notion that religious practice can itself be unjust is provoca-

---

would be the standard *wayyqtl* form used for sequential narration in the past (cf. Gen 21:16). Cf. McCarter, *I Samuel*, pp. 59-60; Ska, *"Our Fathers Have Told Us"*, pp. 23-24.

19. Thus Alter, *Art of Biblical Narrative*, pp. 103-5, views the action of the book as beginning in earnest in 1 Sam 1:9. Both the NRSV and the NJPS also begin a new paragraph with v. 9.

20. E.g., Deut 4:29; 6:5; 10:12; 11:13; 13:4; 26:16; 30:2, 6, 10.

21. Willis, "Cultic Elements."

tive even today — it is striking to encounter an acknowledgement of such a concern within an ancient text. But Hannah is not beyond the reach of God's compassion either; the question to be pursued in the subsequent narrative will be whether Hannah and God can still interact within the sacrificial system in a manner that will finally bring Hannah aid.

The main action of the book therefore begins with Hannah presenting herself — without Elkanah — at the sanctuary (v. 9). She is clearly the protagonist in this narrative episode.[22] She is alone except for Eli the priest. She offers a votive prayer in which she pledges to dedicate the life of her son to God, if God will only give her a son (vv. 11-12).[23] Remarkably, however, Eli thinks that Hannah is drunk because she mumbles the words.[24] Apparently, sanctuary prayer is normally declaimed, good and loud, but Hannah for some reason breaks with this custom. Why? The narrator takes special care to explain the precise nature of the situation: "Now Hannah was praying in her heart; only her lips moved, but her voice could not be heard" (NJPS). Here again the "heart" motif is encountered, but with even greater emphasis on the disjunction between external worship practices and the interior disposition of faith. Hannah is in such severe distress and prays so fervently that her lips move, though her voice goes unheard.[25] She later describes her behavior (1 Sam 1:15) as "pouring out her soul" (*wā'ešpōk 'et-napšî*).[26]

Great irony exists in Eli's misinterpretation of Hannah's condition. He is, after all, a priest. If anyone should understand heartfelt devotion to God, it should be Eli. Yet Eli not only misunderstands it, he attributes it to a highly unflattering cause: Hannah must be drunk, he assumes.[27] Here, already, the

22. Meyers, "Hannah Narrative in Feminist Perspective," pp. 117-26.

23. The Hebrew term "lent" (*šā'ûl*) is identical with Saul's name, although a play on Samuel's name would make more sense. Yet the same Hebrew root (√*š'l*) is used seven times in this chapter, culminating in the wordplay of v. 28. Does this narrative feature represent a historical confusion or literary artistry? On this question, see Amit, *In Praise of Editing the Hebrew Bible*, pp. 172-79. Amit argues for intentional foreshadowing.

24. The LXX places the words in v. 14 into the mouth of Eli's attendant; the MT attributes them to Eli himself.

25. Cf. Ozick, "Hannah and Elkanah," p. 89: "Hannah is a heroine of religious civilization because she invents, out of her own urgent imagining, inward prayer."

26. John Donne neatly associates Hannah's perceived drunkenness with the similar criticism made against Jesus' disciples at Pentecost: "They are filled with new wine" (Acts 2:13). See *Sermons of John Donne*, 10:124. On this reading Hannah becomes a "type" for every Christian disciple.

27. Falk, "Reflections on Hannah's Prayer," p. 99, notes how the Talmud interprets the biblical narrative in this direction by expanding Hannah's response to Eli as follows: "You are no person of authority in this matter, and the Spirit of Holiness is not upon you, since you have presumed me guilty rather than innocent. Are you not aware that I am a woman in anguish?"

two trajectories of the story thus far confront each other. The childless lay-woman whom sacrifices do not help nevertheless bears a passionate devotion to God; the official priest, father of priestly sons, is unable to recognize genuine faith when it appears directly before him, and thus he disparages it. Yet the text does not for a moment imply that the official religion of the Shiloh cult is irredeemably bad. After all, Hannah's prayer and vow may be, in a sense, private and personal, but she still goes to the temple to offer them. Similarly, Eli initially misconstrues Hannah's situation, but he accepts his error and grants her a blessing once he has perceived the nature of his mistake.[28] Moreover, Hannah does conceive and bear a child afterwards.

All of this suggests that the interest of the narrative not only lies in affirming the general importance of worship within Israel, but also privileging worship in which the interior dimension to religious belief is appreciated and valued beyond rote ritualism. The radical nature of this implicit critique should not be overlooked: without the interior disposition of faith, and unmediated beseeching of God, sacrifices may not only be inefficacious, according to this narrative, they may even contribute to the deepening of family misfortune, social conflict, and personal unhappiness. But the ideal is still a form of worship that combines the internal and the external, that unifies personal conviction and ritual form. Thus Hannah forgoes accompanying her husband on his annual trip to Shiloh while her son is an infant, but then brings him, together with goods for sacrifice, to Shiloh in fulfillment of her vow (1 Sam 1:21-28).[29]

The Hebrew text of 1 Samuel 1 suitably concludes with a tableau of worship (v. 28, *wayyištaḥû*).[30] Not only has Hannah's plea for a son has been granted, family conflict also seems to have been resolved, and the sacrificial activity at Shiloh is once again a vibrant and unifying expression of faithfulness to God.

(citing b. Berakot 31b). Falk then criticizes rabbinic tradition for failing to follow through on the social implications of its own insight.

28. Indeed, Chrysostom highlights how Hannah "turned her accuser into a supporter, such being the value of goodness and gentleness." See idem, *Old Testament Homilies*, 1:95.

29. The LXX has Elkanah bringing the sacrifices to Shiloh; he and Hannah offer them together. Some of this same confusion is also evident in the reference to Elkanah's vow in v. 21.

30. The NRSV, following Qumranic and septuagintal evidence, reads "She left him there for the Lord." According to the MT, the reference is instead to Elkanah, who "worshiped there before the Lord." Yet both versions conclude the unit by underscoring the connection between the events that have transpired and the holy place.

Hannah's Song (1 Sam 2:1-10)

The secondary nature of the poem at the beginning of 1 Samuel 2 has long been noted, and for two main reasons.[31] In the first place, the present position of the poem interrupts what is otherwise a direct narrative sequence between 1 Sam 1:28 and 1 Sam 2:11 in the Hebrew text. Thus "he worshiped him there before the Lord" in 1 Sam 1:28 (MT) proceeds without any alteration of subject or scene to "and then Elkanah left for Ramah, to his house, and the boy began to serve the Lord in the presence of Eli the priest" in 1 Sam 2:11 (MT). The song attributed to Hannah, while broadly appropriate in this narrative context, rests uneasily within these two verses that both have Elkanah as their subject.

The other indication of the secondary nature to the song emerges from the details of the poem itself, which presents language and ideas not yet introduced and otherwise unusual within Samuel. Chief among these premature details is the song's culminating reference to God's "king" (*melek*) in v. 10, since at this point in the biblical story Israel does not yet have a king, and the eventual implementation of a kingship cannot be taken for granted. The possibility of a monarchy in Israel is in fact ruled out in Judges 8 by Gideon, who rejects efforts to install him as king, saying "I will not rule over you, neither shall my son rule over you; the Lord will rule over you" (Judg 8:23).[32] The danger at stake is vividly represented in the subsequent narrative by the ephod that Gideon constructs from captured Midianite gold (especially the booty from defeated Midianite kings), an ephod which then becomes an object of inappropriate religious devotion or a "snare" (*môqēš*) to both Gideon and Israel (Judg 8:24-27; cf. Deut 17:20).

Abimelech, Gideon's illegitimate son, whose very name means "my father is/was king," does reach for kingly power (Judg 9:2) and is ultimately frustrated in that ambition, even as the inhabitants of Shechem are punished for supporting him in it. Jotham's antimonarchic fable (Judg 9:8-20) is instead presented in Judges as expressing God's non-monarchic intention for Israel's political organization (see Judg 9:23, 56-57). The strong implication of these central chapters of Judges is thus that *God* is to be considered "king" in Israel.[33] Within

---

31. See, e.g., Bailey, "Redemption of YHWH"; Becker-Spörl, '*Und Hanna betete und sprach . . .*'; Eynikel, "Das Lied der Hanna," pp. 57-72.

32. The term "rule" is Hebrew √*mšl*. That the issue at hand is ruling as a king is made clear by the reference in Judg 8:18 to Gideon and the two kings of Midian as sharing a common appearance, looking like "sons of a king" (*kĕtō'ar bĕnê hammelek*). For reasons why Gideon's remark in Judg 8:23 might be interpreted as false humility rather than genuine piety, see Olson, "Buber, Kingship, and the Book of Judges."

33. Cf. Num 23:21. Such a view may also be reflected in Deut 33:5 according to several

the present literary form of Samuel, this same conviction is signaled early on (1 Sam 8:7, "for it is not you they have rejected, but me they have rejected from reigning [*mimmĕlōk*] over them"). In this way 1 Samuel 2:1-10 contrasts with the surrounding narrative, in which monarchy is viewed as fundamentally at odds with the worship of God.

By the end of Samuel, however, both the poems in 2 Samuel 22 and 2 Samuel 23:1-7, granting their differences, project a vision of shared authority between David, Israel's rightful king, and God.[34] God is depicted as possessing ultimate control over situations and events, including the defeat of enemies (e.g., 2 Sam 22:4, 18), and yet David is also presented as, in effect, deputized by virtue of his righteousness (e.g., 2 Sam 22:35-46) to "become a head of nations" (*lĕrō'š gôyîm*, 2 Sam 22:44). In other words, the office of king has been literarily negotiated in such a manner by the conclusion of Samuel that it can function without necessarily undermining God's sovereignty (2 Sam 22:47-50). God can now be said to have "his king" (*malkô*, 2 Sam 22:51),[35] to have implemented an eternal covenant (*bĕrît 'ôlām*) with David, and to have established David's royal house (2 Sam 23:5).

Retrospectively, however, the contradiction between God and king set out earlier in 1 Samuel still implies that the *desire* for a human monarchy is at odds with the continued worship of God. A just monarchy in which God remains the ultimate sovereign only fully emerges as a new religious possibility by the end of the book. From the broader perspective of the narrative, both in Samuel and within the Deuteronomistic History more widely, the allusion to a "king" in 1 Sam 2:10 is not at all thematically out of place even though it does appear temporally dislocated, at least upon first encounter. The secondary addition of Hannah's song to the 1 Samuel prose narrative remains the most plausible historical explanation for the initial sense of literary confusion.

Yet the probable secondary nature of 1 Sam 2:1-10 need not eliminate the possibility of other thematic links with the surrounding prose narrative or

---

commentators, most notably Weinfeld, *Deuteronomy and the Deuteronomic School*, p. 66 n. 1. Others have been skeptical, however; see Nicholson, *God and His People*, p. 71. No one would dispute the eventual emergence in Israel of a belief in the kingship of God. At issue is primarily how early to date it. See further Brettler, *God Is King*. Schmidt, *Königtum Gottes in Ugarit und Israel*, argues for a date after the emergence of the monarchy in Israel. But the notion that Israel could only conceive of God as king after it had a human king of its own seems unnecessary, even fatuous. The biblical narrative depicts pre-state Israelites as already having an awareness of how other nations had human kings.

34. Childs, *Introduction to the Old Testament as Scripture*, p. 274.

35. There is some uncertainty about the referents for this expression; I take the suffix as referring to God and *malkô*, in parallel with *limšîḥô*, *lĕdāwid*, and *lĕzar'ô* in the following lines, as a reference to David.

diminish the significance of those connections, as the example of the king motif has already shown. Even though the song was likely added later to the narrative in which it is now found, there is no reason to assume that the addition was done in a slapdash manner without regard to literary context — and in fact there is good evidence to the contrary. The basic theme of thanksgiving in the song serves well as a poetic response to Hannah's deliverance and the birth of her son. The ascription of power and knowledge to God (1 Sam 2:2-3) reinforces the notion, already implied within the first chapter (e.g., 1 Sam 1:5, 27), that God is purposeful and actively at work behind the unfolding of the plot.

Even more important, however, is the theme of social reversal given explicit expression in the song. Those who were hungry are now fed, and those who were full are now hungry; formerly barren women conceive, and the mother of many loses her fertility (*'ūmĕlālâ*, 1 Sam 2:5). God does this — not arbitrarily, but based on the moral/religious stance of individuals and their relation to God's purposes. Those who set themselves against God, the "wicked" (*rĕšā'îm*, 1 Sam 2:9), will be removed from the positions of earthly power and wealth to which they gravitate (1 Sam 2:7). The "footsteps of [God's] faithful" (*rāglê ḥăsîdāyw*, 1 Sam 2:9) are by contrast tenderly overseen by God, who corrects the social disadvantages to which the faithful are naturally heir. The assumption of the song is that social structures favor the disobedient and prevent God's faithful from attaining a "seat of honor" (*kissē' kābôd*, 1 Sam 2:8), and that therefore God rectifies social inequality through social reversal. The point, however, is not simply reversal for its own sake but reversal as a guarantee of ultimate success for the faithful, who keep and promote God's justice. Such a goal is strikingly depicted as in line with the structure and purpose of creation itself, as God has established it (1 Sam 2:8).

This deeply theological understanding works backwards and forwards with respect to its present narrative context. On the one hand, the motif of social reversal for the poor and the righteous comments obliquely on the interaction between Hannah and Eli in the first chapter. The mistreatment Hannah received from Peninnah was a continually painful taunting, but ultimately merely interpersonal in nature. Hannah's patronizing reception by Eli is instead now revealed to stand for a wider social problem within Israel, and Hannah's deliverance by God becomes a paradigmatic instance of divine rescue.[36] The realization of this socio-theological agenda in the song, as well as in the narrative, leads to the further recognition that earthly power and di-

---

36. The paradigmatic quality of Hannah's song can be recognized within the Jewish liturgical tradition, which includes it, along with the first chapter of Samuel, in the *haftarah* (or lectionary reading from the Prophets) for Rosh Hashanah, the Jewish New Year.

vine power are being juxtaposed. They are on something of a collision course already in this story of Samuel — although the precise path of that course is only available thus far in the form of a hint: "for not by might will a person prevail" (*kî-lō' bĕkōaḥ yigbar-'îš*, 1 Sam 2:9).

There has not yet been any military action within the book, but the language of Hannah's song points ahead to such activity. Her story and her song pose questions in advance about the relationship between Israel's assumptions regarding warfare, privilege, and power — and the nature of the God who created the world, who retains expectations for it, and who is able to transgress customary social transactions in order to achieve true justice. In this manner Hannah's song focuses a reading of its surrounding narrative through the lens of its own implicit questions.

Sons and Power (1 Sam 2:11-36)

When the narrative resumes after Hannah's song, it alternates in its attentions between Hannah's son Samuel and Eli's sons Hophni and Phinehas. As other commentators have helpfully described, Hebrew narrative is often "scenic" in a manner suggestive of modern cinematography.[37] First a certain narrative context is introduced — usually with great concision, however, so that the focus of the narrative remains on presenting actions rather than providing explicit description. The context is established by an identification of the characters involved in the scene and sometimes by brief geographical or temporal specifications. The flow of the scene is then constituted by a recounting of the actions of those characters, often employing direct discourse. The conclusion of the scene frequently features a comment from the narrator that acknowledges the passage of time and occasionally offers a quick evaluative judgment. Usually, however, there is no explicit evaluation at all. A narrative space, or lacuna, with its implication of time passing and a change of location, often exists between the scene just concluded and the introduction of the next.[38] The analogy with filmmaking is a close one. The Bible's episodic narrative style mirrors the establishment of a film's scenes through the use of particular camera angles and "cuts."

As detailed by Walter Brueggemann, the first chapter of Samuel contains four such scenes, structured geographically: Ramah, Shiloh, Ramah, Shiloh.[39]

---

37. Alter, *Art of Biblical Narrative*, pp. 79-80; Amit, *Reading Biblical Narratives*, pp. 49-57; Berlin, *Poetics and Interpretation of Biblical Narrative*, pp. 43-55; Brueggemann, "1 Samuel 1."
38. Bar-Efrat, *Narrative Art in the Bible*, pp. 130-32.
39. Brueggemann, "1 Samuel 1."

By comparison, 1 Sam 2:11-36 is noteworthy for heightening the disjunctive aspect of this scenic technique. Once again the scenes are structured geographically, but the alternation between scenes is more abrupt, and there is a greater emphasis on contrast than continuity. After rounding out the action of 1 Samuel 1 with the concluding statement in 1 Sam 2:11, a new scene is introduced in 1 Sam 2:12. Explicit indications are provided for evaluation at the scene's beginning and at its end. So 1 Sam 2:12 reads, "Now Eli's sons were no good (*běnê běliyyā'al*); they did not know the Lord." These "good-for-nothings" are thus implicitly contrasted with Hannah, who has told Eli that she is *not* a "worthless woman" (*bat-běliyyā'al*, 1 Sam 2:16). At issue here is not just how people behave, but specifically how people comport themselves at the sacred shrine. Eli's sons do this quite badly; 1 Samuel 2:17 concludes, "The sin of the young men (*hannĕ'ārîm*) was very great before the Lord for the people treated contemptuously (√*n's*) the Lord's offering." The sons' wickedness is shown above all in their habitual threats of violence toward worshipers (v. 16) and their illicit sexual activity at the shrine. What makes this wickedness even worse is how it leads to contempt for worship itself on the part of the people.

Sixteenth-century commentator Joseph Hall insightfully develops the narrative significance of these irreligious priests:

> If they had not been sons of Eli, yet being priests of God, who would not have hoped their very calling should have infused some holiness into them? But now, even their white ephod covers foul sins; yea, rather, if they which serve at the altar degenerate, their wickedness is so much more above others, as their place is holier. A wicked priest is the worst creature upon earth.

Hall acerbically adds, "the altar cannot sanctify the priest."[40] In this way the narrative once again thematizes a distinction between religion as a cultural inheritance, with its institutions, roles, and customs, and religion as the personal knowledge of God, knowledge that cannot simply be transmitted or gained through the performance of religious ritual.[41]

The narrative then moves immediately to a new scene (vv. 18-21) in which Samuel's priestly development is detailed and evaluated with the final statement, "The young man (*hanna'ar*) Samuel grew up with the Lord" (v. 21). Thus a contrast is made evident between Eli's "young men," his own sons who

---

40. Hall, *Contemplations on the Historical Passages*, pp. 154-55.

41. Cf. Hall, *Contemplations on the Historical Passages*, p. 154: "If the goodness of examples, precepts, education, profession, could have been preservatives from extremity of sin, these sons of a holy father had not been wicked; now neither parentage, nor breeding, nor priesthood, can keep the sons of Eli from the sons of Belial."

were "no good" and "did not know the Lord," and Samuel — a contrast that is further confirmed by Samuel's steady progress in divine instruction (note, however, 1 Sam 3:7, "Samuel did not yet know the Lord"). Over time Samuel remains "*with* the Lord," whereas Hophni and Phinehas sin repeatedly and greatly "*before* the Lord."

This contrast is reinforced by an even briefer scene (vv. 22-25), in which Eli challenges his sons' behavior and his sons turn a deaf ear to his criticism. The odd (anachronistic?) reference to the "tent of meeting" (v. 22) may signal that this scene has been added later to the narrative, possibly in order to summarize the narrative situation thus far and prepare for the oracle of the unnamed "man of God" in vv. 27-36. There is a totalizing emphasis in the phrases "all Israel" (v. 22) and "all these people" (v. 23). Moreover, this narrative unit stresses the unpardonable seriousness of the sons' sins against God ("if someone sins against the Lord, who can make intercession [√*pll* Hithp.]?"), while also indicating God's resolve that the sons must therefore die (v. 25; cf. v. 34). The failure of Eli's sons then leads to another contrastive, laudatory reference concerning Samuel in v. 26: "The young man Samuel kept on (*hōlēk*) growing and gaining favor (*wĕgādēl wāṭôb*) with both the Lord and with people."

The present form of the "man of God" oracle (vv. 27-36), with its deuteronomistic language, its disproportional length and its anonymous speaker, likely also represents a secondary expansion of the earlier narrative.[42] Still, the speech now contributes importantly to the surrounding narrative by explicitly naming the tension between "honoring" (√*kbd*) sons and honoring God (v. 29). For the immorality of Hophni and Phinehas, and for Eli's all-too-weak protests against it, God's intention is proclaimed by the unnamed prophet to consist in the removal of Eli's priestly house from power, and the establishment of a new priestly house headed by a similarly unnamed "faithful priest (*kōhēn ne'ĕmān*)" (v. 35). In addition to performing duties in keeping with God's intention, the faithful priest will "go before" (*wĕhithallēk lipnê*) another shadowy figure described by God as "my anointed" (*mĕšîḥî*). At least in the present form of the book, the reference to this anointed figure recalls the ending to Hannah's song, in which the same term (*mĕšîḥô*) is used in parallelism with "king" (*malkô*, 2:10). In contrast, God will cause Eli's eyes to become "used up" (*lĕkallôt 'et-'ênêkā*, v. 33), presumably from weeping, although the prediction may also refer to a resulting lack of vision (spiritual as well as physical).[43] The deaths of Hophni and Phinehas are confirmed (v. 34). In the future the few remaining members of Eli's priestly line will be forced to beg for bread (v. 36).

42. McCarter, *I Samuel*, pp. 91-93.
43. See further Sasson, "Eyes of Eli."

The constituent scenes in 1 Samuel 2 are thus all the more sharply framed because of what they share: an emphasis on sons and a concern about lineal-biological succession. Here the "cross-cutting" style of the chapter's presentation reinforces the differences between the sons being described. Hophni and Phinehas abuse the privileges of their priestly office in shameful ways; the narrative takes more time to make its case against them and to portray the impotence of Eli's response. Samuel, on the other hand, steadily grows into his duties organically and unproblematically, living uninterruptedly under divine oversight and blessing. The irony is of course that Hophni and Phinehas are the natural heirs of Eli, while Samuel is only on loan (1 Sam 1:28), an adopted son-like figure.

Within this contrast the narrative develops the question of succession in a rather pointed and surprising manner. Is it not the case, the narrative suggests, that sons are sometimes inferior to their fathers? That social institutions dependent upon lineal succession sometimes suffer because of the vagaries of history? That religious conviction and behavior are not reliably transmitted from generation to generation? Why does Samuel possess religious conviction and maintain moral integrity while Hophni and Phinehas do not? By posing such questions the narrative lays the thin edge of a wedge against customary assumptions relating to inheritance, suggesting that God's proper service requires a devotion that is independent of simple biological succession. At the same time, since Eli and his house are going to be replaced by *another* priest and *another* house (as opposed to having no priests and no houses at all), the narrative does not dismiss society's need for institutions and leaders to direct them. The narrative asks instead how institutions and leaders can retain moral accountability and spiritual vigor in the face of shifting generations.[44] Yet the Samuel narrative never views Eli without sympathy either. Every parent knows that children will make their own decisions in the end, whatever parental guidance they receive, and that the responsibility of parents for their children is at best partial and inexact. Eli's greater fault is not the kind of children he has produced, but how he fails to punish them for their failings — and protect others from their bad behavior.

The second chapter of 1 Samuel therefore hinges again on the nature of faith and true worship. The introduction of this theme in 1 Samuel 1 (i.e., Hannah's personal devotion, as contrasted with Eli's institutional obliviousness)

---

44. A similar perspective is offered in 1 Tim 3:4-5 regarding the family life of a bishop: "He must manage his own household well, keeping his children submissive and respectful in every way — for if someone does not know how to manage his own household, how can he take care of God's church?"

has deepened into a searching meditation on the transmission of spiritual faith and practices from one generation to the next. The empty faith of Hophni and Phinehas is depicted precisely in their cynical manipulation of worship practices for self-gain.[45] By contrast Samuel, born out of Hannah's personal faith and not from any priestly line, is clothed with the priestly garments of worship (v. 18). The point is that lineal descent and religious institutions do not provide sufficient guarantees for the maintenance of spiritual conviction, which at times can exist and even flourish within the framework those institutions provide, but is also not reducible to family trees and institutional flow charts.

There is a peculiar imbalance in the way this issue is presented by the narrative. Hophni and Phinehas disqualify themselves from the service of God through the immorality of their behavior. This immorality expresses itself in their cynical manipulation of worship and the deterioration of Israel's worship practices. Yet the difficulty with Hophni and Phinehas is not a matter of neglecting proper procedure, of merely failing to use the proper fork when overseeing sacrifices (vv. 13-14), but in the fact that they steal portions for themselves, threatening force (v. 16), and engaging in possibly coercive sexual relations with serving women at the worship site (v. 22). It is their *immorality* that disqualifies their worship and leads to their rejection.[46] However, very little information is given about the morality of Samuel's actions or even about the nature of Samuel's *actions* at all. Beyond reporting that he would make the annual pilgrimage to Shiloh with his parents (v. 19), the narrative is silent about the reasons for Samuel's success.

The implication is that Samuel's success has not been so much earned as granted, that Samuel represents the fruit of Hannah's profound faith, even as Hophni and Phinehas reflect Eli's own cynicism. When he does criticize his sons, Eli appears more concerned about correcting their public reputation (vv. 23-24) than redressing their crimes. Without explicitly saying so, the narrative suggests in this way that both faith and apostasy descend from one generation to the next in complex and unreliable but perhaps still identifiable ways. Children do benefit from their parents' religious faith and suffer from their doubts. The main point, however, remains that social and religious in-

---

45. In a nice turn of phrase, Murphy, *1 Samuel*, p. 24, calls Hophni and Phinehas "antipriests."

46. This moral failing is therefore also viewed as a religious one. In 1 Sam 3:13, God will characterize what Eli's sons have done as "cursing God." In some translations this line is rendered "cursing themselves," because the MT changes the word "God" into the pronoun "themselves" (through the simple expedient of dropping an *aleph*) in order to avoid reproducing the words "cursing God," although this is clearly the sense of the verse. See Parry, "Unique Readings in 4QSam^a," p. 218 n. 13.

stitutions themselves cannot guarantee a successful transmission of religious conviction. In the world of this narrative, a priest must be more than a priest in order to secure the inheritance of his priestly sons: he must be "faithful" (*ne'ĕmān*).

Samuel and Eli (1 Sam 3:1–4:1a)

Central to this chapter is the notion of reversal or paradox. The double story line of the preceding material, which depicted Eli's sons and Hannah's son in separate but contrasting narrative scenes, now unites in a series of scenes involving Eli and Samuel. The numbered structure of the narrative is hard to miss, and conforms to a standard convention of folklore ("and then the *last* time . . ."). [47] In this account, however, the two characters' roles are persistently reversed, as are the expectations of the reader/hearer regarding their behavior and the outcome of the story. No commentator has perceived the paradoxical quality of the narrative more acutely than Joseph Hall. Describing how 1 Samuel 3 is presented as a logical consequence of the preceding narrative, Hall writes, "Old Eli rebuked not his young sons, therefore young Samuel is sent to rebuke him." [48] In this chapter God chooses to speak to the serving boy rather than to the boy's priestly master. Eli is no longer the one to whom God speaks. "He which was wont to be the mouth of God to the people, must now receive the message of God from the mouth of another . . ." [49] God's action thereby confirms two narrative impulses that have been building since the first chapter: Eli's deterioration and Samuel's promise.

Less obvious, and sometimes neglected, is how when God speaks to Samuel in this episode Samuel mistakenly assumes that he is being called by Eli. Hall observes a further reversal within Samuel's confusion:

He that meant to use Samuel's voice to Eli, imitates the voice of Eli to Samuel; Samuel had so accustomed himself to obedience, and to answer the call of Eli, that lying in the further cells of the Levites, he is easily raised from his sleep; and even in the night runs for his message to him who was rather to receive it from him. [50]

---

47. For threefold repetition in accounts of dream verification from Mari, see Gnuse, *Dream Theophany of Samuel*.

48. Hall, *Contemplations on the Historical Passages*, p. 156.

49. Hall, *Contemplations on the Historical Passages*, p. 156.

50. Hall, *Contemplations on the Historical Passages*, p. 156.

If Eli is not the one to receive God's message, Samuel is not the one who recognizes it. By use of this literary device Samuel's obedience is foregrounded throughout the narrative, even while his initial response is shown to be in error.

Conversely, Eli's response is correct, although his disobedience is precisely what is at issue. Hall again notes, "Thrice is the old man disquieted with the diligence of his servant; and, though visions were rare in his days, yet is he not so unacquainted with God, as not to attribute that voice to him which himself heard not."[51] In other words, even in his state of physical (v. 2) and moral decay, Eli remains a priest of God, familiar with God's ways and acquainted with God's voice. In order to draw out this contrast the narrative makes a point of commenting on young Samuel's lack of religious experience: "Now Samuel did not yet [*ṭerem*] know the Lord; the word of the Lord had not yet been revealed to him" (v. 7). This comment is conspicuously placed between the second and third instances of God's calling out to Samuel, instead of at the beginning of the chapter, as a way of explaining Samuel's repeated lack of understanding and heightening narrative suspense.

The chapter begins by emphasizing the symbolic significance of Eli's blindness. "Vision" (*ḥāzôn*) was not exactly "bursting out" (√*prṣ* Niph.) all over, the narrative wryly reports (v. 1), leading directly to the statement that Eli himself increasingly could not "see" because his aged eyes had grown dim (v. 2, perhaps in fulfillment of 1 Sam 2:33). In this fashion his personal deterioration mirrors the spiritual decline of his era. There is deep irony in the idea of Eli as a priest who cannot "see," a description with a metaphorical valence.[52] Similarly, we read that "the lamp of God had not yet [*ṭerem*] gone out" (v. 3) — a statement that possesses a symbolic as well as a realistic resonance within this narrative world. The "night" of this chapter is ordinary night, and yet more than that; the lamp of God is the ordinary light within the temple, and yet more; Eli is old and understandably weak-eyed, but his physical decline signifies spiritual decadence.

By contrast, David and his dynasty will come to be called the "lamp of Israel" (e.g., 2 Sam 21:17; 1 Kgs 11:36; 15:4; 2 Kgs 8:19; 2 Chr 21:7), even as he himself will ultimately attribute the source of that light to God (2 Sam 22:29). There remains hope in the darkness. Eli, for all of his physical and spiritual weakness, does understand both the nature of what is occurring and how to offer a proper response — although his comprehension also seems to require

---

51. Hall, *Contemplations on the Historical Passages*, p. 156.
52. Eli's blindness also sits uneasily with later (?) rules about who could become a priest; see Avalos, *Illness and Health Care*, pp. 334-35.

repeated promptings before it crystallizes. Indeed, Eli provides Samuel with the procedural key needed to receive God's message in its fullness. "Go lie down, and if he calls to you again, say 'Speak, Lord, for your servant is listening'" (v. 9). When Samuel then employs this verbal formula, and only when he does so, God proceeds to deliver a message of judgment against Eli (constituting a further reversal). Still, the character of that oracle should not be taken as a warrant for demonizing Eli or completely discounting his religious sensibility.

The greatest paradox in the chapter is the one right at its core: Samuel is the person to whom God chooses to speak, but Samuel does not know what to say; Eli is the person to whom God does not choose to speak, but Eli knows what must be said. As much as Samuel's seemingly innate religious genius is celebrated by the narrative, a note of appreciation for religious institutions and their leaders is therefore also struck. Even in the midst of his personal deterioration and the abuses of worship in which his sons are engaged, Eli maintains a crucial religious memory and sensibility. Not only does he understand — finally — what is happening to the boy, he provides him with the formula needed in order to receive a word from the Lord. Moreover, when Samuel, at Eli's prompting, tells Eli the nature of the divine message he has received, Eli's response is neither self-justifying nor grudging: "He is the Lord; He will do what looks right to him" (v. 18). In this response Eli exhibits great strength of character, as well as an awareness of God that is both dynamic and personal.[53]

Previous characters such as Peninnah, Hophni, and Phinehas were rather one-dimensional in the narrative, serving mostly as literary foils to advance the plot;[54] but the character of Eli is more fully nuanced. The main characters of biblical narrative are hardly ever portrayed in white hats and black hats, as in classic cowboy movies. In that kind of movie the good guys wear white and bad guys sport black, and the plot unfolds consistently according to the clear, acknowledged difference between the two.[55] The good cowboys are all good and the bad cowboys are all bad — but not so in biblical narrative. Eli's portrait

---

53. Hall, *Contemplations on the Historical Passages,* p. 157. Hall sees Eli's deep faith precisely in Eli's willingness to expose himself to "the afflicting hand of our maker." As Doody fairly notes, however, Eli still does not take any action with respect to his sons; see her "Infant Piety and the Infant Samuel," p. 120: "God couldn't speak to Eli because Eli could not — would not — listen. Eli made doublings and equivalents and evasive equations. To Eli it seemed just as good for God to talk to Samuel as to himself, and just as good for God to punish him and his [sons] as for Eli to try to set matters right. Eli thinks in equations and the poise of stupid inertia."

54. On literary "foils" in biblical narrative, see Ska, *"Our Fathers Have Told Us"*, pp. 86-87.

55. See further Tompkins, *West of Everything.*

conveys remarkable sympathy for him, even while the judgment against him (and his family) manages to appear accurate and just. This sympathy cannot be viewed as an accidental effect of the narrative, since its central reversal motif would not otherwise succeed. Instead, the narrative makes a point of expressing sympathy with someone who is at the same time a recipient of God's judgment. This same quality of sympathy will be even more pronounced in the stories about Saul, so the employment of it here anticipates and predisposes the reader/hearer toward its presence as a sustained narrative feature.

Beyond the narrative's evident sympathy for Eli, however, there is also the related quality of appreciation for religious tradition and institutional leadership, as has already been noted. The first chapter of Samuel involved worship at Shiloh, and the narrative section of the second chapter focused on the worship practices of Eli's sons and Samuel. The third chapter is set again in the temple at Shiloh. Samuel is sleeping by the ark (v. 3). On the one hand, a distinction between material objects (e.g., temple, lamp, ark) and the dynamic reality of God's presence is underscored. Even *with* the temple, the priesthood, and all the sacrificial accoutrements, "The word of the Lord was rare in those days; no vision had broken out [$\sqrt{prṣ}$ Niph.]" (v. 1). In other words, the religious institutions of temple and priesthood are not in themselves sufficient to guarantee the presence of God, especially during a time in which priests are morally lax.

Yet neither are such religious institutions, personnel, and objects negligible, for they do contain within themselves the legacy of the former faithful, who developed habits and practices for maintaining a sense for God's presence in their lives.[56] Traditional wisdom continues to have its usefulness, as is shown in the verbal formula Eli gives to Samuel so as to invite God's further speech. The high value of worship is emphasized by the conclusion to the chapter, which reports that God continued to appear at Shiloh and reveal the word of the Lord to Samuel (v. 21). The problems that have been depicted in the narrative thus far, particularly the corruptions of the priestly role, are not judged to be essential failings of the worship site at Shiloh or its religious traditions. The site and its traditions are not rejected out of hand. Rather, the narrative specifically indicts worship that has lost its connection to moral righteousness and lacks a genuine openness to God. The narrative attributes both of these positive features to Samuel by implication (e.g., his differences

---

56. On 1 Samuel 3 as an example of the divinatory practice termed "incubation" (= sleeping in a holy place in an effort to induce revelatory dreams), see Porter, "Ancient Israel," p. 202. A case is also made for reading Hannah's story as an incubation "type scene" in Kim, *Incubation as a Type-Scene*, but unconvincingly in my view.

from Hophni and Phinehas; God's choice to speak with him rather than Eli) as well as outright assertion (vv. 19-21). Yet the ideal remains a purified worship of God in which tradition and moral/spiritual sensibility can be united.

One way in which the combination of tradition and faith can be combined is apparently in the role of the prophet. Thus references to prophecy appear in the narrative introduction and conclusion to this chapter. Samuel's receptivity to God's word is contrasted with the rarity of prophecy generally at this point in Israel's history (3:1). The narrative conclusion (3:19–4:1a) emphasizes how all of Samuel's predictions came true over time (3:19). This stress upon fulfillment as a criterion for distinguishing true and false prophecy is in fact formulated as a rule in deuteronomic tradition (Deut 18:22; cf. 13:3). The statement that "all Israel" recognized how Samuel was "faithful" (*ne'ĕmān*) as a prophet of the Lord (3:20) reinforces the successful portrait of Samuel's prophetic activity. In its narrative context, the term "faithful" also recalls the earlier reference to a "faithful priest" (*kōhēn ne'ĕmān*) in 1 Sam 2:35, inviting the suspicion that Samuel may well be the one to whom the prophecy referred, even though he has been characterized as a prophet more than as a priest.

Moreover, Samuel's prophetic capability is demonstrated by the continued presence of God at the Shiloh temple (3:21). The "word of the Lord" (*dĕbar-yhwh*) comes to Samuel at Shiloh and the "word of Samuel" (*dĕbar-šĕmû'ēl*) then goes forth to "all Israel." The resultant narrative portrayal of Samuel is therefore not only one in which he has become the central intermediary figure between the people of Israel and God, but one in which Samuel speaks *for* God. In arriving at such a conclusion the narrator thus aligns the normative stance of the narrative with the perspective of Samuel as a character within that narrative. If Samuel speaks for God, he will be expected to speak the truth in the future unfolding of the plot.

The Ark Narrative (1 Sam 4:1b–7:1)

The internal coherence of this section, and its difference from the surrounding narrative, has long given rise to the speculation that its origin was separate and that it has only been added secondarily to Samuel.[57] Even

---

57. For a brief review of scholarship advocating a separate origin for the Ark Narrative, as well as a historical-critical argument in support of its coherence with the wider Samuel narrative, see Smelik, *Converting the Past*, pp. 35-58. For a more detailed history of scholarship, with analysis, see Eynikel, "Relation between the Eli Narratives." On the literary aspects of the Ark Narrative, see Gitay, "Reflections on the Poetics of the Samuel Narratives." For theological reflection, see Brueggemann, *Ichabod toward Home*.

though it may have been added later, however, its origins could still be quite old.[58] One of the most prominent difficulties in relating it to the rest of the book is the complete absence of Samuel as a character in the events it relates.[59] Samuel clearly emerges as the main character in the first three chapters of the book. He is styled deuteronomistically as a prophet like Moses (3:19–4:1a). Moreover, as soon as the sojourns of the ark have ended, the narrative resumes again with Samuel and his prophetic activity, once more depicted in stereotypically deuteronomistic terms (7:2-4). Yet in the intervening material the ark of the covenant effectively replaces Samuel as the narrative's focal point.[60]

The ark is in fact personified in this account, although subtly and with only a vague suggestion of the fantastic elements that would be associated today with the literary style known as "magical realism."[61] After a military defeat against the Philistines, the Israelite elders propose bringing the ark into battle in order to ensure that God will be with them and their next hostile encounter will be successful. From the outset, therefore, the ark is a visible and concrete symbol of God's presence within the narrative. To speak of one is to speak of the other: "Let us take for ourselves [*niqḥâ 'ēlênû*] the ark of the covenant of the Lord from Shiloh so that he/it [the pronoun in Hebrew is the same] will come into our midst and deliver us from the hand of our enemies" (4:3). The ark "enters" (√*bw'*, 4:5-6) the Israelite camp, is captured or "taken" by the Philistines in turn (√*lqḥ*, 4:11, 17, 19, 21-22; 5:1-2), and duels mysteriously with the image of Dagon in the Ashdod temple. (The mechanics of the duel are left undescribed; only its effects are related.)

Repeatedly the identity between the ark and Israel's God is acknowledged: "And when they realized that the ark of the Lord had come into the camp, the Philistines were afraid, for they said, '*God* has come into the camp.'" (4:6-7, my emphasis). The Philistines fear the power of the ark, as a divine talisman, to generate the kinds of plagues they remember to have struck the Egyptians. Indeed, wherever the ark is sent within the Philistine pentapolis, disease and death break out at the hand of Israel's God, until the Philistines finally decide to expel the ark from their midst. At this surface level of the story, the ark

---

58. See, e.g., Ahlström, "Travels of the Ark."

59. See further Spina, "A Prophet's 'Pregnant Pause.'" For an overview of recent scholarship and other efforts to read the Ark Narrative within the wider horizon of the Samuel narrative, see Bodner, "Ark-Eology."

60. For a general historical overview of the ark, see de Vaux, *Ancient Israel*, pp. 297-302.

61. For a quick introduction, see Bowers, *Magic(al) Realism*. One hallmark of this literary style is its use of miracle and the fantastic, deliberately flouting Enlightenment assumptions regarding causation.

narrative celebrates (with not a little humor) the power of God over Dagon, and the religious faith of the Israelites over that of the Philistines.

On a deeper, more ironic level, however, the narrative suggests that the Israelites and the Philistines are not all that different: both use the ark inappropriately and both confuse the ark with the deity that the ark represents. The Israelites initially bring the ark into battle because a previous military engagement has not gone well and they believe the presence of the ark will secure their subsequent victory (4:3). Yet such an action threatens to force God's hand; central to the world of this text is the freedom of God to act in the way God so chooses (3:18).[62] It is true that there is no explicit word of negative evaluation from the narrator regarding Israel's initiative with the ark. One of the most challenging features of the Samuel narrative is in fact the evaluative reticence of the narrator, who prefers to suggest indirectly rather than to issue explicit moral judgments.[63] This narrative technique engenders tremendous sympathy for the story's characters, who thus appear to be neither all good nor all bad but complex mixtures of traits and inclinations. That it is Hophni and Phinehas, the disgraceful sons of Eli, who lead the ark from the temple to the battlefield nevertheless sends an ominous signal (4:4). The stance of the narrator is only fully revealed by Israel's defeat, the ark's capture, and the death of Eli's sons (4:10-11). The nature of the deed is known by its outcome. The Israelites' effort to compel God's favor through the military use of a religious image brings about disastrous consequences.

So the ark is the crucial issue in these chapters, as shown not only by its prominence and personification but by the way in which the loss of the ark outweighs all of the other aspects of Israel's defeat. Eli's heart trembles for the "ark of God" while he awaits news from the battle (4:13).[64] Even though Eli also hears from a messenger that Israel has suffered great losses and that his two sons have been killed (as previously predicted, 1 Sam 2:34), the narrator makes clear that it is the news of the ark's capture that shocks Eli into falling off his chair and breaking his neck ("when he mentioned the ark of God," 4:18).[65] So, too, Phinehas' wife is reported to mourn the loss of the ark just as much as the loss of her husband, naming her son Ichabod, which the narrative glosses as meaning "the glory has departed from Israel" (4:21-22). The repeated use of the phrase "the ark was taken/captured" (4:11, 17, 19, 21-22; 5:1) throughout the

---

62. Cf. Buber, *Prophetic Faith*, p. 62: "There can be no forcing YHVH's hand, even against the Philistines; the duration of their supremacy is a concern of His acting and planning for Israel."

63. Ska, *"Our Fathers Have Told Us"*, pp. 53-54.

64. Berger, "On Patterning in the Book of Samuel."

65. On the motif of Eli's chair, see Spina, "Eli's Seat."

same passage underscores this sense of religious tragedy and loss. The ark is "captive" outside the territory of Israel in a manner that the narrative associates with the captivity of the Israelites in Egypt (6:6; cf. 4:8).

Yet by subsequently depicting the power of the ark on its own to cause the destruction of Dagon's image (5:1-5) and bring about sickness and death among the inhabitants of the Philistine cities (5:6-12),[66] the narrative implies both that the ark had possessed the necessary power at the outset to guarantee an Israelite victory in battle — and that God had permitted military defeat and the ark's capture precisely as punishment for Israel's manipulation of it. From this vantage point the thematic connection between the ark material and the surrounding narrative becomes clearer. Whatever the origin of the ark material may have been, in its present form and location it provides an extended illustration of misplaced faith. The Israelite elders had asked *themselves* why God had given victory to the Philistines (4:3), but they had not consulted God. Instead, they used the ark in a mechanical way without sufficient regard for God's freedom. This misuse of a central religious object strengthens, deepens, and complicates the theme of worship inherited from the first three chapters of Samuel.

It must be stressed that the narrative does not present the Israelites as cynical manipulators of the ark. To the contrary, they seem to act sincerely. Nor are they wrong in viewing the ark as more than merely symbolic; the narrative depicts the ark as representing the "real presence" of God precisely by personifying it. In addition, the biblical tradition found in Num 10:33-36, whatever its historical date and provenance, provides apparent support for moving the ark from camp to camp and using it in battle. Indeed, David will also later use the ark in battle (2 Sam 11:11; 15:24-25). So military deployment of the ark in general is not the issue, but rather *how* the ark is to be used militarily. In this way the ark narrative in Samuel demonstrates how sincere faith and genuinely holy objects can be bankrupted through an application of religious ritual that does not account sufficiently for the freedom and identity of Israel's God.[67]

A final irony emerges because the Philistines are in fact more respectful of the ark than the Israelites were, especially Hophni and Phinehas, since the Philistines *do* consider the ark to be unpredictable. After their various sufferings, the Philistines finally ask their priests and diviners how best to send the ark "to its own place" (*limqômô*, 6:2), and the priests — in addition to coming

---

66. The nature of the Philistines' physical affliction and their attempted method to ward it off are highly obscure. For a recent examination of the historical question, as well as the proposal that "hemorrhoid" might be better translated "phallus," see Maeir, "A New Interpretation of the Term *'opalim* (עפלים)."

67. Cf. Mosis, *Welterfahrung und Gottesglaube*, pp. 116-20.

up with a nice bit of sympathetic magic — devise a scheme in which the ark is placed upon a cart to which two cows are harnessed and then turned loose. The Philistines not only intend to determine through this divinatory procedure the right location for the ark but also to gain a final confirmation as to whether their misfortunes have truly been caused by the Israelite deity (6:9).[68]

To make things more difficult for Israel's God in this exercise, the Philistines use two cows that have recently calved and are heavy with milk. Their calves are taken from them and kept indoors. In order for the ark to return to the territory of the Israelites, therefore, Israel's God must not only somehow direct the milk cows to travel in that specific direction, God must do so contrary to the strong pull of nature. That is the miracle of what occurs next: "The cows went straight ahead along the road to Beth-shemesh, along a single highway, lowing as they went, and not turning to the right or the left" (6:12). As Robert Polzin has noted, there is thus an echo in this episode of the difficulties between parents and children featured in the first three chapters of 1 Samuel.[69] As previously observed, here again is the sense that natural succession, whether in the human world or in the animal kingdom, cannot be a sufficient guarantee that God's purposes will be accomplished. This uneasiness with succession plants seeds of doubt about the religious adequacy of the monarchy before it is even begun. Counter to the implication at the end of the book of Judges and the beginning of 1 Samuel, in which the breakdown of social institutions is apparently detailed in order to provide a justification for the rise of the monarchy, 1 Samuel 4–6 deepens the worry that a hereditary kingship may only exacerbate the patent inconstancy and unreliability of natural generation.

That Israel has not learned from its mistake with the ark is evident in the curious postscript regarding the punishment of the inhabitants of Beth-shemesh and the subsequent movement of the ark to Kiriath-jearim (6:19–7:1). The Israelites in Beth-shemesh are struck down either because they looked into the ark (as the MT has it) or because some of them ("the descendants of Jeconiah," as LXX tradition explains) did not rejoice with the others when the ark was returned from the Philistines. Either way there is a lingering impression that the Israelites as an entire group have not yet fully understood how to use the ark or how best to worship God.[70] Their rhetorical question points in the direction that ironically identifies the narrator's own theological concern: "Who is able to stand before the Lord, this holy God, and to whom will he go

---

68. On such divinatory practices, see Porter, "Ancient Israel," p. 197.

69. Polzin, *Samuel and the Deuteronomist*, pp. 66-67.

70. On the role of group comments like this as representing a "collective" character, see Bar-Efrat, *Narrative Art in the Bible*, pp. 96-97.

from us?" (6:20).[71] The presence of God can be a threat to Israel (no less than to the Philistines) as well as a blessing.

How then can this dangerous, unpredictable deity be worshiped? How does one live with a God like this? The next two chapters of 1 Samuel address this question and offer a provisional answer.

Samuel's Leadership (1 Samuel 7:2–8:22)

Although the ark is now housed in Kiriath-jearim and the house of Abinadab is charged with looking after it, the narrative treats this resolution to the ark narrative as incomplete and undesirable. Israel continues to "lament" ($\sqrt{nhh}$ Niph.?, 7:2) God's presence, which is regarded as prolongedly absent. Suddenly Samuel is in the forefront of the narrative again, however, and he now speaks a prophetic word in standard deuteronomistic dress: "If with all your heart you are returning to the Lord, remove the foreign gods and sacred poles (*ʿaštārôt*) from among you and fix [$\sqrt{kwn}$ Hiph.] your heart on the Lord and serve him only; then he will deliver you from the hand of the Philistines" (7:3). Samuel's pronouncement assumes that the Israelites have been worshiping foreign gods, something the narrative has not yet reported, and to this extent his speech represents a good candidate for a later addition to the narrative. Yet the words of Samuel only amplify what the narrative has already identified as an issue — namely, the absence of God from Israel — and they lay the responsibility for that absence squarely at Israel's own feet. Thus the presenting problem in this chapter is not how God can be returned to Israel but how Israel can return to God.

To achieve this return, Israel's interior disposition, the proper stance of Israel's "heart" (*lēbāb*), will be crucial. It goes without saying that in deuteronomistic understanding this return to faithfulness must entail the setting aside of other deities because impiety arises from the lack of single-minded devotion to God (cf. Deut 6:4-5; 26:16-19). To that extent, the deuteronomistic expansion in this chapter expresses a spiritual sensibility already present in the narrative, but develops it in line with later deuteronomistic insight. This kind of heart devotion is not to be construed, however, as "spiritual" in such a way as to obviate corporate ritual action. Samuel leads "all Israel" in gathering at Mizpah, engaging in a water rite, fasting, and confession (7:5-6).[72] The episode

---

71. The NRSV translates the second part of the question as "To whom shall he go so that we may be rid of him?" While this rendering is a little free, it does make plain the force of the Hebrew term *mēʿālênû* ("from over us"), which is difficult to render literally in English.

72. As Wellhausen observes (*Prolegomena to the History of Israel*, p. 256), this rite of pouring water is foreign to later priestly practice.

thus provides, in a brief but telling manner, baseline expectations for questions about what will constitute proper worship later in the book. Here Israel is led by Samuel — already depicted in the narrative as priest and prophet, and now judge/ruler (*wayyišpōṭ*, 7:6, 15-17) — who intercedes on Israel's behalf by praying (√*pll* Hithp.) to God directly. The people of Israel in turn engage in corporate ritual action that expresses outwardly their individual and interior commitment to pure devotion. This form and manner of worship should be contrasted sharply with the decision in 1 Samuel 4 to bring the ark into battle. In 1 Samuel 4, no prayer and no religious rites were reported by the narrative at all. The previous use of the ark in battle was not somehow "secular" (the distinction between "sacred" and "secular" is a modern one) but rather *forced*, and therefore inadequately reverent.

A similar function is served by the following passage (7:7-14), which, however, points forward in the narrative rather than backward. When the Philistines move against Israel militarily, the Israelites at Mizpah become afraid and plead with Samuel to help them by continuing to intercede with God for their deliverance (7:7-8). Samuel responds by making an offering and "crying out" (√*z'q*) to the Lord on Israel's behalf, a plea to which the Lord is said to "respond" (√*'nh*, 7:9). Simultaneity is used as a way of depicting God's mysterious intervention: "Just as (*wayhî* + participle) Samuel was making the offering (*hā'ôlâ*), the Philistines drew near (√*ngš* perf.) to do battle against Israel, and the Lord thundered mightily on that day against the Philistines; he confused them and they were defeated before Israel" (7:10). Use of the verb "thundered" (√*r'm* Hiph.) recalls 1 Sam 2:10 and points ahead to 2 Sam 22:14. In the world of this narrative, the appearance of God on behalf of Israel in battle is an index of Israel's faithfulness.

Comparison between this account of Samuel's successful intercession and the story of Saul's unsuccessful leadership in 1 Samuel 13 reveals many of the same narrative elements. In 1 Samuel 13 the Philistines gather again to attack; the Israelites become fearful; Saul presents offerings; simultaneity is employed: "Just as he was finishing the offerings (*wayhî* + inf. cstr. + *ha'ălôt*), behold, Samuel arrived (√*bw'* perf.), and Saul went out to meet him and to bless him" (13:10). But in 1 Samuel 13 the intercession is judged by Samuel to be faulty. The explicit reason given by Samuel is that, by acting before Samuel had arrived, Saul neglected to follow his instructions to the letter. Especially when viewed in relation to the narrative in 1 Samuel 7, however, another reason emerges. Unlike Samuel's behavior when confronted by a similar Philistine threat, Saul's actions consist of routinized ritual without a clear vertical dimension. While Samuel had led the Israelites in corporate worship, fasting, and confession, Saul later does none of that. While Samuel had prayed to God, interceding for Israel, Saul does not. Saul's offering, like the earlier effort to bring the ark into battle, is neither cynical nor secular. Yet it is suspiciously made in isolation from other actions that in crucial respects preserve the connection between ritual activity and the person of God. The description of Samuel's intercession in 1 Samuel 7 thus also functions *prospectively* to establish readerly expectations. These expectations become crucial for the evaluation of the Saul material that follows.

The conclusion to 1 Samuel 7 marks the culmination of the initial section of the book and styles Samuel as a judge (in line with the major figures found in the book of Judges). In addition to emphasizing how all of the most significant social roles (e.g., prophet, priest, judge) are now combined in a single individual, the generic similarity with the Judges narrative at this point underscores the fit between a more "charismatic" (i.e., non-hereditary) form of leadership and Israel's traditional religious convictions ("he built there an altar to the Lord," 7:17). No sense is given in 1 Samuel 7 that the role of the judge is flawed or imperfect; to the contrary, it appears ideal. The problem is that, as in the past, Samuel cannot perform all of these functions forever, and his sons — like those of Eli before him — have grown greedy and abuse their authority (8:1-3). This situation preemptively exposes the faulty logic of the Israelite elders, who proceed to ask for a king (*melek*). They wish Samuel to appoint them a king because Samuel's sons have been corrupted (8:5). Yet a kingship, with hereditary rights and privileges as well as expanded social power, will only make the problem of disobedient sons *more* difficult to resolve.[73]

1 Samuel 8 is often treated as the beginning of a new literary section, one that relates the rise of the monarchy (1 Samuel 8–12). Yet the present form of the narrative offers 1 Samuel 8 as a continuation of 1 Samuel 7 ("When Samuel grew old . . .," 8:1) and instead positions 1 Samuel 9 as a fresh departure, one reminiscent of the beginning of the book ("Now there was a man of Benjamin . . .," 9:1).[74] Accordingly 1 Samuel 8 continues to depict Samuel as Israel's chief leader and to portray more fully its normative vision of the proper relationship between power and worship. If 1 Samuel 7 offers a portrait of Samuel's activity primarily as a blessing for Israel, 1 Samuel 8 treats his activity mostly as warning or curse. In both respects Samuel's interactions with God are shown to be "conversational" in nature ("Samuel prayed to the Lord and the Lord said to Samuel . . .," 8:6-7). Even though Samuel personally disapproves of the elders' request for a king, he asks God about it before responding to them himself (8:10).

73. Hubmaier, "On the Sword," , p. 192, identifies the problem slightly differently. For Hubmaier, the people are not wrong to ask for a monarchy per se, they are wrong to ask it of Samuel (instead of God).

74. For a comprehensive argument in favor of reading 1 Samuel 8 together with the first seven chapters of the book, see Frolov, *Turn of the Cycle*.

The words that Samuel receives from God are curious. On the one hand, God makes explicit what is likely at the root of Samuel's own misgivings: for the people of Israel to request a king for themselves is in effect to depose God from the same role ("for it is me they have rejected from reigning over them," 8:7; 10:19; cf. Judg 8:23). God also acknowledges that this rejection entails the repudiation of Samuel's authority and conforms to a pattern of behavior extending back to the time of the Israelites' exodus from Egypt (8:8).[75] As in the previous chapter, here, too, the Israelites are said to be worshiping "other gods." On the other hand, however, God surprisingly tells Samuel to "obey" the Israelites' demand (šĕmaʿ bĕqôlām; lit., "listen to their voice," 8:7, cf. 8:9, 22). God wants Samuel to warn the Israelites about the consequences of a monarchy, but not apparently because they might then decide to retract their proposal. From the very beginning God is prepared to accede to their request, although fully opposed to their aim. Why?

In content and structure Samuel's warning to the people mirrors other examples of prophetic testimony to the impossibility of faith. Isaiah is commissioned *not* to let the people of Israel understand him, so that God's judgment of exile will not be forestalled (Isa 6:9-10). In response to the people's optimistic commitment to serve God, Joshua responds by telling them that they will *not* be able to serve God no matter what they do because God is holy and jealous (Josh 24:19). When the people insist on serving God regardless, Joshua styles them "witnesses against yourselves" (ʿēdîm ʾatem bākem, Josh 24:22, cf. 24:27). In the same manner Samuel is not just to "warn" but to "witness against" the Israelites (kî-hēʿēd tāʿîd bāhem, 8:9) by describing the excesses to which a monarchy will be prone (8:10-18).[76] The perspective recalls Deut 17:14-20, with its conception of the monarchy as a concession and its anticipation of royal abuse.[77] The king's future excesses are not described in 1 Samuel 8 as conditional but ultimately unavoidable, although there is probably an implied conditionality to Samuel's entire speech.[78]

Fundamental to the activities of the new king will be "taking" (√lqḥ, 8:11,

---

75. Steussy, *Samuel and His God*, pp. 78-79, characterizes God's words here as just as much a rebuke to Samuel as the people.

76. On the appropriateness of reading "witness against," see Jenni, *Die hebräischen Präpositionen*, 1:263.

77. See Clements, "Deuteronomic Interpretation of the Founding of the Monarchy." Note particularly the implied inevitability of the phrases "when you come into the land" and "like all the nations round about" in Deut 17:14-20. On this point see Patrick, *Old Testament Law*, pp. 119-20.

78. For this point, and for an exploration into the ancient Near Eastern background of this passage, see Kaplan, "1 Samuel 8:11-18 as 'A Mirror for Princes.'"

13, 14, 16) and "taxing" (*'śr*, 8:15, 17).[79] Because the main job of the king will apparently be to keep a standing army, young Israelite men will be drafted, and seasoned warriors will be retained in order to command the troops, farm the king's land, and fashion the king's weapons. Young women will be needed for other jobs, and additional lands and livestock will be required for the king and his court. However, the ultimate consequence of these broad changes throughout society will be that the Israelites are reduced to the status of "slaves" in their own land (8:18).

The similarity between the description of the monarchy in 1 Samuel 8 and the details of Solomon's reign, especially in 1 Kings 10–11, has long been noted.[80] Here again it is likely that Samuel's speech reflects Israel's experience in later history. Not only were the excesses described by Samuel typical of subsequent Israelite kings, the same royal offenses were later viewed as responsible for the eventual downfall of both the monarchy and the Israelite nation. After the Exile, even when they had returned to their land, the Israelites continued to perceive themselves as "slaves" (Ezra 9:8-9; Neh 9:36), a situation attributed to the errant leadership of the kings and other leaders within pre-exilic society: "Even when they were in their own kingdom . . . they did not serve you" (Neh 9:34-35). The point is that in the present form of the Samuel narrative the eventual tragedy of exile is already implied at the very introduction of the monarchy. An ominous note is struck, leading the reader to anticipate not only that kingship in Israel will be problematic but also that as an institution it is fundamentally flawed. According to 1 Samuel 8, the purpose of God finally lies in one direction and the course of the monarchy in another.

It is all the more strange, then, that God is depicted as sanctioning the monarchy from the beginning, too. The danger of the monarchy is the same as its most crucial benefit: dynastic continuity. At its best a monarchy promises a way past the instability of charismatic leadership. With a monarchy, a royal figure can represent the people before God and represent God to the people.[81] Such a governmental structure is never demonized within the biblical narrative, although it can and will be abused. Instead it is perceived and treated as a means of providing a tangible benefit to Israel, not only in terms of military

79. This aspect of the narrative is emphasized by Silber, "Anarchy and Monarchy Part One," pp. 44-46.

80. E.g., Clements, "Deuteronomic Interpretation of the Founding of the Monarchy," 408-9; McCarter, *I Samuel*, p. 162; but cf. Leuchter, "King Like All the Nations," who argues for an implied critique of Assyrian rulers rather than Israelite kings.

81. According to Frankfort, *Kingship and the Gods*, all ancient Near Eastern monarchs served as mediators between the gods and humankind. On a distinctive need for such mediation in Israel's tradition, see O'Donovan, *Desire of Nations*, pp. 49-53.

self-defense but also as a form of social organization providing insight into the ways of God, and able to preserve the community of faith. Along these lines Lyle Eslinger has argued that the people should be considered right to ask for a king within this narrative, that their request is not on its face evidence of their unfaith. The problem with Eslinger's interpretation is that he understands the people to want a "profane monarchy," as if the goal of their request is something like the separation of church and state.[82] Yet monarchy was never "secular" in the ancient Near East. The king always represented one god or another. The people's request is therefore better understood — as the narrative itself understands it — as "pagan" rather than "profane." There are in fact grounds to view this narrative as laying the foundation for something like a separation of church and state, but that distinction emerges not in the success of the people's request but in Saul's eventual demise.

God's ultimate intention is seemingly to use the monarchy as a kind of negative lesson for the Israelites, one in which they will eventually be thrown back upon their own misguided demand: "You will cry out on that day because of the king you have chosen for yourselves, but the Lord will not answer you on that day" (8:18). By the same token, the error of the people in asking for a king exculpates the monarchy somewhat, keeping it ambiguous rather than a straightforward evil.[83] As a lesson, it will be a costly one for both Israel and God. Yet God is portrayed as being quite determined to see it through. The ambiguity of the monarchy as an institution within Israel is at the center of this interpretive conundrum, and the later difficulties surrounding the reigns of Saul and David will only build upon this basic dilemma within the nature of the monarchy itself.

Although the elders had initially justified the need for Israel to be "like all other nations" by appealing to the deficiency of Samuel's sons (8:5), the same goal is revealed at the conclusion of this narrative section to arise from a rather different motivation as well. The people want a king to "go out before us and fight our battles" (8:20). In this request is both an implied criticism of Samuel, who was not (the reader now realizes) previously depicted in 1 Samuel 7 as leading the Israelite troops, and also of God, who was.[84] Rather than encouraged by the presence of God in battle and their victory, the Israelites see themselves as suffering from a military deficiency. They want a king who will lead their army rather than merely relying upon God to be present somehow

82. Eslinger, *Into the Hands of the Living God*, pp. 353-57.

83. Noth, *Deuteronomistic History*, p. 80.

84. As emphasized by Newman, "Wilfulness of Israel," in idem, *Parochial and Plain Sermons*, 3:497-98. Israel's proper task, Newman insists, was to "wait and be still" (cf. Exod 14:13-14; Deut 1:21; 2 Chr 20:15-17; Isa 7:4).

in the fray. Perhaps this desire stems from the military unpredictability of God, who in any given context might agree to fight on Israel's behalf (7:10) or might not (4:10).[85] Perhaps it is because even when God does so, God fights for Israel more by confusing Israel's enemies and encouraging Israel's army (7:10-11) than by appearing as an observable, easily identifiable figure, who personally takes part in the fighting. A visible king could be counted on.

On this point there is a conceptual similarity between the implied critique of the self-fought battle within the Samuel narrative and the denunciation of militarism as misplaced trust within the prophetic tradition (see 1 Sam 17:47; Isa 30:15-17; 31:1; Hos 1:7; cf. Pss 33:16-17; 147:10-11), although for the prophets kingship itself is not criticized as strongly as military alliances and physical might (e.g., "Woe to those who go down to Egypt for help and rely upon horses," Isa 31:1).[86] A closer parallel exists in Judges, when God has Gideon reduce the size of his troops so that the Israelites will not think they have won their own victory (Judg 7:2; cf. Deuteronomy 20). For Samuel, Israel's becoming like "all the nations" means for Israel to have a human king in such a way that God will no longer be acknowledged "king" as fully as he was before. The two loyalties can coexist, even harmoniously at times, but they will still be fundamentally at odds. This transition in spiritual understanding marks a turning point in the book and within the larger story of Israel. After this moment it will continue to be possible for the Israelites, and even their kings, to be faithful believers in God, and that possibility can and will be celebrated by the Samuel narrative as it proceeds. But henceforth, until the Exile, the Israelites will be unable to confess resolutely that God alone is king over Israel — apart from any human viceroy or partner. This sad loss of ultimate spiritual loyalty at the expense of a more pragmatic national politics is the profound point of 1 Samuel 8.

Some commentators have made much of the fact that the narrative does not detail Samuel's fulfillment of God's command to appoint a king.[87] It is indeed strange that 1 Sam 8:22 reads, "The Lord said to Samuel, 'Obey their voice and make a king for them' and Samuel said to the men of Israel, 'Each one go to his own city.'" God's command and Samuel's announcement are placed into

---

85. From this perspective Noth, *Deuteronomistic History*, p. 49, views the advent of the monarchy as "a refusal to be dependent on occasional divine help."

86. For a sympathetic evaluation of the royal tradition, see Roberts, "In Defense of the Monarchy."

87. For Polzin, *Samuel and the Deuteronomist*, p. 84, Samuel intentionally attempts to short-circuit God's command by sending everyone home. Cf. Sternberg, "Time and Space in Biblical (Hi)story Telling," pp. 86-87, who refers to Samuel's "obstructionism" and God's "stage management."

the closest rhetorical proximity and yet they do not match. Is Samuel's execution of God's command implied? Or does Samuel dismiss the men *instead of* appointing a king? Is the narrative suggesting the possible disobedience of Samuel? If so, then the narrative would introduce for the first time a theological distinction between the views of Samuel and the will of God.[88] The figure of Samuel could then be read from here on out as a less reliable indicator of God's perspective with regard to the action of the unfolding narrative.[89]

Yet this interpretation fails to convince. Is Samuel to go about making a king *on the spot*? Who should be chosen? Much more likely is that Samuel sends the Israelites home as a preparatory step on the road to selecting a king.[90] "His (own) city" (*lĕ'îrô*) is technical language denoting an individual's hometown within a traditional tribal allotment (e.g., 1 Sam 1:3).[91] By dismissing the Israelites and sending them home, Samuel is laying the groundwork for a necessary process of discernment. His act of disbandment fits the more charismatic pattern of leadership familiar from the book of Judges (e.g., Judg 2:6) and represents a strategy — whether conscious or not — of retaining a charismatic aspect with regard to the new monarchy. The king will presumably need to be chosen by God, identified by the Israelites (initially at a local level), and installed in a proper manner. The details of these expectations are not yet clear; Samuel's dismissal of the people only implies the fact that such expectations exist.

These expectations are then subtly confirmed by the beginning of chapter 9, which refocuses the attention of the narrative by introducing a new figure, Saul, who is possessed with excellent qualities and living quietly at home. He is just as unknown to the reader as he is to the rest of the Israelites. Yet because of the implications of Samuel's dismissal, the reader immediately expects that Saul is more than some hometown nobody. The simple juxtaposition of God's intention to make a king and Saul's abrupt narrative introduction already indicates that he is likely the one to be chosen.

88. Some commentators have read 1 Sam 8:1-3 as implying Samuel's disobedience by reporting the failure of his sons. Thus Heller, *Power, Politics, and Prophecy*, argues that 1 Samuel 8–16 presents a more ambiguous portrait of Samuel than 1 Samuel 1–7, in which he is viewed in completely positive terms. In 1 Samuel 8–16, by contrast, the earlier criticisms against Eli are implicitly redeployed with regard to Samuel, beginning in 1 Sam 8:1-3. Cf. Kammerer, "Mißratenen Söhne Samuels." Yet even allowing for greater ambiguity on this point in the narrative, it is important to see that the explicit stance of the narrator remains explicitly positive with regard to Samuel (1 Sam 8:10).

89. Samuel's speech in 1 Samuel 8 is read as a defensive justification for his own authority and status in Bar, *God's First King*, pp. 8-9.

90. Dietrich, *Early Monarchy in Israel*, p. 32.

91. Cf. Judg 21:23-24.

Saul's Introduction (1 Sam 9:1–10:16)

Saul, like Samuel, is a Benjaminite. It bears noting, however, that the introductory information in 1 Sam 9:1 is properly about Saul's father Kish. Saul himself is then introduced in 9:2 as Kish's son, a designation further emphasizing the parallelism between Saul and Samuel. They are both Benjaminite *sons*. The narrative additionally provides two significant items of information: that Saul is "choice and good" (*bāḥûr wāṭôb*) and that no one in Israel was "better looking" (*wĕʾên ʾîš mibbĕnê yiśrāʾēl ṭôb mimmennû*) or "taller from the shoulders up" (*miššikmô wāmaʿlâ gābōah mikkol-haʿām*).[92] The word "choice" could be a substantive (= "a young man in his prime"; cf. 1 Sam 8:16, MT) or a passive participle functioning adjectivally (= "chosen one"; cf. 1 Sam 24:3). In either case the Hebrew root is the same (√*bḥr*), and the term is also used in the Hebrew Bible to express divine election (although not all of its uses are theological in nature). By announcing from the outset that Saul is "choice," however, the narrative is again establishing readerly expectations in line with the hanging conclusion of 1 Samuel 8. Who is to be "chosen" as Israel's new king? How about this "choice" young man Saul from Benjamin?

Saul's "goodness" (*ṭôb*) can be taken as a physical quality ("handsome") or a moral trait ("virtuous").[93] It is also possible here that the narrative is using the term to make a double point. In one sense Saul's "goodness" is related to how he appears, how he is perceived. This kind of "goodness," already suspect within the world of the story thus far, will be persistently subverted in the narrative's telling of subsequent events. In another sense, however, Saul's "goodness" is moral and actual; he is not a bad man. Pronouncing Saul "good" at the outset of his story functions in a broadly similar way to the repeated statement that creation is "good" at the beginning of Genesis: the difficulties that will arise later are not the inevitable consequences of something that began "bad" or had an inherent tendency to "go bad." Things here start out well and could have turned out differently. Saul began fundamentally good.

However, the other item of information given in Saul's introduction is more ambiguous: Saul is "a head taller than any of the people" (NJPS). This characteristic of Saul is presented as if it is something positive; after all, it appears in tandem with the reference to Saul as "choice and good." Yet the same adjective translated as "tall" has already appeared with a negative nuance in

---

92. At the same time it is possible that a double meaning may lurk in the term *maʿlâ* ("upwards"), based on the wordplay with the similar root √*mʿl* ("act unfaithfully, treacherously") in 1 Chr 10:13. See Downey, *Perverse Midrash*, p. 123 n. 40.

93. Avioz, "Motif of Beauty," p. 346. See further, Sternberg, *Poetics of Biblical Narrative*, pp. 354-56.

Hannah's Song, used adverbially: "Do not speak any more so high and mighty" (*'al-tarbû tĕdabbĕrû gĕbōhâ gĕbōhâ*, 1 Sam 2:3). Moreover, the song went on to use the distinction between "high" and "low" in order to illustrate the way in which God *reverses* the customary social order. "He lays low; he also lifts high. He raises the poor from the dust; from the ash heap he lifts up the needy" (1 Sam 2:7b-8a). "The bows of the valiant (*gibbōrîm*) are broken" (1 Sam 2:4a). "For not by strength does one prevail (*yigbar*)" (1 Sam 2:9b). In this fashion Hannah's song built upon the reversal of expectations and norms found in the first chapter of the book (e.g., the childless woman bears a son; men in power are not favored by God as much as the powerless woman, etc.) and attributed this reversal to the essential nature of God.

So the ordinarily appealing characteristic of height begs a particular question in the narrative world of this book: Is Saul's height a sign of divine favor or an indication that he may be in need of divine diminishment? Either way — as a purely physical characteristic or a personality trait — the quality of his tallness suggests that something innate to Saul is somehow at issue. Furthermore, the significance of this personal detail is not limited to Saul's narrative introduction.[94] The same phrase will be repeated almost verbatim in 1 Sam 10:23: "he was taller than all of the people from the shoulders up" (*wayyigbah mikkol-hā'ām miššikmô wāmā'lâ*). In fact, Saul's physical size will be revealed in the course of the narrative to be the ironic source of an inflated sense of personal insecurity (1 Sam 9:21; 15:17) and a wrong-headed approach to national defense (1 Sam 14:52). Just as Samuel and God had feared, the course of the monarchy in Israel, at least as pursued initially by Saul, will be to weaken reliance upon God in warfare and political affairs by fostering a seemingly more pragmatic politics, in which physical strength is favored over prayer and physical appearance over spiritual fortitude.

All this is merely hinted in Saul's introduction. The narrative proper begins with the presentation of a quest. Kish sends Saul out into the wider territory of Benjamin to look for his lost donkeys (*'ătōnôt*). The ability of a hero to prove himself through the performance of a successful mission is a well-known theme from classical literature, especially in the tradition of the Romance,[95] thus further confirming the great expectations evoked by Saul's introduction.[96]

94. Hawkins, "First Glimpse of Saul," pp. 353-62.
95. Frye, *Anatomy of Criticism*; Ryken, *Words of Delight*, pp. 186-206.
96. The symbolic resonance of the donkeys or "she-asses" has been explored by Rudman, "Commissioning Stories." Not only are the people of Israel said in Isa 1:3 to be less intelligent than the "he-ass," use of the verb √*ṣr* ("restrain") in 1 Sam 9:17 as a description of Saul's political destiny suggests a parallel between the two actions of shepherding and ruling. Both the NRSV ("rule") and NJPS ("govern") obscure this verbal link. It should be remembered that

The rest of this narrative unit, through 10:16, is a tightly constructed, brilliant example of literary artistry.⁹⁷ At his servant's suggestion, Saul seeks out a local prophet in order to gain additional information about the lost asses. The servant knows this dignitary to be a true prophet, according to the standard deuteronomistic criterion of truthful prediction (10:6), and suspects that he may even already know about their current situation ("perhaps he will tell us about the way upon which we have set out," 9:6).

The reader anticipates, of course, that this local prophet is none other than Samuel, but Samuel's name is skillfully withheld until Saul and his servant finally encounter him (9:14). In this way, the reader "meets" Samuel in the narrative just when Saul does. Samuel's access to superhuman knowledge is reemphasized through the addition of a narrative analepsis or "flashback" (9:15-16), in which Samuel is told by God that Saul is to be anointed Israel's "leader" (*nāgîd*).⁹⁸ The flashback is confirmed by the inclusion of another (private) word from God to Samuel (9:17), of which Saul is unaware, and Samuel's uncanny provision of information about the lost asses ("As for the asses that were lost three days ago, do not fret over them [lit. 'do not set your heart on them'], for they have been found" (9:20). Samuel is a mind reader to boot ("all that is in your heart I will tell you," 9:19). He will go on to predict three encounters that Saul will experience on his return home: one with two men near Rachel's tomb (10:2), another with three men going up to Bethel (10:3-4) and a final encounter with a band of prophets outside Gibeah (10:5). All three incidents are eventually reported to occur just as they were predicted, although only the fulfillment of the last one is actually narrated (10:9-10) — a success rate that not only contributes additional authority to the figure of Samuel but lends extra credence to his other words and actions, specifically those regarding Saul's anointing.

---

the she-asses also connote wealth; cf. the reference to Kish as a *gibbôr ḥāyil* ("man of wealth") in 1 Sam 9:1.

97. Dell, "Incongruity in the Story of Samuel," has helpfully seen the oddity of how "trivial" stories are interwoven with momentous events in this narrative, but she explains the significance of the combination by an appeal to the narrative's oral prehistory. By contrast I see a highly sophisticated narrative strategy at work. See further Gilmour, "Suspense and Anticipation in 1 Samuel 9:1-14." The narrative's coincidences lend an air of mystery and providence to the story. See Deist, "Coincidence as a Motif." On "coincidence miracles" in the Bible more generally, see Jacob, *Theology of the Old Testament*, p. 225. Cf. Zakovich, *Concept of the Miracle*, pp. 26-29, on some biblical miracles as "fortuitous occurrences."

98. McCarter, *I Samuel*, pp. 178-79, argues for this term as referring to a distinctive office of "king designate" or "crown prince," drawing on the work of Mettinger, *King and Messiah*, pp. 151-84. However, more recent scholarship has been skeptical of such an office and tended instead to view *nāgîd* and *melek* more or less as synonyms. See Ishida, *History and Historical Writing*, pp. 57-67.

Samuel's religious credibility, in combination with God's explicit direction (9:17), rules out any sense that the choice of Saul is a mistaken one. Nevertheless, subtle ambiguities continue to pervade the narrative. Why is it that Saul's servant knows about the prophet in Benjamin but not Saul (9:6)?[99] Rather than being concerned about the truthfulness of this prophet's words, Saul instead focuses on the idea that a prophet will need payment (9:7). While such payment was apparently nothing out of the ordinary,[100] Saul's cast of mind suggests a fairly pragmatic approach to religious life and institutions. When Saul and Samuel do meet, Samuel's initial words about Saul and the kingship are framed as a question and as a matter of Israel's desire (*ḥemdat-yiśrā'ēl*) rather than God's choice (9:20): "And on whom is all Israel's desire fixed, if not on you and on all your ancestral house?"

Later the people respond skeptically to Saul's own prophetic behavior (10:11); those who have known him in the past have difficulty viewing him now as filled with the spirit of God. Although the narrator adds another anonymous voice ("someone from there," 10:12) to suggest that it is no less likely for Saul to be filled with the spirit, based on his background and parentage, than for any of the other prophets, it is still the people's doubt that survives as a nagging proverb: "Is Saul really among the prophets, too?" (10:12).[101] Even if the narratives regarding Saul's prophetic activity were once more positive, as they currently exist they serve to call into question the authenticity of his religious experience.[102] There is something about Saul's relation to prophets and prophecy that does not seem right or convincing.[103] A. B. Davidson catches this dimension of the narrative particularly well:

99. Simon, "Minor Characters in Biblical Narrative," p. 16, suggests that minor characters are sometimes employed by the biblical narrator in order to express irony; cf. Jacobs, "Role of the Secondary Characters."

100. Paul, "1 Samuel 9,7."

101. For a sense of the earlier critical discussion about this proverb, see Sturdy, "Original Meaning of 'Is Saul also among the Prophets?'" For more recent scholarship, see Nihan, "Saul among the Prophets," pp. 88-118.

102. Heller, *Power, Politics, and Prophecy*, p. 104 n. 33, helpfully observes that in biblical Hebrew the interrogative particle *hăgam* usually implies disbelief (see Gen 16:13; 1 Kgs 17:20; Esth 7:8; Job 41:1; Ps 78:20). Perhaps a better translation might therefore be, "Saul isn't among the prophets, is he?"

103. Polzin, *Samuel and the Deuteronomist*, pp. 184-85, makes the point that Saul's misuse of prophecy constitutes a misuse of religion more broadly. Mowinckel, *Spirit and the Word: Prophecy and Tradition in Ancient Israel*, p. 109, goes even further, characterizing Saul's behavior among the prophets as "blind, religious fanaticism." If Mowinckel is correct in this assessment (and it seems a little one-sided to me), then one might further conclude that for this narrative there is as little of God in blind fanaticism as in pragmatic atheism — indeed, that in the end the two are not all that different.

It was incongruous to [the people], this consorting with men of profound religious convictions and experiences, on the part of one who hitherto had not only shown no liking for such company, but, who, anyone could see, had no capacity for such a life and such duties as the prophets undertook.[104]

The artistry of the narrative is evident in how it establishes this kind of doubt without collapsing the ambiguity of the episode by offering a more explicit judgment.

Finally, it seems odd that Saul does not report anything about his anointing once he returns home (10:14-16). His withholding of information from his uncle suggests evasion and secrecy. To be fair, such secrecy has already been initiated by Samuel, who spoke with Saul one on one (9:25) and made certain to anoint Saul privately ("'Tell the servant to cross ahead of us' — and he crossed ahead — 'but you stand still and I will communicate the word of God,'" 9:27). The secret anointing of Saul implies that public approval of a specific candidate for the kingship cannot merely be mandated but must still be earned. The lingering question, however, is what the earning of the kingship will entail.

Perhaps part of the answer lies with the development of Saul's own character. The quest theme in literature usually illustrates the moral and spiritual growth of the hero, in addition to his discovery of the object of his quest. Often it is implied that the true object of his quest was in fact such growth in the first place.[105] Similarly, Saul is depicted as being changed in some fundamental manner because of his receptivity to the spirit of God (10:10). The narrative describes this change using highly theological language: "God transformed his heart" (*wayyahăpok-lô' 'ĕlōhîm lēb 'ahēr*, 10:9). Samuel had earlier predicted this change as Saul's becoming a "transformed person" (*wĕnehpaktā lĕ'îš 'ahēr*, 10:6). After engaging in prophetic behavior (perhaps an indication of his changed heart?),[106] Saul is said to visit the shrine at Gibeah (10:13), one of the few reports within the book indicating that he might be participating in worship. However, only the Masoretic text provides this information, and even so does not relate any specific acts of piety or devotion; the Greek tradition reads instead that Saul returned home (which makes more sense in

---

104. Davidson, "Saul's Reprobation," p. 154.

105. Auden, "Quest Hero." On the hero pattern more broadly, see Miller, *Epic Hero*. Still valuable is also Somerset, *Hero*.

106. Eslinger, *Into the Hands of the Living God*, pp. 322-23, views Saul's prophetic activity as another way in which Samuel's prediction of transformation in 1 Samuel 10 is being fulfilled. But to my mind the narrative establishes the connection between the two episodes more as a question than a straightforward fulfillment: *has* Saul in fact changed? *Can* Saul truly change?

light of the narrative's continuation in 1 Sam 9:14). Moreover, the successful fulfillment of the signs predicted by Samuel would appear to put into effect what Samuel had said would be the ultimate outcome for Saul: "You are to do as you see fit (lit. 'do as you find it in your hand [to do]'), for God is with you" (10:7). So along with the notes of ambiguity, Saul is described in terms of great confidence and high optimism for the future. Actually, unlike other quest narratives, Saul does not really have to do anything to earn his election. The events of the narrative are almost exclusively prophecies and signs (10:7), of which he is but the passive recipient.

There is, however, a single condition stipulated by Samuel, one relating to a future event at Gilgal where Saul is to wait for Samuel: "Seven days you will wait until I come to you and make known to you what you shall do" (10:8). This condition represents the test that Saul will be judged to fail in 1 Samuel 13, so it is important to examine it here in its initial narrative context. As several commentators have noted, Samuel's direction is itself ambiguous.[107] Does he mean simply that he will arrive in seven days (= "you will wait") or does he mean that Saul *must* wait seven days (= "you shall wait") and then proceed *only when* Samuel arrives and tells Saul what to do? Conflicting information from the narrative simultaneously strengthens both interpretations. On the one hand, Saul has been told in the preceding verse to "do as you see fit," a directive that suggests flexibility and delegated authority. On the other hand, Saul's earlier chance meeting with the young women drawing water (9:11-14) includes a description of Samuel's customary activity at sacrificial events. The women tell Saul to hurry if he wants to meet Samuel, because the people wait on the prophet to arrive before they eat: "for the people will not eat until he has come, since he must bless the sacrifice; after that the invited eat" (9:13). This practice is later illustrated in the same narrative (9:22-24). Such a description provides a narrative benchmark for a different interpretation of Samuel's later directive to Saul, suggesting that the condition of waiting for the prophet is customary and firm.

Remarkably, given its brevity, this entire section of the narrative thus establishes multiple opportunities for a variety of interpretations of Saul and his advance to the kingship. Several events in the narrative are not clearly evaluated by the narrator but are instead presented for further reflection and interrogation, sometimes through the use of unnamed characters or groups who express (through their discourse) counter-readings or ambiguities at odds with the main plot (10:11-12, 14-16).[108] In this manner the narrative at this

107. The best discussion is found in Gunn, *Fate of King Saul*, esp. 39-40.
108. Jacobs, "Role of Secondary Characters"; Reinhartz, "Anonymity and Characterization."

juncture raises more questions than it provides answers. Saul simultaneously appears as both full of promise and dogged by intimations of inadequacy. Chief among these intimations is his own sense of self-doubt: "Am I not a Benjaminite, from the smallest of the tribes of Israel, and my clan the most insignificant of all the clans of the tribes of Benjamin? Why do you speak in this way to me?" (9:21). Even Saul finds the prospect of his becoming king to be strange and confusing.

Such self-doubt can be evidence of noble modesty in a narrative hero (e.g., Exod 3:11). Yet here such doubt takes the form of a concern about physical size, and it deepens the worry introduced in 1 Samuel 8 and implied at the beginning of 1 Samuel 9: will the kingship be able to maintain Israel's traditional reliance upon God for its national defense and political well-being? Or will the monarchy contribute to a competition of loyalties between God and country, as Samuel seems to fear? Samuel will take exactly this concern directly to the people in the next section of the narrative.

King by Acclamation (1 Sam 10:17-27)

A noticeable shift exists between 1 Sam 10:16 and 10:17. Without any narrative preparation or transition, Samuel calls "the people" to Mizpah and addresses them with a standard prophetic formula: "Thus says the Lord, the God of Israel" (*kōh 'āmar yhwh 'ĕlōhê yiśrā'ēl*, 10:18). Other than the reference to the "people," the narrative initially gives no indication that Saul is also present at the gathering. Yet after Samuel in his brief address again equates the establishment of the kingship with the rejection of God (10:19), he then casts sacred lots to identify the individual that *God* desires to become king.

The nature of the lots and the procedure for their use are assumed rather than explained. That is true not only in this narrative but throughout the Old Testament. It would appear from ancient Near Eastern evidence that lots were either stones, sticks, boards, or dice, and that they were thrown or manipulated in a certain manner in order to divine God's will.[109] Old Testament narratives such as this one imply that the information provided by the lots was binary in nature, that is, of a "yes" or "no" variety. (Sometimes the answer could also be inclusive.) For this reason a winnowing process was used in which at first

109. For concise descriptions of lots in antiquity and their usage, see Hallo, "First Purim" (with photographs); Weinfeld, *Deuteronomy and the Deuteronomic School*. For more detailed overviews, see Kitz, "Hebrew Terminology of Lot Casting"; Nigosian, *Magic and Divination in the Old Testament*; Van Dam, *Urim and Thummim*. On the use of the lots in this part of the Samuel narrative, see Cooley, "Story of Saul's Election."

an entire group was tested by the lots. If the answer was "yes," then half of the group was tested again. If the answer was still "yes," then half of that group would be tested. If the answer was "no," then the other (first) half would be tested — and so forth, until the group had been thoroughly sorted and the lots had identified a single individual. That procedure is followed in this brief narrative, with the exception that the lots are somehow able to identify Saul in spite of the fact that he is not present. (The implication for the actual procedure is not explained; perhaps individuals were sometimes identified by proxy according to lists or tokens?)[110]

In response to the people's question about whether Saul is present, God is then more forthcoming (by providing more than only a "yes" or "no" answer): "Behold, he is hiding among the equipment" (hakkēlîm, 10:22). Saul is brought forward and, especially when his impressive height is observed, Samuel identifies him as God's chosen and the people accept him with a great shout as king (melek). On the surface, this narrative moment would seem to be a successful culmination of the movement toward the monarchy, one that has been building in the book ever since the people made known their request for a king. Saul's effort to hide could even be viewed as an admirable act of modesty. Yet once again worrisome details cluster below the narrative's surface. The "equipment" among which Saul hides might well consist of or include weapons of war. The Hebrew term kēlîm has a very broad range ("vessels," "implements," "utensils," "stuff"), but its customary translation of "baggage" in this passage (NRSV, NJPS) masks its associations in Samuel, in which it tends to refer to pagan religious objects (1 Sam 6:8, 15) and weapons or armor (1 Sam 8:12; 17:54; 20:40; 21:9; 2 Sam 1:27; cf. the fixed expression nōśē' kēlîm or "arms-bearer," as in 1 Sam 14:1, 6-7, 12-14, 17; 16:21; 31:4-6; 2 Sam 18:15; 23:37). While the term can also refer to non-military "baggage" (e.g., 1 Sam 9:7; 17:22), the other associations provoke an unsettling question. Where will Saul be located in the future, with God or with the tools of war — those implements with which Saul appears to identify himself?

110. Van Dam, Urim and Thummim, pp. 185-86, believes that the use of lots was distinct from that of the Urim and Thummim, and that there are two different procedures detailed in this narrative: first, the binary use of the lots; and, second, a priestly inquiry without the same binary limitation. Van Dam's reading cannot call upon any explicit narrative evidence for this conclusion other than the presence of the expression "šā'al b- + divine name." Yet this expression does provide strong evidence. It is used consistently for priestly inquiry involving the ark (1 Sam 14:36-37; 22:10-15; 23:2, 4; 30:8; 2 Sam 2:1; 5:23-24), as Van Dam persuasively illustrates (pp. 182-90). However, there is also no reason why the Urim and Thummim may not have been used in the same manner as a lot oracle, in addition to whatever other purpose they had, as Van Dam concedes (p. 186). See further Madl, "Gottesbefragung mit dem Verb šā'al."

Another indication that this brief narrative passage seeks to make a larger statement is signaled by a play on Saul's name. When the people inquire of God about Saul's absence from the scene, the Hebrew verb used for "inquire" is *šā'al* (10:22), a word sharing the same Hebrew root with Saul's own name. The people thus "requested" (*wayyiš'ălû*) "the requested one" (*šā'ûl*). The subtle wordplay associates Saul's identity with this particular scene, with his absence and the people's inquiry about him. From the very beginning, therefore, Saul is somehow "missing." The story of Saul's kingship originates in uncertainty and Saul's name is treated as a kind of implicit question.[111]

The uncertainty also underscores the strangeness of Samuel's behavior in this episode. Although he explicitly indicates that the establishment of the kingship entails the rejection of God (10:19), again appealing to the Exodus and the tradition of God's compassionate care for Israel without any human king (10:17; cf. 1 Sam 8:17; Judg 8:23), Samuel nevertheless leads the people in establishing this monarchy. He even prompts the people to accept Saul by coyly calling attention to his kingly appearance ("There is no one like him among all the people," 10:24). Yet Saul's physical appearance, as the narrative has already indicated, is the most ambiguous thing about him.

Surprisingly easy to overlook at this point in the narrative, however, is the fact that Samuel himself has not only known all along that Saul will be chosen king (9:17), he has even already secretly anointed him as "leader" (*nāgîd*, 10:1).[112] Of course, diachronic reconstructions have typically separated 1 Sam 10:17-27 from 9:1–10:16 and treated them as two different sources, but such a move does not adequately address the present form of the narrative. Some literary commentators have resolved the difficulty by attributing a selfish motivation to Samuel. On this reading he sets up the kingship for failure by choosing a candidate who is bound to be unsuccessful because he views the request for a king as a rejection of his own leadership.[113] There are three major problems with such a view. In the first place, the narrative at no point states or implies the kind of selfishness to Samuel that these

111. Indeed, Saul is introduced as a character who typically asks questions himself (e.g., 1 Sam 9:7, 11, 18, 21). See Polzin, *Samuel and the Deuteronomist*, p. 103. In retrospect the reader may recall that Samuel was also introduced as "the requested one" (*šā'ûl*, 1 Sam 1:28), a verbal link further contributing to the narrative's resistance to any quick closure. Who is really the "requested one," Samuel or Saul?

112. For more recent study of this important term, see Kim and Human, "Nāgîd"; Murray, *Divine Prerogative and Royal Pretension*, pp. 281-301.

113. Or, as Polzin, *Samuel and the Deuteronomist*, pp. 105-8, argues, Samuel proceeds with Saul's selection because he thinks he can then keep Saul under his thumb and hold on to power. Polzin thinks there is just as much a critique of prophecy here as of monarchy.

commentators have invented. To the contrary, Samuel is treated consistently throughout the narrative (with the possible exception of 8:1-3) as an exemplary Israelite leader whose views accurately represent God's will (see also 8:10). Second, the narrative explicitly attributes both the decision to establish the monarchy (8:7, 9, 22) and the selection of Saul as "leader" (9:17) directly to God rather than Samuel. Any attribution of selfishness to Samuel would have to attribute a similar selfishness to God, who would become by extension the ultimate source of Saul's "setup." Finally, although Samuel may conceal some of his actions, he explicitly discloses his point of view: "Today you have rejected your God, who delivered you from all your misfortunes and troubles, but you said 'No, set up a king over us'" (10:19).[114] Samuel is thus open about his conviction that the monarchy is a mistake and will eventually result in catastrophe. If he meant to trick the people, why communicate his disagreement at all?

More likely is that the establishment of the kingship is viewed by Samuel, and thus the narrator for whom Samuel speaks, as a prophetic "sign act." In the Old Testament, prophets often engage in symbolic actions in addition to speaking symbolic words.[115] Sometimes these symbolic actions involve other individuals (e.g., Hosea's marriage) or entail a historical experience for the entire people (e.g., exile). Treating the monarchy as a prophetic sign act would not only remove the taint of self-interest from Samuel (and God), it would also make sense of the way in which both God and Samuel criticize Israel's desire for a king but then accede to it. As a sign act, the monarchy's failure will provide a continuing testimony to God's righteousness, to the people's faithlessness, and to the difference between a human kingdom and the kingdom of God.

However, the nature of this sign act does not mean that everything associated with the monarchy will be bad. If that were so, then God would not have agreed to it, even for the purpose of teaching a lesson, for God continues to be righteous and faithful to Israel within this narrative world. But the monarchy as "sign act" will mean that every king and every generation of Israelites ruled by a king will be forced to wrestle with the tension between the form of government they have inherited and the fundamental convictions of their

114. An equally possible reading of the last clause is, "but you said to him, 'Set up a king over us.'" However, see also Samuel's later citation of this same remark in 1 Sam 12:12.

115. See further von Rad, *Old Testament Theology*, 2:95-98; Robinson, "Prophetic Symbolism." Both von Rad and Wheeler Robinson stress how such actions are not merely visual illustrations but enactments of the prophet's message. Von Rad describes the prophetic sign act as "a creative prefiguration of the future" (p. 96), and Robinson invokes sacramental language in order to characterize these prophetic actions as "partial realizations" (p. 10).

religious faith. There will be kings who rise above their office by pointing beyond themselves to God as Israel's true king, and there will be kings who will lead the Israelites further astray by taking them farther away from God. The crucial issue will be whether kings maintain God's sovereignty by limiting their own. One basic safeguard that kings are to observe, it seems, is to submit to the authority of the prophets, who function as the ambassadors of God's kingdom.[116]

After Saul has been accepted by the people, Samuel goes on to provide rules for Israel's new monarchy (*mišpaṭ hammĕlukâ*, 10:25) and then sends everyone home again. His provision of rules is another indication that the kingship is not evil but "freighted with ambivalence."[117] The final narrative marker of this ambivalence occurs at the very end of the unit again through the inclusion of anonymous grumbling.[118] Saul is said to return home with "warriors" (*haḥayil*, MT; *bĕnê haḥayil*, LXX, 4QSamᵃ); but others ask, "How can this one deliver us?" and they are said to "disdain" (√*bzh*) him and give him no gift (10:27). The articulation of this worry and its indication of dissension among the people conclude this narrative portion on a troubled note rather than a celebratory one. Saul's future is called into question preemptively, and uncertainty rather than confidence colors the continuation of the story.

This uncertainty is underscored by the nature of Saul's response to the dissension: "he kept silent" (10:27).[119] Is his silence to be construed as diplomacy or insecurity, fortitude or weakness? The narrative itself keeps silent. For the narrator explicitly to note Saul's silence, and yet not to provide any explanation for it, ensures that such questions will linger. Few things are more mysterious in literature than a character that is explicitly described as refraining from speech,[120] for then he is present in the description but simultaneously inaccessible in his silence. The contrast emphasizes a significant disjunction between appearance and reality, communicating that not all things are as they appear.

---

116. Polzin, *Samuel and the Deuteronomist*, p. 106.

117. Campbell, *1 Samuel*, p. 132.

118. See further Jacobs, "Role of Secondary Characters."

119. On possible *resh–dalet* confusion here, see Klein and Klein, "ויהי כמחריש," pp. 185-92. The LXX and 4QSamᵃ read "after about a month" instead. Cf. McCarter, *I Samuel*, pp. 199-200, who sees no evidence of haplography, only "an extraordinary case of scribal oversight." For McCarter, "he kept silent" is exclusively a later corruption of the text.

120. Alter, *Art of Biblical Narrative*, pp. 100-101. See further Grabher and Jessner, eds., *Semantics of Silences*; Stout, *Strategies of Reticence*.

Saul, Ruler in Battle (1 Samuel 11)

As a result of the discovery of the Dead Sea Scrolls, the transition from 1 Samuel 10 to 1 Samuel 11 has changed considerably. One of the Qumran documents (4QSam[a]) contained a new paragraph of text introducing Nahash and describing his oppression of the Israelites.[121] Various translations have made their own editorial choices about this textual unit, either including it (e.g., NRSV, in unnumbered verses) or not (e.g., NJPS). Although quite new, the paragraph was not entirely unexpected, since the transition between the two chapters had long been viewed as rough. Moreover, the Hellenistic Jewish historian Josephus appeared to preserve additional information about the story.[122] Not only did there seem to be context lacking for the events described at the beginning of 1 Samuel 11, the final phrase of 1 Samuel 10 (MT: "but he kept silent") was also rendered differently in septuagintal tradition. Both Josephus and apparently his Greek source read "about a month later," which shares most of the same Hebrew consonants as "he kept silent" but with the letter *dalet* instead of a *resh* and a *yod* (a common scribal confusion in antiquity). It therefore seems as if the newly found paragraph was an ancient victim of haplography, a scribal error in which the scribe's eye moves prematurely from one word or expression to a similar one later in the text, thus neglecting to copy the intervening material. This explanation could still mean that the phrase "he kept silent" originally concluded that portion of the text now regarded as 1 Samuel 10, but it would also justify the presence of the phrase "about a month later" at the beginning of the MT to 1 Samuel 11, where it is presently missing.[123]

Because the new paragraph will not be included in all translations, it is reproduced here in the form in which it appears in the NRSV:

> Now Nahash, king of the Ammonites, had been grievously oppressing the Gadites and the Reubenites. He would gouge out the right eye of each of them and would not grant Israel a deliverer. No one was left of the Israelites across the Jordan whose right eye Nahash, king of the Ammonites, had not

---

121. Cross, "Ammonite Oppression of the Tribes of Gad and Reuben." For the full text, with critical commentary, of this discovered document, now see Cross, "4Q451," in Cross et al., eds., *Qumran Cave 4.XII*, pp. 65-67. While Cross views the missing text as original but somehow lost, other scholars conclude that the "missing" text is in fact secondary and some form of expansion; see Kallai, "Samuel in Qumran"; Rofé, "4QMidrash Samuel?"

122. Josephus, *Ant.* 6:68.

123. Or perhaps both phrases originally read "about a month later." See further Vander-Kam, *Dead Sea Scrolls and the Bible*, pp. 18-20.

gouged out. But there were seven thousand men who had escaped from the Ammonites and had entered Jabesh-gilead.

Of particular interest for theological interpretation are both the reference to a need for a deliverer and the explanation for the deep loyalty that the people of Jabesh-gilead will later demonstrate to Saul. In the ensuing narrative Saul is depicted as a heroic, divinely authorized warrior after the fashion of the judges. The inhabitants of Jabesh-gilead are not only rescued by him but will remain grateful for Saul even after his death, rescuing his body in turn from Beth Shean so that it can be burned with honor and his bones buried in Jabesh (1 Sam 31:11-13; cf. 2 Sam 2:4-7; 21:12).

Saul's portrait is strikingly different in this chapter from how it has been previously presented.[124] Here he is styled as something like a local chief, residing in his own fiefdom, "Gibeah of Saul" (11:4). His coming in from the field in order to take charge is a motif known from other hero stories in antiquity (cf. the Roman story of Cincinnatus).[125] When he hears of the difficulty faced by those in Jabesh, however, "the spirit of God surges ($\sqrt{slh}$) over Saul" and he becomes very angry (11:6). Not only is the same idea evident in the Samson narrative, the identical terminology is used (cf. Judg 14:6, 19; 15:14).[126] There, as in the Saul account, a link is drawn between anger and spirit possession (cf. Judg 15:14). When Saul was previously gripped by the spirit, it led to prophetic behavior (1 Sam 10:10; cf. 10:6). In 1 Samuel 11, however, the presence of the spirit unleashes Saul's temper. The association with Samson creates further uncertainty about whether this is a good thing. As will become evident, the difference between Saul and David is eventually going to be framed in part by the presence or absence of God's spirit (1 Sam 11:6; 16:13-14; cf. Ps 51:11).

Yet the surface level of the narrative is entirely positive at this point — presenting the most seemingly sympathetic portrait of Saul within the entire book. He takes up the cause of Jabesh-gilead and compels the people of Israel to go to battle against the Ammonites. True, he compels them out of fear as well as a sense of responsibility, but this fear appears to stem ultimately from God (*pahad-yhwh*, 11:7), and Saul's actions are therefore justifiable. Indeed, the Israelites celebrate a great victory over the Ammonites and save Jabesh. After the battle, the people remember those who had earlier questioned Saul's capabilities (1 Sam 10:27) and demand that Samuel give them up to be killed (11:12). At this point it is Saul who refuses them, saying nobly, "Let no one be

---

124. See further Polzin, "On Taking Renewal Seriously."
125. See Livy, *Early History of Rome*, 3:26.
126. Mobley, "Glimpses of the Heroic Saul," p. 82.

put to death on this day because today the Lord has wrought a victory in Israel" (11:13). Saul is thus glowingly portrayed as a merciful leader as well as a tough customer. His refusal to kill captives after battle foreshadows the fateful events of 1 Samuel 15, in which it is precisely his refusal to kill Agag the Amalekite that costs him his kingship. Here, however, Saul's victory and statesmanlike generosity lead instead to the formal inauguration of the monarchy at Gilgal, with Saul — fully and finally — as king (11:14-15).

Once again the narrative poses implicit questions by disclosing judiciously sculpted items of information and simultaneously withholding complete explanations. The people of Jabesh do not enter the narrative neutrally but reflect a problematic pre-history from the final chapters of Judges. It was the people of Jabesh who had been slaughtered in order to rob them of their young women and provide the Benjaminites with wives (Judges 21). It was the Benjaminites in turn who had been decimated by the other Israelite tribes (Judges 20) in response to the Benjaminites' rape of the Levite's concubine in Gibeah (Judges 19). Saul's slaughter of a yoke of oxen as a means of rallying Israel (11:7) mirrors the cutting up of the Levite's concubine into pieces (Judg 19:29). The reference to "Saul of Gibeah" (11:4) provides a common geographical point for the association of the two episodes. If Saul is to be viewed as admirably transcending the troubled history of his people and reunifying Israel, it remains worrisome that he descends from a bloodstained tribe, which was remembered above all for its violation of the ancient obligation of hospitality.

Just as Saul's physicality has been highlighted in the previous narratives as his most noteworthy aspect, his success in warfare is now identified as the pre-eminent feature that validates his accession to the kingship. Saul appears at first to conduct war in such a way that God's sovereignty is still preserved. "Because today the *Lord* has wrought victory in Israel" (11:13, my emphasis), he proclaims to the Israelites after the battle. However, the culmination of the narrative unit occurs not in battle or victory or kingship but in a worship scene (11:15). The people proclaim Saul king "before the Lord" (*lipnê yhwh*) and offer sacrifices "before the Lord" (*lipnê yhwh*). Unclarified in this report is the relationship between these worship practices and the king. Just who is leading the sacrifices? Samuel? Saul? It is another conspicuous silence in relation to the attention to worship given in the book thus far and in light of the worries that have been articulated about both the kingship in general and Saul specifically. What does it now mean for Israel to be "before the Lord" and how is Israel's worship life related to its military activities? Is it enough for Israel to fight its battles as other nations do and then give thanks to its God? Or will maintenance of the worship that is pleasing to God require Israel — and Saul — to do more?

1 Samuel 1–12

Samuel, Worship Leader (1 Samuel 12)

Almost the entirety of the next narrative unit is styled as a speech by Samuel, with only minimal third-person narration and just three brief responses from the people (12:4, 5, 19).[127] The speech apparently occurs at Gilgal since no transitional movement is reported after the concluding events of 1 Samuel 11, which were set at that location. Interestingly, Samuel is portrayed as very much in charge of things, which immediately raises the question not only of the power dynamic between Saul and God but also between Saul and Samuel. Who is now God's viceroy in Israel? And how will the nature of that role shift as Israel moves from a tribal confederacy united under a religious leader like Samuel to a kingdom under a military leader like Saul?

Samuel's speech takes the form of a farewell discourse. Having grown old, and knowing that his sons are unsuitable for leadership (cf. 1 Sam 8:5), Samuel confirms that he has now established a king in Israel, as the Israelites had earlier asked him to do. In fact, he characterizes this action as "obeying the voice" (*šāma'tî běqōlěkem*) of the people (12:1). In spite of the fact that Samuel was not a "king" (*melek*), he appears to conceive of Saul's place within Israel's communal life as largely identical to his own. Samuel has "gone about" (√*hlk* Hithp.) before Israel in the past; now the king will be the one who "goes about" (√*hlk* Hithp., 12:2). This verb can sometimes be used as a technical worship term (e.g., 1 Sam 2:30).[128] Is Saul now to officiate at sacrifices? It should be remembered that the people's request for a king had originally been couched in jurisprudential and military rather than sacrificial terms. They wanted a king so that he could maintain the social order (1 Sam 8:35) and also "go out before us and fight our battles" (1 Sam 8:20).

Samuel's speech and actions in 1 Samuel 12 are all designed to communicate two verities to the Israelites: first, that there can be no protector of justice or keeper of peace who does not also lead Israel in worship; and, second, that leading Israel in worship requires honesty, a spiritual sense for God, and a deep awareness of Israel's overarching story. Rather than a self-righteous self-defense,[129]

---

127. For the most recent comprehensive treatment of this speech, especially within the context of the Deuteronomistic History, see Nentel, *Trägerschaft und Intentionen des deuteronomistischen Geschichtswerks*, pp. 140-65.

128. See further *TLOT*, 1:369. Jenni and Westermann cite Josh 3:6; 6:9; 1 Sam 6:12 in relation to the ark, and note how the Hithp. form of the verb, as in 1 Sam 2:30, can be used in reference to relationship with God (cf. Gen 17:1; 24:40; 48:15; 2 Kgs 20:3).

129. Thus Polzin, "On Taking Renewal Seriously." Cf. Polzin, *Samuel and the Deuteronomist*, p. 118. Noll, *Faces of David*, p. 46, goes even further, characterizing Samuel's speech as "a series of explicit distortions and outright lies."

117

Samuel's description of his own moral conduct (12:2-3) serves as a crucial reminder to the Israelites of the need for their leaders to be honest.[130] Samuel's retelling of salvation history (12:6-13) situates the Israelites within the embrace of an identity that transcends their particular historical moment and underscores the steady faithfulness of God — right up to the point that they rejected God by demanding a king ("you said to me, 'No, a king shall reign over us,' even though the Lord your God is your king," 12:12). In Samuel's retelling of the story it is the Ammonite threat (as in 1 Samuel 11), rather than that of the Philistines (1 Samuel 7), which precipitates the people's desire for a king. Yet either way, the people's demand is based primarily on military insecurity.

Also worth observing is how Samuel's speech characterizes national defense as a matter for repentance. Military threats in the past arose when the Israelites "forgot the Lord their God" (12:9). Such threats are repulsed not by superior arms or artful stratagems but through seeking God's forgiveness ("They cried out to the Lord saying, 'We are guilty, for we have abandoned the Lord and worshiped the Baalim and the Ashtaroth,'" 12:10). Deliverance and right worship go hand in hand ("Now deliver us from the hand of our enemies and we will serve/worship you," 12:10).[131] Only then did God send the warrior judges of the past, Samuel tells them, individuals like Jerubbaal, Bedan, Jephthah and . . . Samuel. Here again, some have read Samuel's inclusion of himself in this list as self-absorbed and self-promoting. Is it not immodest for him to insert himself in such exalted company — and in his own speech? Yet the countervailing option is to credit Samuel with the kind of honesty that goes beyond appearances to the truth of the matter. Samuel *has* been a leader like the judges of old, and it is important for him to draw the connection explicitly so that the Israelites can see the sharp inconsistency between the shape of their common life before God up to now and the enormous change they have initiated.[132]

Still, in contrast to the exclusively negative stance that Samuel had earlier adopted with respect to the kingship (8:18), now he characterizes the Israelites' future success as conditional upon their behavior. "*If* you will fear the Lord

130. The unexceptional nature of a "negative confession" by a leader in the ancient Near East is shown by its ritual place within the Babylonian New Year's festival; see Kuhrt, "Usurpation, Conquest and Ceremonial," p. 33. From this perspective it is a mistake to view Samuel's speech in 12:3 as self-indulgent, pompous, or self-righteous.

131. The Hebrew verb translated "serve" (√'*bd*) can also be used to mean "worship." Only context determines which translation is better employed in any particular narrative.

132. However, as Steussy, *Samuel and His God*, pp. 36-37, rightly notes, Samuel's inclusion of his own name may also be a sign that he views himself, as well as God, as being rejected by the people.

and serve/worship him (√'*bd*) *and* obey his voice *and* do not rebel against the command of the Lord . . ." (12:14, my emphases). These four interlinked criteria are all *theocentric* in nature — that is, they are directed toward Israel's orientation toward God — and thus they preserve a whisper of hope that Israel can maintain a holy loyalty. The request for a king is still viewed as essentially an indication of unbelief (12:17), but by painting the future in conditional terms Samuel indicates that *Israel* remains redeemable, even if the kingship is ultimately not.

In fact, to read this narrative section closely is to see that the issue at stake is the destruction of Israel rather than the failure of the monarchy, which has always been a foregone conclusion as far as the figure of Samuel is concerned. By means of his retelling of Israel's story — and his prayer for thunder and rain — Samuel manages to convince the people that their situation is indeed dire, and that they were wrong to ask for a king in the first place (12:19). The wheat season (v. 17) was the driest period of the year,[133] yet Samuel successfully calls forth rain. Moreover, "harvest" represents a spiritually as well as agriculturally auspicious season (cf. John 4:35-36). In this pregnant moment Samuel again frames his response theocentrically: Israel is to serve/worship (√'*bd*) the Lord with "all your heart" (12:20). If the Israelites worship (√'*bd*) the Lord with all their heart and recall how God has done great things on their behalf in the past (12:24), it is implied, then they will be preserved. The alternative is not only outright rebellion against God but a broader, and perhaps more subtle, "turning away" from God toward "the empty things" (*hattōhû*, the same word used in Gen 1:2 for the emptiness prior to creation, but here treated as a plural noun). By promising to intercede with God on Israel's behalf in the future, Samuel models exactly the same kind of behavior that he advocates. For Israel to survive, it must maintain its God-centered perspective. When this perspective is minimized or lost, then Israel will come under divine threat.

The pressing issue at hand, however, is to what degree the kingship will assist Israel in maintaining that God-centered perspective or how hard Israel will be forced to work to maintain it in spite of the pull of the king toward "empty things." Since "empty things" are by definition those things that lead away from God, the ability of Israel to worship with its whole heart becomes the determining factor for its survival. And the king, will he finally help Israel to survive or tempt it toward destruction?

---

133. Wevers, "1 Samuel," pp. 161-62.

CHAPTER 3

1 Samuel 13–20

A king is not saved by his great army; a warrior is not delivered by his great strength.[1]

To whom shall I have respect, but to him that is poor and little and of a contrite spirit?[2]

Blessed are the meek, for they will inherit the earth.[3]

The First Rejection (1 Samuel 13)

After Samuel anointed Saul he gave him three prophetic "signs" (1 Sam 10:2-6). These signs were predictions of events that would occur as Saul returned home — three meetings on the way. First he is to encounter two men who will confirm for him that his father's asses have been found, just as Samuel had already cryptically implied, and that his father is worried about him. Then Saul will meet three men on their way to Bethel who will offer him two loaves of bread. Finally Saul is to proceed to Gibeah, where he will come across a band of prophets engaged in ecstatic prophesying, and he will be seized by the same manner of ecstasy. As presented by the prophet Samuel, all of these signs are intended to confirm for Saul that he has indeed been anointed king, and also to embolden him to meet his next challenge successfully: a meeting with Samuel at Gilgal. Saul is in effect provided with three meetings in preparation for the one rendezvous that will really matter.

---

1. Ps 33:16.
2. Isa 66:1-2.
3. Matt 5:5.

The anticipated Gilgal meeting has been somewhat awkwardly postponed by the gathering in Mizpah (1 Sam 10:17-26) and the battle against the Ammonites (1 Sam 11:1-13). Samuel gathers the people in Gilgal afterwards (1 Sam 11:14–12:25), but the pattern of events does not exactly match what has been predicted: Saul does not arrive prior to Samuel. In fact, one might well be forgiven for thinking that the situation predicted in 1 Sam 10:8 had long since played itself out. Samuel and Saul have already offered sacrifices of well-being (*zĕbāḥîm šĕlāmîm*) together at Gilgal (1 Sam 11:15), seemingly in line with Samuel's earlier prophecy (1 Sam 10:8). So it comes as a bit of a surprise to find Samuel's previous directive still in force as the narrative now reaches the events of 1 Samuel 13. Saul returns to Gilgal after fighting the Philistines successfully, and the Israelites rally to him there out of fear of another Philistine attack (13:4). At this point the narrative reintroduces the notion of the seven-day waiting period as Saul prepares to offer sacrifices on the eve of yet another military confrontation with the Philistines. Worship and battle are again brought into closest proximity and maximum tension.

In all likelihood the difficulty in moving from Samuel's commission in 1 Sam 10:8 to Saul's enactment of it in 1 Sam 13:8 arises primarily from the composite nature of 1 Samuel 8–12. The material that is deuteronomistic in style and content has probably been added later to earlier material telling of Saul and his rule. Although significant differences exist among the proposed reconstructions of historical-critical scholars who have attempted to identify and isolate the individual strands of this narrative, most researchers have distinguished broadly between earlier, pro-Saul tradition(s) and a later, deuteronomistic and anti-Saul layer.[4] One key indication of this basic shift in perspectives has long been taken to be the use of the term "king" (*melek*) in the deuteronomistic layer (1 Sam 8:5-6, 9-11, 18-20, 22; 10:19, 24; 12:1-2, 12-14, 17, 19, 25; cf. 8:7; 10:16; 11:12, 14-15) and its avoidance in favor of the term "leader" (*nāgîd*) in the earlier layer (1 Sam 9:16; 10:1; 13:14).[5] Originally, so the

---

4. The later layer tended at first to be viewed as pre-deuteronomistic but still anticipating many of the characteristics of full-blown deuteronomism. See Wellhausen, *Composition des Hexateuchs*, pp. 234-46; Birch, *Rise of the Israelite Monarchy*; Eslinger, "Viewpoints and Point of View"; McCarter, *I Samuel*, pp. 23-30; McCarthy, "Inauguration of the Monarchy in Israel." Current scholarship tends to treat 1 Samuel 8–15 as the compilation of numerous sources rather than only two. See, for example, Schmidt, *Old Testament Introduction*, pp. 153-54, who entertains the possibility of up to five discrete sources; cf. Van Seters, *In Search of History*. However, for a different kind of reconstruction see McKenzie, "Trouble with Kingship." For an argument that there did exist an "old story" about Saul, which was then later reconstructed by the deuteronomists, see Na'aman, "Pre-Deuteronomistic Story of King Saul."

5. Smith, *Books of Samuel*, p. 62. Similarly, Cross, *Canaanite Myth and Hebrew Epic*, p. 220.

theory goes, the tradition(s) about Saul told of his life as a tribal chieftain in ancient Israel, and only with the deuteronomistic compilation and substantial recasting of those traditions in the period of the late monarchy was the story of Saul transformed into the present account of Israel's first unsuccessful "king." If one employs this basic terminological criterion to divide the present text of 1 Samuel 8–12 into putative sources, one comes up with two "non-king" narrative passages (9:1-10:16; 11:1-11), now interwoven and book-ended by three "king" texts (8:1-22; 10:17-27; 11:12–12:25).

There are difficulties with this two-source model, not the least of which is that the term "leader" (*nāgîd*) is well represented in late biblical texts like Chronicles and Daniel, undercutting the force of the argument that its presence necessarily indicates an early source in Samuel.[6] Moreover, the fact that the present text is likely to be a composite mixture of various sources, and thus the product of a lengthy process of literary development, does not eliminate the possibility that these sources were artfully combined.[7] To the extent that some of their source(s) were apparently quite sympathetic toward Saul, it is all the more remarkable that the deuteronomistic tradents of the material did not completely eliminate those features but incorporated them into the broader narrative of Israel's story that they constructed. In fact it would be a mistake to imagine that here two ideological strains of tradition have been woodenly joined and that the ambiguities so evident in the present text are an accidental consequence of their admixture. More likely is that such features have not created ambiguity accidentally or even been combined in order to *create* ambiguity, but instead draw out the ambiguities that already existed within the pre-deuteronomistic and deuteronomistic memories of Saul.[8]

One indication of this rhetorical strategy is precisely the apparent delay in following through on Samuel's commission to Saul in 1 Sam 10:8. The delay is not a casualty of careless editing but a narrative device employed to lead the

---

6. Fischer, "Saul-Überlieferung," pp. 170-71, argues convincingly that *nāgîd* is not a pre-monarchic conception but a royal honorific title meaning "shepherd" and cognate with the Akkadian *nāqidu*. See 2 Sam 7:8, where this conception is made explicit. Fischer draws on the work of Lipiński, "Leadership." Fischer also treats both *nāgîd* and *melek* as deuteronomistic and therefore views the layering of the Samuel narrative as a development internal to the deuteronomistic tradition.

7. For a literary defense of such "composite artistry," see Alter, *Art of Biblical Narrative*, pp. 163-92.

8. Hamilton, *Body Royal*, pp. 123-24, insightfully points to the ritualization of opposition to the monarchy in the ancient Near East, represented above all by the slapping of the king by a priest in the New Year's Day festivities in Babylon. This kind of ritual action suggests that "pro" and "anti" positions may well go "all the way down" and cannot be reduced to a temporal sequence.

reader/hearer to forget the matter of Samuel's commission, for a little while, until it returns front and center in 1 Samuel 13.[9] The impact of this narrative forgetting is to increase the reader's sympathy with Saul, who can then be faulted for failing to observe the letter of his instructions only if the reader becomes questionably scrupulous. In other words, the effect of the narrative postponement is not only to engender more sympathy for Saul but to provoke the reader into questioning his or her own sense of justice. Can Saul really be blamed for forgetting exactly what Samuel had told him, especially when as readers we ourselves barely remember what Samuel said?

Furthermore, the chapter starts as if it marks the beginning of another new narrative departure. Even though the first verse is famously fragmentary and absent from the septuagintal tradition altogether, enough of it appears in the MT to indicate its nature as an introduction. Interestingly, Saul's son Jonathan is briefly reported to be more successful in battle than his father, although he possesses half as many troops (13:2-3). This information immediately reestablishes the association between Saul and physical strength, an association that was prominent in earlier chapters, and at the same time calls it into question. Saul has apparently established a standing bodyguard for himself (1 Sam 13:2),[10] yet it is Jonathan who wins the victory (1 Sam 13:3). Moreover, even though the death of the Philistine commander at Gibeah is an accomplishment of Jonathan, Saul — either intentionally or unintentionally — receives credit for the deed (1 Sam 13:4). Thus the narrative subtly renews doubt about Saul even as it continues to construct a literary context that displays profound regard for him.

With Saul moving to Gilgal and the people rallying to him there in the face of a new Philistine threat, the stage is now finally set for the resumption of Samuel's test. Despite some textual difficulty, the narrative states clearly that Saul "waited seven days" and refers pointedly back to Samuel (13:8).[11] But

9. On this literary strategy as one of "temporal deformation," see Long, *Art of Biblical History*, pp. 409-18; more generally, Sternberg, "Telling in Time (III)." The point here is not to insist woodenly that all narrative events between 1 Sam 10:8 and 13:8 must somehow be fitted into the span of one week, but to read 1 Sam 13:1 (despite its apparent textual difficulties) as a focusing device drawing attention to Saul's wider significance. By employing a literary form reminiscent of a reign summary within a royal chronicle, the narrative subtly implies that the conclusion to Saul's reign is already a foregone one — in other words, that *from the perspective of the narrative* Saul is already "dead."

10. Von Rad, *Holy War in Ancient Israel*, p. 75.

11. This time notice implies a seven-day period between chapters 10 and 13, which would thus improbably include Saul's accession to the throne (twice) and his deliverance of Jabesh-gilead. On the further temporal difficulties that this framework presents, see McCarter, *I Samuel*, p. 228, who notes how in 1 Samuel 10 Saul was still "a young man living in his father's

Samuel has still not arrived after the seven days are over, and the people begin to shrink away. At this point Saul orders a burnt offering and a sacrifice of well-being to be prepared (both are stipulated in 10:8, although there both terms are plural), and he himself has just officiated over the burnt offering when Samuel finally shows up (13:10). Not only is Samuel displeased by what Saul has done, Samuel astonishingly treats this small infraction on Saul's part as a crime of such great magnitude that Saul's dynasty is disenfranchised and the days of his own rule are said to be numbered (13:14).[12]

Here the narrative plays a high-stakes game with the reader. The narrative invites the reader to have as much sympathy as possible for Saul without actually leading the reader to resent Samuel's judgment against him. The tilt of the balance is beautifully struck. On the one hand, Saul seems fully justified in his actions in several respects. By offering sacrifices Saul apparently seeks to be a responsible ruler, preparing for battle in a religious manner. Since when is it a sin to engage in worship?[13] Moreover, he is confronted by a situation in which the confidence of the people is waning and waiting has become even more dangerous. Saul can see his army disappearing; surely it cannot be wrong to do something to maintain the morale of his troops. All of this is in addition to what was already observed about the fundamental fuzziness of Samuel's directive in 1 Sam 10:8. When Samuel said "Seven days you shall wait until I come to you" did he mean that Saul should wait seven days exactly or that Saul should wait until Samuel arrived, which he planned to do in seven days?[14] It is particularly difficult to be dogmatic about an answer to this question since Samuel had also told Saul to act on his own initiative: "Act for yourself as you see fit, for God is with you" (1 Sam 10:7). The narrative reinforces the sense of

---

house" but "here he is king of Israel and has a grown son of his own." Polzin, *Samuel and the Deuteronomist*, p. 126 n. 6, argues that Samuel had never specified exactly when the seven-day period was to occur — but this seems like a stretch.

12. Interestingly, the term "leader" (*nāgîd*) is also used in this passage (1 Sam 13:14), suggesting again that — to the extent the usual reconstruction of sources is accepted — even in its early stages the Saul story included an account of Saul's disobedience and rejection.

13. This tension is developed homiletically to good effect in John Henry Newman's sermon, "The Trial of Saul," in his *Parochial and Plain Sermons*, 8:33-47: "Observe, Saul in his way was a religious man; I say, in *his* way, but not in God's way; yet His very disobedience *he* might consider an act of religion. He offered sacrifice *rather* than go to battle without a sacrifice. An openly irreligious man would have drawn up his army and fallen upon the Philistines without any religious service at all" (pp. 44-45; his emphases).

14. Andrew of St. Victor, *Commentary on Samuel and Kings*, pp. 85-89, tries to work out the confusion as a difference in how the seven days were counted by Saul and Samuel, but the operative narrative distinction is actually between Saul's inclination to count and Samuel's insistence on prophetic authorization.

a merely technical violation by having Samuel arrive immediately after Saul had made his first offering. In this way Saul can still be faulted but only by a razor-thin margin.

For his part, Saul seems oblivious to the danger he is in. He does not hide from Samuel but goes out to "bless" him (√*brk*, 13:10) and, in answer to Samuel's query, to explain what he has done. The people were deserting, Samuel had not come, the Philistine troops were massing, and God's favor needed to be entreated:[15] what was a king to do? The unusual verb often translated "so I forced myself" (√*'pq* Hithp., 13:12 NRSV, NJPS) could be used here with that meaning but might also have the sense of "but I restrained myself" (i.e., from heading into battle without making the proper sacrifice).[16] On this reading, Saul did not "force himself" to make the offering, but "restrained himself" from going into battle. He was not focused on sacrifice but war.

By contrast, Samuel seems unsympathetic as a character in this fraught encounter. He is so nitpicky and inflexible that several commentators have questioned his motivation.[17] Has Samuel set up Saul for failure from the start? Samuel made no bones about his expectation that the monarchy would ultimately miscarry (1 Sam 8:18). In response to Saul's explanation, Samuel not only seems to impose the harshest of penalties for the lightest of infractions, he also recalls his own words to Saul in 1 Samuel 10 as the very commandments of God (13:13-14) — a stance that could easily be viewed as arrogant, if not even deranged. Finally, it is certainly true that Samuel is a character in the plot (i.e., not the narrator himself), and therefore his motivations are not above question.[18]

Against such a reading, however, lies the entire characterization of Samuel up to this point. Samuel has been consistently and entirely laudable in his words and actions. He has reliably represented the "orthodox" perspective shared between God and the narrator. The book of Deuteronomy makes quite

15. The Hebrew text reads "before I had entreated before [lit. 'the face of'] the Lord." This reference to God again sounds somewhat distanced and formulaic, an aspect masked by both the NJPS translation ("before I had entreated the Lord") and the NRSV ("and I have not entreated the favor of the Lord").

16. Smith, *Books of Samuel*, p. 97, similarly reads *wā'et'appaq* as "I constrained myself"; i.e., that Saul held back as long as he could. Cf. Alter, *Art of Biblical Narrative*, p. 72.

17. Miscall, *1 Samuel*, p. 88: "a golden opportunity for [Samuel] to denounce Saul"; Polzin, *Samuel and the Deuteronomist*, p. 129: "Verses 1-14 of chapter 13 are thus about Samuel's present failure as prophet as well as Saul's future as king."

18. On the biblical narrator as reliable, see Amit, *Reading the Biblical Narratives*, pp. 93-102. Probably no one has argued for more distance between the narrator and Samuel than Lyle Eslinger; see his reflections on Samuel as a character in his *Kingship of God in Crisis*, pp. 260-62; *Into the Hands*, pp. 81-121.

clear both the need to follow the instructions of a judge or levitical priest exactly (Deut 17:8-13) and for a priestly invocation to precede a battle (Deut 20:2). While one might still point to the absence of any confirmation by the narrator (or by God) of Samuel's verdict — the narrative simply continues with Samuel's exit from Gilgal — an opposite interpretation is more likely: because Samuel has spoken, there is nothing more for the narrator (or God) to add. This blunt reminder of Samuel's reliable orthodoxy compels the reader to return to the matter of Saul's error. If Samuel's judgment is harsh but right, then what exactly has Saul done wrong (despite his apparently good intentions)?

There seem broadly to be three possibilities. In the first case, Saul may have failed his instructions on a technical point, as appeared to be the case on an initial reading. However, as we have seen, here the difference between the nature of Saul's misdeed and Samuel's penalty is so great as to call into question Samuel's righteousness as Israel's judge (1 Sam 7:15-17). Could Saul's failing have therefore entailed a greater mistake? Perhaps the apparently trifling nature of Saul's error has been highlighted in the text precisely to evoke such a question. In this case, another option might then be to question whether Saul as king is supposed to offer sacrifices at all. It is noteworthy how Samuel's original instructions (1 Sam 10:8) presumed that Samuel himself would offer the sacrifices after he had arrived in Gilgal — and not Saul. Saul did seem to be involved in the earlier sacrificial rites at Gilgal (1 Sam 11:14-15), but the text did not actually report any leadership on his part in worship activity. To the contrary, Samuel still appears to be overseeing ritual actions (1 Sam 12:1, 18-19). Yet no hard-and-fast separation exists between Samuel's priestly role and his other functions. Why should it be any different for Saul? Because he is king? Because one way to control the power of the monarchy is to keep it separate from Israel's worship?

Such a "separation" seems unlikely, not only because Saul does proceed to make a sacrifice in 1 Samuel 13, but also because of what will occur throughout the rest of the book of Samuel. Not only is the position of the monarch perceived to be a deeply religious office,[19] the spiritual dimension of the monarchy will become in time the greatest criterion of its success or failure. Not only does David engage in ritual religious action as king, by the end of what is now

---

19. Note how Solomon functions as a priest at the Temple dedication ceremony in 1 Kings 8. Such an understanding is in line with ancient Near Eastern understandings of kingship generally; see Day, "Canaanite Inheritance of the Israelite Monarchy"; Dietrich, "König David"; von Soden, *Herrscher im alten Orient.* Even allowing for its excesses, earlier work on the monarchy's sacral dimensions by the "myth and ritual" school remains useful; see Engnell, *Studies in Divine Kingship in the Ancient Near East*; Johnson, *Sacral Kingship in Ancient Israel.* More recently, see del Olmo Lete, "Royal Aspects of the Ugaritic Cult."

2 Samuel the royal figure of David is presented in a thoroughly religious light (e.g., 2 Sam 22; 23:1-7). Saul can hardly have sinned against an ideally "secular" kingship if that ideal is later revealed instead to be fundamentally sacred. For this reason a third possibility begins to suggest itself. Perhaps the deeper problem with Saul's offering was his reason for proceeding with it. Rather than the seven-day waiting period being an indication that Samuel was hardly fair, perhaps it discloses how Saul was only barely religious. Although the Philistines were quickly assembling and his people were steadily drifting away, Saul was willing to wait the seven days he had been instructed to wait — but not one second more.

On this reading the "technicality" at issue in the incident at Gilgal is the formal quality of Saul's obedience rather than the technical nature of his failure. The deeper problem revealed by his actions is a pragmatic cast of mind that leaves little room for spiritual realities and for God. Not only is his mindset indicated by his focus on the thinning ranks of the people (13:8, 11) and the military threat represented by the Philistines (13:11-12), he seems to feel that he has held out for as long as he possibly could ("but I restrained myself," 13:12). Indeed, Saul cannot even recognize the nature of his misdeed because his entire worldview is shaped according to the strategic considerations of war.[20] Within the world of this text it would not be out of the question — in fact it would be praiseworthy — for a character in such military straits to say, in effect, "I do not care if the enemy is at our door, we must place ourselves in the hands of God; let God do as God will." Yet at no time in the description of Saul's sacrifice or in his comments to Samuel about it does Saul mention God at all. Strikingly absent in his words and deeds is the heartfelt devotion to God so crucial to deuteronomistic theology and to the overall shape of the Samuel narrative thus far. Saul's ritual action has instead the feel of a formality to be observed rather than a genuine act of worship.[21] On exactly this point the lack of Saul's fitness for the kingship is thus painfully exposed.[22] If the one thing, more than any other, that a king in Israel should possess and model for his people is a heartfelt devotion toward God (cf. 2 Kgs 23:25), then Saul is fundamentally unsuited for the task. For this reason, and not for some minor failure of timing, Samuel pitilessly gives Saul notice that he will not for long remain king.

---

20. This narrative theme is also recognized but reduced to a historical datum in van der Toorn, "Saul and the Rise of Israelite State Religion," p. 528: "The religion of the Saulide state was born in the army."

21. Levy, *Waiting for Rain*, p. 190, similarly describes Saul's sacrifice as "pro forma" and "perfunctory."

22. McGlasson, *Invitation to Dogmatic Theology*, p. 251, refers accordingly to this chapter of 1 Samuel as a protest against "the politicization of the sacred."

However, Saul will apparently remain king for as long as it will take Samuel to find a replacement. This task is given time because, as Saul has now shown, a particular type of person must be sought. The right person for the kingship will be "a man after God's own heart" (*'îš kilbābô*, 13:14), thus confirming the centrality of heartfelt devotion to the unfolding of the narrative.[23] This quality of heart is the thing Saul lacks, the reason for his rejection and the one thing above all others to be sought in his replacement. God had given Saul "another heart" (*lēb 'aḥēr*, 1 Sam 10:9) after his anointing, but this change of heart had seemingly been insufficient. Saul's failure not only evokes uncertainty about God's ability to change Saul's heart successfully but also about God's selection of him in the first place (1 Sam 9:15-17). Was God wrong?

Possibly the answer lies in the curious distancing of the phrase "another heart." After all, if God ultimately wanted "a man after his own heart," why did God simply not give Saul a heart like that at the outset? Perhaps such a heart is not entirely in God's power to give, for if God could simply "give" such a heart then God would remove any need for human responsibility and negate any worth to human freedom. Saul can fail despite his election by God and his anointing by Samuel precisely because Saul is ultimately responsible for his actions and his choices. One aspect of the mystery of human existence lies in the givenness of character and context, over which human individuals cannot always exercise full control. From the beginning of the narrative's treatment of Saul, it emphasized how his very nature consists of a focus on physicality and pragmatism. Saul is himself a big man, someone who respects weapons, armies, and brute force. Indeed, the conclusion to 1 Samuel 13 reminds the reader of

23. McCarter, *I Samuel*, p. 229, has argued against any particular emotional implication in this narrative, preferring to take the expression "a man after God's own heart" as an indicator only of Yahweh's free choice: "This has nothing to do with any great fondness of Yahweh's for David or any special quality of David, to whom it patently refers." McCarter notes similar usages in 1 Sam 14:7; Ps 20:5 (Engl. 4); Jer 3:15. There is no need, however, to insist on an either/or at this point. To be sure, "heart" is often used metaphorically in the Hebrew Bible to refer to the location of human will or intellect rather than emotion, which is instead the more modern association. But "heart" does also have an emotional valence in the Bible; see Fabry, "Lēb." Fabry maintains that "heart" is a way of speaking about the whole person, including both the affective and noetic aspects of human nature. Taking this mediating position as well are Arnold, "Love–Fear Antinomy in Deut 5–11"; Becker, "Heart in the Language of the Bible"; Lapsley, "Feeling Our Way"; Rüterswörden, "Liebe zu Gott in Deuteronomium." I therefore understand the term "heart" to refer both to God's choice and God's fondness. I also agree with Johnson, "Heart of YHWH's Chosen One in 1 Samuel," who examines and rejects McCarter's position that the term does not denote any special quality of David, concluding, "It is a key thematic interest in the narrative of 1 Samuel that YHWH's chosen agents have a right heart, and it appears that there is something about David's heart that makes him an ideal candidate to function as YHWH's chosen one" (p. 466).

this basic reality about Saul, just in case it has been forgotten. Rather than some casual historical report, the notice regarding the lack of Israelite weapons (13:19-22) provides further confirmation that the theme of self-reliance has been crucial all along in the events of 1 Samuel 13, and it establishes important background for additional reflection on this theme in 1 Samuel 14.

Yet this narrative attention to Saul's nature also produces greater sympathy for him instead of simply emphasizing his undesirability. Sympathy *and* critique, these two attitudes toward Saul are brilliantly maintained throughout the narrative of 1 Samuel 13 and, for that matter, the entire book of Samuel. However, the lingering question provoked by the intersection of these two attitudes in the arena of worship is this: Is heartfelt devotion finally included in the text's gesture toward responsibility? Is such devotion more of an innate quality for human beings, so that they can be praised for its presence in their lives and criticized for its absence, though ultimately they cannot really be considered responsible for their basic spiritual predisposition? Or is heartfelt devotion something that can be learned, practiced, and maintained, with human beings held fully responsible for their spiritual vitality or lethargy? The book of Samuel will continue to worry about these questions but never fully resolve them — beyond acknowledging that somehow both perspectives are true.

Jonathan and Saul (1 Samuel 14)

The final notice in 1 Samuel 13 has already made the point that none of the Israelite soldiers had adequate weapons because of the scarcity of smiths in Israel. The Israelites could pay the Philistines to have their farming implements sharpened into weapons, but only if the Philistines were willing. This notice underscores the traditional agricultural identity of the Israelites and reinforces the relative foreignness of advanced warfare to their native culture. Because of the constraints involved in procuring weapons, only Saul and his son Jonathan have sword and spear at their disposal (1 Sam 13:22). Although the latest Philistine threat had apparently not fully materialized after Saul had made his offering and Samuel had arrived at Gilgal, the Philistines are now preparing again for battle. Once more there is the ominous sense of impending military jeopardy.

The narrative in 1 Samuel 14 develops an extended contrast between Saul and Jonathan as representing two very different responses to this threat.[24]

24. See further Williams, "Is God Moral?" pp. 181-82.

Saul's response is consistent with his behavior in the book thus far; Jonathan's response illuminates the way in which Saul is falling short and also foreshadows David's perspective and character. What are the two responses? Simply put, Saul continues to rely upon force, technicalities, and pragmatics, whereas Jonathan models a truly "yahwistic" approach to battle, leadership, and faith. As a narrative character, Jonathan reveals Saul's central weakness, lack of faith, by embodying faith's abundance. For Jonathan, God can save "by many or by few" (1 Sam 14:6), but for Saul having the bigger army makes all the difference.

The contrast is introduced at the beginning of the chapter by Jonathan's decision to advance against the Philistines — by himself, with only his armor bearer — without telling his father what he is doing. This secret initiative on Jonathan's part alerts the reader to a distance between father and son, a gap of information that will soon become a difference in character. On the one side is Jonathan's courageous initiative. On the other side is Saul's choice to remain in his camp, and the fact that his camp also contains Eli's great-grandson Ahijah, who has brought a priestly ephod. In other words, not only does Saul fail to display the same battle-ready initiative as his son, by hosting Ahijah and the ephod he also echoes the earlier failure of Eli's sons in bringing the ark into battle (1 Sam 4:14).[25] Use of the ark as a military talisman had been discredited by Israel's defeat and the ark's capture in that context. Now, however, Saul essentially repeats that earlier error.

But, one might be forgiven for asking, can it really have been viewed in the ancient Near East as a spiritual mistake of some sort simply to have a priest or sacred object present at a battle site? Is not such an interpretation anachronistic? As one commentator has stressed, "Nowhere in the ancient world was warfare a purely secular matter. Victory depended on the gods — more so than on the valour of men."[26] Yet the description of Jonathan's sortie suggests a further nuance. Jonathan's brief speech to his armor bearer (14:6) is remarkable for its theocentric character and spiritual dynamism: "Come, let us cross over to the camp of these uncircumcised ones; perhaps (*'ûlay*) the Lord will act for us, for nothing holds back the Lord from victory whether by many or by few."[27] Here Jonathan's enthusiasm for bloodshed is the speech's least noteworthy aspect. Far more important is his firm understanding of God's freedom to act. *Perhaps* God will help him against the Philistines, perhaps not;

---

25. The priestly ephod is used synonymously with the ark (14:18) in this narrative unit. The septuagintal tradition also reads "ephod" in 14:18 to match 14:3.

26. Van der Toorn, "Saul and the Rise of Israelite State Religion," p. 528.

27. The divinatory aspect of Jonathan's speech is emphasized by Porter, "Ancient Israel," p. 197.

that is God's decision and it cannot be compelled or forced.[28] In fact, if God decides to act on Jonathan's behalf, it will not make any difference that Jonathan is vastly outnumbered, for God has the power to achieve a victory even against a superior military force.[29] This religious outlook illumines in relief exactly what is absent in Saul, Jonathan's father.[30] The use of "heart" language again underscores the point. A more literal rendering of the armor bearer's speech in v. 7 would read, "Do whatever is in your heart . . . I shall be with you; my heart is like your heart."[31]

As the narrative proceeds, Jonathan and his armor bearer fight against the Philistines by seeking omens from God in the unfolding of events and in the utterance of certain words by the Philistine sentries (14:8-13).[32] When Jonathan pushes ahead with his attack, he does so with the conviction that God will be fighting on his behalf, and that the victory will be Israel's and not only Jonathan's own (14:12). The narrative report of widespread terror and an earthquake accords with a standard type-scene for so-called "holy war,"[33] which confirms that God does enter into the battle in some way on Jonathan's behalf. Given the negative implications of warfare and weaponry in the narrative up to this point, the success of Jonathan's raid serves the important purpose of signaling

---

28. See further Reimer, "An Overlooked Term in Old Testament Theology – Perhaps."

29. This focus on Jonathan is highlighted by the implicit reference to his own name ("Yhwh has given") in v. 10, "the Lord has given them into our hands." See Garsiel, *First Book of Samuel*, p. 151 n. 48. At the same time, it is perhaps telling that Jonathan's bravery takes the form of a solo action rather than a grand military strategy. Is there already groundwork being laid here for the idea that Jonathan, despite his personal bravery, is in fact unsuited for the throne? Or at least not as suitable as David will prove himself to be? Jonathan is depicted from the outset as a brave and pious warrior, but no general. Cf. Zehnder, "Observations on the Relationship," p. 161.

30. McGinnis, "Swimming with the Divine Tide," p. 259, also points to the spiritual contrast between Jonathan and Saul.

31. I assume haplography in the last clause. McCarter, *I Samuel*, pp. 235-36, once more dismisses any emotional resonance to the term "heart" and instead translates "Do whatever you have in mind . . . I shall be with you! We are of the same mind!"

32. On this scene as a biblical example of cledonomancy (= divination based on chance events, encounters, or remarks), see Nigosian, *Magic and Divination in the Old Testament*, pp. 47-48.

33. Von Rad, *Holy War*, thought that a certain type of battle, with distinctive characteristics, was recognized as a "holy war" in ancient Israel. Scholarship has now abandoned this view, but von Rad's literary observations about Old Testament battle accounts remain of real value. Although the term "holy war" is a misnomer — no war or battle is ever called "holy" in the Old Testament — there is certainly a stream of Old Testament tradition that understands God as being present in battle on Israel's behalf. For further discussion see Chapman, "Martial Memory, Peaceable Vision."

that warfare itself has not been the precise object of criticism. Instead it is a false attitude toward warfare that the narrative has sought to expose and condemn, an attitude according to which warfare is conducted ritualistically and God is brought in only to "baptize" whatever the politicians and generals have already decided to do.

In a manner quite at odds with modern liberal sensibilities, the Samuel narrative maintains the appropriateness of God's presence in battle. What is at issue in the narrative is how that presence is to be sought and understood. Saul approaches God's presence in a manner more superstitious than devout; his main concern lies elsewhere. Jonathan's focus is on God rather than on victory; his perspective ironically ensures his victory just as Saul's lack of concern for God dooms him to failure. Just because the book of Samuel sees a role for God in battle, however, does not mean that Samuel views God as a bloodthirsty deity. To the contrary, the battle scenes involving God exhibit extraordinary restraint. God is never personified in a battle scene within the book. Instead God participates in battle primarily by the manipulation of the natural world — or perhaps, to put it more accurately, by withdrawing from the natural order (cf. Ps 81:11-12 [Engl. 12-13]; Isa 50:11; 64:6 [Engl. 7]; Rom 1:18-32). The battle scenes imply a situation in which God has removed the protective restraints that ordinarily keep the forces of chaos in check, releasing their fury upon Israel's attackers.[34] "Holy war" in this sense is a matter of upsetting and reasserting the divinely sponsored created order.[35] It is a matter of preserving Israel and its place in the created world, of defensive protection, and not of a nationalistic lust for territory, possessions, or political dominance. Although individual military actions like Jonathan's may appear in local contexts to be offensive rather than defensive in nature, in terms of the wider situation within Samuel they are all viewed as defensive actions relating to a preexistent threat to Israel's survival. It is also worth noting that the narratives of Saul's battles never contain cosmological features (cf. 1 Sam 13; 14:20).

Saul's worldview is further revealed by his failure to understand how Philistines could be fleeing (14:16). He assumes that some of his troops must have left and initiated a battle. Yet a count of his men results in the information that only Jonathan and his armor bearer are missing (14:17). Apparently resolving to enter the fray — presumably out of opportunity, perhaps also out of filial concern — Saul instructs Ahijah to bring up the ark for the purpose of divina-

34. Von Waldow, "Concept of War in the Old Testament."
35. The Hebrew text signals this perspective not only by its restraint in depicting God in war but also perhaps by its impersonal use of the term "god" as a superlative. Thus v. 15 can be read as "a god-awful big panic" (cf. Jonah 3:3) rather than an instance of God's name. The NJPS translation ("a terror from God ensued") mediates between these two possibilities.

tion prior to battle.[36] Yet here, as in 1 Samuel 13, time and worship again collide. Because the Philistine camp is increasingly in disarray and there is an urgent need for his troops to react, Saul interrupts the priest before he can finish his ritual (14:19). At this point the contrast between Saul and Jonathan could not be sharper. Jonathan enters into battle prematurely in a worshipful spirit; Saul prematurely concludes worship in order to enter the battle.

Saul's forces are successful in spite of his resistance to the ways of God, but their success has more to do with Jonathan and the spirit that he demonstrates. Not only does Saul fail once more to invoke God's help properly, he also makes things more difficult for his troops by giving an order that they may not eat any food until the fighting is at an end. Septuagintal tradition (LXX) offers an explicit interpretive comment at this point: "Now Saul committed a very rash act on that day" (1 Sam 14:21, NRSV), which in terms of its content is in keeping with the sense of the narrative but not its style. The Hebrew narrative shies away from such vulgar moralism (the MT reads, "The Israelites were distressed that day"). Instead, the selfishness of Saul's order is indicated by its first-person point of reference: "Cursed be the one who eats food before it is evening and *I* have taken revenge against *my* enemies" (14:24, my emphasis).

In contrast to Jonathan, who explicitly fights on behalf of *Israel*, Saul fights for personal vengeance. His self-absorption naturally leads to his blindness with regard to the needs of his men. When honey is found, none of the men will eat of it, even though they are weary from battle and hungry. Only Jonathan, who did not hear his father's curse, eats of the honey.[37] When told what his father had said, Jonathan's critical response again points to the fundamental difference between the two. Jonathan realizes that greater concern for the troops would have led to an even greater victory. His words also reveal that Saul's curse was directed toward the spoils of the Philistines (14:30) rather than food discovered on open ground. Saul did not want any of his men to start dividing up the spoil until he had first pick.

As a consequence of Saul's selfishness and bad decision-making, his troops seize upon the spoil and disregard the traditional religious prohibition against eating bloody meat (14:32). To atone for this violation Saul tells his men to bring him whatever oxen or sheep they have gotten, so that the animals can be slaughtered at an altar and their blood drained properly (14:34). As in 1 Samuel 13, this scene of Saul building an altar and legislating proper worship is a conspicuous rarity. Indeed, the narrative reports that "it was the first altar he erected to the Lord" (1 Sam 14:35, NJPS), which either suggests he had

36. Cf. Davies, "Ark or Ephod in 1 Sam 14:18?"
37. On historical-critical questions, see further Blenkinsopp, "Jonathan's Sacrilege."

been insufficiently attentive to altar-building in the past or perhaps even that he had built altars to other deities.[38] On the whole it is Saul's *lack* of religious activity that has been the more persistent trait in the Samuel narrative, as we have seen.[39] Even with regard to this altar, however, Saul's mindset seems more superstitious than anything else. He is worried that his army's behavior will damage its future prospects in battle. His concern about the meat once again betrays his focus on ritual procedure in abstraction from religious substance. Also, although he refers to God in the third person and erects an altar to God, Saul does not speak to God directly in this incident, nor is it clear from the text that he offers the necessary sacrifices personally.

Saul's distance from God is stressed further in what follows, but in a more nuanced way. Telling his men that he wants to attack the Philistines in the night, he is stayed by a priest (presumably Ahijah; see 1 Sam 14:3, 18) who urges him to discern God's will. Apparently only because of this prompting, and for the first time in the entire Samuel narrative, Saul is explicitly said to "inquire of" God (14:37; otherwise only in 1 Sam 28:6), a technical phrase referring to divination.[40] The play of words in Hebrew is particularly fine: *wayyiš'al šā'ûl* or "the sought (one) sought." The wordplay communicates an essential impossibility about this combination of ideas, as if it is somehow in Saul's nature to be sought but not to seek, as he here attempts to do. That sense of impossibility is confirmed by the lack of any response from God: "but he did not answer him on that day" (14:37).[41] All this reminds the reader that something quite serious did occur in 1 Samuel 13. Although God has never been depicted in the narrative up to now as speaking to Saul, it always seemed as if it *could* happen if Saul *had* sought it. Now, however, that door has apparently been closed and it does not seem likely to reopen.

Saul interprets God's lack of response as the result of someone's violation of his curse and not a consequence of his own rejection. Whether or not the narrative traditions in 1 Samuel 13 and 14 have a common origin, as they now stand they depict Saul as refusing to admit the consequences of his actions

38. As Hawk, "Saul's Altar," observes, the verbal phrase is likely inceptive: "Saul began to build an altar for Yhwh." Perhaps then the subtle implication is that Saul did not finish the job (cf. 1 Chr 27:24).

39. Hawk, "Saul's Altar," pp. 686-87, further argues that Saul's action is in fact viewed positively in this narrative because his altar-building restores the sacred order. Israel does go on to victory against the Philistines, but I would argue that both Saul's willingness to kill his own son and the ensuing reversal of his royal judgment by the people indicate the continuation of internal disorder.

40. Cryer, *Divination in Ancient Israel*, p. 259.

41. Craig, "Rhetorical Aspects of Questions."

in 1 Samuel 13, as Samuel had decreed them. Using the lots, Saul divides and subdivides his troops until at last the culprit is revealed to be either Jonathan or him. This is now the only time that Saul appears to call on God by name in second-person address ("O Lord God of Israel," 1 Sam 14:41).[42] But even (or especially!) here, God's name is invoked as a formula for the manipulation of the lots, which is precisely the point at issue. There is great irony in the way that the choice comes down to one of these two characters: Saul or Jonathan? The choice for the reader from the outset of the chapter has been between these two; here the reader's need for a decision is mirrored by the choice between Saul and Jonathan in the plot. Of course, the lots indicate that Jonathan is the one who has violated Saul's directive. Even though he was ignorant of the prohibition, and even though it was only a bit of honey, Jonathan accepts responsibility for his actions and prepares to die. Saul prepares to kill him, again valuing a formality — this time more than his own son. But the troops intercede with Saul on Jonathan's behalf, reminding Saul (and also the reader) that the day's victory is not due to him but to Jonathan.[43]

In this fascinating turn of events, Jonathan is both rightly and wrongly accused. Rightly, because he did in fact break Saul's oath.[44] Wrongly, because he did not know of the oath when he broke it, and because the oath itself was fundamentally selfish and misguided. Yet why include the account of the oath and Jonathan's near death at all? Perhaps to show that even as Saul, who cannot perceive God fully or accurately, is not to be vilified for his lack of perception, Jonathan, who has a robust sense of God, is not without defects or dangers either. Again, this narrative world is not that of the classic cowboy films; here there are no "black hats" and "white hats." Biblical characterization is differentiated as well as subtle. The figures in classical Hebrew narrative are hardly ever merely "good" or "bad" but represent complex combinations of identity, context, and commitment. Just because Jonathan approaches battle correctly does not mean that he will experience no setbacks and receive only blessings. Just because Saul goes about battle incorrectly does not mean that he will never be successful in military encounters.

---

42. For additional reasons why the form of this speech appearing in the NRSV (with the double vocative) is likely a secondary expansion, see Van Dam, *Urim and Thummim*, pp. 197-203.

43. Patrick, *Old Testament Law*, p. 118, argues that deuteronomic tradition displays "an aversion to the use of the lot and the oath." While Patrick characterizes this aversion as a further instance of the deuteronomists' "rationalism," I take it as evidence of genuine religious insight.

44. On "oaths" and "vows," see Cartledge, *Vows in the Hebrew Bible and the Ancient Near East*; Parker, "Vow in Ugaritic and Israelite Narrative Literature"; Ziegler, *Promises to Keep*.

The concluding reports of the chapter bear out this moral and religious complexity, even as they reaffirm the ongoing central themes of the narrative. Saul now firmly establishes his kingship (14:47-48), despite God's previous judgment against his future rule (1 Sam 13:13-14). Although Saul errs in the ways of God, he delivers Israel from those who would destroy it (14:38). His children increase and his family solidifies its position of power (14:49-51). Yet two brief items perpetuate the larger thread of the narrative in spite of this seemingly successful portrait of Saul and his family. First, although Saul is successful in fighting against the Philistines, he never manages to put an end to the need for war itself. It continues "all the days of Saul" (14:52). In this way Saul and his reign are associated with warfare, and this warfare — even though apparently successful enough to preserve Israel from defeat — does not release its grip over the country for the entirety of Saul's years in power. There is no indication of any real effort at international diplomacy, only more war.[45] The perpetuity of war is the familiar curse of the military leader, who, even when successful, still keeps his nation ready for battle because it is the only mode of governing he knows and understands. The kind of war Saul understands is the war of numbers and force, not the kind of war of which Jonathan's raid had been an example. Saul's way of warfare is given succinct form in the chapter's final verse: "and when Saul would see any strong man or warrior, he would collect him" (14:52). There could be no finer summary of Saul's deepest inclination and manner of life. He puts his trust in strong men rather than in the strength of God.

The Second Rejection (1 Samuel 15)

A narrative disjunction exists between 1 Samuel 14 and 15 because at the outset of 1 Samuel 15, without any narrative transition, the figure of Samuel has apparently returned to speak to Saul.[46] Samuel now gives Saul a new directive from God: he is to attack the Amalekites and slay them all: men, women, children, and animals (1 Sam 15:2-3).[47] In effect, this command sets forth a test for

45. Diplomacy was viewed in the ancient Near East as an activity at which good kings excelled just as much as warfare; see Dietrich, "König David," pp. 8-9.

46. The abrupt transition raises suspicions that 1 Samuel 15 may be a later addition to the Samuel narrative; at least its present form gives the impression of having resulted from significant editorial work. On such questions, see Foresti, *Rejection of Saul*; Giercke-Ungermann, *Niederlage im Sieg*; Yonick, *Rejection of Saul*.

47. A number of interpreters have appropriately registered their horror at this genocidal command; see especially Stark, *Human Faces of God*, pp. 122-24. For an argument that the

Saul, and the failure of that test is here rendered in narrative form as an exact violation of the prophet's instructions.[48]

Yet the command also begs the question of why God is asking Saul to do anything at all, since Saul has already been rejected. As closer attention to 1 Samuel 13–14 disclosed, however, God had not immediately and fully rejected Saul himself from the kingship. The force of the rejection in 1 Samuel 13 focused instead on Saul's future heirs and dynasty. Saul himself was left in place, as an apparently adequate if ultimately temporary ruler, until an appropriate successor could be found. As 1 Samuel 14 demonstrated, Saul can still be effective in battle, even though his manner of warfare finally only underscores the spiritual deficiency that led to his rejection in the first place.[49] So God once more tests Saul's military conduct.

As the chapter depicts, Saul's campaign is victorious; he and his men put all of the Amalekites to the sword, except for Agag, the Amalekite king, "and

---

Amalekites are used symbolically rather than realistically in 1 Samuel 15, just as in the Pentateuch, see Chapman, "Perpetual War." The point of 1 Samuel 15 is to highlight Saul's lack of obedience, not to commend or incite violence against Amalekites.

48. Although the prophet's command is often associated with the pentateuchal injunction to "wipe out" (√*mḥh*) the memory of Amalek (Exod 17:8-15; Deut 25:17-19), it is significant to note that 1 Samuel 15 nowhere presents Samuel's instructions to Saul as bearing Mosaic authority. Also, neither Exodus nor Deuteronomy invokes the term *ḥērem* in relation to the Amalekites, whereas it is strikingly prominent in 1 Samuel 15. The point in 1 Samuel 15 is thus precisely *not* that Saul should destroy the Amalekites because of bad history between the two peoples or an authoritative Mosaic teaching still in force, but that Saul should do so here and now simply because God has told him to. Contra Lind, *Yahweh Is a Warrior*, p. 106. Stern, *Biblical Ḥerem*, pp. 166-69, also argues against the literary dependence of 1 Samuel 15 on Exodus 17 and Deuteronomy 25. Among other consequences, this decoupling would help to explain the association in 1 Samuel 15 of *ḥērem* with sacrifice, an association otherwise mostly absent in the Old Testament. This is pointed out by Nelson, "Ḥerem and the Deuteronomic Social Conscience." To invoke the status of *ḥērem* was to place an object completely in God's possession. Sacrifice does not do this, because sacrifice is something from which humans receive a benefit. According to Nelson, this confusion is "precisely the problem behind Saul's lapse in 1 Samuel 15 . . . One cannot sacrifice to Yahweh what is already his" (p. 48). Cf. Naiden, "Rejected Sacrifice in Greek and Hebrew Religion," p. 207. The artful telling of 1 Samuel 15 thus compels reflection on how even sacrifice might represent insufficient obedience to God. There may also be a contributory warrant for harsh military action against the Amalekites in 1 Sam 14:48, where it is said that the Amalekites had been "plundering" (√*šsh*) the Israelites. Saul is to respond to such "plundering" with *ḥērem*, the complete renunciation of plunder and the devotion of all things to God. See further Younger, "Some Recent Discussion on the Ḥērem."

49. The mention of how Saul mustered his troops by "counting" (√*pqd*, 1 Sam 14:17) them emphasizes this deficiency. As will be the case with David in 2 Sam 24:9-10, such numbering seems to be taken by the narrative as a marker of unfaith, a refusal to rely upon God's capacity to ensure victory without regard to the operation of superior forces.

anything of value" (*wĕʿal-kol-haṭṭôb*, 15:9). The concision and directness of the narrative's structure underscores how this episode has the character of a test.[50] Saul is told explicitly to do a thing completely (15:3); he does not (15:9).[51] Immediately God speaks again to Samuel, confirming Saul's disobedience. On this occasion, however, Samuel is said to be "upset" or "angry" (√*ḥrh*, 15:11), and to cry out to God through the night. The object of Samuel's anger is unspecified, so it is uncertain as to whether he is angry with Saul or with God, but his remonstrance to God during the night seems to indicate a degree of support for Saul — or at least Samuel's resistance to Saul's complete rejection, which is now what God intends. Samuel's resistance is in fact a foreshadowing that a final rejection lies ahead in the narrative.

On going to meet Saul, Samuel finds that he has already left for Gilgal. Samuel is also told by an anonymous narrative voice that Saul had stopped to build a monument to himself (!) en route (15:12). The implied arrogance of such a gesture, along with the time taken to perform it, undercuts the rather more urgent picture that Saul will offer Samuel by way of an explanation for his actions.[52] As in 1 Samuel 13, Saul appears to meet Samuel with a clear conscience. He proclaims his obedience right away (15:13). Samuel, however, greets Saul's words with pure sarcasm: "Then what is this noise of sheep in my ears and the sound of cattle that I hear?" (15:14). Saul's response at first attributes the presence of livestock to his troops rather than accepting responsibility himself: "*They* brought them from the Amalekites because *the army* spared the best of the sheep and cattle in order to sacrifice to the Lord our God. The remainder we committed to destruction" (15:15, my italics). With this remark Saul may be viewed as aware of the instructions that he had been given and only making excuses. He also does not mention Agag. His addendum to the effect that the *remainder* of the Amalekite force was destroyed could be an attempt to explain away his non-compliance with the precise nature of Samuel's command, which clearly stipulated how the destruction of the Amalekites

---

50. To a limited extent, then, the nature of this command as a test provides some counterweight to its moral repulsiveness, in a manner similar to Genesis 22. The "test" character of God's command in both passages reinforces the exceptional quality of the act being required, as well as its repugnance to the one receiving that command. Otherwise it would not be much of a test.

51. Williams, "Is God Moral?" p. 184, notes how the use of a volitional auxiliary verb ("they were not *willing* to destroy them utterly") underscores the character of Saul's disobedience.

52. However, 1 Sam 15:12 LXX also includes words to the effect that "Saul offered a burnt offering to Yahweh, the firstfruits of the spoil that he had brought from Amalek." Some interpreters have used this reference as support for concluding that Saul is sincere in his actions. See Gunn, *Fate of King Saul*, p. 50; Robinson, *Israel's Mysterious God*, p. 44.

was to be total and complete. Joshua's slaying of the king of Ai (Josh 8:23, 29) argues for a customary expectation that a foreign king would be killed under such conditions.

The one potentially exculpatory aspect to Saul's explanation is his protest that his men had saved the best of the livestock in order to sacrifice them to the Lord. Here Saul seems either to be revealing himself as well-intentioned but incompetent or hypocritical and devious. Yet the narrative does not immediately indicate which interpretive option is to be preferred. In fact, the narrative prolongs uncertainty about Saul's rationale so that the reader is drawn into an examination of the precise terms of his remarks to Samuel. Rather than collapsing the interpretive tension, which would have been relatively easy to do through the addition of evaluative commentary, the narrative initially places the burden of decision-making on the reader. This technique has the additional effect of leading the reader to contemplate anew the nature of the command that Saul was given. What could possibly be the purpose of such a merciless order?

Preemptively, Samuel calls a halt to the discussion before it has really even gotten started. "Drop it!" he tells Saul (15:16, √*rph* Hiph.). Then he zeros in on Saul in a way that can only be described as psychological: "Although you are small in your own eyes, are you not the head of the tribes of Israel?" (15:17). The force of Samuel's comment is directed against Saul's attempt to blame his troops for not following through with God's command. As Israel's king, Saul should be able to control his men. Ironically, however, Saul's private sense of himself is at fatal variance with how he appears to others. Saul is a big man, and he values physical strength in others, but in his inability to discipline his own military he shows himself to lack inner stature. This weakness alone calls into question his fitness for the kingship. But Samuel turns back the question of responsibility to Saul personally: "Why did *you* not listen (√*šmʿ*) to the voice of the Lord?" (15:19, my emphasis; the Hebrew verb form is second-person singular, but the pronoun does not appear separately from the verb).

Saul's second response hardly carries conviction either. He now claims to have obeyed his instructions, yet it is inconceivable that he could have misunderstood their main point ("You shall not spare any of them," 15:3).[53] Saul maintains that he has shown obedience by capturing the Amalekite king, destroying everything else, and permitting his troops to sequester the best

---

53. It is sometimes argued on the basis of passages in which booty is kept (Num 21:24; Deut 2:34; 3:6; 10:28-40; 11:10-12; Josh 8:2) that Saul might have legitimately believed he possessed discretionary latitude in obeying his commission in 1 Samuel 15. But 1 Sam 15:3 itself is not phrased in a way that allows for interpretive flexibility.

livestock so that they could be sacrificed to God at Gilgal. Here again Saul claims an overriding intention to sacrifice. Yet once more the question of Saul's sincerity confronts the reader. Can Saul truly believe that he is blameless in what has occurred?[54] However, now Samuel appears to give Saul the benefit of the doubt. Rather than condemning him for lying, Samuel instead criticizes Saul for suggesting that the goal of sacrifice allows him to adjust the letter of the command that God had given him: "Does the Lord delight in burnt offerings and sacrifices as much as in obeying [lit. 'listening to,' √šm'] the voice of the Lord? Behold, obeying [lit. 'listening'] is better than sacrificing, heeding better than the fat of rams" (15:22). These stirring words not only remove all possibility of justification from Saul's explanation of his actions, they also pinpoint precisely the issue that has been at the heart of the book's deepest concern from its very first chapter onward: the nature of true worship.

Saul seems to have believed that his soldiers' removal of Amalekite livestock was justified because they would eventually kill those animals anyway, sacrificing them to God. From this perspective, worship is given a certain respect, but as a form of ritualized activity rather than the "heart" religion promoted by the deuteronomists. By insisting on worship when it conflicts with God's stated instructions, Saul exhibits a perspective in which worship is separable from obedience and performed for its own sake. A rather shocking indication of this difference in perspective occurs three times in Saul's responses to Samuel when Saul refers to "the Lord *your* God" (15:15, 21, 30, my emphasis). Time and again Saul has neglected or refrained from speaking to God directly or making any pronouncements of his own belief.[55] Here he does so once more. His insistence on a form of worship that contradicts what God has specifically commanded betrays a serious spiritual defect.

Samuel's judgment in turn exposes Saul's version of sacrifice as not only a type of false worship but as the equivalent of worshiping false gods (15:23).[56] By making this conceptual link, the theological brilliance of the deuteronomists reaches a new height. Deuteronomistic tradition uses the exclusive worship of God as a litmus test for religious leaders, phenomena, and perspectives (e.g., Deuteronomy 13). The deuteronomistic shaping of Samuel adds to that view by further defining the proper worship of God as worship of the heart. By definition, then, worship not of the heart, even if conducted as worship of the God of Israel, is the equivalent of idolatry. When worship

---

54. The argument that Saul still intended to kill Agag stands in considerable tension with Agag's later realization that he is in fact going to die (1 Sam 15:32). Agag apparently thought he was going to live. For this insight, see Williams, "Is God Moral?" p. 185.

55. Saul uses God's name in 1 Sam 15:3 in a formulaic greeting.

56. Tosato, "La Colpa di Saul."

becomes the worship of worship, worship itself has become a false god. For this failure, above all, Saul is rejected as king (15:23). Even so, this verdict contains an unexpected element of mercy, since Saul's own life has become forfeit due to his failure to devote Agag to the Lord (cf. 1 Kgs 20:42), and yet Saul's life is nevertheless preserved.

The narrative gives no indication that Saul has understood the true nature of his mistake.[57] He accepts responsibility, but he also again blames his men by saying that he was afraid of them and "obeyed [lit. 'listened to' √*šm*ˁ] their voice" (15:24).[58] His claim of fear recalls his earlier hiding among the baggage (1 Sam 10:22), but it is difficult to square this alleged insecurity with his prior actions in 1 Sam 14:31-35. Perhaps then there is also a note of idolatry in the way that Saul obeys the voice of his men rather than the voice of God.[59] Conspicuous at this point, however, is the lack of any attempt on Saul's part to plead directly with God for forgiveness. He pleads instead with Samuel and, ironically, promises to worship God if he is forgiven. Yet the problem all along has been Saul's inability to approach God as a real presence, and here he gives no sign that he has understood what previously had escaped him. Finally, Saul begs Samuel not to embarrass him in front of the people and "the Lord *your* God" (15:30, my emphasis). Saul is still too concerned about what others think of him, and he still does not have a vital sense of his own for God. Nonetheless, Saul's self-characterization arouses the reader's sympathy even though his self-defense is unpersuasive. By contrast, Samuel's blanket indictment precludes sympathy, although he appears to be in the right.

David Gunn, more than any other interpreter, has lodged a powerful protest against interpretive efforts to characterize Saul as religiously deficient. Saul is in fact admirably "religious," Gunn observes:

> He is remarkably attentive (almost to the end) to the ritual acknowledgement of Yahweh. Indeed both times that he is found guilty of breaking a commandment of God he has done what he has done in order to honour

---

57. Barth, *Church Dogmatics II/2*, p. 368, claims that in this chapter Saul repents just as sincerely as David will do later on. This aspect of Barth's interpretation of Samuel is unconvincing to me.

58. See further Frisch, "For I Feared the People."

59. Saul's admission of fear certainly incriminates him in the eyes of the deuteronomists, who treat fear in the face of battle as a mark of unfaith (see Deut 20:1, 3, 8). For an interpretation that stresses the significance of Saul's fear of the people, see Sellars, "An Obedient Servant?" pp. 317-38. Sellars, however, attempts to take Saul's fear positively (i.e., as evidence that he is a "responsive leader" in contrast to "the model of tyrannical kingship" prophesied in 1 Samuel 8).

him by sacrifice. He is prepared to acknowledge his error (whether compre-
hendingly or not), and even in rejection, worship him. Saul is not disloyal
to Yahweh.[60]

Gunn is correct, to a point. What he overlooks, however, is precisely the critique of ritual found throughout the Samuel narrative. Ritual is necessary but
not sufficient for loyalty to Yahweh in this narrative world, and it is Saul's tragedy to illustrate that central point despite starting out with the best of intentions.[61] In order to identify the religious problem at stake as an over-reliance
upon procedure, Saul's failing is twice depicted as technical and seemingly
minor (1 Sam 13; 15). In this way the nature of the infraction mirrors the deeper
dilemma.

Naturally, this turn of events renews the difficult question of Saul's election. Just as in 1 Samuel 13, here again the narrative prompts the reader to ask
why God (and Samuel) had chosen Saul in the first place if he was constitu-
tionally deficient. In response to Saul's request for forgiveness, Samuel tells
him that God has already made a decision and it is final, since "the everlasting
God does not deceive or regret [√nḥm Niph.] because he is not human" (15:29).
Ironically, Samuel uses this reason to explain why God is rejecting Saul even
though it intensifies the problem of Saul's original election. The final verse of
the chapter even boldly contradicts the earlier claim: "and the Lord regretted
[√nḥm Niph.] that he had made Saul king over Israel" (15:35). The same note
had also been struck before: "I regret [√nḥm Niph.] that I made Saul king"
(15:11). In other words, God, being God, absolutely does not regret, except
when God does.[62]

There are at least two interpretive options to explain the tension between
the two references to the actuality of God's regret (15:11, 35) and the one reference to its impossibility (15:29). One alternative is to draw a distinction between the references by God (15:11) and the narrator (15:35), on the one hand,
and the character of Samuel on the other (15:29).[63] Several commentators have
taken this distinction as further evidence that Samuel is playing his own selfish

60. Gunn, *Fate of King Saul*, p. 124.

61. In a seminar paper for me Chad Eggleston insightfully drew attention to the implicit
contrast between 1 Sam 11:11 and Saul's actions in this chapter: "Where the Lord does not
command the ban, Saul leaves 'no two together,' but where the Lord does command the ban
(15:1-3), he fails to finish the job."

62. Thus Chisholm, "Does God Deceive?" argues that the statement "God does not lie"
is not intended as a general philosophical claim but a statement about God's specific will in a
given situation. Cf. Moberly, "'God Is Not a Human.'"

63. Amit, "Glory of Israel."

game, using the situation brought about by Saul's failure in order to get rid of him, even though Saul is hardly guilty of anything requiring the loss of his kingship.[64] Yet there is no explicit evidence anywhere in 1 Samuel 15 that the narrator considers Samuel's actions selfish or self-motivated.[65] To the contrary, Samuel apparently continues to stand symbolically for the narrator's version of religious orthodoxy.

So another alternative to the dilemma concerning God's "regret" involves crediting Samuel with being a consistently reliable figure in the narrative but conceding that here Samuel's conception of God is nevertheless less flexible than God actually is.[66] On this reading Samuel is presented as reliable but human, with his own blind spots, yet not devious. It is interesting to recall in this context that it was after God admitted regret the first time that Samuel had become angry (15:11). God's dynamism is difficult for prophets, who make a living by presenting God's will as consistent and predictable. The prophet Jonah is similarly exasperated by God's flexibility (Jonah 3:10–4:2). In the Bible God *does* regret certain divine actions, and the Samuel narrative is not embarrassed by this characteristic of God at all, although it recognizes something of its apparent scandal.[67] Samuel's words are in fact used in the narrative to voice this very concern: How can God "regret" or "change" in intention if God is God and not human? The theological answer matches the portrait of God offered from a variety of angles in the book from its outset. God is a vital, dynamic presence, who is scandalously like a person in the ways God interacts with human beings. God's rejection of Saul makes the point that *God* confers sovereignty in Israel, and God can therefore take it away. This "personality" of God does not diminish God or prevent God from exercising awesome power, nor does it reduce God's trustworthiness, but it does undermine people's efforts

64. See Polzin, *Samuel and the Deuteronomist*, pp. 145-47. He points to the association of Samuel with "night" (1 Sam 15:11, 16) and the characterization of Samuel's cries to God as "angry."

65. I do acknowledge that Samuel's distress in 15:11 opens up the possibility of a divergence between Samuel's wishes and God's will. The emphatic *'ōtî* in 15:1 should also be observed, although its nuance is difficult to determine. See, for instance, the NJPS translation: "I am the one sent to anoint you."

66. Thus Polzin, *Samuel and the Deuteronomist*, p. 146, also develops a view of Samuel as representing "authoritarian dogmatism": "To believe that God *will* accomplish humanity's idea of mercy is, in this instance at least, as mistaken a position as to believe that God *must* punish according to human views of strict justice" (his italics). Alternatively, Miscall, *1 Samuel*, p. 111, suggests that 1 Sam 15:29 could function as a traditional saying or "pious platitude," perhaps marked by its use of the rare divine title "the Glory of Israel" (*nēṣaḥ yiśrā'ēl*), which the narrative then intentionally subverts.

67. See further Fretheim, "Divine Foreknowledge."

to second-guess God or to assume too much about what God will do. The personhood of God is a consequence and an expression of God's freedom, and the fact of this freedom requires a different quality of interaction on the part of God's human worshipers. If Saul has not adequately perceived the personhood of God, 1 Samuel 15 illustrates that even Samuel resists its truly radical implications.

Samuel's arguable shortcoming is enacted and magnified by his killing of King Agag. Ostensibly simply the correction of Saul's oversight, Samuel's action is usually taken to conform to the stance of the narrator. Then this text is treated as an objectionable "text of terror,"[68] a biblical passage whose religious message presents urgent moral difficulties for modern readers. However, given the immediately preceding exposure of Samuel's inflexible view of God (15:29), and given the tension between worship and warfare throughout the narratives about Saul, the possibility also exists that the narrator actually means to portray this event as reprehensible.[69] Samuel's hewing of Agag "before the Lord" (*lipnê yhwh*, 15:33) indicates that the killing is done at the worship site in Gilgal, perhaps even at the altar.[70] If Saul was criticized for neglecting to bring worship into battle, perhaps Samuel is now depicted as making the opposite mistake by bringing battle into worship. To the extent that Saul's mission against the Amalekites was a test, there is no real reason for Samuel to follow through where Saul had left off, other than being overly rigid.[71]

68. The phrase is borrowed from Trible, *Texts of Terror*.

69. Cf. the powerful statements of Buber, "Autobiographical Fragments," pp. 31-32: "I believe... that Samuel has misunderstood God" and "Nothing can make me believe in a God who punishes Saul because he has not murdered his enemy."

70. Levine, "*Lpny YHWH*." The interpretive difficulty of this verse is compounded by the fact that the Hebrew verb traditionally translated as "hew" ($\sqrt{ssp}$, Piel) appears nowhere else in the Hebrew Bible. The related root *šs'* is often substituted (= "divide, cleave"), although its use in 1 Sam 24:8 suggests a more metaphorical sense. The root *šsp* is also known in post-biblical Hebrew. It remains clear from the narrative context, however, that Samuel does execute Agag. McCarter speculates (*I Samuel*, p. 269) that perhaps the sacrificial slaughter of Agag is being described as punishment for the violation of a covenant ("of which we have no knowledge") between the Amalekites and the Israelites (cf. the covenantal overtones to Saul's dismissal of the Kenites in 15:6).

71. It may be instructive to note that Exod 17:16 tells how God (not Israel!) will be at war with Amalek forever and thereby "utterly blot out [$\sqrt{mhh}$] the memory of Amalek from under heaven," and that Deut 25:19 then extends that same divine activity to Israel (*timḥê 'et-zēker 'ămālēq mittaḥat haššāmāyim*). Yet the nature of this "blotting" is left unspecified. Nowhere does the Pentateuch explicitly characterize this commandment as an order to kill every Amalekite man, woman, and child. The possibility therefore exists that what Saul is being told to do — and what Samuel actually does — goes beyond what the law requires. At the very least it would be an error to use the details of 1 Samuel 15 to explain the metaphorical language of Exod

The narrator does not make this point explicitly; the scandalous image of Samuel, his sword, Agag's body, and God's altar lingers and burns. So perhaps it is supposed to. One stream of rabbinic commentary protests against the scope of the killing throughout 1 Samuel 15, only to be cautioned by a heavenly voice against the sin of "over"-righteousness.[72] Another rabbinic tradition, attributed to Resh Laqish, makes an even more challenging point, refusing to let Saul off the hook: "Whoever is merciful when he should be ruthless in the end is ruthless when he should be merciful."[73] This latter tradition also alludes to the account of Saul's eventual slaughter of Israelites at Nob (1 Sam 21–22). If the saying concedes the possibility of violence to God in a troubling manner, it nevertheless maintains a mysterious disjunction between human and divine justice. What seems like mercy, when it goes against the express instructions of God, may in fact lead to worse violence.[74]

David (1 Samuel 16)

The narrative of 1 Samuel 16 falls neatly into two related halves.[75] The first half concerns Samuel's search for Saul's successor and his anointing of David (16:1-13). The second half describes David's introduction into Saul's royal court (16:14-23). Tying the two halves together is the movement of God's spirit, which descends upon David in his anointing (16:13) and, as suggested by the close juxtaposition of the two reports, simultaneously departs from Saul (16:14). The implication is that God's spirit only rests upon one leader at a time, that God's investment of the spirit in David cannot occur without the removal of that

---

17:16 and Deut 25:19, as nevertheless often occurs. From the other direction, note the absence of the key term *mḥh* in 1 Sam 15:2-3, although the justification provided for God's command is admittedly the same as that given in Exodus and Deuteronomy — Amalek's unprovoked and merciless attack upon Israel in the wilderness. Within Judaism, the command to war against Amalek has in fact sometimes been remembered and interpreted as an ongoing duty to commit genocide (e.g., *Sefer Ha-Chinukh*, Mitzvah #604). However, the Talmud also renders this commandment essentially non-performable, and thus merely theoretical, because of the mixing of people groups after the fall of the Northern Kingdom and Judah's subsequent defeat and exile (b. Berakot 28a). On this point, and for wider reflections, see Helfgot, "Amalek."

72. Ecclesiastes Rabbah on Eccl 7:16 and b. Yoma 22b, quoting Eccl 7:16 ("do not be too righteous"). See Urbach, *Sages*, pp. 518-19.

73. As found in Canticles Rabbah and b. Yoma 22b. Cited in Urbach, *Sages*, 519.

74. A similar interrogation of well-intentioned mercy toward a prisoner of war lies at the heart of Steven Spielberg's film *Saving Private Ryan* (DreamWorks, 1998).

75. For historical-critical treatment of this chapter and the next two, see in particular Seidl, "David statt Saul."

spirit from Saul, an action resulting in bitter consequences. Also connecting the two halves of the chapter is a concern about the unreliability of vision. This theme builds upon the contrast that the book has already established between physical appearance and spiritual fitness but now grounds in the character of God.

The beginning of 1 Samuel 16 follows logically, if abruptly, on the end of 1 Samuel 15. God tells Samuel to stop grieving over Saul's rejection and to set about installing his replacement. God has already decided ("foreseen," √r'h) who will be the next king but will only tell Samuel that it is one of the sons of Jesse the Bethlehemite (16:1). God could have been more specific. Instead the situation is constructed as another test, and this time the test is for Samuel rather than Saul. In response to Samuel's objection that Saul could be dangerous if he discovers how Samuel has gone to locate a new king, God instructs Samuel to engage in some light subterfuge. He is to tell the Bethlehemites that he has come for a sacrificial feast. Ironically, now Samuel must use worship as an excuse. While Jesse is in the process of preparing for the feast, God will indicate which of his sons Samuel is to anoint (16:3). Samuel's cover story is an excuse or half-lie,[76] but it is one that God has told him to employ. Perhaps more significant than the ethics of Samuel's excuse is the fact that its context involves worship. If Saul's justification for his failure to follow through on God's command was all the more reprehensible because it elevated worship's practice above worship's object, here God also appears to view worship as a suitable ruse. But God's greater concern has to do with the political survival of the people rather than merely the operation of religious ritual for its own sake.

What follows employs a sequence format well known from folk tales and legends: Samuel examines Jesse's sons one by one in an effort to determine which is God's chosen. But Samuel initially chooses poorly. His first pick is Jesse's son Eliab — probably the eldest and/or the biggest of the sons because when Samuel thinks to himself that Eliab *must be* the one God has in mind, God responds by drawing a distinction between external appearance and internal suitability. "Do not pay attention to his appearance or to the height of his stature . . . for humans see [√r'h] with their eyes but the Lord looks to the heart [lēbāb]" (MT, 16:7).[77] This same concern was present throughout the

76. The narrative implies that Samuel did eventually organize a sacrificial feast (16:11), although that feast itself is never explicitly narrated. A strategic presentation of information is not the same thing as a flat-out lie.

77. The NRSV follows the LXX at this point, rendering, "for the Lord does not see as mortals see; they look on the outward appearance, but the Lord looks on the heart." For discussion, see Bodner, "Eliab and the Deuteronomist."

description of Saul's rise to power, but the contrast was never put as sharply there as here. Still, it is noteworthy that Eliab's apparently impressive physical stature is reminiscent of Saul's (9:2; 10:23).[78] Not only is outward appearance an unreliable guide for selecting a leader, it actually misleads. If Saul's failure has shown nothing else, it is that.

Of new concern, however, is that Samuel, of all people, is the one who gets this wrong. Samuel has struggled against the difficulties that Saul introduced into Israel's common life precisely because Saul consistently confused the external and the internal, outward form and inner disposition. So Samuel should know better.[79] Moreover, Samuel remains a prophet of God, a "seer" ($\sqrt{r'h}$, 1 Sam 9:19). In 1 Samuel 16, therefore, Samuel has ironically become a "seer" who cannot see properly, in contrast to God who "sees" rightly, even in advance (16:1; cf. Isa 11:3). This lapse on Samuel's part retrospectively calls into question his earlier role in selecting Saul. Was Samuel perhaps also too impressed with Saul's physical appearance? His comment to the people immediately preceding their acclamation of Saul now appears suspect: "Do you *see* ($\sqrt{r'h}$) him whom God has chosen? There is no one like him among all the people" (1 Sam 10:24, my emphasis). These words appeared immediately after the narrator's report that Saul was "a head taller than all the people" (1 Sam 10:23). Samuel himself seems to have been a bit taken in by the desire to have a king who looked the part. But what should a king look like? The customary physical expectations for a king are based on human needs and criteria, according to this passage, not on the will of God. These customary expectations are confirmed by historical evidence throughout ancient Near Eastern cultures: kings are depicted and described as big, strong, and handsome.[80] This passage subverts such expectations in line with Israel's religious values. If there is to be a king in Israel, then the normal expectations for how a king should look will no longer apply.

Chastened, Samuel continues to examine the rest of Jesse's sons and proceeds to reject them all, presumably at least in part because they are all still too physically impressive. The narrative builds suspense by having Samuel exhaust the list and then ask whether there might perhaps be any more sons to review. At this point David, the youngest son, is finally brought in from

---

78. Gunn, *Fate of King Saul*, p. 60, concludes that we are "doubly reminded" of Saul by Eliab, since in addition to the implication of height, the Hebrew verb for "reject" ($\sqrt{m's}$), which has previously been used of Saul (15:23, 26; 16:1), is now applied to Eliab.

79. Cf. Polzin, *Samuel and the Deuteronomist*, p. 155: "[Samuel is] a mistaken prophet who somehow believes that God likes to replace tall kings with tall successors."

80. Dietrich, "König David," pp. 3-31. Cf. Hamilton, *Body Royal*; de Vaux, *Ancient Israel*, pp. 100-138.

tending the flock.[81] He is of course The One, as God indicates to Samuel, who then anoints him in the presence of his family. Ironically, however, when David does finally appear in the narrative he is described as physically attractive (16:12).[82] This detail is commonly thought to subvert the theological point already made about the difference between human and divine choice.[83] After all, the customary expectation, even in Israel, is that the king should model strength and majesty in his own person (cf. Ps 45:3-4 [Engl. 2-3]). Yet the Samuel narrative's witness is sophisticated rather than self-contradictory. Just as Eliab, like Saul, is not to be chosen simply because he looks like a king, David is not to be *dismissed* because he looks attractive either. To choose *or not to choose* a king based upon external characteristics is wrong, because in both cases the physical characteristics become the determining criteria for the choice, rather than the internal qualities that God prizes.[84] Rather than a clumsy inconsistency, David's description provides a crucial check against any moralizing interpretation that might render the narrative's message as in effect: "godly leaders should not be physically prepossessing." Ironically, godly leaders will sometimes be physically impressive and sometimes physically unimpressive, because their aptness for leadership functions on an entirely different basis. God's kingdom inverts the significance normally attached to perceptions of physical capability. As Joseph Hall puts it, "The strength or weakness of means is neither spur nor bridle to the determinate choices of God."[85]

To the extent that David's physical appearance makes any difference at all, it is only as an indication that he is "against type" in comparison to a

81. That David's shepherding has a symbolic valence is brought out well by Rudman, "Commissioning Stories of Saul and David." Throughout the ancient Near East "shepherd" (*rōʿê*) was used as a synonym for "king." God is considered the ultimate "shepherd" in the Old Testament (e.g., Pss 23:1; 80:2). In addition to frequent use of the term "shepherd" and related motifs as descriptors of kingly activity, Rudman points to 2 Sam 5:2, where the analogy between shepherd and king is made explicit. Cf. Ezekiel 34 for a full-blown political allegory employing this same symbolism.

82. On the Samuel narrative's use of physical beauty in characterization, see Avioz, "Motif of Beauty"; MacWilliam, "Ideologies of Male Beauty"; Sternberg, *Poetics of Biblical Narrative*, pp. 354-64.

83. E.g., Avioz, "Motif of Beauty," p. 349: "Here it can be seen how selective and tendentious use is made of the attribute of beauty: When it pertains to David, this attribute is important, whereas when it pertains to Saul and Eliab — they are not worthy in spite of their beauty, because external beauty is not sufficient for becoming a leader."

84. Readers familiar with the Bible might also associate this perspective with Isa 53:2 ("he had no form or majesty that we should look at him, nothing in his appearance that we should desire him").

85. Hall, *Contemplations on the Historical Passages*, p. 169.

warrior like Saul. This dimension of David's characterization is in fact explicitly thematized in the narrative, but only retrospectively. In the next chapter Goliath will disdain David "for he was only a youth, ruddy and handsome in appearance" (*kî-hāyâ na'ar wĕ'admōnî 'im-yĕpê mar'ê*, 17:42). This language links directly back to David's introduction and thus provides guidance for how to interpret it; 1 Sam 16:12 reads, "Now he was ruddy, and had beautiful eyes, and was handsome" (*wĕhû' 'admōnî 'im-yĕpê 'ênayim wĕṭôb rō'î*). David is not chosen because he is handsome; neither is he chosen because he is physically unthreatening. Yet, as things turn out, his slight appearance does equip and predispose him to rely all the more firmly on God's help, and this particular predisposition does prove to be a crucial one for a leader in Israel.

It is still remarkable that David is introduced in such a manner into the narrative. Given his later stature, it would be customary for David's story to begin with a birth narrative filled with arresting portents of future success and glory.[86] Curiously, this absence of a birth narrative is something that Saul and David share in 1 Samuel. The reason for it may well be that fate does not have the same premium within the world of this narrative as it had in other ancient cultures. The well-known legends told and retold about the birth and youth of Alexander the Great, for example, suggest that his later path in life was to a large degree scripted in advance.[87] Absent from the Samuel narrative is precisely this notion of social or even divine "scripted-ness," notwithstanding the narrative's stress on divine sovereignty and coincidence. In other words, inscribed in this particular scripture is a deep acknowledgement of, and appreciation for, human freedom. Of crucial significance in the text-world of Samuel is not what the stars foretell but the choices people make. Even the narrative's tragic awareness that Saul is somehow fatally flawed never negates its understanding of human beings as fundamentally free and therefore responsible for their freedom.

The same is true of David, whose inherent capacity for kingship can be inferred from the way he does not have to be transformed into a new kind of person or given a new heart (like Saul) in order to take up his divinely appointed vocation. Instead the "spirit of the Lord" comes upon him, and apparently in an abiding fashion — unlike Saul, for whom "spirits" come and go. Even so, however, David's predisposition is never understood to diminish the reality of his choices or diminish the courage of his convictions.

---

86. For comparisons with other ancient Near Eastern cultures, see Stott, "Herodotus and the Old Testament"; Hamilton, *Body Royal*.

87. Legends about Alexander the Great, known as the Phyllada, circulated for centuries. For a convenient collection, see Stoneman, ed., *Alexander the Great*, which basically reproduces the venerable "Alexander Romance" of Pseudo-Callisthenes.

That Samuel's anointing of David is secret is not fully clear at first.[88] Yet Samuel could have anointed David in the presence of the Bethlehemite elders or the whole town, but he does not. The secrecy appears to stem from a concern for safety (see 16:2) but also perhaps out of lingering respect for Saul's status. There is in fact a sense throughout the remainder of the book that only one anointed king can be acknowledged at a time, with the difficulty that there are now two anointed figures, one publicly acknowledged and one privately designated. Saul has been rejected but, for some reason the narrative never really explains, not removed. Within the world of this narrative God could simply kill Saul, as God later does with Nabal (1 Sam 25:38). Or God could construct a series of events to remove Saul completely and replace him with David. But neither of those possibilities immediately occurs. Instead David is privately anointed, and Saul and David are largely left to work out for themselves how the transition will transpire. Of course, there continues to be a strong suspicion that God is working providentially behind the scenes, but the reader nevertheless marks the implicit decision of God to work indirectly rather than directly.

Something of this strategy also appears to be related to the nature of what the kingship is. As God's anointed, the king has a kind of freedom, even with respect to God, to participate fully in history and to move historical events in particular directions. Israel's choice to have a king in the first place entailed the distancing of its communal life and leadership from God's direct action with exactly such freedom (1 Sam 8:18; 12:6-12). The rest of the book will chart how the transition between kings occurs *without* God's direct intervention, which means that the figures involved, especially Saul and David, face real decisions and trials of character as they attempt to handle a terribly difficult situation with integrity and honor.

God may not actually remove Saul from the kingship, but God does remove the divine spirit from Saul and replace it with a "bad spirit" (*rûaḥ rā'â*, 16:14).[89] The theological concern of some interpreters about something "evil" coming from God is largely misplaced because of a lack of attention to the range of the Hebrew root *r'*, which does not always mean something objectively wicked but can also refer to something subjectively unhelpful or unpleasant.[90] Even granting this subjective sense of the term (= "bad spirit"), the

---

88. This aspect of secrecy is kept ambiguous by the narrative; see the helpful discussion in Short, *Surprising Election*, pp. 180-86.

89. For a stimulating theological engagement with this aspect of the narrative, see the classic sermon by Phillips Brooks, "An Evil Spirit from the Lord," in his *Twenty Sermons*, pp. 297-315.

90. Wellhausen, *Prolegomena to the History of Israel*, p. 302: "good and evil in Hebrew

narrative still portrays God as sending Saul a spirit that troubles him. But while the narrative therefore indicates that God may chasten and punish, it does not — contrary to the implication of several modern translations (e.g., NJPS, NRSV) — attribute evil to God. This troubling of Saul is presented, moreover, as a continual occurrence, which can only be intermittently relieved by music (16:16, 23). Just as David's private anointing sets the stage for the interactions between Saul and David throughout the rest of the book, Saul's mental instability is introduced here as a recurring motif with great significance for the subsequent narrative.

Saul then asks his servants to "see to" (√*r'h*) someone gifted in music (16:17). Coincidentally, one of Saul's court attendants has "seen" (√*r'h*) a son of Jesse who is musically skilled in just the manner Saul appears to need (16:18). In this way the narrator draws an implicit contrast between how God "sees" and Saul does not "see." God "sees" David even before David is introduced in the narrative (16:1), before David has done anything within the narrative to merit being an object of God's vision. By contrast Saul cannot "see" David, although one of his servants can. Even after the servant's detailed description, Saul is so blind to David's true identity and providential trajectory that he invites him into his own household.

By such acute observation Saul's courtier is also more perceptive than the prophet, for he has noticed a personal quality that goes beyond mere appearance. The courtier knows David to be "a fighter and a man of war" (*gibbôr ḥayil wĕ'îš milḥāmâ*, 16:18) in spite of his youth. The courtier knows as well that "the Lord is with him" (*wayhwh 'immô*, 16:18). This perceptiveness of the servant not only stands in contrast to Samuel's initial difficulty in selecting the right son of Jesse, but also to Saul's lack of ability to recognize David for who he is. After all, Saul invites into his court the very person who has been secretly anointed to supplant him. Yet Saul has no inkling that this youth to whom he takes a liking and finds personally helpful is his divinely appointed rival. A further irony involves David's musical therapy for Saul. Rather than intensifying Saul's distress, as David's presence and his music might be expected to do, David successfully brings Saul the relief he needs from the bad spirit that plagues him (16:23). David is somehow bound to Saul and his personal well-being, even as David cannot avoid undermining him politically. Saul is taken with David's charm and success, and so he does not — at first — view him as a threat.[91]

---

mean primarily nothing more than salutary and hurtful; the application of the words to virtue and sin is a secondary one." See further √*r'* in *TDOT*, esp. 13:564.

91. This turn in the narrative is reminiscent of the relationship between Mozart and Salieri

The rest of the Samuel narrative is therefore driven by a dual tension: How will David become publicly recognized as king, and how will Saul eventually be ousted? Even further, there is a fundamental question about the intersection of these two concerns; namely, will Saul himself ultimately be able to recognize David as king (cf. 24:21), that is, to "see" him rightly? Just as 1 Samuel 15 presented a crucial episode in Saul's life as a drama of "listening," 1 Samuel 16 offers its account as a test of "seeing." The remainder of 1 Samuel continues this theological drama of perception, relentlessly driving toward a true vision of the way things already really are. Crucial to this tension is the theme of violence, which is now transposed into a new key, from violence between Israel and its enemies to violence within Israel. Violence against Saul will henceforth represent a fundamental temptation for David, "to seize his kingship by *force*, to spill *blood*, to establish his reign prematurely before it pleases God."[92]

It is in fact a highly puzzling feature of the narrative: why should David wait "until I know what God will do for me?" (1 Sam 22:3). If David is sure of his anointing, and of Saul's rejection, then why should he not boldly claim what is his and seize the kingship, even through bloodshed if necessary? "If he really was the elect, then every day that passed without him establishing his reign might be viewed as meaningless and lost."[93] Yet David instead enters into a time of waiting and suffering, of persecution and flight, in order to submit to God's own timing.

David and Goliath (1 Samuel 17)

This narrative section is long and complex, giving every indication of a complicated history of literary development.[94] The account does appear somewhat

---

in Peter Shaffer's play *Amadeus*, subsequently appearing as a film with the same title directed by Miloš Forman. In this drama Mozart cannot help but outshine Salieri, who is industrious and accomplished but lacks Mozart's genius.

92. Bonhoeffer, "Bible Study," p. 878 (his emphases).

93. Bonhoeffer, "Bible Study," p. 878.

94. 1 Samuel 17 has often been reconstructed as consisting of two distinct original versions, roughly: (1) 17:1-11, 32-40, 42-48a, 49, 51-54 (only these verses are found in LXX[B]) and (2) 17:12-31, 41, 48b, 50, 55-58; 18:1-5 (these verses are missing in LXX[B]). For a convenient English translation of the Septuagint version, see Pietersma and Wright, eds., *A New English Translation of the Septuagint*. See further McKenzie, *King David*, pp. 78-83. Cf. Barthélemy et al., eds., *Story of David and Goliath*. According to Barthélemy the second version was the shorter, original account of the story (he views this account as more or less consisting of only 17:1-11, 32-40, 42-48a, 49), which was later expanded by the addition of the material now contained in the so-called first version. However, there are also cogent reasons for viewing the

baroque and more theologically articulated than many of the other narrative units in Samuel, but this is not a sufficient basis to conclude that 1 Samuel 17 must be "late" or that more subtle narrative units are necessarily "early" (let alone more "secular").

David and his family are introduced into the narrative as if they have not already appeared in the book (17:12-15). Saul seems at first to know David — or at least he needs no personal introduction (17:31). But then at the end of the episode, Saul appears not to know who David is (17:55-58). Such difficulties may well be due to a combination of multiple prior sources. Still, whatever the prehistory of this text, it now exists in a highly polished and carefully crafted form, even if there are now and again slight discrepancies in the unfolding of the plot. Indeed, as Robert Polzin has suggested, repetition and inconsistency in this narrative contribute to the literary characterization of Saul as unstable and progressively deteriorating.[95]

At the center of the narrative is the confrontation between David, the young shepherd, and the physically impressive Goliath, the Philistine champion[96] — which is to say that this is a narrative about *bodies*.[97] Because David's secret anointing is known to the reader, if not to Saul, there is a strong presumption from the beginning that David will somehow manage to overpower the Philistine strong man. The narrative's suspense derives from this "somehow." How exactly will David pull it off? This question focuses the issue introduced in the last chapter concerning just how the royal transition between Saul and David will be managed. To this extent, Goliath functions from the outset as a placeholder for Saul and a symbol for David's ability to overcome adversaries. In other words, Goliath foreshadows the struggle that David will later have with Saul. But the ultimate outcome is never in doubt, because David's success rests with God. The outcome of this particular episode is actually so secure from the beginning that the narrative can teasingly introduce a

---

Greek version as a later abridgement (and reinterpretation) of the Hebrew version rather than the more original of the two. See as well Auld, "Story of David and Goliath"; Aurelius, "Wie David ursprünglich zu Saul kam"; van der Kooij, "Story of David and Goliath." For additional studies of the historical issues involved in the interpretation of this chapter, see Auld and Ho, "Making of David and Goliath"; DeVries, "David's Victory Over the Philistines"; Dietrich, "Erzählung von David und Goliath"; Hendel, "Plural Texts and Literary Criticism"; Johnson, "Reconsidering 4QSamᵃ"; Nitsche, *David gegen Goliath*; Rofé, "Battle of David and Goliath," pp. 117-22; Tov, "Composition of 1 Samuel 17–18"; Trebolle Barrera, "Story of David and Goliath"; Wénin, *David & Goliath*.

95. Polzin, *Samuel and the Deuteronomist*, pp. 161-62.
96. For cultural background and norms, see de Vaux, "Single Combat."
97. See further George, "Constructing Identity in 1 Samuel 17."

number of obstacles that would appear to disadvantage David and strengthen Goliath's position.

Goliath's physical description emphasizes his great height (17:4) as well as his heavy armor and weaponry (17:5-7). The summary of Goliath's tools of war is extensive and emphasizes their *weight*.[98] The narrative is not only giving a picture of the significant challenge that David faces, it is strengthening Goliath's implicit association with the figure of Saul, who also possesses both height and heavy weapons (17:38-39). Adding extra piquancy to 1 Samuel 17, however, is its repeated motif of "defiance" ($\sqrt{hrp}$ Piel, 6×, in 17:10, 25-26, 36, 45).[99] Goliath describes his challenge as constituting "defiance" or "taunting" or even "belittling" (17:10), just as David portrays his response as standing *against* "defiance" (17:26, 36, 45).[100] Interestingly, however, Goliath claims to defy "the ranks of Israel" (17:10), and the Israelites view his defiance as having the same object (17:25). What sets David apart, then, is his theocentric understanding of the threat that Goliath poses: David considers Goliath to be defying *God* (17:26, 36, 45).

Unlike Saul, who had earlier stayed with the baggage (1 Sam 10:22), David sets down the provisions his father has asked him to bring to his brothers and leaves the baggage area in order to greet his brothers personally (17:20). These details are given in order to deepen the reader's sense that David winds up in proximity to Goliath almost accidentally. Behind the accidental flavor of David's arrival, however, is the firm hunch that God is involved, even though God does not actually appear as a character in this chapter. Once again the narrative emphasizes coincidence. Jesse *just happens* to ask David to bring food to his brothers; David *just happens* to go to the battle line; he *just happens* to overhear Goliath as he utters his defiance. But it is David's concern for divine honor that drives him toward armed engagement with the Philistine. The other Israelites say nothing about this threat as being insulting to God. Only David makes the connection.

The other Israelites understand the object of Goliath's disdain to be Israel, and they discuss with each other the rewards that Saul has promised any Israelite who accepts Goliath's challenge. One might well wonder why Saul, big man that he is, does not decide to meet Goliath in battle himself. But the narrative makes a point of saying early on that Saul was just as afraid of Goliath as all the other Israelites were (17:11). David's rationale is not purely altruistic

---

98. Galling, "Goliath und seine Rüstung"; Millard, "Armor of Goliath"; Yadin, "Goliath's Armor"; Zorn, "Reconsidering Goliath."

99. On the defiance/disgrace motif, see especially Kellenberger, "David als Lehrer der nachexilischen Gemeinde." Kellenberger observes how this theme is recognized as central to the story by subsequent tradition (Sir 47:4; Ps 151:6-7).

100. For further historical context, see Kutler, "Features of the Battle Challenge."

or personally disinterested either; he too is depicted as wanting to know the exact rewards that the king is offering an Israelite victor (17:26-27). Yet David's thirst for battle with the Philistine is not portrayed as being primarily driven by a hope of advancement or riches. To the contrary, David's confidence is based partly on his past experience in saving sheep from marauding predators like bears and lions (17:34-35), but even more by his conviction that if he is fighting for God, then God will fight for him (17:36-37). This conviction, of course, is precisely the faith perspective that Saul has lacked from the beginning. Now Saul is ironically being instructed in it by the very person who has been anointed to succeed him.

Saul's lack of perspective could not be expressed more perfectly than in the scene in which he clothes David in his own armor (17:38-40). Of course Saul cannot imagine any way of meeting Goliath on the field of battle except by wearing the same kind of heavy armor that Goliath sports and carrying the same sort of weaponry. He attempts to have David do so as well, but such implements are too heavy or too awkward for David to use.[101] The narrative reports that David is unable to walk with them because he had not "tried" them before or perhaps even "proven (himself with)" them ($\sqrt{nsh}$ Piel, 17:39; cf. 17:40). David relies upon his familiar shepherding weapons instead: his sling and five smooth stones gathered from a dry streambed. However, it is also slightly ironic that David is the one to employ a sling, since the Benjaminites, Saul's tribe, were apparently known for their skillful use of this weapon (Judg 20:16). So once again David does what Saul cannot or will not do.

Like Jonathan in 1 Samuel 14, David goes into this fight at what appears to be a stark disadvantage, given the received wisdom about such things. He is armed only with "the name of the Lord of hosts" (17:45). But also like Jonathan, David knows that human weapons are meaningless if they are directed against God and God's champions. David approaches battle with Goliath bravely, even though he is seriously outmatched: "for not by sword or by spear does the Lord give victory" (17:47).[102] For David, God's might exceeds the power of

---

101. On this armor scene as a satire, see Alter, *World of Biblical Literature*, pp. 99-100.

102. As Dietrich Bonhoeffer insightfully perceived, Saul's armor amounts to a further "temptation" for David — the temptation to "appear strong in the eyes of the world," which David resists because "He does not wish to become different." In this context Bonhoeffer recalls the words of Jesus at Gethsemane: "Have you come out with swords and clubs to arrest me as though I were a bandit?" (Matt 26:55). Bonhoeffer further reflects: "The enemy and the world must necessarily disdain and insult and curse the defenseless warrior (vv. 42-43). They do not comprehend him, instead considering him crazy or cocky, not understanding that it is David's proper humility toward God and God's word that makes him defenseless." See Bonhoeffer, "Bible Study," p. 878.

the tools of war, and God's strength alone will determine the outcome of this engagement.[103]

That conviction is borne out. Although he has neither sword nor spear, David defeats Goliath and causes the Philistines to flee. David's success is therefore not his victory alone but the victory of God over all those who would defy God, those who rely upon the implements of war to turn events in the direction they wish, those who privilege brute force instead of trusting God to do what is just (cf. 17:50, "there was no sword in David's hand").[104] Perhaps it should then come as no surprise that Saul cannot recognize David after Goliath has been slain. He certainly cannot recognize what David represents. Nor is Saul the only one to have this difficulty: Abner, Saul's general, cannot identify David either. In spite of David's military success against Goliath, David's manner of battle is on such different terms from that of Saul and Abner that they struggle to know who he is. Although some commentators have seen their non-recognition of David as simply evidence of multiple sources and clumsy editing,[105] a more persuasive interpretation of the narrative, as it now exists, attributes Saul's confusion to his spiritual deficiency, as also symbolized by the return of the bad spirit that intermittently plagues him.[106]

Antony Campbell has been scathingly critical of what he terms the "small boy" interpretation of 1 Samuel, particularly with regard to this chapter. Campbell also views 1 Samuel 17 as further detailing the contrast between Saul and David, but he maintains that nothing in the text specifies David's physical size.[107] Campbell acknowledges three narrative details often cited in support of such an interpretation: (1) David's introduction as Jesse's youngest son in 1 Sam 16:11-12; (2) Saul's remark in 1 Sam 17:33 that David cannot hope to defeat Goliath because he is only a "youth" (na'ar); and (3) Goliath's dismissal of David at sight in 1 Sam 17:42. In response Campbell attributes these three features to "different traditions" (which by itself is hardly an adequate objection

103. See further Wong, "Farewell to Arms."

104. Meier, "Sword," stresses how Goliath's own sword is used against him, and how this feature of the story corresponds to a broader, prominent biblical theme regarding weapons: namely, they are in fact a liability rather than an advantage. On v. 50, see especially Moberly, "By Stone and Sling."

105. E.g., McCarter, *I Samuel*, p. 307.

106. Cf. Polzin, *Samuel and the Deuteronomist*, pp. 171-76. See also Gros Louis, "Difficulty of Ruling Well," p. 20.

107. Campbell, *1 Samuel*, p. 164. Cf. Campbell, *Making Sense of the Bible*, p. 255: "There is *no evidence* that David was small" (his emphasis). Campbell's discussion here makes clear that he is reconstructing a history by eliminating "legendary accretions" (p. 256). But the result is then a (reconstructed) story, not the one the Bible tells.

to an interpretation of the present narrative) and suggests that they can be explained in other ways.[108]

Campbell is correct is insisting that the Hebrew term *na'ar* has a wider semantic range than the English word "boy." In Hebrew the term can also refer to a servant, younger soldier, or junior officer.[109] Even so, there is a strong argument in favor of treating *na'ar* as a "life cycle" term that can encompass social roles by extension (much like the English terms "boy" and "lad").[110] A denial of any implication of youth at all for *na'ar* cannot carry conviction. Campbell also quarrels with the English translation "little" for the Hebrew term *qāṭān/qāṭōn*, which he insists properly means "young" and does not necessarily refer to David's diminutive size or stature.[111] However, Campbell's ongoing diatribe against romanticized notions of David as a simple shepherd boy reveals the real nub of his anxiety.[112] Nor is he all wrong; the text attributes considerable physical strength to David, as well as prior brushes with mortal danger (17:34-35). But there is every reason to treat David's youth and his size as two related features, rather than as an either/or.[113] Campbell's weighing of the philological issues is one-sided and dictated in advance by his desire for an interpretation in which David is successful not because of his reliance on

---

108. Campbell, "Structure Analysis and the Art of Exegesis," p. 88.

109. See MacDonald, "Status and Role of the *Na'ar*"; MacDonald stresses the high social status of the *na'ar*, especially within military contexts. For a more recent comprehensive study, see Leeb, *Away from the Father's House*.

110. For a recent reappraisal, see Wilson, *Making Men*.

111. Campbell, *1 Samuel*, p. 172: "the designation of David as small . . ., translating *haqqāṭān* in 1 Sam 16:11 and 17:14, exploits a potential overtone (in my judgment, incorrect), but it is irresponsible not to draw it into relation with the overwhelming meaning in such contexts of 'younger' or 'youngest'" (here Campbell is specifically critiquing the interpretation of 1 Samuel 17 by André Wénin).

112. Campbell, *1 Samuel*, p. 180: "It is often as if a 'God of the gaps' theology is influential here and a 'God of the guts' is ignored as unworthy. David has the physical attributes and the weaponry to do the job; all he needs is the courage and the nerve. He needs to be enabled to do what lies within his power — not to have done for him what lies beyond his grasp." Cf. p. 189.

113. Note that Hannah gives Samuel a "little robe" (*mě'îl qāṭōn*) in 1 Sam 2:19. Also note how in 1 Sam 17:13-14 *haqqāṭān* is contrasted with *haggĕdōlîm* ("the big/biggest ones"). In light of those and other examples, it makes more sense to me to treat the base meaning of √*qtn* as "small," since it can be used in reference to inanimate objects like weights and vessels. The connotation "young" would then be a derived meaning pertaining to "small" people and animals. See also "*qāṭōn*," *TDOT*, 13:4. Cf. the clear use of √*qtn* for "small" in 1 Sam 15:17. Short, *Surprising Election*, p. 149, proposes the translation "least" as a means of catching both the nuance of size and youth. In 1 Sam 9:21 √*qtn* is in fact paralleled with "least" (*haṣṣě'îrâ*).

God but because he possessed the better military strategy: "A big man in Saul's armor has no chance against the giant Philistine. A fast, light-armed slinger, with good reflexes, is militarily Israel's best chance against the big champion."[114]

Such an interpretation moves in exactly the opposite direction from the present narrative's intention.[115] Although biologically possible, it strains belief to imagine Jesse's youngest son as physically imposing in comparison to his older brothers. Saul's proffer of armor to a mere lad is not narrative nonsense but heavy irony. Goliath's taunt of David is not made because he appears to be a "fast, light-armed slinger" but because he does not look like a seasoned soldier at all. There is indeed subterfuge and strategy on David's part: he hides his five stones in his shepherd's bag so that Goliath does not see them (17:40). But if David had not appeared physically negligible to the giant, why would such subterfuge have made any difference?

David and Saul's Family (1 Samuel 18)

Since they share a similar faith in God, it is no surprise that David and Jonathan become fast friends. The language of "love" ($\sqrt{}$'hb) and "covenant" (běrît) resonates with deuteronomistic theology and its conception of the human–divine relationship.[116] Just as Israel is to "love" God and live in "covenant"

---

114. Campbell, "Structure Analysis and the Art of Exegesis," p. 89. See also Campbell, *Making Sense of the Bible*, pp. 255-56. Cf. Ambrose, *De officiis*, 1:77: "[David] spurned the armor offered to him, saying that it would only weigh him down — for bravery depends on its own muscle, rather than on any protection offered by independent resources."

115. For another, more popular, interpretation along these same lines, see Gladwell, *David and Goliath*. Unlike Campbell, Gladwell agrees that David was small, but he considers the slingshot to be a superior weapon and David therefore the better tactician. Yet Gladwell, too, is interested in "the real story of what happened" (as the book cover's front flap suggests), rather than in the biblical account as such (e.g., p. 14: "What many medical experts now believe, in fact, is that Goliath had a serious medical condition."). By contrast, compare the judgment of Garsiel, "Valley of Elah Battle," p. 420: "This is not a story of a contest between warriors in which the weak, the underdog, defeats the stronger. This is a story that delivers a theological message that the outcome of the war is in the hands of God, no matter what weapons are used by the warring parties."

116. On "love" language, see Thompson, "Significance of the Verb *Love*"; cf. Moran, "Ancient Near Eastern Background of the Love of God." Both scholars highlight the political sense of this term within the ancient world in contrast to its more ordinary emotional or sexual usage today. For other ancient Near Eastern examples, including a close parallel to 1 Sam 18:1 found in one of the vassal treaties of Esarhaddon, see Bodi, *Michal Affair*, p. 14. Bodi also calls attention to the political usage of the term in 1 Kgs 5:15, in which Hiram king of Tyre is said to "love" David. Bodi ultimately determines that "love" is used in a double sense in the

with him, so too Jonathan "loves" David and they enter into "covenant" with one another (18:1-4).[117] Their exchange of clothing underscores the covenantal dimension of their interaction.[118] They are making a promise to maintain their friendship with each other in the face of any coming obstacles, as good friends will do. This picture of committed friendship thus reinforces the idea that Jonathan and David both understand God correctly, even as it deepens the reader's sense that they stand together in opposition to Saul.[119] The irony in this stance is not only that Jonathan is Saul's son, but that David himself appears to maintain a very high regard for the man he cannot help but undermine.[120] Saul confidently sends David on military missions, and David is successful every time (18:5). The Hebrew root √*śkl* (Hiph.) is used to describe David's success; it also appears within the wisdom literature of the Old Testament as a term connoting insight, cleverness, and prudence.[121] Yet Saul, always sensitive to public opinion, becomes angry when David's exploits are contrasted favorably by the people to his own (18:6-8). In fact, Saul begins to realize that David is becoming a threat to his kingship. Saul is said to "eye" (*'wyn* Qere) him from this point on (18:9).[122]

Samuel narrative: as a political and an emotional term. For a similar conclusion, see Arnold, "Love–Fear Antinomy in Deut 5–11." Arnold corrects Moran by demonstrating that "love" has both cognitive and affective dimensions in this tradition. Cf. Lapsley, "Feeling Our Way"; Rüterswörden, "Liebe zu Gott in Deuteronomium."

117. Interestingly, Josephus omits these verses from his account of David, which may signal his discomfort with the emotional dimension to David's friendship with Jonathan. Josephus substitutes his own explanation of Jonathan's bond with David: Jonathan "revered him for his virtue." See Josephus, *Ant.* 6:206. Wojcik, "Discriminations against David's Tragedy," p. 23, notes this substitution and also calls attention to Josephus' replacement of the later reference to David's love for Jonathan as "surpassing the love of women" (2 Sam 1:26) with a much more prosaic mention of how Jonathan had once saved David's life (see Joseph, *Ant.* 7:5). These alterations do not provide direct evidence that the David–Jonathan relationship was originally depicted as homoerotic or homosexual, but they do seem to indicate how Josephus already read the narrative in that way — or worried that it could be (mis?)interpreted along those lines by his Graeco-Roman readers. See further Kaiser, "David und Jonathan"; Olyan, "Surpassing the Love of Women."

118. Cf. 2 Kgs 11:10. Thompson, "Significance of the Verb *Love*," p. 335.

119. Joseph Hall nicely notes how Jonathan's (successful) provision of clothing and armor to David (18:4) contrasts with Saul's unsuccessful effort to do the same thing in the previous chapter (17:38-39). See his *Contemplations on the Historical Passages*, pp. 188-89: "It was perhaps not without a mystery, that Saul's clothes fitted not David, but Jonathan's fitted him; and these he is as glad to wear, as he was to be disburdened of the other: that there might be a perfect resemblance, their bodies are suited as well as their hearts."

120. See further Brueggemann, "Narrative Coherence."

121. See √*śkl* in *TDOT* 14:112-28.

122. Interpretation of this section (1 Sam 18:6-16) is made more complicated by the

Saul's insecurity and jealousy invite another visitation from the "bad spirit of God" (18:10), the spirit of God that threatens him. The last time this occurred in the narrative was in 1 Sam 10:10-13; with such repetition the narrative again emphasizes the instability of Saul's personality and his inability to make any genuine progress. Once more Saul is described as "prophesying" or perhaps "raving ecstatically like a prophet" (√nb' Hithp.).[123] This constellation of factors — Saul's internal emotional state, his visitation from the spirit, and his ecstatic possession — paints a portrait of a man wholly obsessed and out of control. It should be no wonder that Saul has often been interpreted as having some sort of physiological or psychological defect; the biblical narrative not only raises the issue of his state of mind, it implies a relationship between his state of mind and his apprehension of God. But the biblical narrative never reduces God to a psychological impression either. There is always an objective character to God's spirit in Saul's encounter with it. The text does suggest that Saul's state of mind disposes him, even constrains him, to experience God as a threat rather than a blessing. Yet the narrative further maintains that God intentionally comes in the form of a threat to Saul. The "bad spirit" and the prophetic raving are not depicted as products of Saul's imagination but as key indicators of a deterioration in the divine–human relationship, which ideally functions in a manner opposite to its depiction here.

Saul's mental and spiritual deterioration are further shown by his hurling a spear at David — twice (18:11; cf. 1 Sam 16:14-23) — while David plays music for him, trying to relieve his distress. The repetition highlights both David's commitment to Saul as well as God's commitment to David. Even after Saul turns violent towards him, David continues to serve him loyally while God loyally protects David.[124] Saul takes account of David's ability to escape and perceives that God is "with him" ('immô), which ironically only adds to Saul's insecurity and fear that David could replace him (18:12). In fact, David's survivability seems to remind Saul that God has "turned from being with him" (mē'im šā'ûl

---

absence of everything except vv. 6b-8a and 9 in LXX[B]. See Smith, *Books of Samuel*, p. 168. Here I simply follow the MT.

123. See Wilson, "Prophecy and Ecstasy." The Hithpael form of √nb' appears to be used in 1 Sam 18:10 to mean something like "act deranged" — given Saul's behavior, its non-prophetic context and the parallel to 1 Sam 16:14-23. Prophetic behavior could clearly violate social conventions. In 2 Kgs 9:11 Jehu (insincerely) dismisses Elijah as "that madman" (hammĕšūg-gā' hazzê) and describes his actions as "aggravation" (śîaḥ), a term also used by Hannah in reference to herself (1 Sam 1:16), in another situation in which social conventions are viewed as having been breached. See further Parker, "Possession, Trance and Prophecy."

124. Chrysostom interprets David's flight as forbearance and concern for Saul: "The reason for withdrawing himself from his enemy's sight was to bring down the swelling, check the inflammation and allay the malice." See his *Old Testament Homilies*, 1:17.

śār, 18:12 [my emphasis]). God's "being with" someone is apparently construed here not only as a zero-sum game — if God is "with" one king, God cannot be "with" another — but also as a quality of relationship that exhibits itself in indications of worldly success.

Saul's fear of David continues, but his strategy for dealing with the problem appears curiously weak. Spear-throwing is an iconic action of ancient Near Eastern gods and kings, sometimes used in pictorial depictions to indicate their physical strength and supreme authority.[125] In this case, however, Saul's action only expresses his impotence, as a king and as a man.[126] Because he cannot eliminate David himself, he sends David away from the royal court by making him a commander in the army (18:13). Since David's success in ad hoc military assignments was precisely the issue that precipitated Saul's anxiety in the first place, giving David further opportunities to achieve military victory hardly seems wise. Perhaps Saul is motivated more by his own survival — keeping David away from court reduces the chance that David might kill Saul — and by a pragmatic inclination to use David's ability to achieve success so long as his initiatives can be fitted within Saul's own goals and initiatives. However, Saul's strategy does nothing to reverse the trend established at the beginning of the chapter. David continues to exhibit "success" (√*śkl* Hiph., 18:14-15), Saul continues to fear him, and the people love (√*'hb*) David all the more (18:16). Once again, the term "love" signals not only personal affection but political allegiance.

Yet Saul then turns to another strategy to deal with the threat presented by David: getting him killed by the Philistines. Saul's attempt to harm David earlier in the chapter was an indication of betrayal, but it was depicted as the effect of Saul's personal deterioration rather than premeditated murder. Saul had not specially procured a weapon; it was simply at hand (18:10). It is not even fully clear that Saul intended to kill David at the time. The narrative reports — in the form of a soliloquy so that the reader overhears Saul's internal motivation firsthand — only that he meant to pin David to the wall (18:11). Yet being struck against a wall by a spear is hardly an incidental injury. Nor perhaps is it any accident that Saul's effort to strike David against a "wall" (*qîr*) foreshadows Saul's own ultimate humiliation on "the wall of Beth Shean" (*bĕḥômat bêt šān*, 1 Sam 31:10). However, should there still be any residual doubt about the conscious, premeditated quality of Saul's animosity against David, the next scene confirms it.

---

125. E.g., see Keel and Uehlinger, *Gods, Goddesses, and Images of God*, pp. 76-77.

126. Hamilton, *Body Royal*, p. 197, calls attention to this contrast, noting, "Once again the narrator uses iconicity ironically." In other words, a conventional sign of strength is paradoxically used to depict weakness.

Saul tells David that he will give him a daughter in marriage (18:17). The narrative again uses the soliloquy form to indicate how Saul's personal calculations are quite different from his public words. He wants to find a way for the Philistines to kill David so that he does not have to do so himself (18:17). At first Saul offers David his daughter Merab; David modestly refuses on the grounds that his background is too humble to be related to the king by marriage, and Merab is subsequently married to someone else. However, when Saul hears that his daughter Michal "loves" ($\sqrt{\ }$'hb) David (18:20), he renews his offer and a soliloquy is once more provided in order to confirm his duplicity (18:21). It can be observed that Saul exhibits little personal regard for his daughters in his scheming.[127] Their happiness is not his concern. Because Saul learns that David's hesitation is based in part on the "bride-price" David thinks he will need to pay in order to acquire a princess, Saul springs his trap by giving David a non-monetary condition: the foreskins of one hundred Philistines. Just to make sure the point is not missed, the narrator once more confirms Saul's state of mind: "Saul thought to make David fall by the hand of the Philistines" (18:25).

But of course — and the narrative does communicate an "of course-ness" about it — David sorties out with his men, procures *two* hundred Philistine foreskins (double the bride-price) and returns alive to gain Michal's hand despite Saul's scheming.[128] Saul has only succeeded in making the situation worse. Not only is it more apparent than ever that God is "with David" ('*im-dāwid*, 18:28), now David is even married to Michal, Saul's own daughter, who in turn "loves" ($\sqrt{\ }$'hb) David.[129] So throughout the course of this chapter, the conflict set out at its beginning is only intensified. Jonathan "loves" David; so do all the people and even Jonathan's own sister Michal.[130] Saul only exacerbates his situation by raging and duplicitously scheming against David. In the end, Saul is said to consider David his "enemy" ('*ōyēb*, 18:29), a status that comes very near to proclaiming God to be his enemy as well, since it is finally clear to Saul — as to the reader — that God is "with" David in all his under-

---

127. On this point, see Exum, "Fate of the House of Saul." On the Michal traditions generally, see Bodi, *Michal Affair*.

128. The number "two hundred" may well be a secondary intensification within the Hebrew text tradition. Septuagintal tradition reads "one hundred," a number also remembered later in the Hebrew text of Samuel (2 Sam 3:14). However, the doubling of the amount, even if a later change, is perfectly in keeping with the spirit of the narrative at this point in describing David's unavoidable and decisive success.

129. Some Greek manuscripts read "Israel loved him" instead. I keep with the MT's reference to Michal at this point in order to catch the parallelism between Michal and Jonathan, both of whom respond to David with love, regardless of their father's disapproval.

130. On the love motif in this chapter, see especially Naumann, "David und die Liebe."

takings. There is now also a finality to Saul's position: David will be his enemy "all the days" (*kol-hayyāmîm*, 18:29) or, in other words, from here on out.

Nothing, however, can impede David's success (√*śkl* Qal, 18:30) — not Saul's plots and not the Philistine threat that is regularly present. There is little attention to worship in this chapter, other than perhaps the festal welcome that the women of Israel give to David early on (18:6), reigniting Saul's suspicions. Still, it is noteworthy in light of this theme throughout the rest of the book that even this type of ritual welcome works to David's benefit and Saul's dissolution. It should also be noted that there are no scenes here of David praying before battle or otherwise inviting divine assistance for his military victories. The full emphasis of the narrative is simply on God's sovereign choice of David as the one on whom God's favor rests, and the utter impossibility of Saul, even at his most devious, to do anything to change that. Not only has Saul's dynasty been refused by God, Saul's children are drawn just as much to David as God is. They have chosen David, too, leaving Saul isolated and unhinged.

For his part, David is a cipher in these verses. Unlike Saul, whose internal thoughts are repeatedly reported to the reader, there is little indication of David's own state of mind.[131] Does he love Saul? Does he speak sincerely? On what basis does he reach his decisions and make his choices? The narrative does not say that David loves Jonathan or Michal, only that they love him. Does David realize that his relationships with members of Saul's family work to his advantage? Is he actively seeking to gain the kingship? Or has he put the outcome of events into God's hands alone? In effect, the narrative poses all of these questions by being entirely silent about them. Only in the subsequent unfolding of the story will bits and pieces of information be introduced for use in retrospectively discovering the answers.

David Escapes from Saul (1 Samuel 19)

In this chapter the focus continues to rest on members of Saul's family and David's interactions with them.[132] The association between Saul and mur-

---

131. Klein, "1 Sam 18."

132. See further Exum, "Fate of the House of Saul"; Willi-Plein, "1 Sam 18–19 und die Davidshausgeschichte." See also the nice summary of the significance of the family theme at this point in the narrative in Zehnder, "Observations on the Relationship," p. 158: "David is loved and helped not only by the one person who might be the biggest means of political promotion (Michal as the king's daughter), but even by the one person who might be the biggest obstacle to pursuing a political career leading to kingship (Jonathan as the king's son and heir to the throne)."

der, introduced in the last chapter, now becomes a recurring theme that ties together the individual events of the narrative and explains why David has to flee for his life.

Saul had secretly plotted against David before; now he encourages Jonathan and other members of his court to kill him (19:1). But Jonathan, who has a covenant of friendship with David (1 Sam 18:3), tells David of Saul's intentions. Jonathan also engages in a further subterfuge of his own. He tells David to hide in a field, and then he brings Saul out to the same place for a conversation. After Jonathan praises David and proclaims his innocence, Saul swears not to hurt him: "By the life of the Lord, let him not be put to death!" (19:6). Jonathan subsequently finds David, gives him the good news and reunites him with Saul. The reconciliation effected by Jonathan patches things up but does not last. Nevertheless, this episode plays an important role in the wider narrative by introducing the idea of bloodguilt for the killing of an innocent person (19:5) and placing Saul under a holy oath not to take David's life.

Just as in 1 Samuel 18, a "bad spirit of the Lord" visits Saul while he is listening to David play music. As before, Saul tries to spear David to the wall and David is forced to make a hasty escape (19:9-10). Even if one account is based on the other or they both once had a common source,[133] these two stories of Saul's attempt on David's life now have different literary functions. This second account points to the hopelessness of the situation by its nature as a repetition. Despite Jonathan's effort, Saul is right back where he was before. His situation has even worsened, since he is in danger not only of incurring bloodguilt for killing David but also for breaking a vow to God in doing so. In this way the narrative constructs a bleak situation of steady, seemingly irreversible decline for Saul, whose bright moments are increasingly few and all too quickly extinguished.

Does Saul have sufficient control to prevent himself from trying to kill David? In the world of the narrative how much is Saul to be blamed for what he does? This question is central to 1 Samuel but difficult to answer. On the one hand, the narrative depicts Saul as making reasoned choices and judgments. He listens to Jonathan's arguments about David and swears his oath out of personal conviction. Yet Saul does not always appear to be himself. He does not attempt to take David's life again until the "bad spirit" from God embraces him. If one cannot say that God "makes" Saul attempt to kill David, one cannot say that Saul acts entirely on his own initiative either. Instead, the narrative

---

133. See Smith, *Books of Samuel*, p. 177. As to the literary effect of the repetition, Smith suggests that perhaps "the two accounts are intended to represent two successive attempts of the same kind, separated by the reconciliation of 19:1-7."

paints Saul as having inconstant mental states — now lucid, now not. In this fashion the complicated question of the cooperation between God and Saul is negotiated temporally, with Saul sometimes alert and sometimes overpowered. Saul is thereby held to be responsible for his actions but not blamed cheaply for things that he has little power to resist. Saul is never demonized in this narrative, even when he flouts God and engages in immoral acts.

This quality of sympathy is partly the result of narrative reticence — the narrator consistently refrains from offering explicit moral condemnations of Saul. But sympathy for Saul also arises from the reader's knowledge of the wider story. In his rejection by God, Saul has seemingly been placed *outside* the loving confines of God's favor. Outside of that relationship, God is encountered as a source of threat rather than blessing, confusion rather than peace, fear rather than hope, insecurity rather than trust. So how can Saul be blamed for exhibiting those things? For whom would it be any different? Who will cast the first stone (John 8:1-11)? To be sure, it was Saul's own failure that led to his rejection. But even then, as the narrative disclosed, Saul's failure was more the failure of not being the right person for the job in the first place than the failure of someone who had every necessary gift and ability but squandered them for some sinful purpose. Saul does not represent a life lived *against* God but a life lived *without* God. That kind of life is perhaps more frightening, but also more sympathetic.

After failing to spear David for the second time, Saul then thinks to have his men kill David on the following morning. He sends men to watch David through the night and prevent him from again escaping (19:11). Just as Jonathan previously informed David of his father's intentions, this time Michal tells David of Saul's plot and aids his nighttime departure through a window. Michal disguises an idol to look like David in his bed so that Saul's men will still think he is sleeping. The selection of an idol for this purpose may only be a matter of finding a household object of the proper size and dimensions, but that would also suggest a very large idol.[134] So perhaps the identification of this object as an "idol" (*těrāpîm*) is also an oblique comment on Saul's obsession with David. In a sense, David has become Saul's idol in Saul's desire to possess and control him.[135] Saul's "idolatry" in turn forces those around him into

---

134. On historical questions regarding *teraphim*, see Bauck, "1 Samuel 19"; Flynn, "*Teraphim*"; Loretz, "Teraphim als 'Ahnen-Götter-Figur(in)en'"; Nigosian, *Magic and Divination in the Old Testament*, pp. 69-70; van der Toorn, "Nature of the Biblical Teraphim." In Genesis 31 the *těrāpîm* somehow fit under Rachel's saddle (v. 34); they are also called "gods" (*'ĕlōhāy*, v. 30; cf. v. 32).

135. As Bodi observes (*Michal Affair*, p. 26), use of the term *těrāpîm* here also suggests a link to its previous appearance in 1 Sam 15:23b, where it was employed as a figure of Saul's

ethically ambiguous stances. Michal justifies her duplicity to her father, saying that David threatened her with death if she did not help him. The statement is clearly a lie, but one that is difficult to begrudge Michal given her father's madness and antipathy to her husband.[136] Within the shape of this unfolding story, it is not inconceivable that Saul might kill his own daughter if he knew she had been supporting his "enemy" (19:17).

At this point in the narrative David flees to Samuel in Ramah. By going to Samuel, David indicates that he continues to be aware of his anointing at Samuel's hands. The destination may also be the result of desperation: where else can David go to protect himself from Saul? Indeed, Saul sends men after David and eventually goes to Ramah himself. But after finding Samuel at the head of a band of prophets, Saul's men weirdly begin prophesying, too. The same thing happens to a second and a third group of messengers until Saul also makes the journey the Ramah, where he is overcome by the prophetic spirit as well, strips off his clothes, raves ecstatically before Samuel, and lies naked all through the day and night (19:23-24).[137] In this scene the power of prophecy takes the form of a spiritual army to protect David against Saul's murderous rage. Interestingly, David is not described as prophesying. He remains a cipher. But all of Saul's strong men are portrayed as powerless before the action of God's spirit as it spreads through Samuel's band of prophets and overwhelms Saul's soldiers.

Saul's presence "before Samuel" (*lipnê šĕmû'ēl*, 19:24) would appear to contradict the statement in 1 Sam 15:35 that "Samuel did not see Saul again until the day of his death." The likely historical explanation for the contradiction is that two different traditions about Samuel and Saul have been imperfectly joined. Yet it is also possible that here the Hebrew preposition *lipnê* ("before") has more of a cultic connotation than a personal one.[138] By having Saul speak "before" Samuel, the narrative may be conceiving of Saul prophesying at the

---

unfaith. This link is often obscured in translation (e.g., in 1 Sam 15:23b the NRSV translates *tĕrāpîm* as "idolatry.").

136. On the ethical implications of Michal's behavior in this chapter, see Rowe, *Michal's Moral Dilemma*.

137. Hamilton, *Body Royal*, p. 199, argues that Saul's naked incapacity in this chapter "exposes Saul . . . as one no longer fit to be king, since he can no longer control his self-presentation." For further evaluation, see Firth, "Is Saul Also among the Prophets?"

138. On *lipnê yhwh* as meaning "at a temple" or "in the forecourt of the sanctuary," especially in priestly usage, see Haran, *Temple and Temple Service*, pp. 26-37; cf. Milgrom, *Leviticus 1–16*, pp. 209-10; Zevit, *Religions of Ancient Israel*, pp. 286-88. Slightly more broadly, Wilson, *Out of the Midst of the Fire*, pp. 131-97, argues that the expression indicates "the localized Presence of the Deity at the 'chosen place'" (p. 204) — at least in Deuteronomy. For further discussion, see Fowler, "Meaning of *lipnê YHWH*."

cultic site where Samuel was in charge. Thus Samuel may not have "seen" him, whether in the sense of an extended meeting or even in the sense of a simple observation. In any case Saul must appear at Ramah himself in this scene, given the literary grammar of the story. There is only one reason for having three different groups of messengers incapacitated in Ramah — to necessitate Saul's own presence there.

Of course, Saul finds the prophetic spirit irresistible, just as he always has and just as the proverbial saying of the people acknowledges: "Is Saul also among the prophets?" (19:24). Both the scene and the saying therefore form something of an *inclusio* with 1 Sam 10:9-13, where the same kind of scene and the same saying previously appeared at what was then the outset of Saul's story. Thus yet another repetition emphasizes and heightens the problematic nature of Saul in all his complexity.[139] He does possess a certain receptivity for spiritual things, as if his brain is hardwired to pick up prophetic "chatter,"[140] but he exhibits the *behavior* of reception without comprehension of the message being communicated, the form without the substance. The irony of this turnaround is both rich and sad. Saul is too spiritual to succeed in killing David, but not spiritual enough to succeed as king.

Jonathan and David (1 Samuel 20)

After fleeing from Ramah, apparently while Saul is incapacitated by the prophetic spirit, David seeks out Jonathan and attempts to formulate a plan for responding to Saul's threats. Because the narrative now reports more of David's speech, his characterization begins to take on clearer dimensions, although much of David's internal motivation remains shadowy.

When David reports Saul's attempt on his life to Jonathan, Jonathan initially disbelieves. After all, Saul has sworn a sacred oath. Moreover, Jonathan maintains that his relationship with his father is so close that Saul could not do such a thing without letting Jonathan know of it (20:2). But David replies by telling Jonathan that Saul knows about their strong tie of friendship and is therefore keeping his actions against David a secret from Jonathan. David then asks Jonathan to participate in a clandestine fact-finding mission regarding his father (20:5-8). Instead of joining the king for a sacred meal at the new

---

139. Weeks, *Sources and Authors*, p. 157.

140. Saul's susceptibility to music underscores this point, as music and prophecy went hand in hand in the ancient world (e.g., 2 Kgs 3:15-16; 1 Chr 25:1-3; Ezek 33:32). See further Franklin, "Lyre Gods of the Bronze Age."

moon, David will hide in the country. Jonathan is to tell the king that David has received permission to celebrate the sacrifice in Bethlehem, his home. If the king approves of David's absence, then David will believe that all is well between Saul and him. If the king becomes angry, however, David's fears will be confirmed.

David presents this plot to Jonathan as a way for David himself to learn the truth of Saul's intentions. But in light of what has already happened to David in the narrative, the point of these actions seems much more geared toward proving Saul's intentions to Jonathan. In fact, David's words to Jonathan seem a bit insincere and manipulative. He not only reminds Jonathan of the covenant they have made with each other, he also grandly tells Jonathan to kill him himself before allowing Saul to do so (20:8). This rhetorical gambit of reverse psychology does the trick; Jonathan quickly rejects any notion of David's death, even if he must betray his own father to prevent it (20:9). In this exchange of words David comes across as crafty, but not wicked. The reader knows already that Saul does in fact desire David's death, that David is engaged in a mortally serious contest for his life (at significant disadvantage), and that Jonathan knows less about the situation than he thinks. Indeed, Jonathan may need special persuading precisely because he willfully resists the implications of what he has already heard and seen (e.g., 19:1).[141] One might even argue that David exhibits consideration for Jonathan in contriving to show him, rather than simply stating, the perfidy of his father. Of course, David's plan is also designed to preserve his friendship with Jonathan while at the same time demonstrating to Jonathan the truth of Saul's actions and intentions.

Jonathan's two-part speech in response to David's suggestion is likewise grand (20:12-16, 18-23). Its most striking feature is the prominence of its "God language." David has mentioned God only in an oath formula (20:3) and in relation to his covenant with Jonathan (20:8). In response, however, Jonathan not only increases the number of oath-related references to God (20:12, 13 [2×], 21, 23), he also articulates an explicitly theological perspective. *God's* faithfulness is ultimately at stake in Jonathan's covenant with David (20:14). *God* favors David and will continue to oppose David's enemies (20:15-16). *God* is at work determining the outcome of events and actions within David's life (20:22).[142] With such statements Jonathan continues to represent the position

---

141. Some commentators view Jonathan as actually not very bright. See, for example, Noll, *Faces of David*, who refers to Jonathan as "dense" (p. 46) and views his lack of intelligence as a further narrative specification regarding his lack of fitness to succeed his father. Cf. Polzin, *Samuel and the Deuteronomist*, pp. 187-94. I view Jonathan's lack of understanding at this point in the narrative as more a matter of will than intelligence.

142. This theocentric perspective is emphasized in the narrative by Jonathan's inclusion

of orthodox deuteronomism. What he says is true from the perspective of the narrative: God has chosen David and favors him, as the narrative has reported. Yet the explicit nature of Jonathan's theological perspective calls David's own outlook somewhat into question. Why is David not more explicitly theological himself? Not only are theological statements relatively absent in his speech, David's plan itself involves using — in fact lying about — a sacred act of worship in order to trick Saul into revealing his hand. At this point David appears to possess a pragmatic attitude toward religious observances and rites that is not unlike Saul's own. Perhaps here the narrative is probing the question of whether a king can act in any other manner. Given the realities of political life and the constraints imposed by the gaining and maintaining of power, even when such power is authorized by God, can a king truly devote himself whole-heartedly to spiritual realities and a robust practice of worship? Or does the exercise of power necessarily infringe upon a king's ability to do so? Is this perhaps why Jonathan is unsuited for the kingship, even beyond God's rejection of Saul's dynasty? Is Jonathan too holy to be king? Is David no better than Saul? These are questions skillfully prompted by the narrative through its silences and its implicit comparisons.

The narrative goes on to detail how David's plan plays out. Saul does become enraged at David's absence but somewhat unexpectedly directs the force of his anger against Jonathan. Saul's insults target family loyalty rather than anything sexual.[143] By trying to help David — as Saul rightly perceives

---

of shooting arrows within the plan (1 Sam 20:20-22, 36-40). Rather than simply a coded means of letting David know that "the coast is clear," the arrows reflect an ancient divinatory practice (belomancy) in which the divine will could be invoked and revealed. See Iwry, "New Evidence for Belomancy"; Porter, "Ancient Israel," p. 203.

143. For discussion of the homoerotic aspects in the narrative, and the possiblity of reading the friendship between David and Jonathan as a sexual one, see Schroer and Staubli, "Saul, David and Jonathan." Cf. Ackerman, *When Heroes Love*; Harding, *Love of David and Jonathan*; Heacock, *Jonathan Loved David*; Horner, *Jonathan Loved David*, pp. 26-39; Naumann, "David und die Liebe"; Nissinen, "Liebe von David und Jonatan"; Peleg, "Love at First Sight?" Against a homosexual interpretation is Zehnder, "Observations on the Relationship." Zehnder offers an explicit critique of Schroer and Staubli, as well as a review of recent literature. Note that Jonathan is later said to have children (2 Sam 21:7; 9:3) and David will acquire multiple wives. Still, Fewell and Gunn, *Gender, Power, and Promise*, p. 150, claim that "it is common in patriarchal societies for men whose primary sexual orientation is homosexual to live out a heterosexual role for at least some part of their lives, and in doing so to father children." While homosexual activity was not unknown among warriors within the ancient world, and perhaps in certain contexts even customary or common, so was highly emotional language between men not involved with each other sexually. Nor did this kind of male bonding only occur in antiquity; see Solomon, "David and Jonathan in Iraq." There is nothing in the Samuel narrative that necessitates the inference of a homosexual relationship between David and Jonathan, just

— Jonathan has betrayed his father and his family in a shameful manner.[144] Saul expects Jonathan to act in the interest of his family, which is also in his own self-interest (20:31). Only when Saul now attempts to spear Jonathan, however, does Jonathan fully understand his father's implacability (20:33). Putting the rest of their plan into motion, Jonathan meets secretly with David on the following day to convey the news (20:35-41). David seems to be sincerely affected. He bows before Jonathan, and as they kiss each other and weep David is said to weep "longer/the more" *('ad-dāwid higdîl*, 20:41).[145] The

as this possibility cannot definitely be ruled out as a historical possibility. As it now stands, however, the narrative provides no indication that their friendship was sexual. The nature of the biblical tradition, with its legal provisions against homosexuality, also suggests that such a reading is unlikely. Exum, *Tragedy and Biblical Narrative*, p. 73, rightly treats the narrative's presentation of their friendship as a matter of "male bonding." The profound nature of their friendship is also stressed by Kaiser, "David und Jonathan"; McKenzie, *King David*, pp. 84-85. The classic Christian exploration of the David–Jonathan relation as a model for how friendship can lead to Christ is found in Aelred of Rievaulx, *Spiritual Friendship*, pp. 72, 111-13. For Aelred, genuine friendship occurs when friends value the well-being of each other beyond calculations of self-advantage. Now see further Stansell, "You've Got a Friend." Stansell stresses how Jonathan is more active than is often thought, that he is the "real emotional energy in the friendship" (p. 227).

144. Saul's words to Jonathan certainly sound sexual: "You son of a perverse, rebellious woman! Do I not know that you have chosen the son of Jesse to your own shame, and to the shame of your mother's nakedness?" (20:30, NRSV). However, Zehnder, "Observations on the Relationship," p. 150, helpfully comments: "According to the traditional Jewish interpretation" of this phrase, the shame lies in the fact that to the outside observer Jonathan simply seems to be plotting with his father's enemies, and that after Saul's death his surviving son Jonathan and Jonathan's mother will be alive as subjects of the new king David." Zehnder takes the term "nakedness" to be a reference to the act of giving birth. Even more convincingly, Davies, "Friendship of Jonathan and David," p. 69, rules out any sexual nuance in Saul's words. Davies notes the commonly accepted critical view that on the basis of the LXX and 4QSam[b] "perverse rebellious woman" (NRSV, rendering MT *na'awat hammardût*) should be emended to "rebellious servant girl" (*na'arat hammardût*), thereby losing any implication of perversity. Cf. Cross et al., eds., *Qumran Cave 4.XII*, pp. 232-33; McCarter, *I Samuel*, 339; Smith, *Books of Samuel*, pp. 193-94. Similarly, Davies persuasively maintains that the reference to "shame" is not about sex but royal succession: "The expression is a typically vivid way of saying that Jonathan is and will be a disgrace to the mother who bore him, nothing more" (p. 70). For further thoughts on shame in Samuel, see Stansell, "Honor and Shame in the David Narratives." For an argument that Saul's remarks are nevertheless still "sexually charged," see Harding, *Love of David and Jonathan*, pp. 201-13.

145. This Hebrew phrase is difficult in its present context and might also be rendered "thus David increased (further)." Kirova, "When Real Men Cry," p. 39, styles David the "second great weeper" in the Hebrew Bible (after Joseph). She calls attention to the competitive nuance here, as if "the two heroic males are outweeping each other," and also to how David's tears in this instance certify him as the "manlier" man.

narrative segment concludes with a mutal oath, a covenant that now includes their offspring (20:42).[146] This commitment toward their children and heirs will prove important later in what is now the book of 2 Samuel, as David consolidates his royal power. In the present context it may also represent one way in which Jonathan attempts to persuade himself of the falsehood of his father's accusations. If David commits himself to the safety and security of Jonathan's children, then Jonathan does not work against his own self-interest and does not betray his own family as Saul has charged.

With this profound commitment between the two fully established, the narrative turns from the relationship between David and Saul's family, and from now on dwells primarily on the interactions between David and Saul alone. For the remainder of the book Saul will pursue David and David will seek to preserve his life, even as David continues to gain popular acclaim and support. The main question arising from the contours of the plot remains precisely the question of how David will come to replace Saul. The inevitability of that outcome has been thoroughly prepared in the events of the narrative thus far, but the details of how exactly it will happen are unknown and therefore remain suspenseful. Bloodshed has not yet been absolutely ruled out. Even beyond the events of the plot, however, what drives the narrative and intrigues the reader above all is increasingly the question of David's character. Who is he really? How different is he from Saul? Can he be king in a manner distinct from Saul? A way that can successfully unite the theological traditions of Israel with the realities of royal power? Is there any true hope for a monarch with "God's own heart"? Or are Samuel's remembered warnings inexorably moving towards catastrophe? The remainder of 1 Samuel will portray a David who steadily matures in his understanding of kingship, as well as in his knowledge of himself. Readers awaiting further revelations will not be disappointed.

---

146. The last portion of this numbered verse in English translations is found as verse 21:1 in the Hebrew Bible. On the "covenant" between the two figures here, see Woźniak, "Drei verschiedene literarische Beschreibungen."

CHAPTER 4

1 Samuel 21–31

You wouldn't go to Macbeth to learn about the history of Scotland — you go to it to learn what a man feels like after he's gained a kingdom and lost his soul.[1]

Since power belongs only to God, it is the tragic story of every man of God that he had to contend for the right of God by placing himself in the wrong. This must be so if the men of God are not to usurp the place of God.[2]

When Jesus realized that they were about to come and take him by force to make him king, he withdrew again to the mountain by himself.[3]

Saul, David, and the Priests at Nob (1 Samuel 21–22)

Just as David fled to a religious site in the last chapter, he now requests provisions from the priests at Nob. He had previously sought Samuel's protection; this time he asks Ahimelech the priest for aid. Despite some difficulties in the Hebrew text, this episode is masterfully told and must be read together with the following chapter (1 Sam 22) in order for its full significance to be gleaned.

The most striking narrative feature of this material is its curious treatment of Doeg the Edomite.[4] When David first speaks to Ahimelech, the narrative

1. Northrop Frye, cited in Smith, *What Is Scripture?* p. 360 n. 23.
2. Barth, *Epistle to the Romans*, p. 57.
3. John 6:15.
4. For extensive discussion of this character and his role in the narrative, see Lozovyy, *Saul, Doeg, Nabal, and the "Son of Jesse"*, pp. 84-120.

gives no indication of anyone else being present. Only in verse 7 is the reader informed that Doeg was also at the scene.[5] After the narrative identifies Doeg, however, neither David nor Ahimelech proceed to speak to him or to have any interaction with him of any kind for the remainder of the chapter. It is not even clear, on the basis of what is explicitly narrated, whether David and Ahimelech are themselves aware of Doeg's presence or whether he can hear their conversation. Not until 1 Samuel 22, when Saul asks his men for information about David, does the narrative resume its attention to Doeg, who at that point reports to Saul how Ahimelech and the other priests have given David provisions. Doeg's report not only persuades Saul to attack Nob and slay the priests, it induces Saul to ask Doeg to do the killing since, as an Edomite, he does not share the scruples of Saul's men about killing priests of the Lord (22:17-18). Doeg is to "surround" (√*sbb*, 22:18, 2×) and slay the priests, since Saul's men would not "surround" (√*sbb*, 22:17) them.

However, when David is informed of the horrific slaughter of the entire priestly city, he admits to knowing all along that Doeg had been listening to his conversation in Nob, already realizing that Doeg could tell Saul what had transpired: "I knew on that day, when Doeg the Edomite was there, that he would tell Saul. *I* have surrounded [√*sbb*] every soul in your father's house" (22:22, emphasis original; the personal pronoun appears in addition to the verb form).[6] In his grief, David probably exaggerates his responsibility. He likely could not have known for certain that Doeg would report to Saul, but David berates himself all the same for not taking the possibility more seriously. Yet the fact that David knew about Doeg's presence at all is somewhat surprising, since that aspect of the story was previously unacknowledged by the narrative, and it provides another example of "retrospective" storytelling. At the conclusion of 1 Samuel 22, with the knowledge that David was in fact aware of being overheard by Doeg in Nob, the reader is sent back to the narrative of 1 Samuel 21 in search of further insight.

Several interpreters have concluded after such a search that David knew of Doeg's presence, although Ahimelech did not, and that David duped the

---

5. Verse 8 in the MT. In 1 Samuel 21 all of the Hebrew verses are numbered one less than they are in English translations because the English text counts the last part of 1 Sam 20:42 as 1 Sam 21:1.

6. Seeing the relationship between the use of √*sbb* in this verse and its use in 22:17-18 greatly helps in understanding its meaning. It is unnecessary to emend v. 22 as has often been done — for example, reading its form of √*sbb* as a confusion of √*ḥwb* ("to be guilty"), an otherwise practically unknown verb in the MT. (There is only one other attestation, in Daniel 1:10 [Piel].) The point being made by David is that he is himself responsible for the killing of the priests of Nob in precisely the manner in which it occurred.

innocent priest into treason and catastrophe.[7] In its defense, this view can point to the apparent lie told by David at the very outset of the episode: "The king charged me with an errand . . ." (21:3). However, other interpreters have argued that David's reference to the "king" in this statement is in fact a reference to God rather than to Saul[8] — a clever evasion or half-truth that Ahimelech may or may not have understood, although 1 Samuel 22:17 later implies that he did.[9]

A more compelling narrative reading of 1 Samuel 21 has been offered by Pamela Tamarkin Reis, based upon the additional information provided by 1 Samuel 22. Reis argues that an awareness of Doeg's presence on the part of David and Ahimelech actually explains the oddity of their words and behavior.[10] Why should Ahimelech "tremble" (√ḥrd, 21:1) on meeting David? Because he knew Doeg was there. Why should David tell Ahimelech a lie about being on a mission for Saul (21:2; cf. 21:8)? Because he knew Doeg was listening. David's pretext gave Ahimelech "plausible deniability," which Ahimelech is then able to invoke later when he is questioned about his actions by Saul (22:14-15). Reis may be correct to emphasize the "overheard" character of the conversation between David and Ahimelech, even if a precise identification of their internal motivations is impossible due to the narrative's reticence. The narrative technique she describes does not call into question the fundamental reliability of the narrative but rather suggests the presence of multiple levels of meaning, that things are not always as they first appear.

Another possible explanation for the narrative's belated introduction of Doeg is the immediately preceding reference (21:6) to the holy bread as being "removed from the presence of the Lord" (*leḥem happānîm hammûsārîm millipnê yhwh*). Although the geography of the scene remains sketchy, Doeg is also said to be "detained before the Lord" (*ne'ṣār lipnê yhwh*, 21:7). As we have seen, the phrase "before the Lord" can refer metaphorically to the altar area of a temple or its inner precinct.[11] It is therefore possible that the first part of the conversation between David and Ahimelech takes place outside of the inner temple precinct, and that only once they enter the temple to retrieve the holy

---

7. E.g., Campbell, *1 Samuel*, p. 226; McCarter, *I Samuel*, pp. 350-51.

8. Bergen, *1, 2 Samuel*, p. 221; Fokkelman, *Narrative Art and Poetry in the Books of Samuel: Vol. 3*, p. 355; cf. Polzin, *Samuel and the Deuteronomist*, pp. 194-95.

9. For further discussion, see Lozovyy, *Saul, Doeg, Nabal, and the "Son of Jesse"*, pp. 22-32.

10. Reis, "Collusion at Nob." Reis's reading is now also supported by Bodner, *David Observed*, pp. 25-37. Bodner emphasizes the literary device of what he terms "flashback" or "delayed exposition" in this narrative.

11. See further Reindl, *Angesicht Gottes*, pp. 24-32; cf. Fowler, "Meaning of *lipnê YHWH*." Fowler overstresses somewhat the presence of the ark when this expression is employed (as is evident, for example, in 1 Sam 23:6-12).

bread are they observed and heard by Ahimelech. After all, Ahimelech does not report the substance of the earlier part of their conversation to Saul, only that Ahimelech inquired of God on David's behalf and gave him food and a weapon (22:9-10). On this reading the structure of the narrative would in fact mirror the perception(s) of the characters themselves, a recognized feature of biblical narrative.[12]

Interestingly, the narrative in 1 Samuel 21 does not explicitly describe Ahimelech as "inquiring" of God on David's behalf, yet that action is later alleged by Doeg to have happened (22:10) and admitted by Ahimelech (22:15). So this aspect of the story, too, only becomes apparent from the retrospective information provided by 1 Samuel 22. The fact that it concerns divination, Saul's characteristic deficiency, is no accident. Just as previous chapters have raised questions about David's character in contrast to Saul's, 1 Samuel 21 seeks to do the same by withholding information about David's thoughts and motivations. At first it appears that David has not sought to inquire of the Lord through Ahimelech since that action is not mentioned in the narrative. But 1 Samuel 22 indicates that it did happen. Similarly, David might seem at first to be much like Saul in the way that he appropriates holy bread for a pragmatic, military purpose. However, David's manner of appropriation is distinct: rather than simply taking the bread by force, David asks for it.[13] Not only that, but when the priest concedes that the bread might be eaten by David's men if they are ritually clean (21:4), David responds with the surprising information that his men keep ritually clean on every trip they take, no matter how routine (21:5).[14] This religious conception of military action contrasts strongly with Saul's reduction of military success to physical strength and brute force. Although the outcome might be viewed as similar (i.e., David puts to personal use and advantage something intended for divine worship), David's words register the possibility of a qualitative difference.

This contrast is then reinforced by the matter of Goliath's sword. Once again what might seem like the same sort of link between worship and weaponry that Saul would make proves distinctive on closer inspection.[15] David

---

12. On "subjective plotting," see Bar-Efrat, *Narrative Art in the Bible*, pp. 117-19; Berlin, *Poetics and Interpretation of Biblical Narrative*, pp. 43-82.

13. It also interesting to note that the provision of food to God's elect is an important motif in the book of Deuteronomy; see MacDonald, *Not Bread Alone*, pp. 88-96; idem, *What Did the Ancient Israelites Eat?*, pp. 100-101.

14. See further Carmichael, "David at the Nob Sanctuary."

15. Short, *Surprising Election*, pp. 81-84, views David's request for a sword as an ironic development, given his earlier disavowal of such weapons (1 Sam 17:45-47). Short also sees irony in David's neglect of the ephod, and he treats David's visit to Nob as a divinatory failure.

does not ask Ahimelech to provide all of his troops with arms. He only asks for a sword or spear for himself. There may be a certain realism reflected in David's request.[16] The narrative has already explained that weapons were rare in Israel generally because of the lack of smiths (1 Sam 13:19-21). Even beyond that difficulty, however, when Ahimelech describes Goliath's sword by saying "there is none here except that one" ('ên 'aḥeret zûlātāh bāzê, 21:10), he indicates that the priestly community at Nob is hardly a military supply center, let alone an armory. In fact, Goliath's sword has been treated as an object with religious significance rather than a weapon. It has been wrapped in a cloth and deposited behind the ephod at the community's worship site (21:10). How the sword arrived in Nob is never explained, but since David apparently took the sword from Goliath (1 Sam 17:50-51, 54), he also must have relinquished it at some point. Yet David makes no claim of ownership in his conversation with Ahimelech; to the contrary it is Ahimelech who makes the prior connection between David and the sword.

So rather than simply a tale of David procuring a weapon, this brief narrative appearance of Goliath's sword depicts Nob as a peaceful priestly community and David as the inheritor of a holy relic. The sword's religious significance is more important to the narrative than its military usefulness. Yet this narrative cannot be viewed as mere folklore either, an ancient Israelite version of the British "sword in the stone" legend.[17] Goliath's sword does not possess supernatural qualities of strength or effectiveness;[18] indeed, except for the passing reference in 1 Sam 22:10, the sword never appears in the Samuel narrative again. The point is rather that David continues to pursue a combination of strength *and* holiness, seeking strength *in* holiness, an impulse also found in Jonathan (1 Sam 14) but utterly lacking in Saul.[19]

The narrative presents this aspect of David's character indirectly, through hints and inferences, and that presentational strategy in turn heightens suspense by preserving a fundamental sense of mystery about David. Who is he

16. Indeed, Samuel A. Meier interprets this request as a mark of David's unfaith; see his "Sword," pp. 160-61.

17. See Geoffrey of Monmouth, *History of the Kings of Britain*. For further discussion, see Jankulak, *Geoffrey of Monmouth*.

18. On heroes and their weapons, see Miller, *Epic Hero*, pp. 206-14. Later epics often feature heroes with named swords; Goliath's sword lacks any such designation.

19. Peterson, *Leap Over a Wall*, p. 67, describes Saul's mentality colloquially, but with devastating effect: "By now, King Saul's ideas of God and religion were thoroughly twisted and completely self-serving. The task of priests wasn't to help fugitives, but to protect kings. Sanctuaries weren't places for hungry and hunted men and women to get help but wayside historical shrines for preserving the memory of God and the traditions of the country. But such religion isn't religion at all, but a form of power politics."

really? What does he want? Since these questions are always posed against the background of Saul and his rejection, they represent another way of asking whether, and if so how, David is different from Saul and therefore possibly in greater conformity with God's intentions for the monarchy. In David's flight from Saul, which will continue through the end of 1 Samuel, his difference from Saul is staged geographically as well as personally. For his part Saul's efforts to capture David are in a sense also efforts to locate something in himself that he knows he lacks. Saul is the pursuer, David the pursued. Despite his own name, Saul is the seeker and David the "sought one." These characteristic stances in the second part of the book reinforce the basic relation of the two figures toward the monarchy itself. Saul, although he realizes himself to be rejected by God, holds on to the kingship by force. David, although he knows himself to be anointed by God, forgoes any effort to place himself on the throne, instead setting himself and his future in God's hands.

After David flees from Nob, he travels to the Philistine town of Gath (21:11). His reputation has preceded him. On his arrival the members of King Achish's court remind the king of the same proverbial chorus that ate away at Saul earlier: "Saul has killed his thousands but David his ten thousands" (21:12; cf. 1 Sam 18:7-8). Now for the first time the reader is given explicit internal information about David's own state of mind: David is said to fear that the knowledge of this chorus in Gath may lead Achish and the others to harm him. However, David's next course of action is completely unexpected: he pretends to be mad by scratching[20] or drumming[21] on the town's gates and drooling (21:14). The ruse works. Achish is convinced that David is insane and determines to have nothing to do with him (21:15-16). For David the king's decision is a reprieve, allowing him to leave Gath and hide at Adullam (22:1).

It is difficult to know what is more worrisome about David's pretense of insanity: that he pursues a plan of deception or that he is so good at it. By also disclosing that David is afraid, the narrative has finally provided some information about David's interior emotional life. But then by depicting him as skilled in deception, the narrative creates new doubts about David's sincerity and righteousness. How can the reader trust a character who is depicted as quite clever at fooling people? Even though one can celebrate David's cleverness, justify his commitment to self-preservation, and chuckle over another

20. Reading the Qere *wytyw* from √*twh* (Piel), "to make or set a mark" (cf. Ezek 9:4 Hiph.).

21. Following the LXX by amending the Ketiv *wytw* to *wytp* from √*tpp* "to beat" (cf. Ps 68:26). Given the context, I am also inclined to consider an emended *wytp* from √*twp* "to spit" (cf. Job 17:6). See McCarter, *I Samuel*, p. 355.

instance of dim-witted Philistines, David's acting ability nevertheless conveys an unsettling slipperiness. Do not those skilled in acting tend to use that skill habitually?

On the other hand, by only *pretending* to be mad David further differentiates himself from Saul, who has previously appeared, on occasion, actually to be mad. So Saul goes mad in phases, while David merely dissembles. From this perspective David can ironically be seen to possess a quality of self-control or judgment (*ṭaʿam*, 21:14) that Saul sorely lacks. His pretending to be mad therefore emphasizes just how sane he is. The absence of adequate spiritual grounding within Saul's character leaves him peculiarly sensitive to any kind of external religious authority or event, like a ship without a rudder. Not a particularly devout person, Saul nonetheless raves with the best of them when exposed to others engaged in prophecy. David, by contrast, does increasingly appear to possess real spiritual depth — although the reader still awaits full confirmation of that suspicion — and this depth seems to enable David to remain himself even when he modulates his external behavior. Saul goes mad; David pretends to be mad. In this way, then, by pretending to be mad David is also in effect pretending to be like Saul. Could David's ability to act insane be particularly convincing because he has had so many opportunities to observe madness firsthand, playing his soothing lyre before his dangerously unhinged king?

In Adullam, David is joined not only by members of his extended family but by everyone in difficulty (*kol-ʾîš māṣôq*), everyone in debt (*kol-ʾîš ʾăšer-lô nōšeʾ*), and everyone embittered (*kol-ʾîš mar-nepeš*, 22:2). This narrative development shows how a sense of crisis is widening in Israel, and how David is becoming a focal point for the hopes of the people. Noteworthy, too, is that the disadvantaged are drawn to David, and that he does not refuse them. Whereas Saul picks out the strong (1 Sam 14:52), David is chosen by the weak. David also displays an openness to national alliances and diplomacy, in contrast to Saul's predisposition toward battle. David leaves his parents in Moab for their protection "until I know what God will do for me" (22:3). Here David's brief words again suggest a surprisingly theocentric perspective. However, he not only expresses such a sentiment, he also obeys the prophetically communicated divine word, as shown by his adherence to the instructions of the prophet Gad (22:5). In essence, what begins to emerge in this brief episode in Adullam is the theological and social profile of David's eventual kingship, a kingship of divinely authorized, compassionate rule, in which the poor are given assistance, parents are cared for, nations live in peaceful interaction, and kings submit to prophets.

No greater contrast could exist between this snapshot of David's royal qualities and the following portrait of Saul. Saul sits enthroned at Gibeah, with his servants waiting upon him (22:6). Already, in retrospect, David's camp looks much more dynamic and egalitarian. Saul's camp represents a court organized by hierarchy, privilege, and coercion. Saul fears — perhaps wrongly, perhaps rightly — that his own men are sympathetic to David, who may have conspired to give them lands (22:7). Saul's increasing sense of isolation is palpable. The first-person pronoun is prominent in his words (22:8). He unfairly berates his men for neglecting to inform him of Jonathan's covenant with David (he already knew about it, according to 1 Sam 20:30-31). Paranoia and tyranny are conspicuous here as two sides of one and the same coin.

It gets worse. Hearing Doeg's report from Nob, Saul summons Ahimelech and all the priests of Nob for an explanation (22:11). Ahimelech defends David (as well as himself by association) for being "faithful" (*ne'ĕmān*, 22:14) to Saul. This term echoes all the way back to the "faithful priest" (*kōhēn ne'ĕmān*) prophesied by the anonymous man of God in 1 Sam 2:35. Ahimelech does not dispute having done what is charged against him, but he denies his acts constitute disloyalty to the king. He also claims to have known nothing about the treasonous intentions of David that Saul alleges (22:13). The inclusion of a charge of "inquiring" suggests a degree of irony because of the linguistic similarity between the term used here for that action (*liš'āl-lô bē'lōhîm* Qere) and Saul's own name. Saul, by virtue of his name, might be expected to possess a particular inclination towards divination, but he is instead conspicuous for his divinatory failures (e.g., 1 Sam 14:37). David, as he makes plans and seeks to preserve his own life, engages in successful divinatory practices because he seeks at the same time God's guidance for his choices and decisions.

And then Saul slays the priests of Nob. The horror of this turn of events is mirrored in the refusal of his own men to raise their hands against "the priests of the Lord" (22:17). Indeed, Saul commits the entire population of Nob to total destruction (22:19), the very thing that he had refused to do with the Amalekites in 1 Samuel 15 (and thus the presenting cause for his rejection)[22] — but the citizens of Nob are fellow Israelites! Even more, in Saul's killing of *priests* there is also a perpetuation of Saul's war *on* religion, his distance from and disregard for those who stand in the kind of proximity to God that he has been denied. No act on Saul's part exhibits to a greater extent the depths to which he has sunk in his obsolescence, despair, and godforsakenness — nor does any

---

22. The scope of 1 Sam 22:19 ("men and women, babes and infants, oxen and asses, and sheep") is very similar to that of 1 Sam 15:3 ("men and women, babes and infants, oxen and sheep, camels and asses"). This language serves to emphasize the connection between the two passages for the reader. What Saul will not do to the Amalekites (1 Sam 15:9) he does to his own people. See further Adar, *Biblical Narrative*, p. 240.

act more clearly depict his unfitness for the kingship. By contrast, David takes care of the Lord's priests and guards them with his own life (22:20-23). The sole surviving priest, Abiathar, Ahimelech's son, flees *to* David (lit. "after": *'aḥărê dāwid*, 22:20), so that David continues to live in the company of prophets and priests even as Saul is completely removed from them (e.g., 1 Sam 15:35).

Saul in Pursuit (1 Samuel 23)

The beginning of this chapter reiterates and further emphasizes the developing narrative portrait of David as a spiritual leader who habitually consults the will of God.[23] In response to a Philistine attack on the Israelite town of Keilah, David is again shown to engage in divination. He twice "asks" ($\sqrt{š'l}$) God for counsel on the best course of action and God twice directs David into battle against the Philistines (23:2, 4). Whether or not David employs a divinatory intermediary is unclear. No intermediary is named or described, but then sometimes such accounts are written as if no intermediary is present even when it is apparent from the context that one is (e.g., 1 Sam 14:36-37). This kind of narrative presentation is possible because the intermediary is conceived as being merely instrumental to the human–divine conversation and not himself a partner in the discussion. Moreover, the binary phrasing of David's initial question implies that once more the sacred lots are likely being used as the actual means of divination — and the narrative has already established the precedent that a priest performs the rite of the lots (e.g., 1 Sam 14:19).[24]

On the other hand, many of Israel's priests have just been killed (22:18) and are therefore no longer available for ritual assistance. So perhaps David is here suggested to engage in divination as his own intermediary. The narrative has not placed any explicit limits on the possibility of a king engaging in or directing religious rites personally. At the same time, one would expect some sort of limitation to be in place, if only because of the existence of an official priesthood. Also, in the narrative world of this text there does exist an awareness that religious objects and actions must be handled with care, and

---

23. On historical-critical issues, see Veijola, "David in Keïla."

24. A conflation of the terms "ephod" and "ark" occurs in the divination episodes of 1 Samuel 14, indicating confusion in the tradition about exactly what kind of ritual action took place. Presumably the lots were housed in the "ephod" or the "ark" when they were not being used. What the "ephod" was, or how it may have been connected with the ark, is now unknown. Alter, *David Story*, p. xxvii, argues that the LXX reading of "ephod" is probably correct, since the later Samuel narrative implies that the ark remained in Kiriath-jearim until it was finally moved to Jerusalem under David.

can be dangerous to those who exceed such limitations (e.g., 1 Sam 6:19-20; 2 Sam 6:6-7).

What matters most for the purpose of this study is not what "really" happened, but how David's divination is being depicted. Whether or not it is conventional, the narration of the divinatory exchange between David and God suggests a degree of personal interaction between the two of them that is all the more striking for being absent with Saul. Not only are Saul's efforts at ritual participation routinely interrupted or bungled, he is almost always portrayed as relying upon the spiritual ability of others rather than interacting with God directly. In comparison, David not only appears to speak to God directly but to receive God's replies personally. The successful outcome of his campaign against the Philistines in Keilah confirms David's prophet-like ability to gain insight into God's intentions and plans (23:5). The likelihood that David is depicted as performing the act of divination himself is increased further by the narrative's subsequent report that Abiathar fled to David at Keilah with a priestly ephod (23:6). In other words, only after David had already successfully divined the will of God on his own was he joined by the priest who would have otherwise customarily performed that rite.

When Saul learns of David's presence in Keilah, he thinks to trap David there. At first glance, Saul's words would seem to contradict any distinction between David as a leader who possesses genuine religious faith and Saul as a leader who lacks it. Saul says of David, "God has sold him into my hand, for he is shut in by entering a town with gates and bars" (23:7).[25] Saul's reference to God is unusual for him, but he makes it without hesitation in what initially appears to be a declaration of faith in God's guidance. Yet there are reasons to doubt this interpretation. First of all, the narrative has been unwavering in its description of God's rejection of Saul, which was presented as absolute. There can be no expectation on the part of the reader that God is now helping Saul against David. Second, Saul does not engage in any divination to arrive at this conclusion — in stark contrast to David's insistent seeking of information both before and after Saul's statement about what *he* thinks God is doing.[26] The

---

25. Although the present text gives a reading of something like "God has made him like a foreigner" or "God has alienated him into my hand," this use of the verb (√*nkr* Pi'el) is uncommon and awkward in conjunction with the prepositional phrase. The frequency of the idiom *limkōr bĕyad*, "to sell into the hand" (see Judg 2:14; 3:8; 4:2, 9; 10:7; 1 Sam 12:9) suggests that √*mkr* "sell/sold" may have been the original reading, a suggestion supported by the LXX. "Sell" in this sense has become a technical term for surrendering someone completely into the power of his enemies. Saul's use of this idiom may be part of a narrative effort to depict him as still conceiving of himself in the mold of the judges.

26. For a similar judgment, see McGinnis, "Swimming with the Divine Tide," pp. 263-64.

problematic quality of Saul's receipt of such information is underscored by the reader's realization that Saul is clearly wrong in what he says about God. But might Saul — even if unreasonably — still conceive of himself as enjoying God's favor? That possibility would seem to be the case, since there is no explicit indication in the narrative that Saul is only pretending to claim divine authorization for his new attempt to capture David. David's use of the verb √*ḥrš* (Hiph., "to devise or fabricate") in reference to Saul's plan (23:9) could suggest insincerity on Saul's part — or at least David's belief that Saul was being insincere. But there is still no conclusive reason to discount Saul's reference to God entirely and refuse to credit it as an indication of sincere religious belief.

Instead, the question implied by the narrative is: "belief" in what? Quite strikingly, in the first part of this chapter David refers to God *by name* again and again. He calls on "Yahweh" in his reported speech (*yhwh*, 23:2, 4, 10-11) and the narrator explicitly confirms that "Yahweh" responds to him (*yhwh*, 23:2, 4, 11, 12). The narrative is particular, almost fussy, about it. In 1 Sam 23:7 Saul instead refers to "God" (*'ĕlōhîm*), the generic term, in the third person. Given the interchangeability of these terms for God throughout the Old Testament, it will not do to press a distinction between them too hard. Indeed Saul will use the personal name "Yahweh" later in this same chapter (23:21). But in this specific narrative context a distinction does seem to exist, even to be at the forefront of the narrative's intention, given the way in which Saul's generic reference to God is presently sandwiched between two accounts of David's references to "Yahweh" (or "the Lord," since many modern translations regularly substitute this title as a sign of respect for the divine name). So if this distinction is real, what is its narrative purpose?

Perhaps the idea is that Saul's notion of God is similarly generic, although sincere. This kind of distinction is fairly sophisticated, and some are sure to dispute the likelihood of its existence in the ancient world. Yet this interpretation fits together seamlessly with the view of Saul that has emerged in this study already. At the heart of the narrative's characterization of Saul is not the idea that he is devoid of religion or entirely lacking in faith, but rather that he mistakes the performance of ritual for genuine conviction, for a sense of individual trust in God, who possesses personal qualities for the true believer. The deuteronomists, who presumably edited this narrative and determined its basic literary shape, typically refer to this kind of religious faith with the language of the "heart" and view it as the central aim of their religious reform. For the deuteronomists, Saul is the abiding example of someone who lacks "heart" religion, and of what happens to Israel when someone without vital faith becomes its ruler. So when Saul says "God" here, he does not name God precisely or properly as far as the deuteronomistic editors are concerned. He names instead a ritual inference, a god of what could be termed — with a degree of admitted anachronism — "civil religion," a nationalistic program seeking to profit from a symbolic association with the divine.[27]

Saul's reference to "God," in other words, is the kind of reference to an institutional and traditional "God" that continues to find its place in contemporary U.S. society on the lips of politicians, on money, in court, and as part of a "pledge of allegiance" to the nation's flag.[28] Those who refer to "God" in this way today are also usually sincere in their belief that they are identifying God accurately, even if only imprecisely or partially or generically. But the deuteronomists' radical response is in effect to insist that to name God generically is not to *name* God at all.[29] In this way Saul's apparent declaration of faith in God is ironically revealed to be an indication that he lacks genuine faith, the kind of faith that David exemplifies.

Once again, however, the narrative refuses to demonize Saul for this deficiency. Saul is treated as if he is sincere in his generic belief in God and not an outright mocker or complete unbeliever. His sincerity is ultimately inadequate, but it creates sympathy for his character on the part of the reader. Is it Saul's fault that he does not move from generic belief to an active, trusting apprehension of God as a dynamic personal agent? This question identifies the ultimate mystery about which the events of this narrative swirl. David has not had to work to gain his accurate perception of God; he has just always had it. No matter what Saul has done, or tried to do, he has been unable to move beyond the limitations of the conventional religious belief that he continues to hold and embody. In the comparison between the two figures therefore lies an assumption, or hunch, that genuine faith includes a quality of giftedness. Saul cannot be blamed for his lack of a deeper faith because, given his nature, he cannot achieve it. On the other hand, however, the giftedness of faith does not remove all responsibility from nominal believers either. They are held accountable to the higher standard of active faith. There are those who can, by dint of effort, maintain and even increase their ability to meet that standard of piety — even as there are also those who cannot. And the

---

27. According to John Henry Newman, "Saul," in his *Parochial and Plain Sermons*, 3:39, Saul's attitude suggests how for him "the established religion was but a useful institution, or a splendid pageant suitable to the dignity of monarchy, but resting on no unseen supernatural sanction."

28. See further Ellis, *To the Flag*; Minear, *I Pledge Allegiance*.

29. Of course, deuteronomistic tradition also uses 'ĕlōhîm (e.g., Deut 4:28, 33; 5:26; 9:10; 21:23; 29:25; 32:17), so this term cannot be said to be used negatively or pejoratively either. For a full treatment of Deuteronomy's views about God, see MacDonald, *Deuteronomy and the Meaning of "Monotheism"*.

precise combination of giftedness and effort that together characterize a truly dynamic and vital faith? This question is the one that the narrative does not yet answer. So far it only acknowledges the boundaries within which such a question must be framed.

After again inquiring of God in response to Saul's threat (23:9-12), David and his men leave Keilah before Saul can maneuver against them. As David hides out in the Judean wilderness, the narrative makes it explicit that "God [*ʼĕlōhîm*] did not give him into his [Saul's] hand" (23:14), thereby also refuting Saul's characterization of God's intention. To the contrary, Saul experiences continuing difficulty in finding David wherever David goes. Saul always seems to discover David's whereabouts too late to move against him successfully. Others who exhibit a greater awareness of God do not have this same problem. Jonathan visits David in Horesh and "strengthens his hand in God" (*wayḥazzēq ʼet-yādô bēʼlōhîm*, 23:16), which further heightens the contrast between the faith of David and Jonathan, on the one side, and Saul, on the other. Jonathan confirms for the reader David's intensifying ascendancy to the kingship, and he and David make a further covenant with each other "before the Lord" (*lipnê yhwh*, 23:18).

When Saul now does use the personal name of God in order to bless the Ziphites, who have come to him with information about David's location, the alert reader is rightly skeptical. And, in fact, although Saul uses the word "Yahweh," the substance of his statement could hardly be more formulaic or perfunctory: "May you all be blessed by Yahweh because of the compassion you are showing me!" (23:21). The reference to Yahweh is still in the third person and occurs in the context of a ritual blessing. The focus of Saul's concern is himself and his fortunes. "Yahweh" figures in as a symbolic guarantor of blessing, but not as a dynamic agent who insists on the righteousness of his followers and determines the future in advance. Saul's instructions to the Ziphites in no way arise from information Saul has sought and received from God. He devises his own stratagems. There is much irony, then, in Saul's description of David as "exceedingly crafty" (*ʻārôm yaʻrim hû*, 23:22), for David's craftiness is finally not entirely his own but ultimately comes from God, while Saul's empty allusions to God only thinly disguise what are solely his personal attempts to outwit David.

The result is again rendered geographically, in almost comedic fashion. As if it were a scene from an old "Keystone Cops" silent film,[30] Saul vainly pursues David along one side of a hill near Maon while David and his men escape along the same hill's other slope (23:26). Then, despite a further effort

30. See further Lott, *Police on Screen.*

to capture David, Saul is forced to interrupt his pursuit in order to respond to another Philistine incursion (23:28). When Saul returns, however, the pursuer will briefly become the pursued.

The First Encounter (1 Samuel 24)

David now moves to the wilderness of En-gedi, where Saul on his return continues to search for him.[31] In another combination of low comedy and high coincidence, Saul decides to "relieve himself" (literally: to "cover his feet") in the very same cave in which David and his men are hiding from him (24:4).[32] "Caves" (*mĕʿārôt*) have played a prominent role in the narrative for some time already, beginning with their introduction as a place in which Israelites sought safety from the Philistines (1 Sam 13:6) and continuing with the mention of the "cave" of Adullam (22:1; cf. 2 Sam 23:13), which was simultaneously described as a "fortress" or "keep" (*mĕṣûdâ*, 22:4-5). Even beyond this realistic acknowledgment of the geographic setting — the Judean wilderness is riddled with caves located high on steep canyon walls[33] — the idea of a cave connotes darkness, sensory deprivation and mental confusion. What better location for a drama about the reliability of perception?

As exemplified in E. M. Forster's *A Passage to India*, the darkness of a cave also creates the conditions for socially transgressive interpersonal interactions by stripping away the conventions of the sunshine world.[34] In 1 Samuel 24 the cave location finally makes possible a meeting between Saul and David, an act that therefore has the potential to lead to a resolution of the intractable

31. For historically oriented reflection on the literary unity of this chapter, see Conrad, "Unschuld des Tollkühnen"; Stein, "Und man berichtete Saul." In most English translations, 23:29 is verse 24:1 of the Hebrew text. The difference in versification carries through the rest of the chapter. I give the Hebrew verse numbers here; for the English verse numbers, subtract one.

32. Weiss, *Figurative Language in Biblical Prose Narrative*, pp. 194-95, treats this expression as a euphemism in which "penis" is replaced by "foot" or "leg" and the substitution is acknowledged through the use of "cover" to mean its opposite ("uncover"). In contrast to interpreters who have taken the expression more literally as a reference to the lowering of a cloak for the purpose of defecation, Weiss agrees with Bar-Efrat that at such times the cloak would have been raised rather than lowered.

33. See "Judean Desert" and "Judean Desert Caves," in Negev and Gibson, eds., *Archaeological Encyclopedia of the Holy Land*, pp. 273-75.

34. "Caves" is the heading for the entire second section of Forster's novel; the pivotal scene with Miss Quested (note the heavy symbolism of the name) occurs in one of the caves in the Marabar Hills. See further Moran, "E. M. Forster's *A Passage to India*"; cf. Allen, "Structure, Symbol, and Theme in E. M. Forster's *A Passage to India*."

drama in which they have found themselves. However, the issue at stake for this chapter, and for the next two chapters to follow, is just what *kind* of resolution needs to occur.

David's men assume from the outset that such a resolution requires blood. They remind him that God has authorized him to defeat his "enemy" (24:5), but the oracle they cite has never actually been narrated by the text, not explicitly at least. In the present context David's men appear to be extending the sense of the oracles in 1 Samuel 23, which encouraged David toward defensive action with respect to Saul, but not to bloodshed (1 Sam 23:10-12). And is Saul truly David's "enemy" (*'ōyēb*), as David's men suppose? David himself has never used such language of Saul, nor has God — although Saul has used it of David (e.g., 19:17).[35] Thus this initial characterization of Saul by the men, and their suggested course of action, is effectively posed as a question for the reader as well as for David.

David's differing appraisal is immediately evident from his own action, which consists of furtively cutting off the "corner" of Saul's cloak (*kĕnap-hammĕ'îl*) in the dark (24:5). Yet even this substitute for violence is too much for him. "His heart strikes him" (*wayyak lēb-dāwid 'ōtô*, 24:6), the narrator reports, after which he forbids his men from any "hand-stretching" (*lišlōaḥ yād*) against "the Lord's anointed" (*mĕšîaḥ yhwh*). Once again the inclusion of information about David's internal emotional life is all the more significant because such information has been rare in the narrative. The full connotations of this designation, "the Lord's anointed," are never explained, but David clearly understands it to rule out all violence and thus preclude taking the throne by force. In articulating this commitment he "rips into" (√*šs'* Piel) his men (and the reader) for possibly thinking otherwise (24:8). The violence of David's objection both confirms his sense of the seriousness of a violent act against Saul and at the same time suggests the fragility of his own commitment to non-violence at this particular moment.

Yet David now bravely seeks reconciliation. Following after Saul, who has left the cave, David calls out to him and reveals the forbearance he has demonstrated, using the evidence of the piece of cloak in order to prove his goodwill (24:9-16). The choice of Saul's cloak is hardly accidental, since this garment has already been associated in the narrative with Saul's rejection and his loss of the kingship (*kĕnap-mĕ'îl*, 1 Sam 15:27-28). David's subsequent speech is noteworthy for its deference to Saul, whom he loyally designates as "king" (*melek*), and for his rhetorical effort to persuade Saul that he has been the recipient of bad advice. The narrative has in fact emphasized precisely the contrary, that

---

35. The narrator has also used this term to describe Saul's view of David (1 Sam 18:29).

Saul has single-mindedly waged a personal campaign against David, even as his retainers have been unwilling to take action (e.g., 1 Sam 22:8). When David says, "I have never wronged you" (*lō'-ḥāṭā'tî lāk*, 24:12), the narrative up to this point bears him out and supports the justice of his allegation that Saul is in the wrong for trying to kill him. From the very beginning of David's interactions with Saul, he has never once responded to Saul with violence or with "treason" (*pešaʿ*). David also appeals to Yahweh to confirm his righteousness (24:13, 16), he signals his awareness that an act of bloodshed would return upon his own head by alluding to proverbial wisdom (24:14), and he minimizes his own importance by referring to himself as the equivalent of a dead dog or flea (24:15).[36]

The speech is a virtuoso rhetorical performance. In making it, David comes off as slick but still sincere. He also appears to underestimate Saul's desire to see him dead, and the degree to which his appeal to Yahweh might serve to rub salt in the wound of Saul's rejection rather than to persuade him to be reconciled. The deep irony — unspoken by David — is of course that he, too, is "the Lord's anointed," something that Saul may know or suspect (cf. 1 Sam 19:22), but the narrative has never been explicit about that. In fact, much of the suspense found in the latter part of 1 Samuel arises from the dramatic irony of the reader's sure knowledge of David's anointing — in contrast to Saul, who seems to suspect more than he knows for certain.

Hearing David's words, Saul "wails" (*wayyiśśā' qōlô*) and weeps (√*bkh*, 24:17). Are these crocodile tears? Most likely not. The report of Saul's tears comes from the narrator, who is persistently reliable in this narrative.[37] Saul's apparent difficulty in recognizing David ("Is that your voice, my son David?") signals instead his continuing instability of mood and perception (cf. 1 Sam 17:58). Although he now refers to "Yahweh," this deity is still merely a cosmic inference for the events in his life, not a source of independent information or personal guidance. The scene is portrayed as a moment of temporary clarity for Saul, who remains impressively capable of kingly dignity and breadth of spirit, as well as self-critique. Saul now acknowledges that David will one day become king (24:21), and he asks David only for a pledge that he will not seek to kill Saul's descendants and thereby obliterate Saul's name (24:22). David swears to this condition, further demonstrating his loyalty, but the reader already knows that such an outcome will ultimately be impossible (cf. 1 Sam 13:14).

36. As noted by Weiss, *Figurative Language in Biblical Prose Narrative*, pp. 201-2, the dog metaphor echoes the dog reference in Goliath's speech (1 Sam 17:43) and points ahead to later challenges to David's just rule (2 Sam 9:8; 16:9). On the further nuances of both animal metaphors, see Riede, "David und der Floh."

37. On the biblical narrator as reliable, see also Walsh, *Old Testament Narrative*, pp. 82-83, 98-99. On the biblical narrator more broadly, see Bar-Efrat, *Narrative Art in the Bible*.

The most important feature of this chapter is its revelation of David's internal character, which has previously been mostly unavailable to the reader. David genuinely seems loyal to Saul, in spite of everything, and committed to placing the resolution of the urgently needed "regime change" into God's hands rather than taking it upon himself to effect. In short, this chapter functions as a major check against an interpretation of David as being exclusively or primarily self-promoting, an interpretation that the narrative has strategically allowed to develop by its reticence in describing David's interior life as a character. Now the narrative reveals even further that David is more like Jonathan than Saul, although David remains righteous and loyal to Saul, and thereby righteous and loyal before God. David puts his cleverness to work on behalf of his faith, not his faith on behalf of his cleverness.

However, even David's sly piety has its blind spots. As his reaction to his men has already demonstrated (24:8), David has a temper. Can his commitment to non-violence concerning Saul really last, especially considering the likelihood that Saul's mood may again modulate, as it has done previously? The genuine danger of bloodshed against the Lord's anointed has now at last been confronted head on, and its seriousness underscored, but its danger has not yet been fully averted.

Abigail (1 Samuel 25)

This lengthy chapter contains an artful narrative[38] taking the literary form of a "story within a story," a familiar technique in the Old Testament (e.g., Gen 38; 1 Sam 4–6). Such stories were once routinely viewed as later additions to the wider narratives in which they are now found because they appeared to depart substantially from the main plot line. However, they have increasingly become recognized as a literary device used to establish another angle of vision on the main plot, with which they have more connections than it initially seems. Exactly that revised judgment has also been applied to 1 Samuel 25, with illuminating results.[39]

The name Nabal means "fool" in Hebrew and alerts the reader right away to the presence of an unusual feature in Biblical Hebrew narrative: allegory.[40] The name's symbolic meaning is reported explicitly in the text (25:25).

38. See, for example, Biddle, "Ancestral Motifs in 1 Samuel 25"; Garsiel, "Wit, Words, and a Woman"; van Wolde, "Leader Led by a Lady."

39. E.g., Green, "Enacting Imaginatively the Unthinkable"; Levenson, "1 Samuel 25 as Literature and History"; Polzin, *Samuel and the Deuteronomist*, pp. 210-12.

40. For objections to this approach, see Barr, "Symbolism of Names." In my view, the

Ordinarily, the glory of Hebrew narrative lies in its astonishing three-dimensional characterizations, in which persons are hardly ever all good or all bad but thoroughly realistic composites.[41] It is highly exceptional to find characters that are all good (e.g., Joshua)[42] or all bad (e.g., Nabal). Even more unusual is the symbolic identification between a particular character and a representative virtue or vice (e.g., foolishness). Not only does the presence here of such an identification provide a presumptive interpretative direction for the narrative at its outset (i.e., Nabal will likely remain "foolish"), it indicates a level of oblique commentary directed back toward the main plot (i.e., what other forms does "foolishness" take in the ongoing story of Saul and David?).

The brief notice concerning Samuel's death (25:1) is not incidental, but establishes the larger context for the story to follow: the absence of prophetic guidance for Israel and David.[43] The introductory section of the story presents Nabal as a wealthy, "hard" (*qāšê*) man, "harmful in (his) deeds" (*ra' ma'ălālîm*), with a beautiful wife of "good insight" (*ṭôbat-śekel*) named Abigail (25:2-3).[44] As Nabal and his men are shearing sheep in Carmel, David approaches them for provisions. Nabal owns thousands of sheep and goats (25:2), but he rudely rejects David's request, inciting David to respond militarily against him (25:13). Here Nabal's offense is not only his insolence but his attribution of rebellion to David ("Today slaves multiply, each one breaking away from his master," 25:10). At the core of Nabal's foolishness is his inability to see David for who he really is. David's exact reasons for approaching him armed and ready for battle are not provided, so that the reader also has to make a choice. Whose response is more appropriate, Nabal's or Abigail's?

Abigail fears the worst. Learning from one of Nabal's men that he had unjustly and insultingly "shrieked" at David's men (√'yṭ, 25:14),[45] Abigail takes matters into her own hands in order to avert bloodshed.[46] She prepares provisions for David and his troops, places the provisions on asses, and sets out to

---

symbolic valence of Nabal's name is clearly indicated by Abigail's reference to that valence in v. 25 of this chapter.

41. Alter, *Art of Biblical Narrative*, pp. 143-62.

42. On Joshua's characterization as a leader without flaws or errors, see Chapman, "Joshua Son of Nun." For different point of view, see Spina, "Moses and Joshua."

43. Fischer, "Abigajil."

44. Note the linguistic link between Abigail's "insight" (√śkl) and David's earlier canny "success" (√śkl Hiph., 1 Sam 18:5).

45. The related noun *'ayiṭ* refers to a bird of prey, which presumably makes a similar sound.

46. As Barth observes, Abigail is presented from the beginning as the "wise" counterpart to her husband's foolishness. See Barth, *Church Dogmatics IV*, p. 427. Nonetheless, Abigail is much more than a "type"; on this point, see Bach, "Pleasure of Her Text."

encounter these men herself.[47] Immediately prior to the meeting, the narrative does provide some insight into David's state of mind. From his perspective he was helping to *protect* Nabal and his possessions — something already confirmed by the young man who reports to Abigail (25:15-16) — but, just as Nabal was reputed to do in his narrative introduction, he has "returned harm (*rā'â*) for good (*ṭôbâ*)" (25:21). The allusion to Saul is difficult to miss.[48] Like Nabal, Saul had earlier returned David's "goodness" (*haṭṭôbâ*) with "harm" (*hārā'â*, 24:18). The problem with such a response is not merely the ingratitude it displays but the offense it represents against God's established order, which mandates a framework of justice in which goodness is to be returned for goodness and harm for harm (25:22).

This sense of retributive justice was also a crucial component of David's argument to Saul in the last chapter (24:12-16). It is important to recognize that David is not simply being overly sensitive in his response to Nabal, that in fact he sees himself as defending *God's* righteousness — even at the same time that one takes account of his intemperance. Is it going too far to see a relationship between David's present vow (25:22) to kill every "one who pisses against a wall" (*maštîn bĕqîr*, an earthy Hebrew circumlocution for "male")[49] and his previous decision not to kill Saul while Saul relieved himself in the cave in En-gedi (24:4)? The difficulty emerging is that the righteous logic of David's response to Nabal calls into question David's own prior actions with respect to Saul and undermines David's decision to *refrain* from violence then. From the perspective of the narrative, David is not wrong to move against Nabal but right. By the same token, however, should not David have upheld God's righteousness by attacking Saul?

Abigail's subsequent speech to David proves crucial, not only in defusing the narrative situation at hand but in responding to this deeper question about the logic of retribution and David's responsibility for the maintenance of God's righteousness. First Abigail calls renewed attention to Nabal's name and its meaning (25:25); this remark on her part is a clear confirmation of the symbolic dimension to his characterization within the narrative. Then Abigail reminds David that God has thus far kept him from shedding blood by ensuring his opponents' misfortune. Her vow that David's "enemies and those who seek my lord's harm" should have the same fate as Nabal (25:26) makes the connection between Nabal and Saul explicit. Yet if David truly

---

47. See further Shields, "Feast Fit for a King."

48. Some translations obscure the verbal echoes; on the Saul–Nabal relation, see Gordon, "David's Rise and Saul's Demise."

49. Is this phrase also more than a euphemism? Smith, "Pisser against a Wall," argues that it preserves a cultural memory of an ancient Near Eastern divinatory rite involving urine.

wants to uphold God's righteousness, Abigail argues, he must not put himself in the wrong by exacting retribution on his own (25:28). God will give David a lasting dynasty so long as David trusts God to act against those who threaten him (25:29).[50] Abigail playfully describes God as targeting the lives of David's enemies as if with a "sling," thus recalling David's victory against Goliath while at the same time reminding David that God has always been the true agent of David's defense. Not only would it weaken David's later reign to have the pall of prior bloodshed hanging over his head, it would be just as much of a stumbling block for David to think that he could save himself (*lĕhôšîaʿ ʾădōnî lô*, 25:31). David can fight "the battles of the Lord" (*milḥămôt yhwh*, 25:28) most effectively by trusting God to fight his battles for him.[51]

This speech brilliantly connects with the themes of warfare and worship from earlier in 1 Samuel at the same time that it counteracts the temptation for David to compromise his theocentric outlook. As David gains power and moves closer to the throne, can he continue to maintain the trust in God that was so evident in his early encounter with Goliath? It says much about David that he immediately recognizes the truth of Abigail's words and straightaway adjusts his course of action (25:32-36).[52] Left to God's vengeance, and *not* David's, Nabal is struck down and dies (25:37-38).[53] David understands this outcome to be the result of God's defense, not only of David but of the

---

50. On the metaphorical complexity of Abigail's speech, see further Weiss, *Figurative Language in Biblical Prose Narrative*, pp. 58-72.

51. Peterson, *Leap Over a Wall*, p. 84, paraphrases Abigail's speech to David quite effectively: "Please, please don't do this. This isn't an action worthy of a prince of Israel. Remember who you are. Remember God's anointing, God's mercy. Don't stoop to fighting grudge battles; your task is to fight the battles of the Lord."

52. As Fischer, "Abigajil," has argued, Abigail's words to David demonstrate not only her tact and skill in diplomacy but her prophetic gift of wisdom. Yet what is most striking — precisely because of the reticence on this point in the chapter so far — is Abigail's remarkable insight into David's true identity and purpose. Karl Barth, *Church Dogmatics IV*, p. 429: "The point is that the name David means something to her. She knows and solemnly declares who he is and will be. Since the wordless anointing of David by Samuel in 1 Sam 16:1-8 — and it is not for nothing that the death of Samuel is reported at the beginning of this chapter — it has not been reported that anyone has said anything to this effect either of or to David . . . Everything else depends on, and has its meaning and power in the fact that Abigail knows and has to say this of David, and therefore of the will and promise, the secret of the covenant, of the God of Israel." One might well then compare Abigail to the New Testament figure of Peter, who first among the disciples penetrates Jesus' "messianic secret."

53. Weiss, *Figurative Language in Biblical Prose Narrative*, pp. 74-76, offers an interesting treatment of the phrase that is usually translated "he became like a stone" but literally reads "he became a stone." It may be that what is being described is something like catatonic shock, which would mean in turn that the report of Nabal's death ten days later is not simple redundancy.

established order of retribution built into the very fabric of creation (25:39). Abigail now becomes David's second wife, in addition to Ahinoam (25:39-43). Here the narrative mentions that Saul had taken Michal from David and given her to another man named Palti (25:44). This brief comment at the end of the chapter not only provides a transition back to the main narrative thread about to resume at the beginning of 1 Samuel 26, it also underscores how Saul has not really corrected his injustices to David.

The tale of Abigail and Nabal has everything to do with the larger story of David and Saul. By disclosing how the issue of bloodshed is a test of faith in God, perhaps even the ultimate test of faith, the narrative recalls and deepens the theological perspective of the book — according to which true faith is personal trust in God rather than an effort to control or manipulate God, even when that effort is made with good intentions (cf. 1 Sam 2:1-10). Whether in the form of ritual or retribution, not in themselves bad things in the world of this narrative, people of faith can come to think of themselves as substituting for God. But the God of this narrative will have no substitutions. Not even those delegated to positions of leadership within the community may exceed the limitations basic to the qualitative difference between God and humankind (1 Sam 15:29). In fact, the fundamental challenge to be faced in the establishment of a monarchy in Israel is precisely how to allow for such an exalted office without having the king think that such limitations no longer apply to him. Saul never seems to have known faith as *trust* in the first place; David certainly has known such trust, but he also exhibits in this chapter how, even so, he can jeopardize that attitude of faith in his zeal and the heat of the moment.

Abigail's lesson to David proves crucial for the next chapter as well, when David will be even more severely tempted to use violence against Saul.

The Second Encounter (1 Samuel 26)

Saul now attempts to locate David in the wilderness again. His previous reconciliation with David (1 Sam 24:17-22) appears to have made no lasting difference to Saul's prior intention to kill him. A second time, David stealthily creeps up on Saul — on this occasion in his camp while Saul and his men are asleep. In classic historical-critical approaches to Samuel, this chapter was often viewed as a "doublet" of 1 Samuel 24, the assumption being that both were later literary elaborations of what had originally been a single tale, probably in oral form.[54] Such a speculation could be accurate; both chapters possess a

54. See, e.g., Koch, "Saul and David in the Wilderness," in his *Growth of the Biblical Tra-*

basically parallel structure and address some of the same questions (e.g., Saul's status as "the Lord's anointed," the issue of bloodshed, etc.). Yet just because there may once have been only a single story of a personal encounter in the wilderness between Saul and David it would be a mistake to ignore the fact that the present narrative contains two distinct encounters. Also, even if the two encounters have been embellished, that does not mean such embellishment was without purpose or careless. Viewing 1 Samuel 26 as a "doublet" tends to push its similarities with 1 Samuel 24 into the foreground and move its distinctive literary features and purpose out of critical focus.[55]

In the narrative as it now exists it is in fact crucial that 1 Samuel 26 be read as the *second* encounter between Saul and David, both to make the point that Saul's kind words at the end of 1 Samuel 24 did not last, and also to exhibit how Abigail's words about bloodshed in 1 Samuel 25 have made a real impact on David and his outlook.[56] All three chapters (1 Sam 24, 25, and 26) actually form a kind of literary triptych, with each chapter providing a distinct panel in what is ultimately a single tableau. Recent literary approaches to biblical narrative have been extremely helpful in countering the assumption of ineffectual editing that was often fundamental to the historical-critical work of previous generations.

The Achilles' heel of such work was not so much its effort to pierce the veil of time by reconstructing the history behind the text, but instead its subsequent reliance upon the idea of bad editing to explain how, given the historical reconstruction, the biblical text came to be as it now is. There is no necessary reason that both things could not be simultaneously true — that the biblical text formed gradually over time *and* that those who compiled and edited portions of the text did so carefully and artistically.[57] This would mean, however, that appeals to the "author" of this material are problematic, unless by "author" one means the "implied author," that is, the "author" one infers from the narrative. For that reason the effort in this study has been to

---

dition, pp. 132-48. More recently, see Edenburg, "How (Not) to Murder a King." Making this point visually, Klein, *1 Samuel*, pp. 236-37, prints the two accounts in double columns. However, Walter Dietrich has more recently argued that there were originally two stories here, which were later edited toward each other; see his "Die zweifache Verschonung Sauls durch David." On the basic methodological difficulty, see Nahkola, *Double Narratives in the Old Testament*.

55. For continuing debate about the historical priority of one of the two accounts over the other, see Conrad, "Unschuld des Tollkühnen"; McKenzie, "Elaborated Evidence"; Stoebe, "Gedanken zur Heldensage in den Samuelbüchern"; Van Seters, "Two Stories of David Sparing Saul's Life in 1 Samuel 24 and 26."

56. Gordon, "David's Rise and Saul's Demise."

57. Alter, *Art of Biblical Narrative*, pp. 163-92; Polzin, *Samuel and the Deuteronomist*, pp. 1-6.

make literary observations on the basis of the narrative without couching those observations as evidence of a hypothetical author's "intention." Such a stance does not remove the possibility for an ascription of intentionality or purposefulness to the narrative itself.[58] Indeed, the argument here is that the present narrative of Samuel is quite "intentional" in moving through the three chapters now appearing as 1 Samuel 24–26, and that 1 Samuel 26 provides their (provisional) conclusion.

Asleep, Saul is once more in the dark, with his sleep signifying the same sort of sensory deprivation that the location of the "cave" did in 1 Samuel 24. This time David and Abishai, one of David's men, approach Saul together (26:7). Seeing Saul's spear stuck in the ground close to Saul's head, Abishai asks David for permission to kill him. As David's men did previously, Abishai wrongly interprets Saul's vulnerability and David's opportunity as evidence that God wants Abishai to kill Saul (26:8; cf. 24:5).[59] The difference this time, however, is that Abishai would be the proximate agent of Saul's death rather than David. It might be thought that by delegating Saul's death to someone else David could escape the burden of bloodguilt himself. In fact, if he had not met Abigail it would have been extremely difficult for David to resist this technical solution to his dilemma. But the force of Abigail's argument rules out any move on David's part to cause Saul's death, even indirectly, because such a move would be to assume God's own prerogative.

For this reason David orders Abishai not to hurt Saul: "By the life of the Lord, the Lord himself will strike him down, or his day will come and he will die naturally, or he will go down into battle and perish. But the Lord forbid that my hand should stretch out against the Lord's anointed" (26:10-11). Crucial for David, as a follower of the God of Israel but especially as God's anointed servant, is to preserve God's authority in matters of life and death. This religious understanding is basic not only to David's success, as if it were simply a matter of self-interest, but to the ongoing existence of Israel. When God's

58. Some would say that such an ascription inappropriately personifies the text, that only readers have intentions. My experience of texts is quite different. I find they challenge and contradict me, and that I change in response to them. I do not agree that it inappropriately "personifies" a text to describe it as possessing intention or purpose because in my reading of texts I believe that I encounter more than just myself.

59. See Bonhoeffer, "Bible Study," p. 879: "Thus does the devil argue with God's own words from paradise all the way to the temptation of Jesus, here in connection with the given — 'God given' — situation. But David turns the tempter away . . . For the sake of his reign, David remains defenseless, persecuted, and suffering. And by repaying evil with good, he twice brings Saul to a realization of his own sin. It is not through violence but through love that he wins the heart of the rejected Saul."

position as the guarantor of justice is acknowledged and maintained with due deference, then justice will continue to prosper throughout the land of Israel. But when God's role in justice is usurped, as kings are especially tempted to do, then a dangerous fissure forms within the structure of the created world, a world designed by God to operate according to the principle of justice.[60] Far more is at stake here than simply what will happen to Saul, David realizes. At stake is the continued success of God's creation.

David takes Saul's spear and water jar so he can again prove to Saul that while he had the opportunity to do him harm he did not (26:12). Saul and his men sleep throughout; the narrator credits their sleep to God (26:13), thereby conveying to the reader a sense that God's providential activity exists between the lines of the unfolding plot. David then mounts a hill and shouts back to the camp, awakening Saul, his general Abner and the rest of Saul's men. David criticizes Abner for failing to guard Saul adequately. In doing so, of course, David also proclaims his own honor, not only in refraining from violence but also in preventing Abishai from causing Saul any harm. In effect, David contrasts himself favorably with Abner. They both have a responsibility for the well-being of the king, but Abner has neglected his duty. By contrast, Abner appears to treat David as rude riffraff, someone who has the temerity to "shout" ($\sqrt{qr'}$) at the king.

Overhearing David's speech, Saul is said to "recognize" ($\sqrt{nkr}$ Hiph.) his voice, but then nevertheless asks, "Is that your voice, my son David?" (26:17). In contrast to 1 Sam 24:17, in which Saul seemed truly confused, the combination of a report confirming Saul's recognition of David alongside a simultaneous profession of uncertainty on his part instead suggests that Saul is being duplicitous. David appears not to suspect anything is amiss but continues to make his case. David concedes that Yahweh might have set Saul against him for some reason. An offering could put this problem right, he thinks. But more likely is that Saul's men have poisoned him against David (26:19), a charge David has made before (24:10). David seems to want to believe the best about Saul; his suggestions would all enable Saul to share the blame for the injustice done to him. David's resentment against Saul's supporters stems not only from his having had to flee from Saul's court. Apparently David is also a virtual exile, no longer possessing property rights and unable to participate in the worship rites of Israel (26:19-20).

David has in effect been told, "Go worship other gods" — a possibility that always horrified the deuteronomists. In this way his mistreatment at Saul's

---

60. See further Schmid, *Altorientalische Welt in der alttestamentlichen Theologie*; idem, *Gerechtigkeit als Weltordnung*; cf. Chapman, "Reading the Bible as Witness."

hands ultimately takes the form of *religious* deprivation. David does not seem nearly as worried about being killed as he does about being prevented from engaging in the worship of God regularly and fully. David's speech again concludes with a characterization of himself as a hunted "flea" (26:20, as in 24:15), but this time he also employs the figure of "the partridge" (*haqqōrē'*). At one level, this colorful analogy subtly mocks Saul's over-the-top determination to find and destroy him; some interpreters have also seen in this choice of terms a reference and a rejoinder to Abner's charge that David had dared to "shout" at the king, since "partridge" can also be read as "calling bird" or even "the one who shouts" (*haqqōrē'*).[61]

For a second time, Saul appears to repent. He admits his wrong and once more promises not to seek David's harm (26:21). Saul even says he has "acted the fool" (√*skl* Hiph.), a term that may allude in some way to 1 Samuel 25 (although there the Hebrew term for "fool" is *nābāl*), but more importantly echoes Samuel's condemnation of Saul in 1 Sam 13:13 (*niskāltā* [Niph.], "You have been a fool").[62] It is almost as if in searching for how to apologize to David, Saul can only fall back upon his same old shortcomings. David in turn has two responses to Saul's words. First, he uses his apparent rapprochement with Saul to reaffirm God's control over justice. Just as God has seen David through this particular encounter with David's own righteousness preserved, God will mete out punishment for all who are guilty and deliver all those living lives of righteousness (*ṣĕdāqâ*) and faithfulness (*'ĕmûnâ*, 26:23). God's position of authority is secure. Even Saul seems to agree with this perspective.

But then David responds further in a surprising way. After reporting that David leaves Saul and proceeds on his own, the narrative communicates David's private thoughts (*wayyō'mer dāwid 'el-libbô*, 27:1). And what does David really think? "One day I will surely perish at the hand of Saul." This interior reflection is almost shocking within its narrative context. Although it is historically possible that the material beginning 1 Samuel 27 was not originally intended to follow so closely upon the encounter between Saul and David at the end of 1 Samuel 26, in the present narrative they are so closely juxtaposed that the one cannot be read apart from the other. David's suspicion of Saul compels a rereading of their preceding conversation and suggests that David was all along less trusting of Saul than it appeared. This late acknowledgement of his suspicion confirms for the reader the subtle narrative clues to Saul's duplicity that have already been mentioned. Unlike the end of 1 Samuel 24, when Saul appeared

---

61. Here see Weiss, *Figurative Language in Biblical Prose Narrative*, p. 204. Cf. Cartledge, *1 and 2 Samuel*, p. 304.

62. Morgan, "Playing the Fool."

to be sincere in his regret, Saul was play-acting this time around, and at some point during or immediately after their conversation David has realized it.[63]

Here then is another example of "retrospective" narrative as a literary technique. Certain information is at first withheld in order to heighten suspense and to provoke interpretive questions on the part of the reader. Then further information is given, leading to a reexamination of the narrative thus far, the confirmation of certain developing theses and the disconfirmation of others. At this point David has been strengthened in his commitment to non-violence with respect to Saul. Thanks to Abigail he has made a crucial connection between his response to Saul and his faith in God. David has placed himself and his future in God's hands, to do as God wills (26:24). However, this kind of trust does not imply that David can be foolhardy. He still has a responsibility to defend himself through evasive action. As he now realizes, Saul will never stop hunting him. What David must therefore do is to keep a healthy distance between Saul and himself. Such a strategy is not merely a ploy to protect David's reputation if and when Saul should die, but a commitment to let God unfold events in accordance with *divine* righteousness and faithfulness.

To keep his distance from Saul will not be easy. David will need to remain outside the territory under Saul's control, but keep close enough that he can respond quickly if it becomes time for him to assume the throne. So David daringly decides to call the bluff of Saul's supporters, who had told him to leave and worship other gods. He will go to the land of the Philistines.

David in Gath (1 Sam 27:1–28:2)

David's private thought that he will perish by Saul's hand is an apprehension, not a prophecy.[64] He will not be killed by Saul in the end, although one can certainly understand his anxiety about the future. He has finally come to realize that Saul really does want him dead, cannot be trusted to be sincere, and will never stop trying to capture him so long as David remains in the land of Israel. But where can David go to protect himself as he waits for God to fix Saul's proper destiny?[65]

---

63. For an alternative reading, in which Saul is treated as a tragic hero in this chapter and his portrayal is directly influenced by Greek tragedy, see Adam, "Nocturnal Intrusions and Divine Interventions on Behalf of Judah." However, I do not find the argument very persuasive.

64. On *'āmar 'el libbô* as a marker for "internal monologues," see Ska, *"Our Fathers Have Told Us"*, pp. 67-68.

65. The thematic coherence of the final chapters of 1 Samuel is ably demonstrated by Firth, "Accession Narrative."

The land of the Philistines is David's choice. He returns to Gath, where he had earlier pretended to be mad (1 Sam 21:11-16), and Saul gives up his pursuit for the time being (27:4). On this occasion Achish appears to welcome David without concern, at least initially.[66] David brings men and resources that he commits to Achish's service; in return Achish permits him to take control of the city of Ziklag (27:5-6). Yet David and his men use their base in Ziklag to mount military operations against Israel's enemies (Geshurites, Gizrites, and Amalekites are mentioned) rather than against the Israelites. Indeed, David plays the tricky game of double agent, telling Achish that he has fought against Israelites when in reality he has completely slaughtered the other peoples he raided so that there are no witnesses to disclose his deceit. Achish is persuaded. In fact he thinks that David has so fully alienated himself from his own people that he will be forced to serve Achish indefinitely (26:12).

There may be a note of nervousness here in the narrative as it describes David's practice of total slaughter. On the one hand, David is protecting himself and his men by what he does. He is also protecting Israel. Yet the totality of the slaughter is apparently only truly necessary so that he can hide his actions from Achish (27:11). Are the lives of all those men and women worth so little that they can be forfeited simply for the purpose of a cover story? One might note as well that, in contrast to some of his earlier military engagements, David is not depicted in this passage as engaging in divinatory practices to shape his plans. However, by enforcing a total ban David also now does what Saul did not do in 1 Samuel 15. If Saul had done what he was supposed to do, no Amalekites would presumably have been left for David to worry about. But in 1 Samuel 15 God had specifically told Saul, through Samuel, to kill all of the Amalekites without exception, while in 1 Samuel 27 no explicit word from God has been reported. The notice that David only did this horrific thing so long as he remained in Philistine territory (27:11) betrays a moral worry and represents an attempt to justify David's actions.[67]

The narrative strategy at this point is difficult to ascertain with confidence. The reason for mentioning this appalling and wanton shedding of blood on David's part is most likely to raise a further question about the nature of blood-

---

66. Indeed, Achish and his men give no sign that they have met David before. For further discussion and historical-critical proposals, see Edenburg, "Notes on the Origin"; Klein, "Davids Flucht zu den Philistern."

67. On the other hand, the continued existence of Amalekites in 1 Samuel 30 may indicate that comments like the one found in 1 Samuel 27:9 ("leaving neither man nor woman alive") are to be read as military hyperbole. On this phenomenon more broadly and its implications for dealing with violence in the Old Testament, see Copan, *Is God a Moral Monster?* pp. 170-77; Goldingay, *Old Testament Theology: Volume 3*, pp. 570-72; Wolterstorff, "Reading Joshua."

shed, as just explored in 1 Samuel 24–26. There the issue was, more narrowly, whether bloodshed was justified in order to remove Saul from the throne, and it was resolved in the negative. But the deep logic of that resolution was a theology of creation in which bloodshed by mortals was ruled out so as to preserve God's role in decisions of life and death. This logic is sweeping in scope and quickly moves beyond the presenting issue of dynastic succession. If God is the one to decide matters of life and death, then what of warfare itself? Earlier in the book a distinction appeared to be drawn between battles that were committed to God and therefore considered to be in some sense under God's guiding authority, and battles in which human beings took military matters into their own hands, effectively displacing God's rule. David's genocidal campaigns in 1 Samuel 27 seem more in the mold of the second type of battle than the first. Why narrate them at all, though? Especially if David is to be viewed as the hero of this story?

Once again the narrative of Samuel resists the reduction of characters into "black hats" and "white hats." The bad guys are not all bad; even the heroes have their weaknesses and shortcomings. In this case the narrative is willing to report something less than attractive about David, not just to remind the reader of his humanity (although that is partly the reason) but also to keep alive the issue of bloodshed. If the question of the theological relationship between God and king remains the primary one for the Samuel narrative, the affirmation of God's ultimate authority in matters of life and death poses profounder questions that go beyond even the issue of the monarchy (1 Sam 2:6). If God is truly Israel's king and can be trusted for Israel's security, then why fight battles at all? If they are defensive in nature, perhaps they can be justified once God's guidance has been appropriately sought. But if the logic of bloodshed that David has articulated and adopted is true, then there cannot ever be a possibility of offensive warfare for Israel except at the express bidding of God (e.g., 1 Sam 15:2-3?). David's raids result from no divine mandate and therefore become a negative example in the text, an implicit question for consideration. And the narrative is finally willing to show David in an unsavory light if it will prod the reader into such further reflection.

David's situation becomes more complicated, and more dangerous for him, when Achish himself decides to do battle against Israel (28:1).[68] Although David seems unhesitating in his agreement to march with Achish's forces,

---

68. This approaching confrontation now emerges as the goal to which the wider narrative is moving, even as different narrative strands are explored in the process. See Oiry, "Raconter le simultané."

the reader recognizes this development as a serious challenge.[69] Surely David cannot go to war against his own people, can he? How will he be able to avoid doing so? David is stuck between two kings and two lands, neither one of which is any longer safe for him.

Saul and the Medium at Endor (1 Sam 28:3-25)

The account of Saul in Endor is not the end of Saul's story, but it is the beginning of the end.[70] The repeated announcement of Samuel's death (28:3; cf. 25:1) sets a new scope for Saul's isolation; now Samuel is seemingly not even theoretically possible for him to consult. There also exists in this announcement a confirmation of what the narrative had previously predicted: that after his rejection in 1 Samuel 15, Saul would never see Samuel again until his death (1 Sam 15:35). However, the inclusion of the phrase "until his death" appears, strictly speaking, unnecessary — unless there is perhaps a double meaning to this phrase, that Saul will in fact see Samuel *after* his death. And this is exactly what happens, just as 1 Sam 15:35 had subtly foreshadowed. The report of Samuel's death at the outset of 1 Samuel 28 is paired with the information that Saul had sometime previously "removed" (√*swr* Hiph.) "the ghosts" (*hā'ōbôt*) and "the familiar spirits" (*hayyid'ōnîm*) from the land. This action on Saul's part should not be viewed as an act of piety (in line with Deut 18:10-11) as much as a worrisome signal that in the past Saul had been involved in spiritualism (rather than genuine spirituality), and that he may choose to do so again.[71]

The setting for Saul's army is at Gilboa where Saul will soon die (1 Sam 31:1), so that the final four chapters of 1 Samuel form a cohesive literary section. With the Philistines moving against Saul, the dramatic question regarding how Saul is to be succeeded by David gains fresh urgency. When is Saul to be removed from the throne? Will he be killed? How will such a transition be engineered in a way that respects his status as God's anointed? How will David be able to avoid getting blood on his own hands, especially since the Philistine

---

69. On this point, see further Shemesh, "David in the Service of King Achish of Gath." Shemesh attempts to make the case that the narrative does not seriously entertain the possibility that David might go into battle against his own people; to my mind the text wants to raise precisely this outcome as a real dilemma.

70. On philological and historical issues in this chapter, see Cogan, "Road to En-Dor"; Kleiner, *Saul in En-Dor*; Schmidt, "'Witch' of En-Dor"; Tropper, *Nekromantie*; Vattioni, "Necromanzia nell'Antico Testamento." On 1 Samuel 28 as a subversion of Saul's prophetic capabilities, see Michael, "The Prophet, the Witch and the Ghost."

71. Cf. van der Toorn, *Family Religion*, pp. 318-19.

king Achish has made David the "protector of his head" (*šōmēr lĕrō'šî*, 28:2) or personal bodyguard? If David is forced to accompany Achish's troops into battle against Saul, how can he be prevented from killing Saul while at the same time maintaining his cover with Achish?

As the narrative notes, Saul's heart trembles at the sight of the Philistines (28:5). Sight and size have always been decisive for Saul. He proceeds to "inquire" (√*š'l*) of God, but in those modes of mediation that are still available to him in theory (dreams, lots, prophets) there is nothing by way of a response (28:6).[72] Here again Saul's resistance to God takes the form of improper divination (cf. 1 Sam 15:23), and leads to God's refusal to communicate with him at all. So Saul (once more?) turns to a spiritualist, a woman who communicates with ghosts (28:7).[73] Not only does Saul attempt to hide himself by disguising his clothes, he also seeks out the woman by night (28:8). His request that the woman "conjure up" (√*qsm*) a ghost is met with her ironic reply that King Saul has forbidden doing so. The horror of such sorcery, and its fundamental foreignness to orthodox Israelite belief, is a clear deuteronomistic tenet (Exod 22:17; Deut 18:9-14; cf. Lev 19:31; 20:6, 27).[74] One of the central theological dilemmas presented by this text, however, is that the procedure followed by the spiritualist in fact appears to be successful (after Saul persuades her to proceed). Several early Christian writers worried a good deal about whether the medium had succeeded in raising Samuel's ghost, because her action might then confirm the power of witchcraft.[75] One alternative adopted by some commentators ever since has therefore been to conclude that the medium only *claimed* to summon Samuel or even that a demon impersonated him.

This kind of reading is at least as old as Tertullian, and is fully elaborated by Eustathius.[76] The impersonation theory found some support in the New Testament saying that "Even Satan disguises himself as an angel of light"

---

72. See Craig, "Rhetorical Aspects of Questions."

73. Polzin, *Samuel and the Deuteronomist*, p. 218, views 1 Samuel 28 as the culmination of Saul's "growing divinatory obsession" throughout the wider narrative.

74. Rudyard Kipling's poem "En-dor" stands out in the modern period as a devastating critique of this sort of spiritualism: "And nothing has changed of the sorrow in store / For such as go down on the road to En-dor!" Kipling, *Collected Works, Vol. 26*, pp. 358-59. On the relation between witchcraft and Israelite ritual, see Regev, "Priestly Dynamic Holiness and Deuteronomistic Static Holiness." For a broader discussion of the Old Testament texts regarding witchcraft, including attention to their abuse in later history, see Harvey, "Suffering of Witches and Children." Although lines of distinction can usefully be drawn between terms such as "spiritualist," "medium," "witch," "sorceress," and the like, I use them broadly and interchangeably here.

75. See Smelik, "Witch of Endor."

76. See Greer and Mitchell, eds., *"Belly-Myther" of Endor*, pp. xxxi-lxxxiii.

(2 Cor 11:14). Eustathius further insists that the ghost was not really Samuel because his message was not true: Saul and his sons do not die the very next day as predicted (1 Sam 28:19).[77] Eustathius thus reads the time expression in v. 20 ("all day and all night") as relating to a period *after* the prophecy had been pronounced, so that Saul ate nothing for an entire day and night after receiving this message, subsequently departing from Endor on the second day. But the Hebrew text understands the time expression as describing the period *prior* to Saul's arrival in Endor: "since he *had eaten* nothing all day and all night." So Saul does in fact depart on the morrow. The timeline then admittedly becomes murky, because in chapters 29 and 30 the action shifts to David. But in their present form these two chapters can be read without difficulty as a description of action roughly simultaneous to what is happening to Saul, and of themselves they do not call into question either the inevitability of Saul's fate or the truthfulness of the ghost's prediction.[78]

The wider narrative's tight temporal link between prophecy and fulfillment is presented affectingly in Henry Purcell's musical setting of the story, "In guilty night" (Z 134). Having been summoned by the witch, Samuel sings:

Art thou forlorn of God and com'st to me?
What can I tell you then but misery?
Thy kingdom's gone into thy neighbor's race,
Thine host shall fall by sword before thy face.
Tomorrow, then, til then farewell, and breathe:
Thou and thy son tomorrow shall be with me beneath.[79]

As this text suggests, from this moment on there is a ticking clock over Saul's head. He had sought guidance and aid; he receives a report of his impending doom. However, the truthfulness of this prophecy — as Eustathius perceived — also supports the view that Samuel really was summoned up, and it reinforces the dilemma of discovering a successful witch in the Bible.

One theological alternative to crediting the witch with her own success is to view her activity as having been allowed success by God.[80] One might

77. Eustathius, "A Critical Investigation on the Subject of the Belly-Myther, Against Origen," in Greer and Mitchell, eds., *"Belly-Myther" of Endor*, p. 103.

78. For a detailed treatment of the complicated timeline(s) in 1 Samuel 27–31, see Fokkelman, "Structural Reading."

79. The author of the libretto is unknown. On its political dimensions and the setting by Purcell, see Chan, "*Witch of Endor* and Seventeenth-Century Propaganda."

80. Tradition credits this position to Theodore bar Konai, according to Smelik, "Witch of Endor," pp. 174-75. Cf. Cox, "Origen and the Witch of Endor."

invoke as a parallel the example of Balaam, the foreign seer (Num 22–24), who prophesies beyond his native capacity because of God's leading — as well as other biblical examples of divine concessions that can be understood as heightening, rather than diminishing, God's sovereignty.[81]

Still, it does seem a bit odd that Saul cannot see Samuel's ghost himself and must rely upon the medium to report Samuel's appearance (28:14). Although Saul and Samuel subsequently converse (28:15-19), their exchange of words could be understood as taking place through the medium, even though the narrative does not state this explicitly. However, a few Greek manuscripts read "Saul" instead of "Samuel" in 28:12, which would then explain the medium's expostulation ("You are Saul") as well as the fact that she subsequently appears unable to recognize the identity of the shade in question ("An old man is rising," 28:14). Saul seemingly works out for himself that the shade is Samuel from the medium's description. These narrative features might be developed into an interpretation in which the medium was either unsuccessful and duplicitous or successful but dense.

For Origen, the success of the witch's conjuring must be conceded on the basis of 1 Sam 28:12, in which the *narrator* reports how the medium "sees Samuel" (*wattēre' hā'iššâ 'et-šĕmû'ēl*).[82] Employing what might be considered a surprisingly modern distinction between the discourse of a character (which may or may not be reliable) and the voice of the narrator (which must be truthful because the narrator is held to be reliable), Origen accordingly treats the episode as an authentic instance of witchcraft.[83] Origen's judgment receives support from the realization that Samuel's shade offers a true description of Saul's difficulty ("The Lord has turned away from you and has become your adversary," 28:16)[84] and delivers a prophecy that turns out to be accurate ("Tomorrow you and your son will be with me," 28:19).[85]

81. See further Chapman, "Brevard Childs as a Historical Critic."

82. Origen, "Homily 5 on 1 Kingdoms 28," in Greer and Mitchell, eds., *"Belly-Myther" of Endor*, pp. 38-45.

83. For Origen, the narrator is reliable because the narrator is the Holy Spirit. A comparison between Origen and Gregory of Nyssa on this key point is instructive because their opposing interpretations rest on broader judgments about the nature of biblical poetics. For Origen, if the narrator meant that the medium had in fact seen a demon pretending to be Samuel, he would have naturally said so. For Gregory, the narrator's remark "And Samuel said" can be construed as referring to appearance rather than reality, since "we find it characteristic of scripture often to relate what seems to be instead of what is." See Gregory of Nyssa, "Letter to Theodosius concerning the Belly-Myther," in Greer and Mitchell, eds., *"Belly-Myther" of Endor*, p. 173.

84. Reading *ṣārekā* (from √*ṣrr*) instead of *'ārekā*, which appears only here in the Hebrew Bible. Ps 139:20 does include a form *'ārêkā*, but it is also likely a corruption of the text.

85. Augustine was at first also inclined to deny that the medium had in fact raised Samuel,

In deuteronomistic thought an important test of a prophecy's truthfulness is whether or not it eventually comes to pass (Deut 18:21-22). One of the genuine complexities with regard to prophecy is that sometimes God speaks through non-Israelites (e.g., Balaam in Num 22–24) and often communicates more than the prophet himself or herself, whether non-Israelite or Israelite, can understand. So lack of knowledge on the part of the medium in 1 Samuel 28 does not necessarily call into question her ability to summon up Samuel's shade; it is part of an overarching literary-theological perspective. It also helps to notice how the reason given for Saul's prior rejection by God is explicitly said to be his refusal to enact God's judgment upon the Amalekites (28:18), thus linking this chapter closely with 1 Samuel 15 (and perhaps 2 Samuel 1). Once more Saul's failure to "obey (lit. 'listen to') the voice of the Lord" (28:18; cf. 1 Sam 15:22) is recognized as Saul's chief deficiency.

The force of the specification "this day" ("Therefore this is the word that the Lord has done to you this day," 28:18) is intriguing. On the one hand it could be a general rhetorical device, used in combination with the following temporal specification "tomorrow." Yet "this day" might also be taken to mean that Saul's failure in seeking mediation earlier in the day, whether by dreams or lots or prophets, was the particular consequence brought about by Saul's disobedience with the Amalekites. 1 Samuel 15 did suggest a connection between Saul's disobedience and false divination ($\sqrt{qsm}$, 15:23), which in retrospect looks almost predictive of 1 Samuel 28. The underlying idea in both passages would seem to be that those who are disobedient to God can no longer receive information directly from God, but are put into the same religious position as soothsayers and heretics (cf. 1 Chr 10:13-14).

Just as the presence of the prophetic word indicates a vital relationship with God, a broken relationship with God results in the absence of divine communication and the impossibility of normal modes of mediation ("God ['ĕlōhîm] has turned away from me and no longer responds to me whether by the hand of the prophets or in dreams," 28:15). It does matter that Saul tried to inquire of God (28:6),[86] but once again the precipitating event was his fear at the sight of the Philistine force and not primarily a desire to do God's will whatever the consequences (28:5). According to the deuteronomistic ideal, the one thing the Israelites were not to do above all when they encountered

---

but he later concludes that this did occur — on the basis of additional canonical evidence, namely, Sir 46:20: "Even after [Samuel] had fallen asleep, he prophesied and made known to the king his death, and lifted up his voice from the ground in prophecy, to blot out the wickedness of the people." See Murphy, 1 Samuel, p. 267.

86. Miscall, 1 Samuel, p. 169, points out that while Saul says "God" once, Samuel goes on to refer to "the Lord" (Yhwh) seven times. The disparity is obvious.

an army in opposition to them was to be afraid, for this fear is an implicit rejection of God's power to save (Deut 20:1-4).

It also matters that in Samuel's speech to Saul there is an explicit confirmation of how David will be the one to succeed him (28:17). Saul had seemed to realize this fact on his own (1 Sam 24:21), but hearing it now from the ghost of Samuel sets the terms of the book's denouement for both Saul and the reader. Saul now knows for certain that he will die tomorrow and that David will take the throne. No wonder that he is horrified by Samuel's words and entirely without "strength" (*kōaḥ*, 28:20). Physical strength has always been Saul's preeminent characteristic and the interpretive lens for his personal worldview. Yet faced with absolute rejection and imminent death, his strength vanishes. The ground is being prepared for David's upcoming lament on behalf of Saul (and Jonathan): "How the mighty have fallen!" (2 Sam 1:19).

The concluding events of this chapter (28:21-25) are curious. The medium insists on taking care of Saul by giving him food. The aspect of apparent urgency to her behavior is precisely Saul's sudden loss of strength, and her actions are directed toward restoring it (*kōaḥ*, 28:22). While her concern for Saul at first appears touching, her intention for him is thus precisely the opposite of what he truly needs.[87] The problem with Saul has always been his physical strength, which has gotten in the way of following God adequately and prevented him from serving spiritually as Israel's king. Now when Saul has finally lost that strength and is therefore at perhaps the most spiritually open moment of his life, the medium — who, it must be remembered, is in this narrative a representative of false, if effective, religious practice — can only think to induce Saul away from such vulnerability.[88] There are also cultic overtones to the medium's sacrificial killing (√*zbḥ*) of a calf and baking of cakes (28:24).[89] Saul is then depicted as regaining his strength entirely, but at the cost of engaging in heterodox worship practices.

In helping Saul to recover his strength, the medium confirms her own

---

87. In this way one can think of the medium as a kind of anti-Abigail, a woman who mis-feeds and thereby engenders further strife. Kent, *Say It Again Sam*, has drawn attention to other important links between 1 Samuel 28 and 1 Samuel 25.

88. The medium's provision also recalls how Samuel had given Saul food and lodging in 1 Samuel 9, a reminiscence suggesting that the medium is a kind of anti-Samuel, a false mentor to Saul.

89. For a compelling exegetical argument that the medium is motivated by "self-preservation, not hospitality," see Reis, *Reading the Lines*, pp. 147-67. Since the medium becomes the conduit for ill tidings to Saul, Reis concludes that the medium believed her life to be in jeopardy. In Reis's reading, the medium therefore offers an "idolatrous sacrifice to the spirits of the dead" (p. 159) in an effort to convince Saul that he will not die, as Samuel has foretold. Tragically, according to Reis, Saul goes to his death believing her.

distance from the authentic spirituality of Yahweh worship and demonstrates the tragic impossibility of Saul ever to change.[90] This was Saul's last chance to learn weakness. Not only because his death is now imminent, but also because his separation from God is fully complete, the scene ends, as the chapter began, in the darkness of night (28:25).[91]

David's Dilemma (1 Samuel 29)

As the Philistine generals prepare their troops for war with Saul, they see David and question Achish about David's loyalty. Achish is himself satisfied with David and does not question the truth of his defection from Saul. The other Philistine leaders worry that David may betray them and support Saul once they are all in battle together (29:4). For them, Saul is still David's "lord" (*'ădōnāyw*) and they therefore suspect — rightly, as the reader knows — that David continues to owe him some type of deference. They also cite, for one last time in the narrative of 1 Samuel, the saying about David's skill at arms excelling Saul's (29:5). There is a dangerous quality to this man, the Philistine leaders realize; there is something about him that suggests he is more than he seems. They want David kept out of the upcoming battle, a possibility that the reader immediately recognizes as a serendipitous solution to what has already emerged as a tricky problem: how to keep David from getting Saul's blood on his hands.[92]

Achish is genuinely sorry to dismiss David and persuaded (wrongly) of his honesty (29:6-7). Interestingly, Achish refers to Yahweh when speaking to David ("By the Lord's life," 29:6). Is this reference an oversight on the part of the narrator or simply a naïve use of a rhetorical formula? Perhaps not. It is also possible that Achish's words are meant to imply the subtle effect of "evangelism" by David. After knowing David for a considerable length of time,

---

90. Interestingly, a more positive interpretation of the medium has apparently always prevailed among interpreters; see, e.g., Beuken, "1 Samuel 28"; Cox, "Origen and the Witch of Endor"; Page, "Dynamics of Scripturalization," p. 58; Reis, *Reading the Lines*, pp. 150-51. Cf. Simon, "1 Samuel 28:3-25." This interpretive tendency is at least as old as Josephus; see his *Ant.* 6:340-42. Even if earlier Israelite attitudes might have been more accepting of witchcraft practices, and broader in their understanding of religious orthodoxy, it seems quite difficult to read the present canonical narrative of Samuel as approving of the witch, given the harsh prohibitions of witchcraft found in the Pentateuch (e.g., Exod 22:7; Deut 18:10).

91. For an intriguing grouping of biblical nighttime tales, see March, *Night Scenes in the Bible*. For a motivic link between nighttime and disaster, see Fields, "Motif of 'Night as Danger.'"

92. Brueggemann, "Narrative Intentionality."

Achish has not only become convinced of his moral goodness — a somewhat ironic judgment, since although it is ultimately accurate, David has in fact been misleading Achish — he has also presumably been impressed by David's God. Such a possibility would not necessarily imply that Achish had "converted" to Yahwism, which is both historically unlikely and literarily implausible. Yet polytheistic religion typically exhibits a flexible approach to foreign deities. Achish may simply be politely acknowledging David's God when speaking to David.

All the same, this rhetorical accommodation by Achish to David's religious belief demonstrates to the reader the continued strong link between David and Yahweh. To know the one is to be aware of the other, presumably because David's words and behavior consistently and reliably give honor to this deity. To that extent David does appear to bring a knowledge of God with him, even to a Philistine pagan like Achish (for a narrative precedent, see 1 Sam 17:47). As Achish puts it — somewhat ironically again, given David's duplicity — David is "as pleasing to me as a messenger of God" (*kî ṭôb 'attâ bĕʿênay kĕmalʾak 'ĕlōhîm*, 29:9). Even in deceit, then, David honors God and extends God's reputation. Beyond providing David with an alibi for the time of Saul's approaching death, this chapter therefore contributes substantially to an emerging portrait of David as a successful leader in Israel, a true king.

David's objection is difficult to interpret: is he sincere in feeling offended by his dismissal? Does he truly desire to go fight Israel on behalf of Achish and the Philistines? Most likely not. The suspicions of the Philistines have rescued him — at least for the moment — from a dangerous course of action. As David and his men leave to return to Ziklag in the light of morning, they contrast with Saul and his men, who traveled by night.

David and the Amalekites (1 Samuel 30)

With the narrative moving steadily toward the anticipated battle between the Philistine army and Saul's men at Mount Gilboa, this chapter relates an unexpected turn of events. David and his men, dismissed from service in the Philistine army because of its leaders' suspicion they would not prove loyal in battle, return to Ziklag to find that Amalekites have raided it and taken their families captive (30:3). David has lost two wives himself, Ahinoam and Abigail (30:5), but his troops still direct their grief and anger towards him, threatening his life (30:6).

The narrative has not provided any precedent for such a setback. David has appeared to be charmed in his ability to secure goodwill and meet with political success ever since his introduction in 1 Samuel 16. At the same time, the vulnerability of David in this episode strikes another contrast with Saul. David and his men "weep until they have no more strength (*kōaḥ*) for weeping" (30:4).[93] Unlike Saul, for whom the lack of personal strength represents failure (28:20-25), David's lack of personal strength provides him with the necessary vulnerability to strengthen himself in God (√*ḥzq* Hithp., 30:6). Rather than presuming that he knows what to do, David inquires (√*š'l*) of the Lord through the mediation of Abiathar the priest, Ahimelech's son. Given that the families of David and his men are being held hostage, David's query to God shows considerable restraint. "Shall I chase after these marauders?" he asks (30:8). The form of the question and the mention of the ephod indicate that lots are likely being used as the means of divination.

One cannot easily imagine Saul pausing in this fashion before reacting militarily. The fact that the adversaries at issue are Amalekites further reminds the reader of 1 Samuel 15 and Saul's own engagement with the same group of people. It was arguably unnecessary on that occasion for Saul to inquire of God prior to battle because he had already received specific instructions from God through the prophet Samuel (1 Sam 15:2-3). Nevertheless, Saul's story has shown a persistent neglect for such inquiry, particularly in pressing military situations. Warfare represents the fundamental temptation toward human self-sufficiency for Saul, a temptation away from reliance upon God. Like Jonathan (e.g., 1 Sam 14), David now demonstrates how to conduct military action in a manner that honors God as overlord.

After receiving a positive answer, David pursues the Amalekites. He allows some of his men who are fatigued to remain behind at the Wadi Besor (30:9). This siphoning off of his troop strength not only recalls Jonathan's disregard for numbers (1 Sam 14:6), it also aligns with the deuteronomic ideal for warfare (Deut 20:5-9). Finding the Egyptian slave of an Amalekite alone in open country, David and his men treat him kindly and gather information from him about the Amalekites' movements (30:11-14). The slave agrees to lead them to the Amalekite camp, where the Israelites battle against them, killing most of them and rescuing every single thing taken from Ziklag (30:15-19). The success of the Israelites confirms the accuracy of the word from God that David had received through his use of the lots.

David then takes a portion of the additional spoil for himself (30:20). This action should not be viewed as selfishness on his part, but as an indication that the following episode regarding the further division of the spoil (30:21-30) will affect David personally. However, this turn of events naturally compels a

---

93. See further Josipovici, "David and Tears."

rereading of 1 Samuel 15 at the same time: why was it wrong for Saul to hold back Amalekite spoil but not for David? The answer is partly that God has not commanded David to enforce the ban and destroy all the spoil, as God had ordered Saul through Samuel. Retrospectively, this comparison lends support to the view that Saul's error lay partly in taking the best of the spoil for himself instead of sharing it with his men.[94] This retrospective comparison between David and Saul is reinforced in 1 Samuel 30 by David's use of the expression "the one who sits by the baggage" (*hayyōšēb ʿal-hakkēlîm*, 1 Sam 30:24; cf. 1 Sam 10:22, in which Saul is the one "hiding in the baggage [*neḥbā' 'el-hakkēlîm*]").[95]

Returning to the men left behind at the Wadi Besor, the question arises as to whether they also are entitled to some of the spoils. Certain anonymous voices among the men who had accompanied David selfishly argue against it; those who remained behind are only entitled to their own wives and children, they maintain (30:22). David, however, forcefully rejects their view on a theocentric basis: since the victory is really the Lord's, who is to say that one is more deserving than another (30:23)? David concludes that all should share alike (30:24). In spite of its obvious affront to the self-interest of his men who already possessed spoil, not to mention his own self-interest, David's logic is nevertheless found to be persuasive — as is evidenced by its elevation to a "fixed ordinance" (*lěḥōq ûlěmišpāṭ*, 30:25) within Israel. Rather than violating the spirit of the ban, equal distribution among the men is now viewed as consistent with divine "ownership."[96]

In this way David leads not only by personal example but by the example of his faith. The respect he receives from his men derives not simply from the fact that he shares his wealth with all of them, but that he provides them with a persuasive vision of what it means to follow God together (cf. 1 Sam 22:1-2). Just as there is a theocentric basis to their conduct of warfare, so also there is a theocentric aim to the fabric of their military community. This sense of community even extends beyond the boundaries of the army. David gives gifts of the spoil to various elders and towns in Judah and among the Jerahmeelites and Kenites (30:26-31). Such a move is smart politics on David's part, too, and demonstrates his skill in diplomacy (something not much evident with Saul). Because David and his men had previously journeyed through these areas, they had likely received provisions from the townspeople in the past, just as in

94. Lind, *Yahweh Is a Warrior*, p. 106. In 1 Sam 15:15, 21 Saul says that the people took "the best" of the spoil, but not that he shared it with them.

95. On this narrative link, see Herzfeld, "David and Batsheva," pp. 240-42. Herzfeld terms 1 Samuel 30 "the best example of transposition between the lives of Saul and David" (p. 240).

96. Longman and Reid, *God Is a Warrior*, p. 46. A similar shift can be seen in the book of Joshua; see Chapman, "Israel's Covenant God."

1 Samuel 25. As those who had supported David's troops, therefore, although they did not have an actual part in the fighting either, these elders and towns also deserve to share in God's largesse.[97]

What this chapter offers is finally a model of how the kingship, even though it does represent a fundamental compromise or concession with regard to Israel's religious heritage, can still function in concert with Israel's faith in God. A king will not necessarily detract from Israel's divine allegiance; in fact, if the king possesses the right religious spirit he can actually inspire Israel to maintain a higher degree of faithfulness — at least on occasion. With this realization firmly in place, David has finally arrived at the foot of the throne. Saul can now die because David is fully ready to assume the leadership in Israel.

Saul's Death (1 Samuel 31)

The action reverts to Mount Gilboa, where Saul and his forces are overrun by the Philistines. Following the death of Jonathan and his other sons, and knowing the battle is lost, Saul asks his armor bearer to kill him so that he can be spared the indignity of a death at Philistine hands (31:4). When his armor bearer refuses, Saul falls on his own sword, dying a death that therefore is and is not a suicide.[98] It does amount to suicide because technically Saul kills himself, but the context makes clear that Saul does not want to end his life so much as to die with dignity, given the certainty that he will not survive this battle (31:3).[99] Such a death is entirely fitting for Saul, who has responded to the perceived urgency of military situations throughout the Samuel narrative by taking steps of his own initiative. A man of war, he dies by the sword. His death is neither cowardly nor ignoble. There is courage in his final action and honor in his desire to spare himself and others the possible spectacle of his abuse at Philistine hands (cf. Samson in Gaza, Judg 16:23-31).

97. Dietrich, "König David," p. 13, stresses how the Samuel narrative depicts David rising to power in an "almost democratic manner."

98. For a discussion of other instances of suicide in the Bible, the ancient Near East, and early Judaism, see Shemesh, "Suicide in the Bible"; Dietrich, "Der Tod von eigener Hand im Alten Testament und Alten Orient."

99. The later Jewish suicides at Masada (AD 73-74) lend strength to the view that Saul's manner of death may have been considered noble in ancient Israel. However, the display of his corpse at Beth Shean was most likely thought to be disgraceful and dishonoring — although there are also historical questions about this aspect of the narrative. As Amihai Mazar observes in his essay, "Was King Saul Impaled on the Wall of Beth Shean?" no fortification wall has yet been discovered at Beth Shean. See further Arubas, "Impact of Town Planning at Scythopolis on the Topography of Tel Beth-Shean."

Yet in the very nobility of his act also lies its unfaithfulness. Is this the end for Saul that God desires? The narrative is powerfully silent on that point. Instead, it depicts Saul grasping this death, just as he grasps his own sword, once more acting as opposed to waiting. Of course, Saul expects to die after receiving Samuel's prophecy to that effect (1 Sam 28:19). But in choosing the moment of his death for himself, he circumvents what has been planned and forecloses any other course of action that God might have preferred. Prophetic fulfillment is inexorable but dynamic; there is always the chance that fulfillment may alter its course, although fulfillment itself is never in question.

Saul's death thus mirrors the manner of his life. The Philistines cut off his head — an ironic detail, considering that Saul had come to power because he was "head and shoulders above Israel."[100] One thinks again of Goliath as well (1 Sam 17:51). Saul's headless kingship has led Israel into colossal defeat and disarray. The Israelites have looked to Saul in vain and now can only flee (31:7). Not only does Saul lead Israel to destruction, he gives occasion to the Philistines to celebrate their pagan religion (31:9-10). In contrast to David, Saul's model of kingship diminishes the God of Israel's reputation among the nations. Only the inhabitants of tiny Jabesh-gilead maintain respect for Saul, recalling his early support for them (1 Sam 11). They rescue his body for proper burial (31:11-13; cf. 2 Sam 2:4b-7; 21:12-14).[101] Yet the tamarisk tree (*'ešel*) under which they bury Saul's bones in Jabesh (31:13) also calls to mind the last time Saul sat under a tamarisk in 1 Sam 22:6, when he lorded himself over his men.[102]

The biblical narrative continues into what is now 2 Samuel 1 without pause or interruption. Only the phrase "after the death of Saul" indicates any awareness — at either the original or editorial level — of a larger narrative transition. Similar expressions do mark the introductions of other books of the Former Prophets (Josh 1:1; Judg 1:1; 2 Kgs 1:1). Although the separation of Samuel into two "books" occurred well after the narrative had stabilized in more or less its present literary shape, the current division at the conclusion of 1 Samuel 31 makes good sense. The death of Saul marks a major shift in the broader narrative, even though the first two chapters of 2 Samuel continue to deal with Saul's death, and even though David's moving poetic lament in honor of Saul and Jonathan can be viewed as a literary *inclusio* in concert with

100. Downey, *Perverse Midrash*, p. 121 n. 4.
101. Hamilton, "Creation of Saul's Body," p. 151, calls attention to the narrative detail given to the destruction of Saul's body and relates it to the narrative's broader preoccupation with Saul's body and Israel's "body politic."
102. Leithart, *Son to Me*, pp. 157-58.

Hannah's Song in 1 Samuel 2.[103] As much as what is now 1 Samuel must be read against the horizon of the entire Samuel narrative, pausing to consider 1 Samuel from the particular vantage point of 1 Samuel 31 brings the contrast between Saul and David into especially sharp relief. Saul's way of being king could only end in tragedy; if there is to be a king in Israel at all, then he will need to be a king like David.

In a previous era of scholarship, interpreters quickly latched onto the alternate versions of Saul's death in 1 Samuel 31 and 2 Samuel 1 as evidence of two originally different accounts. But more recent, literarily informed interpretation has perceived their shared unity.[104] Saul's death is recounted by the biblical narrator in 1 Samuel 31, while in 2 Samuel 1 a narrative character relates another course of events (2 Sam 1:1-16). The possibility exists, therefore, that this character may not be telling the truth, although the narrative does not explicitly call him a liar. That this character is an Amalekite, however, is a narrative red flag. As Adele Berlin has pointed out as well, his description of what happened is oddly vague and sounds for all the world as if he is making it up: "*I happened to be* on Mount Gilboa; and *there was Saul* leaning on his spear . . ." (2 Sam 1:6).[105] Perhaps he merely found Saul's crown after the battle and brought it to David expecting a reward (v. 10). Calum Carmichael has noted how in carrying away Saul's crown, the Amalekite literally, and finally, fulfills Samuel's judgment against Saul in 1 Sam 15:28: that the kingship will be taken away from him.[106]

Ironically, of course, David kills the Amalekite because he believes his lie (2 Sam 1:15-16). If the Amalekite had told the truth, he might have lived. In a

103. With the death of Saul occurs the death of Jonathan as well, which entails a genuine loss for David. David's lament for this friendship, "surpassing the love of women," has also been taken as evidence that the relationship between the two had a sexual dimension. More likely, however, is that this genitive construction is subjective rather than objective: i.e., not "surpassing the love that is expressed toward women" but "surpassing the love that women express." For another view, see Olyan, "Surpassing the Love of Women." Keren, "David and Jonathan," has argued that David's regard for Jonathan is calculating rather than heartfelt, and that his public eulogy is delivered for public consumption. The basic reason for this judgment is that David never seems to be forthcoming about his affection for Jonathan until this surprisingly emotional farewell — but as we have seen, David's interior life is withheld altogether throughout the narrative. His later emotional outbursts should not be interpreted as the insincere expressions of a cool customer but the public revelations of a discreet religious poet.

104. Galpaz-Feller, "David and the Messenger."

105. Berlin, *Poetics and Interpretation of Biblical Narrative*, pp. 79-82. Berlin also points out the unusual double instance of *hinnê* in this verse, which she likens to the usage of this term in dream reports.

106. Carmichael, *Spirit of Biblical Law*, p. 146.

further irony, David again succeeds at something Saul had failed to do (i.e., kill Amalekites). At the same time, however, the Amalekite armor bearer lays claim to killing Saul — something that David, Saul's former armor bearer (1 Sam 16:21-22), would not or could not do.[107] But perhaps the deepest irony is that Saul, although rejected by God from the kingship, remained "the Lord's anointed" and under divine protection to the last (2 Sam 1:14). Yet he could not protect himself from himself.

107. Miscall, *1 Samuel*, p. 182.

PART THREE

Reflecting on History and Theology

CHAPTER FIVE

1 Samuel and the Christian Faith

Why do I overlive,
Why am I mocked with death, and lengthened out
To deathless pain?[1]

But he said to them: "The kings of the Gentiles lord it over them;
and those in authority over them are called benefactors. But not
so with you; rather the greatest among you must become like the
youngest, and the leader like one who serves."[2]

Holiness does not consist in one exercise or another, but in a
disposition of the heart, which renders us humble and little in
the hands of God.[3]

Now that a reading of 1 Samuel has been offered on the basis of the narrative's literary features, the question as to the historical plausibility of that reading must be addressed. Could what the Samuel narrative appears to mean in a contemporary reading also have been what it meant in an ancient context? Such a way of putting the question is actually precisely the opposite of Krister Stendahl's well-known and influential description of biblical theology as first determining what a biblical passage meant and then reflecting on what it means.[4] In fact, my intention all along has been to approach this methodological task in reverse.

1. Milton, *Paradise Lost*, 10.773-75 (Adam).
2. Luke 22:25-26.
3. Thérèse of Lisieux, as cited in Johnson, ed., *Spiritual Childhood*, p. 54.
4. Stendahl, "Biblical Theology, Contemporary." Of all the ink that has been spilled in response to Stendahl's proposal, the most trenchant riposte may be that of Clines, "Story and

Most of the recent work on Samuel has followed Stendahl's prescription with a vengeance by reconstructing a much different history from the story the narrative now tells.[5] What *really* happened was "David's usurpation of the Saulide throne and assassination of all who stood in his way."[6] Basically the same sort of interpretation has now been advocated by a number of influential and highly skilled historical scholars.[7] I have no significant quarrel with their choice to pursue historical investigation as such other than to question the prevailing cynicism of their method, which reads the biblical text according to an extreme hermeneutic of suspicion.[8] Is it really adequate to assume from the outset of the task, as this stream of scholarship admittedly does, that the historical reality behind the biblical narrative is likely to be the *opposite* of what the narrative presents?[9] Or that historical agents act only, primarily or even predictably out of a very narrow range of self-interest?[10]

Poem," p. 127: "*We* do not make the leap into the past, *we* do not have to devise some scheme for bridging the gap between the 'then' of the text and the 'now' of the hearer. Any literature worth the name jumps the time-gap of its own accord" (his italics). For further critique of Stendahl's formulation, see Ollenburger, "What Krister Stendahl 'Meant.'"

5. As also described in Bosworth, "Evaluating King David."

6. Thus White, "Saul and Jonathan in 1 Sam 1 and 14," p. 129. Cf. idem, "History of Saul's Rise."

7. See in particular Baden, *Historical David*; Halpern, *David's Secret Demons*; McKenzie, *King David*. For an influential forerunner to this revisionist perspective on David, see McCarter, "Historical David." In fact there is nothing particularly novel about this view; it has been voiced by some interpreters since at least the eighteenth century. See Barber, "'I Resolved to Give an Account.'" Stefan Heym's twentieth-century novel *The King David Report* (1973) adroitly employs the same notion of the biblical narrative as untrustworthy propaganda in order to register a sly protest against totalitarianism.

8. The hermeneutical principles employed are succinctly summarized in McKenzie, "David's Enemies." For other criticisms of this approach, see Weitzman, "King David's Spin Doctors." For instance, Weitzman asks quite sensibly why pro-Davidic propaganda would have included the damning episode with Bathsheba and Uriah.

9. Thus the way that David is distanced from violence in the narrative is used as evidence that historically he was likely steeped in blood, while his biblical portrayal has intentionally prettied him up. See Whitelam, "Defence of David," *JSOT* 29 (1984): 61-87; VanderKam, "Davidic Complicity"; Weiser, "Legitimation des Königs David."

10. The reduction of human action to self-interest is typically supported by the claim that altruism is a naïve fiction. Rather than making a case for altruism, whose existence seems real to me but is difficult to prove, I have argued previously that *various kinds* of self-interest exist. In fact some kinds of self-interest conflict with and mitigate others, thus revealing the inadequacy of assuming that self-interest only concerns immediate personal or social advantage. When it is blithely said that the biblical texts are "really about power," the first question in response should always be "what *kind* of power"? See further Chapman, *Law and the Prophets*, pp. 93-97.

The "principle of analogy" (i.e., people back then were just like us) is fraught with numerous pitfalls and cannot be employed uncritically. Unsurprisingly, this kind of approach tends to flatten the narrative and silence its literary sophistication.[11] After all, "propaganda" cannot be too complex if it is to be effective.[12] Still, if there are those who want to indulge in this type of highly speculative analysis I think they have every right to do so. I agree that a historical reality exists behind the Samuel narrative and that saying what we can about that reality is necessary and important.[13] But my primary concern throughout the exploration of that narrative has been with *depiction* — how Samuel, Saul, and David are portrayed narratively — and not how they might have existed in history.

No, my primary quarrel with this body of scholarship stems not from the way it chooses to understand the Samuel narrative, but from the fact that it hypothetically reconstructs a new narrative to read.[14] By applying the same hermeneutic of suspicion, portions of the narrative more favorable to David are identified as later additions and removed from consideration. Anything that smacks of deuteronomistic language or ideas is usually assumed to be secondary and grinding an ideological axe. Although such efforts claim the mantle of Stendahl's supposedly objective "descriptive task," the value judgments that go into an identification of the "original" story are massive. Just to give one rather obvious reason why: while deuteronomistic additions and interpolations can be identified with a fair degree of reliability because of their formulaic language, their "removal" cannot accurately provide the contours

---

11. See, for example, the judgment of McKenzie, "Saul in the Deuteronomistic History," p. 68: "Saul in the Deuteronomistic History is, for all practical purposes, a one-dimensional character who provides a contrast to David." McKenzie thinks that there are hints of "a more complex and intriguing character" in the "original story," but also that the present narrative reduces Saul to the status of David's necessary foil. In this way McKenzie seeks a Saul who conforms to his own presuppositions rather than the rich, nuanced portrait of Saul on offer in the biblical text.

12. Gunn, *Story of King David*, p. 23. For the counterargument that propaganda must often be subtle in order to succeed, see Whitelam, "Defence of David."

13. For a spirited historical critique of revisionist scholarship regarding David, see Short, *Surprising Election*. Short focuses on the narrative from 1 Samuel 16 to 2 Samuel 5, successfully critiquing the interpretation of this narrative as a self-contained unit and politically propagandistic. The biblical narrative's resistance to being read exclusively in line with the immediate circumstances of its origins, however those are reconstructed, is persuasively identified by Short as a major obstacle to its characterization as propaganda or ideology. For a recent defense of the David story as an example of ancient Near Eastern royal apologetic, see Knapp, *Royal Apologetic*, esp. pp. 218-48.

14. This kind of textual reconstructionism is advocated quite openly by Scheffler, "Saving Saul from the Deuteronomist."

of a pre-deuteronomistic story because the deuteronomists may have deleted material from that story at the same time that they added to it. Usually this methodological point is met with a vague affirmation regarding the inherent conservatism of scribal tradition (i.e., in transmission the scribes characteristically retained even the text's challenging features), but such an affirmation carries little conviction when it comes from the same scholars who also view the scribes as fundamentally ideological and self-interested.

The other problem with viewing the historical David as a "terrorist" or "assassin"[15] or "serial killer"[16] is precisely the way that other biblical texts treat him as a good and noble king — indeed, the model for later Israelite rulers (e.g., 1 Kgs 8:25; 9:4; 15:3-5; Isa 9:1-7; 11:1-9; Mic 5:2-5). Later layers of the biblical tradition thus already view David quite positively. Is it really historically likely that these layers would misunderstand David's portrait so thoroughly or could conspire so successfully in such a whitewash?

Although the received narrative of Samuel (LXX or MT) appears to contain some literary features from after the time of the deuteronomists,[17] I maintain that the present form of Samuel took on its basic dimensions in its deuteronomistic redaction.[18] One can speculate about earlier versions, but interpreting the narrative now means accounting for its meaning *in its deuteronomistic shape*, which again is what largely exists anyway.[19] (There is no actual manuscript evidence for a pre-deuteronomistic Samuel.) For me, this type of literary appraisal shifts the goal of the descriptive task, even when construed historically. The historical aim of a close exegetical reading of Samuel, beyond the basic goal of gaining a deeper sense of the complexity of the text,

15. McKenzie, *King David*, pp. 89, 111.

16. Halpern, *David's Secret Demons*, p. 73.

17. On the presence of "anachronisms" indicative of a considerably later date than the ostensible time depicted by the narrative, see Redford, *Egypt, Canaan and Israel*, p. 305. However, see also, in opposition, Millard, "Are There Anachronisms in the Books of Samuel?"

18. For a discussion of archaic narrative details that may have survived from an earlier time period, see Na'aman, "Sources and Composition." Some scholars hold that the books of Samuel have only been very lightly edited by the deuteronomists and should thus be viewed as predominantly representing an earlier tradition; e.g., McCarter, *I Samuel*, pp. 15-17. Other scholars prefer to view the received form of these books as much later; for example, Garbini, *Myth and History in the Bible*, pp. 76-77, suggests a late (second-century!) date and a priestly source. However, his examples of later additions to the text consist largely of isolated phrases, which do not necessitate such a late date for the narrative as such.

19. On the possibility of a ninth-century "prophetic record" underlying the Samuel narrative, see Campbell, *Of Prophets and Kings*; McCarter, *I Samuel*, p. 18. See as well the interesting study by Gilmour, *Representing the Past*. Gilmour investigates the *kind* of historiography Samuel may be said to represent, a question with obvious implications for its use as a historical source today.

entails the contextualization of the narrative in the ancient context most fully implicated by its present literary shape: the deuteronomistic movement of the mid- to late seventh century BC onward.

Adopting this position prevents my literary reading from becoming disconnected from history; it also admits the possibility that historical concerns may sway interpretive choices.[20] Conversely, if the Samuel narrative is in fact to be set within the historical context of seventh-/sixth-century deuteronomism, then what does this conclusion add to our understanding of the period and "deuteronomism" itself?

Samuel and Deuteronomism

Because of the influential work of Martin Noth,[21] the books of the Former Prophets have widely been viewed as to some extent the product of deuteronomistic tradition.[22] Following his lead, the formulaic language shared between the book of Deuteronomy and certain passages in the Former Prophets has been seen as pointing to a like-minded group of writers and editors that began to be active in the seventh century BC and then largely dominated Israel's written traditions during the Exile.[23] It has been thought that originally the deuteronomists were reform-minded priests who engineered the discovery — or simply wrote — the "book of the law" discovered in the Jerusalem Temple during the eighteenth year of the reign of Josiah (2 Kgs 22:3-10). Ever since W. M. L. de Wette's 1805 dissertation, this "book of the law" was taken to be an earlier version of Deuteronomy, largely on the basis of the similarity between the laws in Deuteronomy and the narratively depicted response to

20. For overviews of recent historically oriented scholarship, but also with an eye toward the need to chart the synchronic dimensions of the Samuel narrative, see Dietrich, "Tendenzen neuester Forschung an den Samuelbüchern"; Dietrich and Naumann, "David-Saul Narrative."

21. Noth, *Deuteronomistic History*. Noth thought in terms of a single author; subsequent scholarship broadened the identification to that of a group, school, or stream. For evaluation of Noth's legacy, see Dietrich, "Martin Noth"; McKenzie and Graham, eds., *History of Israel's Traditions*; Rüterswörden, *Martin Noth*; Thiel, "Martin Noths Arbeit."

22. While most subsequent exegetical work has accepted Noth's thesis in one form or another, it bears noting that a few significant scholars have always opposed his proposal; see, e.g., Westermann, *Die Geschichtsbücher des Alten Testaments*. For further examples, see Römer, *So-Called Deuteronomistic History*, pp. 38-41.

23. For lists of characteristic words and idiomatic expressions attributed to this tradition, see Weinfeld, *Deuteronomy and the Deuteronomic School*, pp. 320-65; and Hoffmann, *Reform und Reformen*, pp. 323-66.

REFLECTING ON HISTORY AND THEOLOGY

the newly discovered lawbook in 2 Kgs 22:11–23:25.[24] From this vantage point Deuteronomy has frequently been interpreted as a revision of earlier practices and laws in Israel.[25] The first legal innovation presented by its central section of laws, often thought to have been the beginning of the original book, stipulates the centralization of all worship in Jerusalem (Deut 12). This stunning change in religious practice, it is usually thought, would have simultaneously abolished local sanctuaries throughout Israel.

However, Noth's interpretive framework is presently under considerable fire.[26] Its major difficulty has always been that it amounts to a sociological inference based upon the similarity of linguistic usage in various ancient texts, a rather dubious methodological proposition. No hard evidence for the existence of a deuteronomistic "group" has ever been discovered.[27] To the contrary, recent archaeological work is increasingly skeptical about the degree to which deuteronomistic reforms were ever put into practice.[28] So when it is now suggested that 2 Kings 22–23 may have influenced Deuteronomy,[29] rather than the other way around, the whole conceptual structure threatens to collapse like a historical house of cards.

There remains nonetheless the fact of the formulaic language itself.[30] Even with all its problems, the deuteronomistic theory still offers the best explana-

---

24. On the history of scholarship, see Römer, *So-Called Deuteronomistic History*, pp. 13-37; Römer and de Pury, "Deuteronomistic Historiography."

25. Most recently in Levinson, *Deuteronomy and the Hermeneutics of Legal Innovation*.

26. See, e.g., Knauf, "Does 'Deuteronomistic Historiography' (DtrH) Exist?"; Noll, "Deuteronomistic History or Deuteronomic Debate?"; Rösel, "Does a Comprehensive 'Leitmotiv' Exist"; Stipp, ed., *Deuteronomistischen Geschichtswerk*; Veijola, "Deuteronomismusforschung zwischen Tradition und Innovation (III)."

27. For a comprehensive overview of the historical evidence, see Lohfink, "Was There a 'Deuteromomistic Movement'?"

28. E.g., Fried, "High Places (*Bāmôt*)." But also note the apparent disappearance of astral motifs from seventh-century Judean seals, first pointed out by Uehlinger, "Gibt es eine joschijanische Kultreform?" pp. 65-67. Cf. Keel and Uehlinger, *Gods, Goddesses, and Images of God*, pp. 354-67. Frank Moore Cross had also previously called attention to the similarities between deuteronomistic rhetoric and the Arad letters, *Canaanite Myth and Hebrew Epic*, pp. 275-76.

29. For a sense of this recent trend in the discussion, see Arneth, "Antiassyrische Reform Josias von Juda"; Davies, "Josiah and the Law Book"; Eynikel, *Reform of King Josiah*; Handy, "Historical Probability"; Hardmeier, "König Joschija in der Klimax des DtrG"; Hollenstein, "Literarkritische Erwägungen"; Lohfink, "Zur neuesten Diskussion über 2 Kön 22–23"; idem, "Cult Reform of Josiah of Judah"; Monroe, *Josiah's Reform and the Dynamics of Defilement*; Niehr, "Reform des Joschija"; Uehlinger, "Was There Cult Reform under King Josiah?"

30. Wilson, "Who Was the Deuteronomist?" p. 78: ". . . the most persuasive case for Deuteronomistic influence can be made on linguistic grounds."

tion for the phenomenon.[31] There are also impressive verbal parallels between portions of Deuteronomy and Assyrian vassal treaties, as demonstrated by Eckart Otto.[32] Otto uses these parallels to date an early version of Deuteronomy between 672 and 612 BC. Whether the parallels suggest direct influence or require a date prior to the fall of the Assyrian empire remain open questions.[33] However, the newly discovered Tell Tayinat inscription (2008), containing another exemplar of a vassal treaty of Esarhaddon, and dated by its colophon to 672 BC, lends further weight to Otto's argument by providing evidence that the text of Esarhaddon's treaty was highly stable and known at that time in the western region of Assyria.[34]

Thus despite the various uncertainties and unknowns, in this section I want to compare my close reading of 1 Samuel to critical scholarship on the book of Deuteronomy and deuteronomism. Until now, I have used the term "deuteronomism" primarily as a literary trope rather than as a historical assertion. However, at this point my interest is to see if the historical hypothesis of deuteronomism — wobbly as it is — can contribute additional plausibility to my literary reading of 1 Samuel, or whether the two seem unrelated or even at odds. Similarities between the two might also lend additional historical support to the idea of a deuteronomistic reform beginning in late seventh-century Judah, just as differences might contribute further to that idea's demise.[35] The major historical alternative to a deuteronomistic setting for Samuel is probably the post-exilic Persian period. I have no doubt that this period will have also left its traces on the Samuel narrative,[36] but I find it more likely that the bulk of Samuel preceded Israel's postexilic situation and, indeed, then assisted postexilic Jews by helping them to understand their religious past, present, and

---

31. See further Römer, *So-Called Deuteronomistic History,* pp. 40-43, for the state of the question.

32. Otto, "Treueid und Gesetz."

33. For further discussion, see Levinson and Stackert, "Between the Covenant Code and Esarhaddon's Succession Treaty."

34. On the find, see Harrison and Osborne, "Building XVI"; Lauinger, "Esarhaddon's Succession Treaty at Tell Tayinat." However, in "Bundestheologie und autoritativer Text im Deuteronomium," Christoph Koch argues for the possibility that the treaty was also used later on (sixth century) as a school text or perhaps liturgically, and so might have exercised influence in Israel even after the time of Josiah.

35. In this discussion I basically attempt to follow the rough convention of referring to the early traditions of Deuteronomy as "deuteronomic" and the similar (but later?) traditions in the Former Prophets as "deuteronomistic." As has often been noted, this distinction quickly proves unstable, not least because there are later layers in the book of Deuteronomy itself. But if not pressed too hard, the distinction is serviceable enough for my purpose.

36. See, e.g., Amit, "Saul Polemic in the Persian Period"; Blenkinsopp, *David Remembered.*

future. I consider it probable as well that an early form of the Samuel narrative, or at least portions of it, preceded the deuteronomists, who nevertheless placed that narrative into roughly the form it still possesses.[37]

I suspect that one of the most controversial aspects of my close reading of 1 Samuel may be the attitude toward worship that I locate at the center of Samuel's narrative world: specifically, the idea that faith in God properly takes the character of personal trust. The language of "personal faith" is sure to sound like an anachronistic imposition, not only onto the narrative of Samuel but onto the ancient world generally.[38] Criticism will likely come from three directions. On one side will be those who work on the Bible within a history-of-religions framework and object to a distinction between ritual and "personal" belief. In the ancient world, *all* religion had a ritual character, they will insist. It recognizably expressed itself in "repetitive, symbolic behavior."[39] They will stress that this ritual basis of religion is true both of more elaborate worship practices, such as some forms of public sacrifice, as well as of brief private prayers. To draw a line between ritual practices and personal belief is illegitimate because it suggests that ritual practices are somehow separate from or devoid of such belief, and this kind of distinction simply did not exist in antiquity. No genuine difference was recognized in the ancient world between cultic and moral failings: each was viewed as related to the

---

37. For a recent presentation of the view that the bulk of Samuel preceded the deuteronomists, whose impact on the narrative was in fact fairly meager, see Garsiel, "Book of Samuel." Garsiel's main argument centers on the assessment that there are different views of the monarchy in Samuel (negative) and Deuteronomy (positive). By contrast I would see a more ambiguous, and thus more similar, perspective in both. That the deuteronomists would have let stand earlier references to sanctuaries outside of Jerusalem and cultic practices they considered heterodox need not indicate an oversight on their part. They knew full well that the time of the narrative, indeed the time prior to Josiah's reform, was characterized by religious diversity and idolatry. It was not necessary for them to rephrase the entire narrative with explicitly deuteronomistic language in order for them to use it in the service of their reform program. Dietrich, *1 Samuel 1–12*, p. 41, agrees that deuteronomistic work on Samuel was fairly minimal because the deuteronomists largely approved of the traditions about David and Saul which they had inherited.

38. For a good summary statement of what has since become the default historical-critical view, see Smith, *Religion of the Semites*, p. 55: "Religion is not an arbitrary relation of the individual man to a supernatural power, it is a relation of all the members of a community to a power that has the good of the community at heart, and protects its law and moral order." Even if the antiquity of personal piety is granted, to identify such a theology as distinctively Israelite would neglect how the notion of a "personal God" was itself neither a Jewish nor a Christian innovation but a well-established religious phenomenon throughout the ancient Near East. See further van der Toorn, *Family Religion*; Vorländer, *Mein Gott*.

39. Bremmer, "Ritual," p. 32.

other.[40] From such a perspective, the idea that a cultic act requires personal belief overlooks how in Israel, as in the rest of the ancient Near East, the materiality of the ritual act was itself efficacious.[41] To suggest otherwise is unfairly and confusingly to introduce a pietistic Protestant bias, perhaps one uncritically beholden to the problematic distinction between "religion" and "faith" asserted by Karl Barth and neo-orthodox theology in the first half of the twentieth century. So the critique.

Another direction from which criticism will likely come is itself thoroughly theological and Christian as well as historical. A number of works, especially in mid-twentieth-century biblical scholarship, viewed the history of worship in ancient Israel as a progressive ascent from primitive cultic practices reflecting pre-monotheistic cultures to the development of more belief-oriented attitudes and practices that found their eventual culmination in the perfected "spiritual religion" of Christianity.[42] Only at the time of the Exile, with the loss of the Jerusalem Temple and the traditional sacrificial system of pre-exilic Israelite religion, did prayer and scripture reading move to the foreground of religious life, showing that "the spirit without the ritual act could suffice."[43] From this viewpoint, although it is no longer nearly as influential as it once was, there will thus be resistance to the idea that a fully "spiritual" attitude toward worship could have existed in pre-exilic Israel, especially in tandem with cultic rituals such as sacrifice.

Both of these objections can be met to some degree with the evidence of the text itself and a careful formulation of the thesis. To the history-of-religions critique, I would respond by saying that ritual is nowhere condemned as such in Samuel. It is unimaginable within the narrative world of this text that ritual might not exist. The question is rather what kind of ritual is pleasing to God, and — I agree, somewhat surprisingly for an ancient text — the narrative engages in a polemic against any ritual that exists apart from personal conviction.[44] This aspect of Samuel is still one of its most radical qualities, literarily

40. E.g., Attridge, "Pollution, Sin, Atonement, Salvation," p. 73: "Modern categories of cultic, social, and moral infractions were simply not part of the conceptual scene at the earliest stages of the religious traditions of antiquity."

41. E.g., Brueggemann, *Worship in Ancient Israel*, pp. 20-22. Brueggemann writes here out of a theological perspective, not a history-of-religions model, but his point supports and amplifies the position being described.

42. Rowley, *Worship in Ancient Israel* is a prime example. For treatments with a similarly progressive framework, see Fohrer, *History of Israelite Religion*; Oesterley and Robinson, *Hebrew Religion*.

43. Rowley, *Worship in Ancient Israel*, p. 246.

44. For another biblical example of this motif or theme, see the account of Hezekiah's illness in 2 Kgs 20:1-16.

as well as historically. It is no longer the case in scholarship, however, that "personal religion" is taken to be a late development within Israelite religion.[45] If some earlier authorities were inclined to trace the roots of personal religion to the biblical prophets,[46] the antiquity of such a phenomenon throughout the ancient Near East has in fact long been recognized.[47] Personal religion is now viewed not as a developmental achievement but a mode of religious activity operating simultaneously with other modes (e.g., national observances, rites for the dead, temple rituals, etc.).[48] In fact, worship of the heart continues to be remembered and known in Jewish tradition to this day as *avodah she-ba-lev*.[49]

As for the theological progressivists, I would admit that indeed Samuel does *not* fit their interpretive framework very well, but I would further maintain that the problem is their framework rather than Samuel. There is no way to ignore the growth in traditions, concepts and theological understanding throughout the story that the Old Testament tells, but much of what has passed for an account of "progressive revelation" has been built on a historically deficient (and neo-Marcionite) appraisal of ancient Israelite religion.[50] One way to salvage the approach might be to date the Samuel narrative quite late, well into the Persian or even Hellenistic period, and then to claim that the theologically "sophisticated" ideas of the text are there because they have had time to develop. I myself suspect that this kind of logic partially lies behind the push within biblical studies, even when made in the name of "objective history," to date texts as late as possible. Yet nothing comes from nothing, and it is inconceivable that a profound Persian-period Israelite faith did not have roots in the pre-exilic era. Furthermore, even if the present Samuel narrative was in fact a Persian-period product, those who framed it apparently did not think that the attitudes and ideas they highlighted in the story would have been foreign to the story's characters in their own day and age. So it is better to take the narrative as a presumptive historical datum in its own right: perhaps in ancient Israel there was indeed what some today would consider a sophisticated understanding of personal faith.[51]

45. See further Lang, *Hebrew God*, pp. 111-14. Lang gives a brief but helpful overview of scholarship on this question. His own analysis of personal religion as a psychological coping mechanism (p. 114) is nevertheless woefully inadequate.

46. Lang cites the example of Skinner, *Prophecy and Religion*.

47. Lang cites Breasted, *Development of Religion and Thought in Ancient Egypt*, pp. 348-49; Jacobsen, *Treasures of Darkness*, p. 147.

48. See Albertz, *Persönliche Frommigkeit und offizielle Religion*; Berlinerblau, "'Popular Religion' Paradigm in Old Testament Research."

49. See Soloveitchik, *Worship of the Heart*.

50. As noted in Barr, *Bible in the Modern World*, p. 146.

51. Rowley could also write of "an invariable prophetic principle" in the Old Testament; namely, that "It is the spirit that gives meaning to the act of worship, and the spirit that reveals

The third objection to this central claim of my close reading will no doubt come from those who view deuteronomism as a "secularizing" movement. Here the arguments are complex and require fuller exposition. The "secularizing" interpretation was first expressed in a comprehensive manner by Moshe Weinfeld in his magisterial treatment of Deuteronomy.[52] It should be noted at the outset that Weinfeld, following Yehezkel Kaufmann,[53] rejects Wellhausen's model of Israelite religion in which the priestly material (P) of the Pentateuch is dated later than the deuteronomic literature (D).[54] This move naturally has significant repercussions for his own reconstruction of Israelite religion. It means, among other things, that Weinfeld is forced to argue against the idea that an exclusive centralization of the Israelite cult in Jerusalem is presupposed by P.[55]

On the other hand, Weinfeld is persuasive in demonstrating that many of the worship practices depicted in the narratives of the Former Prophets — for example, use of the lots, procedures for holy war, sacrifices and libations, purifications and taboos, the setting aside of days for holy meals, religious pilgrimages, and assemblies — seem comfortably at home in the religious worldview of the priestly writings.[56] However, and by stark contrast, the book of Deuteronomy "rests on a distinctly secular foundation," Weinfeld claims.[57] With this phrase he wants to describe the deuteronomic alteration in Israel's religious life as primarily concerned with those institutions and laws that existed apart from the specific priestly sphere of activity — institutions like

---

itself in the act to the eye of God." See Rowley, *Missionary Messsage of the Old Testament*, p. 73. Greenberg, *Biblical Prose Prayer*, pp. 36, 47-52, similarly points out that for biblical prayer to work it had to be sincere, citing 1 Kgs 8:38; Isa 29:13; Pss 78:36-37; 145:18; Lam 2:19.

52. Weinfeld, *Deuteronomy and the Deuteronomic School*.

53. Kaufmann, *Religion of Israel*.

54. Weinfeld, *Deuteronomy and the Deuteronomic School*, pp. 179-80. Weinfeld's justification for viewing D and P as chronologically "concurrent" depends in part on reading D as basically a literary unity stemming from a single period. For example, he argues for the presence of priestly idioms in Deuteronomy 4 without considering — as most historical-critical scholars would conclude — that such idioms could be the result of later redaction. See Weinfeld, *Deuteronomy and the Deuteronomic School*, pp. 180-81 n. 3.

55. Weinfeld, *Deuteronomy and the Deuteronomic School*, p. 183 n. 4. Otherwise, given that P is dated earlier, it would be challenging to explain the innovative quality of D's injunction to centralize worship. However, Weinfeld's solution is to imagine a (non-exclusive) "central sanctuary" in Jerusalem already for the priestly writers. The difficulty of two "concurrent" groups, one of which demands exclusive centralization and one of which does not, is left undeveloped. This key example reveals the underlying difficulty with Weinfeld's thesis and helps explain why historical-critical scholars have usually viewed the two groups as successive.

56. Weinfeld, *Deuteronomy and the Deuteronomic School*, pp. 186-87.

57. Weinfeld, *Deuteronomy and the Deuteronomic School*, p. 188.

the judiciary, the monarchy, the military, as well as civil/criminal laws regarding the family, loans/debts, and trespassing. Even beyond simply having such wider interests, though, Deuteronomy is viewed by Weinfeld as purposely ignoring priestly activities and as thus "secularizing" key aspects of Israel's life, which had previously been considered basically sacred.[58] The social movement that produced the book of Deuteronomy is then further characterized as rationalistic, humanistic, and eudaemonistic.[59]

Weinfeld's most potentially damaging argument to my reading of Samuel is therefore that deuteronomic tradition is "secularizing." As I intend to show, however, his understanding of what "secular" means actually turns out to support my view. In Weinfeld's reconstruction, the deuteronomists seek to take control of Israel's religious life away from the priests and transform it "into an abstract religion which did not require any external expression."[60] His parade example of what he considers the secularizing tendency in Deuteronomy is its rejection of the anthropomorphic language and concepts relating to God (which exist so prominently and unproblematically throughout P), and their replacement with a more abstract notion of God's "name." Quite consistently throughout Deuteronomy and the deuteronomistic literature, Weinfeld illustrates, God's "name" rather than God's person is said to dwell in the Temple. Weinfeld, drawing on Gerhard von Rad,[61] views this move as a rejection of the "popular belief" that God actually dwelled there, and instead a conceptual development in the direction of an abstract, heavenly deity.[62] Similarly, the ark is treated as a repository for the tablets of the covenant (Deut 10:1-5) rather than as a visible representation of God, and the Temple itself is increasingly viewed as a house of prayer rather than a sacrificial site.[63]

To these examples must be added the evidence of the deuteronomic view of sacrifice and Israel's holy days. According to Weinfeld, in priestly theology

58. Weinfeld, *Deuteronomy and the Deuteronomic School*, p. 188. Again, Weinfeld can interpret D as ignoring the full-blown cultic rites of P only because he dates P to the same time as D or, in this case, to a time somewhat earlier than that of D. The earlier he dates P, the more "secular" D looks. The majority of scholars would instead be inclined to attribute the absence of some of the things Weinfeld mentions to the fact that they did not yet exist, not at least in P's fully developed version of them. Another alternative, which Weinfeld acknowledges, would be that D presupposes the priestly regulations of P and therefore did not feel it necessary to reiterate them.

59. Weinfeld, *Deuteronomy and the Deuteronomic School*, p. 189.

60. Weinfeld, *Deuteronomy and the Deuteronomic School*, p. 190.

61. Von Rad, *Studies in Deuteronomy*, pp. 37-44.

62. Weinfeld, *Deuteronomy and the Deuteronomic School*, p. 193. Now see Richter, *Deuteronomistic History and the Name Theology*.

63. Weinfeld, *Deuteronomy and the Deuteronomic School*, pp. 208-9.

the priest himself makes expiation for sin in the sacrificial ritual, which does not include spoken prayers or confessions.[64] In deuteronomic theology, however, God is the agent of expiation, and confession and prayer are necessary for sacrificial rites to be fully adequate.[65] There is also a strong emphasis in Deuteronomy on the purpose of sacrifice as being to provide food for the worshippers present, especially the less fortunate of society.[66] Sacrifice functions for the deuteronomists as a "personal" rather than an "institutional" practice, according to Weinfeld.

For deuteronomic theology, the point of the sacrificial act was thus either "humanitarian" (i.e., providing food for the poor) or "private" (fulfilling a personal vow with a votive offering and extending thanksgiving to God).[67] Sacrifice is further to be controlled and regulated, according to the deuteronomists, by eliminating local shrines and centralizing worship at the Jerusalem Temple. In order to make centralization possible, however, non-sacrificial slaughter will be permitted at the local level. "Non-sacrificial" slaughter means that animals could now be killed without having to dash their blood against an altar (Deut 12:15-16, 20-24). Where once an essential connection between bloodshed and worship existed for Israelites in their daily lives and local communities, with the deuteronomic reform that connection was broken and bloodshed could be viewed as a "secular" act.

Because religious festivals would no longer be observed locally, Deuteronomy reworks the mode of their observance, disconnecting them from their earlier associations with the agricultural year and turning them into regularized occasions for votive offerings and thanksgiving. Weinfeld concludes:

> The centralization of the cult was itself, of course, a sweeping innovation in the history of the Israelite cultus, but its consequences were . . . decisively more revolutionary in nature, in that they involved the collapse of an entire system of concepts which for centuries had been regarded as sacrosanct. With the elimination of the provincial cultus, Israelite religious life was completely wrested from the control of priest and temple. It was freed from its ties to the cult and was transformed into an abstract religion which did not necessarily require any external expression. Indeed the very purpose

---

64. See further Knohl, *Sanctuary of Silence.*

65. Weinfeld, *Deuteronomy and the Deuteronomic School,* pp. 210-11.

66. See further MacDonald, *Not Bread Alone,* pp. 88-96; idem, *What Did the Ancient Israelites Eat?* pp. 100-101.

67. Weinfeld, *Deuteronomy and the Deuteronomic School,* p. 212.

of the book of Deuteronomy, as has been correctly observed, was to curtail and circumscribe the cultus and not to extend or enhance it.[68]

In this formulation, Deuteronomy not only carves out secular space in ancient Israelite society, it does so in order to restrict priestly religion. Yet the question is whether the vision of religious life advanced by Deuteronomy is truly "abstract" and opposed to "external expression."[69]

In a more recent exploration of Deuteronomy, Bernard Levinson supports this aspect of Weinfeld's position by further arguing that the deuteronomists allowed the earlier Covenant Code (Exod 21–23) to stand, but wrote new provisions of their own in order to elaborate and revise that set of laws through the use of "transformative exegesis."[70] Because animal slaughter could no longer occur regularly in the form of an offering at the local sanctuary, which had earlier been the case (Exod 20:24), non-cultic or "profane" slaughter of animals was permitted by the deuteronomists (Deut 12:15-16). Passover, not previously a festival at all (Exod 23:17), was also to be observed in Jerusalem (Deut 16:16). Because local priests had been involved in the administration of justice, the abolition of local sanctuaries created a jurisprudential vacuum that was then filled by the creation of something like an independent judiciary (Deut 16:18-20).

Like Weinfeld, Levinson also describes this process as "secularization." Yet Levinson, drawing on the work of Norbert Lohfink, resists the further conclusion that:

in draining the local sphere of all cultic content, the authors of Deuteronomy . . . leave it as a profane religious void. The local sphere continues to have fundamentally religious structure. One continues to receive divine blessing in the local sphere, although it is now mediated. The compensation for the loss of direct access to the divine, with the eradication of local altars, does not only take place at the cultic center, with the repeated emphasis on the "joy" available there to the pilgrim. That restitution is equally provided in the local sphere with this noncultic, although still religiously conceived, "blessing of Yahweh your God."[71]

68. Weinfeld, *Deuteronomy and the Deuteronomic School*, p. 190.

69. This same question was posed early on by Milgrom, "Alleged 'Demythologization' and 'Secularization' in Deuteronomy."

70. Levinson, *Deuteronomy and the Hermeneutics of Legal Innovation*.

71. Levinson, *Deuteronomy and the Hermeneutics of Legal Innovation*, p. 49. Here Levinson cites Lohfink, "Cult Reform of Josiah of Judah"; idem, "Opfer und Säkularisierung im Deuteronomium," p. 31.

To imagine a "profane religious void" in local Israelite communities outside of Jerusalem not only violates common sense regarding the character of life in ancient societies generally, it also stands in the way of a persuasive description of the deuteronomic reform program. For how could the deuteronomic reformers have convinced their audience to relinquish their local sanctuaries if the alternative had truly been "complete loss of local access to God"?[72]

Still, Weinfeld's basic insight into deuteronomic theology remains that "sacrifice is only of subordinate importance and that the essential requisite for atonement is the sincere intentions of the worshipper; sacrifice alone cannot expiate sin."[73] In Weinfeld's description of Deuteronomy, and especially in this central observation about deuteronomic theology, quite a lot of overlap actually exists with my close reading of 1 Samuel, which identifies a preoccupation in the narrative with a wide variety of ritual practices, and yet also treats the narrative as turning on the need for a subjective dimension to worship. My reading has similarly registered a humanitarian attitude toward worship in Samuel (e.g., 1 Sam 1; 20).

This overlap should therefore provide historical support for my reading and counteract the criticism that it may be anachronistic. As for Weinfeld's characterization of the historical specifics of the deuteronomic transformation of Israelite religion, he seems largely correct to me (although I remain unconvinced that D modifies an earlier P).[74] The confusing aspect of Weinfeld's presentation, however, is his insistence on describing deuteronomic theology

72. Levinson, *Deuteronomy and the Hermeneutics of Legal Innovation*, p. 49. Even so, there remains an odd tension in Levinson's work between historical explanations that credit religious impulses positively and cynical descriptions of the historical factors supposedly at play. E.g., "[The text's editors] attempted to camouflage those innovations by feigning a cunning piety with respect to the very authoritative texts that they had subverted" (p. 48). I find myself wondering to what extent this tension reflects the book's "comprehensive rethinking and complete revision" that Levinson describes in his preface. Interestingly, Lohfink was apparently a key figure in this rethinking, which occurred while Levinson was in Germany.

73. Weinfeld, *Deuteronomy and the Deuteronomic School*, p. 213. He further notes, "The cultic ceremonies described in Deuteronomy are always accompanied by prayers and thanksgiving, in contrast to the rituals described by P, which are conducted in complete silence."

74. See now, however, the historical and exegetical criticism of Weinfeld in Vogt, *Deuteronomic Theology*. In the end I am not persuaded that Vogt succeeds in adequately characterizing the discontinuous, innovative quality of the deuteronomic reform. Indeed, he begs off from situating Deuteronomy within the overarching development of Israelite religion. However, he does score several localized points in his running critique of Weinfeld. More recently, Vogt has argued that while Deuteronomy centralizes *sacrifice*, it actually decentralizes and extends *worship* to the people of the land; see Vogt, "Centralization and Decentralization in Deuteronomy." That the "profane slaughter" of Deuteronomy 12 is still marked as "slaughter" (√*zbḥ*) is crucial for his argument.

as "secularizing." Other scholars have criticized Weinfeld precisely on this point; their criticism will help to demonstrate how Weinfeld's label need not stand in the way of my contention that 1 Samuel, as a prime exemplar of deuteronomistic literature, is intensely interested in worship and thus not "secularizing" at all.

Norbert Lohfink, for example, agrees with Weinfeld that the deuteronomic legal code initiated a major restructuring of Israel's religious life. Yet Lohfink views Deuteronomy's intention as in fact an extension and more thorough integration of religious faith within the Israelite community.[75] Yes, the local sanctuaries are abolished, but the emphasis on religious festivals in Jerusalem is hardly "secular." The deuteronomic platform is neither "abstract" nor independent of "external expression." One could well argue, taking cues from Lohfink, that the restriction of certain religious activities to Jerusalem might have had as its twin goals the elevation of the significance of those activities and the intensification of religion within the functioning of Israelite society generally — or at least that the deuteronomists thought so. From their perspective, the location of religious observances primarily within local sanctuaries could have served to equate religious devotion so much with ordinary life that, as a consequence, religious faith came to lack sufficient conceptual and sociological differentiation. Identifying a need for personal religious conviction actually makes religious practice *less* abstract and *more* binding in individual lives and decisions. Lohfink's stance thus leads to a view of deuteronomism as a religious, rather than secularizing, reform. Its reform aspect lies in its intention not to restrict but to broaden, in a sense to democratize, the sphere of the sacred so that all Israelites truly share in the burdens and blessings of faith.[76] Whether one agrees with this deuteronomistic platform is less important at this point than recognizing how the deuteronomists' perspective might well have been thoroughly religious in nature.

A similar approach comes from Peter Vogt, who has criticized Weinfeld strongly for concluding that particular features of deuteronomic thought are

75. Lohfink, "Opfer, und Säkularisierung im Deuteronomium," p. 41: "Der Umbau, der stattgefunden hat, dient nicht dazu, immer mehr menschliche Lebensbereiche aus der Nähe Gottes zu entlassen, sondern umgekehrt, alle Lebensbereiche Israels in diese Nähe Gottes hineinzuholen." ("The transformation that took place did not aim to remove ever more realms of human life out of proximity to God, but rather the opposite: to bring all realms of human life into this proximity to God.")

76. Cf. Eichrodt, *Theology of the Old Testament*, 1:91: "Those who speak to us in the pages of Deuteronomy are men who know that a natural law can never attain its goal so long as it remains a system reluctantly endured and effective only by compulsion; it must be founded on the inward assent of the people."

"secular" when in fact there are good grounds for viewing those features as religious but still non-cultic.[77] Vogt agrees that Lohfink's idea of an extension of the sacred is preferable to Weinfeld's secularization thesis.[78] For example, Vogt successfully problematizes the view that √zbḥ in Deuteronomy 12 necessarily refers to profane slaughter, since the term is nowhere else used with that meaning in the Hebrew Bible and, moreover, the different term √ṭbḥ consistently does appear with the meaning of profane slaughter.[79] So if "profane slaughter" was meant in Deuteronomy 12, why not use √ṭbḥ instead to describe it?

In sum, Weinfeld's suggestion that the deuteronomists were "secularizing" falls fully short of the mark, but once his insights regarding the deuteronomic agenda are viewed as, in effect, an alternate program of spirituality, there is considerable agreement between what he suggests and what I have located at the heart of the 1 Samuel narrative. Thus, 1 Samuel is still best read as a deuteronomistic construction, notwithstanding the relative absence of deuteronomistic vocabulary and motifs.[80] Its focus on worship and spirituality is grounded historically in the deuteronomic program for reform, even as that focus provides further historical evidence for how such a reform once occurred in ancient Israel. Of course, treating Samuel as a deuteronomistic literary work does not preclude the possibility of earlier sources and compositions, but I remain skeptical of our ability to reconstruct them with a high degree of accuracy or confidence. This stance does not preclude the possibility of later alterations and additions either. In my judgment, however, any such changes have not altered the narrative substantially from its basic deuteronomistic proportions and fundamental literary shape.

1 Samuel as Tragedy

In one of the most recent major commentaries on 1 Samuel to appear, David Tsumura impressively treats the linguistic features of the biblical text, considers historical questions with a bearing on its interpretation, and locates several of the same broad theological themes that I have also identified in my close reading: the kingship of God, God's providential guidance, God's

77. Vogt, *Deuteronomic Theology*, esp. pp. 70-93.
78. Vogt, *Deuteronomic Theology*, pp. 89-91.
79. Vogt, *Deuteronomic Theology*, pp. 181-83.
80. Kratz, *Composition*, pp. 170-74. For further investigation of the issues at stake, see Edenburg and Pakkala, eds., *Is Samuel among the Deuteronomists?* and Schäfer-Lichtenberger, ed., *Samuelbücher und die Deuteronomisten*.

sovereign will and power.[81] Then, however, Tsumura describes the "purpose" of 1 Samuel as follows:

> The purpose of the book of 1 Samuel is to highlight two major events: first, the establishment of the monarchy in Israel (chs. 8–12) and, then, the preparation of David to sit on the royal throne after Saul (chs. 16–31).[82]

Historical reportage is therefore the primary aim of the book, according to Tsumura. The book tells about particular episodes in Israel's history — accurately, he also maintains — and those historical episodes continue to be meaningful by virtue of their location within the overarching sweep of salvation history. Tsumura does perceive a (single) "principle" at work within this history, namely that "the king in Israel is to be subject to the prophet through whom God conveys his word."[83] A true king is obedient to the word of God. From this vantage point Tsumura also suggests a link with the New Testament's account of Jesus, "the Messiah-king," who was obedient to God, "even to death on a cross" (Phil 2:8).

Tsumura's work on 1 Samuel is both comprehensive and learned, and he does offer explicitly Christian reflections on the book. With a focus on the MT and the use of discourse analysis, he exhibits in his treatment the impact of literary ideas and methods on Old Testament scholarship, and he therefore shares a loose kinship with my own approach. In his identification of Samuel's purpose as "highlighting events," however, he presumes that history is the primary bearer of theological significance and that the narrative of Samuel is to be read for the ways in which it makes that history transparent. This appeal to history is common in contemporary biblical interpretation (especially interpretation of the Bible's narrative books) and is largely shared by theological liberals and conservatives, so Tsumura has extensive company. I do not mean to single him out unfairly. Yet in my judgment fatal problems are created — or rather prolonged, since they have existed within biblical interpretation for some time — by this kind of appeal to history. First, the rich subtlety of the biblical narrative is streamlined in order to favor the "history-likeness" of its plot.[84] At most — and to his credit Tsumura attempts this much — one can point to "principles" or "themes" evident in the unfolding of that plot, so that a didactic aspect emerges in the book's rehearsal of history. However, such

---

81. Tsumura, *First Book of Samuel*, esp. pp. 69–73.

82. Tsumura, *First Book of Samuel*, p. 73.

83. Tsumura, *First Book of Samuel*, p. 73.

84. Here I am borrowing the term "history-likeness" from the work of Frei, *Eclipse of Biblical Narrative*, pp. 10-12.

principles and themes typically operate at such a high level of abstraction that in the process they lose much of their literary persuasiveness and theological appeal. "Obedience to God's word" neither illuminates the complexity of 1 Samuel nor carries palpable rhetorical force for the reader. Do not other biblical books also enjoin obedience to God's word? Is there nothing more *specific* about the narrative of 1 Samuel to be said?

The second difficulty reinforced by Tsumura's approach is that it makes his theological interpretation a hostage to historical verification. In Tsumura's case he clearly does not believe this "hostage situation" to be a problem because he possesses a high opinion of 1 Samuel's historical accuracy. Yet many, if not most, biblical scholars and archaeologists who investigate the history of Israel today exhibit great skepticism regarding the historicity of the events that 1 Samuel relates. For example, in one recent treatment Israel Finkelstein and Neil Silberman take the position that "many of the famous episodes in the biblical story of David and Solomon are fictitious, historically questionable, or highly exaggerated."[85] Finkelstein and Silberman are not mere debunkers — nor the most radical of critics — and they have their own historical reconstruction to offer. In the "complex stratigraphy" of the biblical text itself, they recognize a "literary and historical evolution [that], backed by archaeological evidence, is the key to understanding the true character of the biblical David and Solomon story."[86] As this formulation indicates, Finkelstein and Silberman have more in common with Tsumura than one at first might think. Like Tsumura, they not only view their primary task as that of reconstructing history, they also locate the meaning ("true character") of the biblical narrative *in* history. Or, to put it more recognizably in their own terms, the "story" is no longer the story the Bible tells but the story of what "really" happened.

Little difference, if any, is made to that same underlying assumption by Tsumura's effort to offer a more optimistic account of 1 Samuel's verisimilitude. Because the historical issues are in fact disputed, the choice left to Tsumura is either to offer a sanitized version of history or to withhold theological judgments until the historical issues are fully clarified. Like most religiously conservative biblical scholars, he opts for the former course.[87] This choice not

85. Finkelstein and Silberman, *David and Solomon*, p. 21.

86. Finkelstein and Silberman, *David and Solomon*, pp. 22-23.

87. Tsumura, *First Book of Samuel*, p. 31, dates 1 Samuel 1–15 to the time of Samuel and 1 Samuel 16–31 to the early part of David's "era." Tsumura does recognize the presence in the narrative of secondary editing, but he views this editorial work to have consisted of adding minimal transitions between preexistent, free-standing narrative blocks and inserting a few new short passages. In this appraisal, he explicitly follows the literary critic Alter, *David Story*, p. xii. For broader discussion of the predilection within evangelical biblical

only further shifts the focus of his own interpretive attention from theology to history,[88] it also somewhat ironically reinforces the sense among his readership that the meaning of the Bible lies in the history behind it, a perspective that actually erodes the high theological view of scripture that Tsumura presumably intends to affirm. Also, in terms of methodological consistency, if Tsumura's intention is to describe the history to which the text provides a witness, he would do better to use a critically reconstructed text, rather than privileging the MT as he does, since at times the historical priority of other manuscript witnesses seems likely. Tsumura's method therefore undermines the importance that he himself places on the MT, on the text's historical accuracy, and on the role of the Bible as scripture. Each of these three commitments is rendered weaker in his handling, rather than stronger, as he surely had hoped.

The alternative, as I have attempted to demonstrate already, consists in the exploration of the biblical narrative's literary contours themselves as instead representing the "story" that matters. This exploration can be done in a manner that holds open historical questions and seeks historically plausible solutions to interpretive choices. At the same time, such an exploration views the biblical narrative as *more than* a historical witness and endeavors to tease out and *extend* the theological perspectives already operative within that narrative. For the purpose of Christian theology, the "story" as it currently exists within the biblical text is the story that counts. With this formulation I do not mean to reject or denigrate the theological validity of historical investigations of ancient Israel, but I do wish to question their theological decisiveness. The meaning or purpose of a biblical narrative is not *exclusively* a function of its background or genesis; the biblical narrative conveys meaning in excess of the circumstances of its making, including the intentions of its author(s).[89]

To be sure, such "meaning" is articulated in conjunction with specific readers and *partly* derived from the sociohistorical forces that led to its production. Yet the narrative also has a particularity that grants it a "relative determinacy"[90]

---

scholarship to dodge difficult historical questions, see Sparks, *God's Word in Human Words*, pp. 133-70.

88. His discussion of the "purpose" of 1 Samuel consists of a single paragraph. He covers the "theology of 1 Samuel" in 4 pages (out of 698).

89. Something that is indeed true of all art, including history-writing; see Gadamer, "Aesthetics and Hermeneutics," esp. p. 103: "For the real task of historical study is not to understand the subjective intentions, plans, and experiences of the men who are involved in history . . . The subjective intentions of men standing within the historical process are seldom or never such that a later historical evaluation of events confirms their assessment by contemporaries." Cf. Ricoeur, "Hermeneutical Function of Distanciation."

90. For this language, see Hays, *Moral Vision of the New Testament*, p. 8.

and thus a controlling authority over both its origins and its readers. In Christian theological terms this hermeneutical authority is traditionally expressed by the doctrine of inspiration and, despite significant modern debate in Christian circles about the character of inspiration, I would maintain that a biblical view of inspiration locates scriptural authority in the biblical *text* (cf. 2 Tim 3:16!) rather than in the intentions of the biblical authors or in the faithfulness of the reading community. Again, this position does not mean that authorial intention (especially when reformulated as the inferred rhetorical aim of the implied author) and "ruled readings" (by both individuals and church communities) are insignificant and play no role, but it does stake the claim that the narrative itself remains the source and test of both.[91]

What emerges from my own literary exploration of 1 Samuel is the importance of the spiritual relationship between God and Israel, especially Israel's leaders. The book of 1 Samuel does not merely detail the historical beginnings of the Israelite monarchy. It tells how the origin of the monarchy presented Israel with a challenge to its fundamental allegiance to God, a challenge represented above all by the twin threats of expedient politics and formulaic worship. Indeed, the book's emphasis on personal piety subverts its ostensible description of the institutionalization of religion in the form of a monarchy. Saul proves unfit for the true task of leadership, while David rises to the occasion.

Even with David, some doubt is raised by the narrative as to the basic compatibility between a monarchic form of government and God's spiritual kingship over Israel. In the end, David's royal success can be celebrated as a symbol that points beyond itself to God's supreme sovereignty — but always also with a wistful sense of accommodation and loss. Although the story of David's accession to the throne and subsequent reign is religiously instructive, even he can never fully meet the standard that the role demands. However, David's ultimate strength (which is not entirely his own accomplishment) lies in his innately spiritual orientation, and leads him consistently to seek God's guidance and forgiveness, even when he succumbs to the worldly temptations that surround him thanks to the nature of the royal office. By contrast, Saul's weakness (for which he is not completely responsible) arises from his innate lack of a spiritual disposition, and this spiritual deficiency prevents him from seeking God personally, over time destroying him.

As David Gunn has skillfully shown, Christian interpreters have often been uneasy about the tragic quality of Saul's story and have generally responded by attempting to identify Saul's specific sin — "the" reason that will

---

91. For a fuller exposition of this argument, see Chapman, "Reclaiming Inspiration for the Bible," pp. 167-206.

justify his rejection and failure.[92] The squeamishness of Christian interpreters in relation to Saul has in fact been rooted in an unwillingness to entertain the possibility of Christian "tragedy" as a theological category or genre.[93] Within the Bible and within life, the spirit of this resistance insists, the knowledge of God's goodness and decisive victory over death in Jesus Christ finally allows only for a happy ending, that is, for "comedy" in the classical literary sense.[94] Certainly there can be moments of tragedy in Christian scripture (e.g., Israel's exile, Christ's crucifixion), just as such periods exist in the lives of individual Christians, but these moments are circumscribed by God's providential justice and the possibility of further divine action (e.g., Israel's return, Christ's resurrection).[95] In its most extreme form this perspective equates the perception of tragedy with unbelief or willful disbelief.[96] However, some writers have instead seen a kinship between the tragic tradition and Christian emphasis on the impossibility of human beings to secure their own righteousness through effort or an act of personal will.[97] Gunn himself distinguishes between a "tragedy of flaw" and a "tragedy of fate," arguing strongly for the latter as the operative category within the Saul narrative. But he distinguishes these two types too sharply from each other.[98] My own reading suggests that the Saul narrative is precisely concerned to illustrate how "fate" and "flaw" coexist in mysterious interrelation.

I have done something like what Gunn criticizes but also something dif-

---

92. Gunn, *Fate of King Saul*, pp. 23-31. Karl Barth is noteworthy for his insistence that David's shortcomings are, if anything, actually worse than Saul's. See his contrast in *Church Dogmatics II*, p. 370, between the "microscopic sins of Saul" and "the crimson sins of David."

93. There has also been resistance to the idea that tragedy is compatible with Judaism. See Steiner, *Death of Tragedy*, p. 4: "Tragedy is alien to the Judaic sense of the world."

94. Although not himself such an interpreter, Frye, *Great Code*, p. 169, also recognizes the literary shape of the Bible as a "divine comedy." Yet he nevertheless considers Saul "the one great tragic hero of the Bible" (p. 181). Frye locates the essence of Saul's tragedy in the narrative's "suggestion of malice within the divine nature, a suggestion that is perhaps essential to all great tragedy." Although rhetorically forceful, the characterization of God as possessing "malice" misunderstands the theological drama at the heart of the Samuel story.

95. For discussion, see Krook, *Elements of Tragedy*, pp. 267-71. She identifies the crucifixion as the "paradigm of paradigms" for Christian tragedy.

96. See, e.g., Cherbonnier, "Biblical Faith and the Idea of Tragedy"; Niebuhr, *Beyond Tragedy*, p. 155: "Christianity is a religion which transcends tragedy." For more recent discussion, see Farley, *Tragic Vision and Divine Compassion*; Sands, *Escape from Paradise*. For Farley, tragedy does not turn on "pathetic inevitability" but human suffering.

97. See, e.g., Cox, *Between Earth and Heaven*. According to von Rad, *Old Testament Theology*, 1:325, Saul's story is the only one in the Old Testament that has "close affinity with the spirit of Greek tragedy."

98. See further Williams, "Is God Moral?" p. 177.

ferent. I, too, have identified a shortcoming on Saul's part, one that I believe further illuminates the literary details of the 1 Samuel narrative: namely, his incapacity for personal faith.[99] This interpretation is beautifully expressed in a classic essay on Saul by A. B. Davidson:

> Religious incapacity was his fault — was the characteristic of his mind. He had not the faculty of knowing what religion meant. He might know that religion meant a full surrender of one's will to God, but he was too blunt, in a religious sense, to understand what a full surrender was . . . He wanted religious depth. He was not quite an irreligious man, least of all was he an immoral man; but religion was not able to make much of him.[100]

However, in contrast to some interpretive arguments like this I do not consider such an incapacity to be primarily Saul's fault, although I judge that he is not thereby released from all responsibility for what he does or does not do either.[101] In my reading of the narrative, Saul is partly held responsible for what occurs and partly excused from such responsibility. This complex portrait may ultimately stem from the mixture of ancient sources that were once compiled in order to form the book as we now know it. But given the subtlety of the present narrative, I would be wary of assuming too quickly that there had ever been literary sources that were exclusively pro- or anti-monarchic, exclusively pro- or anti-Saul. Much more likely, in my view, is that the character of Saul and the emergence of the monarchy in Israel were *always* viewed as they still appear in the biblical text — as confusing and complex.[102] The present narrative has not developed primarily out of an effort to harmonize earlier oppositional traditions or strike ideological compromises between opposed groups, but in order to witness as faithfully and clearly as possible to theological tensions and ambiguities that likely existed as early as the events themselves.

99. Gunn, *Fate of King Saul*, 38, rejects a version of this explanation, maintaining that Saul is pious throughout the Samuel narrative, anxious to perform religious duties and committed to YHWH alone. Gunn does allow that 1 Sam 15:22 might provide a warrant for the kind of interpretation I am offering. Gunn also concedes that an interpretation of Samuel might attempt to distinguish between external piety and genuine faith, between outward form and inward disposition. This distinction is precisely the one that I have sought to draw in a consistent manner. Without saying exactly why, Gunn rejects it as "very much an explanation of last resort."

100. Davidson, "Saul's Reprobation," pp. 143-44.

101. Even with his heavy emphasis on fate and the collusion of God and Samuel against Saul, Gunn, *Fate of King Saul*, p. 166, does not claim that Saul is completely without responsibility for all that happens. As Williams, "Is God Moral?" p. 185, points out, 1 Sam 13:13b implies that Saul had a real choice.

102. Cf. the similar judgment of Dietrich, "König David," p. 19.

The issue of Saul's culpability only indirectly contributes to the identification of 1 Samuel as a tragedy. Even though Saul is portrayed as partly responsible for his own rejection, I hold that it still makes sense to interpret the Samuel narrative as "tragic" in its features and goals. The real question, I would argue, is not whether the story of Saul is a tragedy, but what kind of tragedy it is. By partly telling its story as scripted by God in advance (e.g., 1 Sam 8:7-9), the narrative does exhibit some similarity with ancient Greek tragedy (which characteristically turns on the inescapability of fate).[103] Yet 1 Samuel as a whole never communicates the same inevitability of time that is central to the Greek genre. To the contrary, despite localized instances in which events function according to a prophesied timetable, the real problem with time in 1 Samuel is instead its open-endedness, the lack of any precise date for Saul's final destiny.[104] After his rejection from the kingship (1 Sam 15), Saul is somewhat surprisingly neither deposed nor placed under a schedule for deposition. The entire second half of the book turns on a *search* for the timing and the circumstances according to which a change in Israel's rulers can finally be effected. A sense remains that God is active and involved in the events that transpire, and that the anticipated "regime change" is God's to negotiate, but in the latter half of the book the character of God, like that of Samuel, moves from the forefront of the narrative into the background. David and Saul, along with the rest of Israel, are left to wonder how and when God will act, and how and when they themselves should act in light of God's apparent delay.

Here tragedy takes a different shape from how Greek tragedy is usually understood. I find it illuminating at this point to appropriate Emily Wilson's work on the tragic tradition and her identification of one stream within that tradition as the tragedy of "overliving."[105] Although Wilson herself does not discuss the story of Saul, she argues for "a central thread in the tragic tradition that is concerned not with dying too early but living too long."[106] She locates this tradition in Greek drama (Sophocles' *Oedipus* plays, Euripides' *Heracles*), Seneca, Shakespeare (*King Lear, Macbeth*), and Milton (*Samson Agonistes, Paradise Lost*). In her description, this thread of the tragic tradition "presents a character who experiences an apparently intolerable sense of suffering and

---

103. See further Exum and Whedbee, "Isaac, Samson and Saul."

104. By contrast, Moses' characterization also possesses an element of tragedy: he is told beforehand (Num 20) that he will not live to enter the Promised Land. But in this case the tragic element is dying too soon instead of not dying soon enough. See further Barzel, "Moses: Tragedy and Sublimity."

105. Wilson, *Mocked with Death.*

106. Wilson, *Mocked with Death,* p. 1.

loss, and feels that he has lived too long but, nevertheless, decides to resist suicide."[107] Although the literary works cited attempt to suppress the difficulties
brought about by this character's resultant "overliving," such efforts invariably
fall short, leaving the reader or hearer disturbed by the idea that "life may feel
too long and endings may seem to have come too late."[108] Tragedies of overliving query their audiences' own sense of timing and meaning.

Wilson further characterizes tragedies of overliving as distinct from the
tropes of physical frailty and old age, which can be used in literature to similar
effect. But in the tragic tradition identified by Wilson, overliving results from a
specific crisis that would appear to necessitate the imminent end of a particular character's life, even a character who may be physically strong and not yet
advanced in years. In this way Wilson's subset of tragedy primarily concerns
a "failure to die" rather than a death.[109] Such an idea casts fresh light on the
narrative of 1 Samuel. Fascinatingly, Wilson associates the "failure to die" in
tragedies of overliving with many of the same features found in the story of
Saul. There is a basic confusion on the part of the other characters in the story,
and the narrative order itself sometimes becomes jumbled. That something
seems out of kilter is also expressed through tropes of blindness and hiding.[110]
Time, dates, and schedules become a source of confusion and an occasion
for conflict. The character who overlives thus poses implicit questions to the
reader or hearer: In what way is my experience of life similar? Has life gone
on too long for me? Is there not a kind of death that can occur within life as
well as at life's end?

Repetition and duplication without significant alteration underscore the
presence of the overliving theme.[111] The central character of the tragedy often sinks into despair and madness, both of which are related to the contrast
between the character's own subjective sense of time and the character's apprehension of another dimension to time, a dimension less accessible and less
favorable. However, the main character typically refuses suicide as ignoble or
even ineffective:

> Suicide is never presented as a wholly satisfactory solution to the problem
> of overliving because once a character has lived too long, any death must
> come too late.[112]

---

107. Wilson, *Mocked with Death*, p. 1.
108. Wilson, *Mocked with Death*, pp. 1-2.
109. Wilson, *Mocked with Death*, p. 4.
110. Wilson, *Mocked with Death*, p. 4.
111. Wilson, *Mocked with Death*, p. 8.
112. Wilson, *Mocked with Death*, p. 6.

Instead, other characters frequently try to heal or cure the main character's sickness but are unsuccessful.[113] His sickness is a symbolic substitute for death, just as their healing efforts are symbolic attempts to help him die. In his madness the main character "tends toward ambivalence, rupture, and irresoluble conflict," and he further interrogates the audience about its own attitude to life.

> Once he has lived too long, the tragic protagonist becomes opaque; the audience no longer knows what to expect from him, his role is no longer clearly defined, and nothing is inevitable. The tragic mode is often concerned with the middle times of life, not its ends. Tragedies of overliving remind us of the illegibility of life when we are in it, and the difficulty or impossibility of making sense of our stories as a coherent narrative.[114]

The difficulty that the reader or hearer experiences in making sense of a life that has gone on too long is reflected in the character's own difficulty of the same type, often reinforced in the narrative or drama using motifs of darkness (as well as blindness).[115] Other dead characters return as ghosts as if they have trouble dying, too.[116]

Saul's tragedy fits this tradition like a glove. Because of disagreements about time (e.g., how long to wait before the sacrifice in 1 Sam 13) and death (e.g., whether to kill Agag in 1 Sam 15), Saul is rejected from the kingship but does not die. He enters a period of overliving in which his role and his destiny are confused and uncertain. As a consequence of his "premature" sacrifice, Saul himself becomes "belated" for the rest of the book.[117] By contrast, David comes to understand that it is God's timing that counts (1 Sam 22:13), that in truth God is always "on time."

Robert Alter notes something similar going on in the proliferation of paired and even tripled repetitions:

> Three different coronation scenes are required for the reluctant Saul; two tales of Saul among the prophets, the first elevating him at the beginning of his career and the second devastating him at the end; two incidents of Saul's hurling his spear at David; two encounters with the fugitive David,

---

113. Wilson, *Mocked with Death*, p. 10.
114. Wilson, *Mocked with Death*, p. 11.
115. Wilson, *Mocked with Death*, p. 11.
116. Wilson, *Mocked with Death*, p. 19.
117. Miscall, *1 Samuel*, p. 93, also characterizes Saul as having a problem with "timing." Cf. the reflections of Polzin, *Samuel and the Deuteronomist*, pp. 213-15, on "providential delay" in Samuel.

1 Samuel and the Christian Faith

who spares his life and receives a pledge of love and a kind of endorsement from Saul, still not to be trusted by David as the older man veers wildly between opposed feelings.[118]

Rather than necessarily an indication of different editorial hands and a mechanical history of literary development, such features are in fact structural reflections of the essence of the tragic tale being told. The temporal interruptions and reduplications within the narrative compel the reader to reflect on the relationship between human time and God's time.

Saul's character disintegrates in response to the brutal contradiction between his rejection by God and his continued retention of the throne, leading to:

- his madness,
- his lack of vision (prefigured by Eli's blindness),
- his persistent posing of questions,
- the repetitive cat-and-mouse plotting of his interactions with David,
- the notable nighttime scenes in the book,
- Saul's inability to secure information from God through intermediaries,
- Saul's increasing disregard for sanctity (e.g., his killing of the priests at Nob),
- his susceptibility to prophetic ecstasy (which symbolically slays him),
- his difficulties with perception (e.g., he has trouble recognizing David),
- and the eventual character of his death, which is and is not a suicide (cf. 1 Chr 10:14, "the Lord put him to death").

Furthermore, Samuel's return from the dead can be understood in part as a mockery of Saul, who should be dead but is still alive. If the figure of Samuel in 1 Samuel 28 represents life in death, then Saul is by contrast an emblem of death in life.

From the vantage point of the tragic tradition of overliving identified by Wilson, the details of Saul's story snap together with a new coherence and focus.[119] But how does it assist the theological interpretation of 1 Samuel? As

118. Alter, *David Story*, p. xix.

119. Cf. Adar, *Biblical Narrative*, pp. 234-35: "The tragedy is painful because Saul's decline is not gradual or the result of old age, like those of Eli, Samuel and David; Saul collapses under the weight of the evil spirit while he is yet in his full strength, and up to his last moment he is described as being in full possession of his powers. The tragedy is painful because it is not a war between good and evil; both Saul and David are very human and win our sympathy: we do not know which of them to blame, or with which of them we sympathise more, for we have caught a glimpse of something mysterious and terrifying which is beyond good and evil."

243

REFLECTING ON HISTORY AND THEOLOGY

Wilson observes, Christian writers in this tragic tradition have struggled with the problem of overliving in ways foreign to their classical Greek forebears. There is a double move on the part of later Christian authors, both to justify the longevity of the overliving character and to criticize his (subjective) sense of having lived past his time.[120] Christian authors were typically concerned to register how ultimately — so from God's perspective — overliving was not overliving at all. The problem is rather a human being's *perception* of overliving. Still, this perception is far from negligible.

In effect, Wilson argues for the existence of a subcategory of "Christian tragedy," seen from a literary perspective. In this genre, represented above all by Milton's *Samson Agonistes* and *Paradise Lost*, the central concern lies

> with the sense of overliving that may afflict all postlapsarian human beings, even those who have a glimpse of God's plan for humanity. Christian tragedy draws attention to the human suffering and despair that may exist even in an ultimately good universe.[121]

> Even though circumscribed by resurrection and bounded by praise, the Christian life passes through dark nights of the soul that are not any less faithful for being so dark — and this tragic literary tradition aims to explore how that can be.[122]

Tragedy is especially appealing and valuable in the present, since ours is a time in which the cultural myths of measurable progress and civic improvement have become more and more difficult to sustain. Tragedy has regained attention in contemporary arts and letters, precisely because it dramatizes our current anxiety about teleology and our insecurity about time.[123] The way this temporal dissonance has become manifest in popular culture is a theme insightfully explored by several cultural critics, most notably by Michel Maffesoli.[124] For Maffesoli, modern society's various ways of restricting and immersing itself in the present reveal both an evasion of the future and a deep longing for

120. Wilson, *Mocked with Death*, p. 18.
121. Wilson, *Mocked with Death*, p. 20.
122. Cf. the view of Auden, "Christian Tragic Hero," p. 143: "Greek tragedy is the tragedy of necessity; i.e., the feeling aroused in the spectator is 'What a pity it had to be this way'; Christian tragedy is the tragedy of possibility, 'What a pity it was this way when it might have been otherwise . . .'" The category of "overliving" moves in the direction of the latter by calling greater attention to what might have been. Perhaps Auden would have done better to draw his distinction between Greek and *biblical* (rather than "Christian") tragedy.
123. See further Scott, "Tragedy's Time."
124. Maffesoli, "Return of the Tragic."

an "intensely lived fate."[125] In other words, the present time is precisely an age *without* a sense of destiny. "Living fast," repudiating personal responsibility, and dying young (and "beautiful") are all glorified, especially within youth subcultures, as a false "doom" that in fact substitutes for a true sense of purpose, or a noble cause, or the kind of lived adventure that gives time meaning.

Samuel and Jesus

To read 1 Samuel against the horizon of tragedy, when construed as the tragedy of overliving, means that Saul's life becomes an account of death within life or, in Christian terms, of crucifixion. Within the New Testament, crucifixion is not only something that Jesus once suffered but something occurring in every Christian's life (Matt 16:24-25//Mark 8:34-35//Luke 9:23-24). In this respect Saul can be viewed as a type for Christ.[126] Saul's agony, his struggle to die, even his distance from God can be viewed as adumbrating the Christ of Gethsemane and Calvary, the Christ of divine forsakenness. From such a vantage point Saul might then be viewed as an icon for those who struggle with religious belief or who experience God as absent from their lives: the middle-aged person who despairs of making a mark in life or others who have "lived too long" — those who are elderly and alone, those who are young and hopeless, those who are physically impaired or sick and isolated, those who see no sense or shape or future for their lives. The Saul tradition invites and compels reflection on suffering as part of the life of faith, as well as on the resistance of human experience to meaning. Experience is messy and confusing, and no less so for Christians. The decision to live life before God is not a comfortable intellectual embrace of principles but a risky commitment to a relationship based upon trust: "It is the Lord; let him do what seems good to him" (1 Sam 3:18).

Rather than an unfair Christian imposition upon the Old Testament text, this kind of typological interpretation arguably preserves the authentic voice of the Old Testament text. In fact, a christological interpretation along these lines can honor the contours of the Old Testament narrative in a highly effective manner, so long as the integrity of that narrative is kept firmly in view.

---

125. Maffesoli, "Return of the Tragic," p. 335.

126. Robert Browning hints at this connection in his poem "Saul"; see his *Shorter Poems*, pp. 167-75. Browning describes one of Saul's fits of madness in cruciform terms: "He stood as erect as that tent-prop, both arms stretched out wide / On the great cross-support in the centre, that goes to each side" (lines 28-29). Browning goes on to compare Saul to a "king-serpent," employing the rhetoric of John 3:14.

As I have argued, the Samuel narrative persistently refuses to demonize Saul; neither does it paint a triumphalistic portrait of David. Viewing Saul alongside David as a type for Christ can thus prevent a narrative interpretation in which David simply becomes the hero and Saul a villain. Usually, it is true, Christian interpreters have done just that, more or less.[127] But the biblical narrative also recalls how the curse of Shimei is pronounced on David, and that curse continues to echo within the tradition: "you are a man of blood" (2 Sam 16:8).[128]

By contrast, the primary theological contribution of the Samuel narrative to Christian theology, throughout church history, has been its provision of David as a type for Christ. Often this typology was based just as much on a reading of David in the Psalms as in Samuel. Here is an extended example from the early tradition:

David too was persecuted, and Jesus was persecuted. David was anointed by Samuel to be king in the place of Saul who had sinned (1 Sam 16:1-3); Jesus was anointed by John to be the high priest instead of the priests (who) had transgressed the law. David was persecuted after his anointing; Jesus was persecuted after his anointing. David ruled at first over one tribe and afterwards over all Israel; Jesus ruled at first over the few who had believed in him, and at the end he will rule over the whole world. Samuel anointed David (when) he was thirty years old (2 Sam 5:4); Jesus received from John the laying on of the hand (when) he was about thirty years old (Luke 3:23). David took two royal daughters; Jesus took two royal daughters, the congregation of the People and the congregation of the Peoples. David returned good to Saul, his enemy; Jesus taught "Pray for your enemies" (Luke 6:28). David was the heart of God (1 Sam 13:14); Jesus is the son of God. David received the kingdom of Saul, his persecutor; Jesus received the kingdom of Israel, his persecutor. David wept with lamentation over Saul his enemy when he died (2 Sam 1:12); Jesus wept over Jerusalem, his persecutor, for it was destined to be laid waste (Luke 19:41-44). David handed over the kingdom to Solomon and was gathered to his people; Jesus handed over the keys to Simon (Matt 16:19) and ascended and went to the One who sent

127. Augustine's interpretation of the David and Goliath story is illustrative of this tradition. In his telling, David stands for Christ and Goliath for Satan; see his treatment of Psalm 143 in Augustine, *Expositions on the Psalms*. See further Gosselin, *King's Progress to Jerusalem*, pp. 11-24.

128. Shimei, of course, later asks forgiveness for these words (2 Sam 19:16-23), but that later development does not prevent them from continuing to resonate, particularly because of the way this motif resurfaces in Chronicles (1 Chr 22:8; 28:3).

him. Because of David the sins of his offspring were forgiven. Because of Jesus the sins of the Peoples were forgiven.[129]

By extension, this analogy between David and Christ could be, and over time was, applied to every faithful Christian. More than anyone else, the medieval theologian Nicholas of Lyra insisted on the possibility, even the necessity, for all Christians to engage in an *imitatio davidis*, breaking with earlier tradition's narrower use of typology. David became the supreme biblical example of the virtuous Christian man.[130] As was increasingly emphasized in Reformation theology, something urgently needed was:

> a conscious involvement and empathy on the part of the Christian not only with Christ but also with David, the sterling example of God's beloved who goes astray and yet can, with God's help, find his way back to the path of salvation.[131]

This typological extension in turn affirms and strengthens what might be called an "analogy of faith" between the Old Testament believer and the Christian: the sense that then and now what is at stake is the same God, the same promise, and the same hope.

The typology is actually already present within the Old Testament in the form of a Davidic "standard" applied to later Judean kings (2 Kgs 14:3; 16:2; 18:3; 22:2). Yet as central as the David typology was to both the New Testament and the Christian theological tradition, it has not been without its problems.[132]

---

129. Aphrahat, *Demonstrations*, 2:215-16 (§21:13). Samuel was in fact dead by the time that David was anointed king at Hebron. This section of the *Demonstrations* includes similar christological typologies involving other Old Testament figures as well.

130. See, e.g., Nicholas of Lyra, *Postilla super psalmos*, on Psalm 88. For further background on the typological interpretations of David by Lyra and Reformation theologians, see Gosselin, *King's Progress to Jerusalem*, pp. 67-89. This interpretive impulse appears to have already been adumbrated in the shaping of the Psalter; see Hossfeld, "David als exemplarischer Mensch."

131. Gosselin, *King's Progress to Jerusalem*, p. 38.

132. Gordon, *I and II Samuel*, pp. 49-53, locates three contrasts between David and Christ: 1) David dies and experiences "corruption," whereas Christ is raised from the dead; 2) David represents killing, whereas Christ is a figure of healing; 3) David stands for the submission of the Gentiles, whereas Christ brings the Gentiles redemption. Cf. the wry comment of Bowers, *Legend of Jonah*, p. 51: "I must admit that I get nervous when an exegete writes 'David significat Christum' (or carelessly: David, id est Christus), mainly because I cannot quite forget Bathsheba and Abishag the Shunammite, even though I know that I am reading a bit of syncopated typology."

It is also not quite as prominent in the New Testament, or as straightforward, as many might assume.[133] To be sure, certain New Testament passages convey a claim involving a genealogical connection between David and Jesus, which elevates the significance of the typological relationship between them. Even so, specific references to Jesus as "Son of David" do not predominate and are often oblique.[134] In the gospels only Matthew invokes the title as a significant motif, and even there its use is still limited.[135]

This feature of the New Testament may reflect an anxiety that the military and imperial aspects of the Davidic legacy can cloud Christ's true identity, misleading Christian believers as to the peaceable nature of Christ's kingdom.[136] Yet this worry also appears already within the Old Testament, which itself expresses a critique of the bloodshed committed by David (1 Chr 22:8).[137]

133. See further Karrer, "Von David zu Christus." Davidic references do appear throughout the New Testament: Matt 1:6, 17, 20; 9:27; 12:3, 23; 15:22; 20:30-31; 21:9, 15; 22:42-43, 45; Mark 2:25; 10:47-48; 11:10; 12:35-37; Luke 1:27(32); 2:4; 3:31; 6:3; 18:38-39; 20:41-42, 44; Acts 1:16; 2:25, 29, 34; 4:25; 7:45; 13:22, 34, 36; 15:16; Rom 1:3; 4:6; 11:9; 2 Tim 2:8; Rev 3:7; 5:5; 22:16. At issue is how to evaluate their meaning and function.

134. They occur primarily in healing stories (e.g., Matt 9:27; 12:23; 15:22; 20:30-31; Mark 10:47-48; Luke 18:38-39) and superscriptions (e.g., Matt 1:1; Rom 1:3). Yet Jesus himself appears to resist the association on at least one occasion (Matt 22:41-45; Mark 12:35-37; Luke 20:41-44). Uncertainty on this point also seems to have been a feature of his popular reception (John 7:41-42). De Jonge, "Jesus, Son of David and Son of God," attributes the connection between David and healing to the description of David as "exorcist" in 1 Sam 16:14-23; cf. Baxter, "Healing and the 'Son of David'"; Mrázek, "Messiah, the Healer of the Sick"; Römer and Rückl, "Jesus, Son of Joseph and Son of David"; Wojcik, "Discriminations against David's Tragedy," pp. 29-31. The name of David also appears frequently in the apostolic speeches in Acts (see Acts 1:16; 2:25, 29, 34; 4:25; 7:45; 13:22, 34, 36; 15:16); see Jipp, "Luke's Scriptural Suffering Messiah."

135. See Kingsbury, "Title 'Son of David' in Matthew's Gospel." Cf. Barber, "Jesus as the Davidic Temple Builder"; Burger, *Jesus als Davidssohn*; Duling, "Promises to David." Blenkinsopp, *David Remembered*, p. 179, concludes that in the gospels "the Davidic identity of the profile of Jesus . . . is marginal." On the patristic reception of this aspect of the New Testament's witness, see Heither, *David*, pp. 164-224.

136. Wojcik, "Discriminations against David's Tragedy," p. 30. See also Wootton, "Monstrosity of David," p. 127, who objects to the Christian tradition's move to read "the story of David back into the Christ event," characterizing it as nullifying "any radical outcome of Jesus' life . . .[,] the establishment of centralized and exclusive control over state and religion, with all the trappings of the Davidic monarchy to churches — both hierarchical and conservative or neo-conservative evangelical — without making contact with the critique offered by the life of Jesus in the Gospels." As I hope I have shown, however, this reading of David, and this understanding of the relationship between David and Jesus, is only part of the picture. Still it bears keeping in mind, even as one part.

137. The precise nature of David's bloodshed is open to question; there are reasons to resist interpreting the charge "man of blood" as a reference to all of his military activities, pure and simple. See Kelly, "David's Disqualification in 1 Chronicles 22:8." Yet even if one grants a

Within Samuel, it is noteworthy that David's rise to the throne does not involve outright rebellion, civil war or any major battle internal to Israel. The Samuel narrative's insistence on separating David from violence as much as possible does not constitute a propagandistic apology for Davidic rule but rather a theological vindication of God's continuing effort to redeem Israel by virtue of a royal exemplar. It remains highly suggestive that postexilic Israel did not ultimately resume a monarchic form of government.[138]

That this worry about the violence of kings was not misplaced can be further seen in the history of Western civilization, in which David's mantle has been continually appropriated by rulers and empires.[139] Although language about Jesus as "Son of David" could in fact be employed as an anti-imperialistic confession, in practice it has contributed to the conflation of church and state by metaphorically generating new Davidic monarchs.[140] The biblical David story was applied to emperors (such as Theodosius) as early as Ambrose of Milan (AD 340–397),[141] but gained strength at the Council of Chalcedon (AD 451).[142] It was then occasionally exploited in Byzantine imperial ideology (beginning with Justinian) and became the

---

distinction between legitimate and illegitimate violence, the fact remains that David's reign is remembered as having led to some type of illegitimate violence. The monarchy and illegitimate violence are therefore problematically linked.

138. This is one of the ways in which John Howard Yoder's argument for an exilic or "Jeremianic" turn in Israel's identity finds traction with the biblical narrative; see his *For the Nations*, pp. 51-78. For critical discussion of Yoder's proposal, see Yoder, *Jewish–Christian Schism Revisited*; Chapman, "Old Testament and the Church." All the same, the role of the high priest took on many of the same symbols and functions; see Rooke, *Zadok's Heirs*; VanderKam, *From Joshua to Caiaphas*.

139. Wojcik, "Transformations of the Myth, of David," pp. 5-6. For an argument that David imagery was not heavily employed early on but then grew in importance in Byzantium, see Rapp, "Comparison, Paradigm and the Case of Moses in Panegyric and Hagiography."

140. On Charlemagne as a new David, see Sypeck, *Becoming Charlemagne*, pp. 15, 94. See also Hobbs, "Bucer's Use of King David"; King, "Henry VIII as David"; Tudor-Craig, "Henry VIII and King David." Revolutionaries as well as monarchs claimed the Davidic mantle in the early modern period; on Cromwell, see Barber, "I Resolved to Give an Account," p. 232. Especially in the medieval period, all of these typological reflexes were visual as well as verbal; see Steger, *David Rex et Propheta*.

141. Ambrose of Milan, *Apol. Dav.* A comparison between secular rulers and Moses seems to have been more prevalent in the early church; see Cameron, *Christianity and the Rhetoric of Empire*, pp. 54-57.

142. Rapp, "Old Testament Models," pp. 188-89. Ludwig, "David – Christus – Basileus," argues that the Davidic model was not actually invoked all that much in the Byzantine empire, except during the reigns of Herakleios (AD 610-641) and Basileios I (AD 867-886), when it was used to considerable effect.

prevailing model for European monarchy in the Carolingian era.[143] Starting with Pippin at Soissons (AD 751), kings were explicitly termed *novus david* and consecrated with holy oil (as David had been anointed by Samuel).[144] Charlemagne's state seal bore the legend: *Samuel renovavit imperium* (= "Samuel renewed the empire"; cf. Sir 46:13).[145] His throne in Aachen was built with six steps because that is how the Bible portrays Solomon's.[146] The famous imperial crown of Otto I contains depictions of David, Solomon, and Hezekiah, with twelve stones in the front for the twelve apostles and twelve at the back for the twelve tribes of Israel.[147]

Over time this new, biblically based understanding of monarchy eventually developed into the complex set of traditions and practices known by the

143. See Chazelle and Van Name Edwards, eds., *Study of the Bible in the Carolingian Era*; Contreni, "Carolingian Biblical Culture"; Herkommer, "Typus Christi"; Laistner, "Some Early Medieval Commentaries on the Old Testament"; Ullmann, *Carolingian Renaissance and the Idea of Kingship*; Wallace-Hadrill, *Frankish Church*.

144. Oakley, *Kingship*, pp. 92-99. Previously, kings and emperors had generally not been anointed, although there is debate about the ultimate origin of the practice. Some evidence exists for earlier anointing, prior to Pippin, among the Visigoths in Spain (Wamba in 672?) and the Irish (Columba in 574?); see Bradley, *God Save the Queen*, p. 77. For further discussion of the evidence for early royal anointing in Ireland, see Enright, *Iona, Tara and Soissons*. Foundational studies of this royal practice are Bouman, *Sacring and Crowning*; Kantorowicz, *King's Two Bodies*; idem, *Laudes regiae*. More recently, see Bautier, "Sacres et couronnements"; Chevalier-Royet, "Saül et David, Premiers Rois Oints." According to Nelson, "Lord's Anointed and the People's Choice," p. 150, "the "prime authority" for Carolingian royal anointing derived from the Old Testament, although there may have been other influences. Interestingly, anointing in episcopal ordination also appears to have begun among the Franks around this same time, which may indicate that the practice of priestly anointing developed on analogy with royal anointing rather than the other way around. See further Kleinheyer, *Die Preisterweihe im römischen Ritus*. Ellard, *Ordination Anointings in the Western Church before 1000 A.D.*, pp. 20-21, notes that the Missal of the Franks mentions Samuel and David explicitly in relation to priestly ordination, but the earlier Bobbio Missal (ca. 700 AD) includes references to Samuel and David in the context of anointing for the dying (cf. p. 31). Either way, baptismal anointing preceded both. See further Halliburton, "Anointing in the Early Church." Still, the Franks certainly viewed themselves as a new "Israel of God," a notion that achieved prominent expression in the Lex Salica. See Godman, *Poetry of the Carolingian Renaissance*, p. 5. On the ancient Near Eastern background of anointing, still valuable is Kutsch, *Salbung als Rechtsakt*.

145. Ullmann, "Bible and Principles of Government in the Middle Ages," p. 197.

146. Schäfer, *Bibelauslegung in der Geschichte der Kirche*, pp. 63-67; Schramm, *Kaiser, Könige und Päpste*, 1:206-12.

147. Schramm, "Alte und das Neue Testament," p. 238. The crown (ca. 960-70 AD) still exists and is held by the Kunsthistorisches Museum in Vienna. For further description and illustrations, see Bakalova, "King David as a Model for the Christian Ruler"; and Kuyumdzhieva, "David Rex Penitent."

shorthand expression "the divine right of kings."[148] In early modern debates about kingship, both sides — royalists and republicans — could, and would, appeal to the Bible.[149] A nice literary example of the biblical analogy at work can be found in John Dryden's epic poem "Absalom and Achitophel," which celebrates the political success of England's Charles II by retelling the biblical narrative in 2 Samuel 15-18: "Once more the godlike David was restored, / And willing nations knew their lawful lord."[150] Thus typological interpretations of the Samuel narrative throughout Western history amply illustrate the persistent danger of political cooption and corruption.

A final problem with the David–Jesus typology in Christian tradition has been its reflexive impact on the narrative of Samuel. As Gunn has rightly noted, the long association between David and Christ has led to an interpretive censure of Saul that stands in tension with his portrait in the biblical narrative itself. As I emphasized throughout my close reading, the Samuel narrative refuses to condemn Saul unreservedly and actually exhibits remarkable sympathy with his character throughout its telling of his story. Moreover, the characterizations of David and Saul emphasize their similarity. This narrative strategy has the effect of subverting a morally framed difference between the two — the distinction between them is real, but it is ultimately located in God's election rather than in their respective personal merits. Yet because David is so thoroughly aligned with Christ in the Christian tradition, Saul has usually been caricatured and condemned by Christian interpreters. One control for this claim can be provided by the treatment of Saul in Jewish tradition, which is surprisingly positive.[151] Not only does the David–Jesus typology often occlude the narrative's patent sympathy for Saul, it also obscures the tensions and weaknesses within David's own narrative portrait, transforming him into a two-dimensional cartoon, a cardboard cutout of cheap triumphalistic faith. At its core the Samuel narrative is more concerned to illustrate God's loyalty to David than David's loyalty to God.

By contrast, the one interpreter who, more than any other, has ventured the kind of interpretation that I am proposing is the twentieth-century theologian

---

148. Gosselin, *King's Progress to Jerusalem*, p. 6. For the classic work, see Figgis, *Divine Right of Kings*.

149. See Ditchfield, "Divine Right Theory"; Metzger, "David und Saul."

150. John Dryden, "Absalom and Achitophel," lines 1030-31, as cited in Ditchfield, "Divine Right Theory," p. 160.

151. For a contemporary example, see Wiesel, *Five Biblical Portraits*. Such sympathy has ancient roots; see Liss, "Innocent King"; Feldman, "Josephus' Portrait of Saul." Josephus reads Saul as a good man corrupted by the power of the monarchy. This traditional sympathy finds modern expression in Milgrom, *Numbers*, p. 430 (on 1 Samuel 15).

Karl Barth. In Barth's powerful excursus on election in Volume II/2 of his *Church Dogmatics*, he treats Saul and other *rejected* figures within the Old Testament as also witnessing to Christ, who as the One despised and rejected, completes and fulfills their witnesses just as much as the witness of David.

> The king of Israel rejected by God, whether he be called Saul or Jeroboam, is the prototype and copy of Jesus Christ . . . it is not at any rate an absolute riddle if the rejected one too, in his own way, bears the marks of one elected and sanctified by God; if he, too . . . does not appear without grandeur, even in his misdeeds and downfall — an object of awe and not of contempt, and his end a serious and necessary act of judgment, but not a triumphant *coup de grace*. Saul is therefore legitimately and in all seriousness among the prophets. He and the Samarian kings who follow him, even while they are allowed to fall, do not fall out of the hand of God. In all the frightful blossoming of their sin, which is much more the sin of their people than their personal sin, and in all the terrible darkness of the divine wrath under which their government stands, they prophesy and exhibit the King who, himself innocent, has interposed himself as a Leader and Representative at the head of all sinful men, and between them and God. Who but the Son of God can be the King of men in this terrible function? Clearly a King of men like this cannot be deprived of the honour which in the Old Testament presentation of history is peculiar to Saul and the other rejected kings of Israel . . . For He who died a criminal's death on Golgotha is as such, overtaken by the divine rejection, the legitimate bearer of this glory, and the King of grace.[152]

For Barth, Christ completes the entire history of God's way with Israel, which means that Christ in fact fulfills God's rejection as well as God's election. God "made him to be sin who knew no sin, so that in him we might become the righteousness of God" (2 Cor 5:21). That divine calling in turn speaks ultimately to the very nature of God:

> God is really like this. He is the One who is both gracious and wrathful, who both makes alive and kills, who both elects and rejects in this way. And this has been actualised in a single person, so that we cannot deny either aspect, or separate them, but can and must understand the one by the other, and see in the whole, i.e., in the one human figure, the kingship of God as it has drawn near.[153]

152. Barth, *Church Dogmatics* II/2, pp. 390-91.
153. Barth, *Church Dogmatics* II/2, p. 393. A pointed and illuminating contrast is

Both the rejected of God and the elected of God in the Old Testament find their fulfillment in Jesus Christ, which means that they *both* participate in his significance.[154]

The obvious rejoinder to such an interpretive move is that only David, and not Saul, is called "servant of YHWH" *('ebed yhwh)* in the Old Testament (e.g., 2 Sam 3:18; 7:5, 8; cf. 1 Sam 23:10-11; 25:39; 2 Sam 7:19-29; 1 Kgs 3:6; 8:24-26; 11:13, 32, 34, 36, 38; 14:8; 2 Kgs 19:34; 20:6).[155] Unlike Saul, David is a true prophet (Acts 1:16; 2:30; 4:25). Neither is there a "covenant" with Saul but only with David (2 Sam 23:5; cf. Jer 33:20-22; Psalm 89; 2 Chr 7:18; 13:5; 21:7). Yet in the end the typological link between David and Christ depends upon more than such phrases, and their absence does not need to rule out a similar link, albeit of a different kind, between Saul and Christ.[156] Saul is nonetheless anointed of God (1 Sam 10:1), just as David is. Saul does receive the epithet "anointed of the Lord" *(měšîaḥ yhwh,* 1 Sam 24:6 [Heb. 7], 10 [Heb. 11], 26:9, 11, 16, 23; cf. 1 Sam 10:1; 12:3, 5; 15:17),[157] which supports his inclusion within the biblical framework of christological typology.

The effect of taking the literary shape of 1 Samuel with utmost seriousness is in fact to preclude the kind of triumphalistic appropriation of David that is nevertheless widespread in Christian tradition. Just as the narrative intentionally subverts an equation between chosenness and moral rectitude, so too a christological reading must embrace the rejection of Saul no less than the election of David. In other words, the question is not so much *whether* to read 1 Samuel christologically, if the goal is to read 1 Samuel as Christian scripture, but rather *how* 1 Samuel will be read christologically — or, to put the point even more precisely, what kind of christology an interpreter will both bring

---

provided by Steussy, *Samuel and His God,* p. 101, who understands the God of Samuel as "a partisan warrior who will champion our cause as long as we repay the favor with obedience and flattery" and a "God who is not particularly loving or lovable and who is not a champion of the oppressed." Steussy seems tone-deaf to the rich complexity and nuance of the Samuel narrative, characterizing its perspective as one in which "simple obedience would solve everything" (p. 100). Whatever obedience may be in Samuel, it is certainly not simple.

154. Barth powerfully adduces John 19:22 (i.e., the sign on the cross reading "Jesus Christ, the king of the Jews") as a confirmation of Christ's culmination and fulfillment of the rejected Old Testament monarch.

155. Kang, *Divine War,* p. 213. Kang points out that no other Israelite king receives this epithet (with 2 Chr 32:16 as the exception that proves the rule).

156. For a recent study of 1 Samuel in which multiple types are identified and explored, see Lefebvre, *Livres de Samuel et récits de résurrection.*

157. As emphasized by von Orelli, *Old Testament Prophecy of the Consummation of God's Kingdom,* p. 148.

to 1 Samuel and employ 1 Samuel to reinforce. My argument is that a close reading of the biblical text compels a Christian reader to see adumbrations and types of Christ not only in David but also in Saul.[158] Jesus is indeed the Son of David, but he is also the One who is rejected by God despite his best efforts, who does not always know the will of his Father, and who is strung up in shame outside the walls of the city.[159]

Moreover, an explicit "Saul typology" is not absent within the New Testament. Pilate's acclamation "behold the man" (John 19:5) is in fact a partial quotation of God's words to Samuel concerning Saul: "Behold the man of whom I spoke to you. He is the one to rule over my people" (1 Sam 9:17).[160] Also, the apostle Paul initially bears Saul's name, and he witnesses in his own life to both rejection and election by God.[161] To the extent that all Christians, like Paul, shoulder the cross of Christ, they therefore know in their suffering and humiliation not only the grief of their Lord but the sorrow of Saul:

> In the lives of many men there comes a moment like this which had come on Saul . . . a moment when it is made clear to us that we are not going to re-ceive that which we had set our heart upon . . . a moment when we are told, as clearly as by a voice from heaven, that we shall not rise to that position in the world . . . or in the Church of God, that we had looked forward to . . . or when we felt that the evil in us, which we had struggled against and prayed to have removed . . . will not yield in this life, and are made conscious that we must stand aside and take a lower place.[162]

---

158. Cf. Hertzberg, *I & II Samuel*, p. 133: "The first king is like a sign pointing toward the true kingly office, but at the same time also a sign showing that the man who holds this office can come to grief in it."

159. For a description of how the David–Jesus typology can center on forbearance and suffering rather than triumphalism in relation to the Psalms, see Anderson, "King David and the Psalms of Imprecation"; cf. Hill, "Chrysostom's Homilies on David and Saul,." Note also the historical judgment of Kuyumdzhieva, "David Rex Penitent," p. 134: "David became the main Old Testament type of penitence for Christianity."

160. See Azar, "Scriptural King"; Böhler, "Ecce homo!" Azar makes a number of other intriguing proposals for intertextual echoes between the Saul stories and John's account of Jesus, particularly its royal dimension.

161. For an exploration of the relationship between the Saul account in 1 Samuel and the portrayal of Paul in Acts, see Chapman, "Saul/Paul." Cf. Compton, "From Saul to Paul"; Davies, "Son of David and Son of Saul."

162. Davidson, "Saul's Reprobation," p. 151. Cf. Robinson, *Israel's Mysterious God*, p. 49: "Anyone whose life suffers a reverse (and whose does not?) — whether one is jilted in love, or passed over for a job, or loses one's position — can make the Saul story his own."

From this profound vantage point, Saul is not somehow rehabilitated but finally viewed with his proper theological significance.[163]

Reading 1 Samuel "in two directions" turns out to be fully analogous to what it means to read the Old Testament in light of the New. An awareness of the "conclusion" to the Christian story gives needed bearings for an approach to the Old Testament, and yet need not, indeed must not, flatten the rich texture of the Old Testament narrative itself. Within Christian theological interpretation, the Christian "conclusion" provided by the New Testament can and should, however, provide a reservoir of hermeneutical cues for the successful adjudication of interpretive issues within the Old Testament. In the case of 1 Samuel, the story of Jesus both supports and discourages possible interpretations.

Uncivil Religion

Because the narrative of 1 Samuel, like the book of Deuteronomy, locates true religion in the internal, subjective aspect of ritual (i.e., trust in God) and in the humanitarian impact of communal worship practices, 1 Samuel "separates" faith from the pragmatic needs of the state, which was perceived to be encroaching upon piety more dangerously with the development of a dynastic monarchy. Paradoxically, this emphasis on the subjective is made in an effort to infuse *all* of life with the religious spirit. To this extent, the primary deuteronomistic response to the dilemma created by the political need for a monarchy was to look for a holier king.[164] Yet even with that ideal in view, the Samuel narrative also appears to register doubt about the ability of *any* human king to serve successfully as God's viceroy. History bore out that suspicion for Israel, as it has continued to do for other nations ever since.[165] For precisely this reason,

---

163. John Henry Newman also treats Saul as a kind of "everyman" figure in his sermon "Saul," in his *Parochial and Plain Sermons*, 3:29-43. For Newman, Saul's sins after being given a new heart by God are like the sins that Christians commit after their baptism. Cf. Davidson, "Saul's Reprobation," p. 157: "Saul was used to teach a great lesson to the Church of God, and to the world: to show what profound qualities the king of God's kingdom needs, what consecration to God, what perfect obedience and spirituality; and Saul's failure taught this more conspicuously than his success would have done."

164. For a contemporary Jewish argument in favor of declaring the present State of Israel to be "a Davidic monarchy without a reigning king" because "any view of Jewish sovereignty that is not based on the House of David is . . . not fully legitimate," see Wyschograd, "Judaism, the Political, and the Monarchy."

165. For a theological argument against the idea that what is needed today is simply to "convert the king," see Ellul, *False Presence of the Kingdom*, p. 121 and *passim*. Cf. Yoder, "Exodus and Exile," p. 309: "What the world most needs is not a new Caesar but a new style. A style is

the best way in the contemporary world to safeguard the deuteronomists' most precious legacy, the freedom of the worshiping heart, lies not in the institution of a sacral monarchy, or some other version of established religion, no matter how enlightened or benign, but paradoxically in the modern solution of a "separation of church and state."[166]

The seed of this modern idea lies in the Old Testament's insistence that only God is Israel's true king, which thus reduces the perennially vaunting ambitions of human government to more modest ends, even "secularizes" it. Such a political arrangement actually protects "heart religion" by preserving the heart's ability to participate only in rituals it believes in:

> Any machinery of government which men have yet devised is too coarse and clumsy for so delicate a task as the inculcation and encouragement of the faith. Government works by compulsion; faith by inspirations. Government lays its hand on actions; faith nestles into unseen affections. Government estimates appearances; faith looks only on realities. And so government, though all the land were unanimously and harmoniously Christian, would still be a poor ministry of Christianity.[167]

The roots of this political vision lie in deuteronomic theology, which therefore charts a collision course with all notions of "civil religion." Why does Saul exist in the biblical narrative at all? To ensure that David's story is *not* read as warranting the baptism of the state and its offices. Needed instead are persons of faith who engage in public service, but whose religious faith remains vital, heartfelt and alert, who have here "no lasting city" but are "looking for the city that is to come" (Heb 13:14).[168]

---

created, updated, projected, not by a nation or a government, but by a people. This is what moral minorities do — what they have done time and again."

166. According to Witte, "Facts and Fictions," some form of church–state separation is not only "Anabaptist" but in fact basic to the entire Christian tradition. For a theological and cultural defense of monarchic systems of government, especially in Britain, see Bradley, *God Save the Queen*. He notes the Book of Common Prayer's explicit support for "Christian kings, princes and governors." Avis, *Church, State and Establishment*, attempts to make the case that having one established church body in a given society can strengthen an awareness of all religious traditions in that society and prevent political decisions from being made completely apart from moral considerations. This argument strikes me as historically quite dubious and amounting to little more than special pleading on the part of those with social advantage as a means of retaining their advantage.

167. From Phillips Brooks's Bohlen Lectures of 1879, as cited in Chesebrough, *Phillips Brooks*, p. 96. Cf. Buchanan, *Cut the Connection*.

168. See further Hauerwas and Willimon, *Resident Aliens*.

On an individual as well as a communal level, this manner of living out the faith calls for humility and forbearance, the utter relinquishment of all ambitions for a Christian nation, theocracy or empire.[169] If Saul was too big, perhaps his final lesson to us is to embrace being "little" as central to an authentic expression of post-Constantinian Christian conviction for today. No one has described this quality of faith more insightfully or persuasively in the modern era than Thérèse of Lisieux, the nineteenth-century French Carmelite nun, who only lived to be twenty-four years old. For Thérèse, Christianity was the "little way" of being a child of God:

> It is to recognize our nothingness, to expect everything from God as a little child expects everything from its father; it is to be disquieted about nothing, and not to be set on gaining our living . . . to be little is not attributing to oneself the virtues that one practices, believing oneself capable of anything, but to recognize that God places this treasure in the hands of His little child to be used when necessary; but it remains always God's treasure. Finally, it is not to become discouraged over one's little faults, for children fall often, but they are too little to hurt themselves very much.[170]

This profound expression of faith, instantly recognizable as deeply Christian,[171] is far removed in its language and metaphors from the narrative world of 1 Samuel — except, that is, for the suggestive cultivation of "littleness" as the prime metaphor for faith itself.[172]

Such language can come across as excessively Romantic, naïve, or even merely cute, but rightly understood Thérèse's "little way" is a radical embrace

169. For a study of how christological language has been highjacked for nationalistic purposes within recent U.S. politics, see Chapman, "Imperial Exegesis." On religious power being made manifest in weakness rather than political force, see further McConville, *God and Earthly Power*.

170. Frohlich, ed., *St. Thérèse of Lisieux*, p. 149.

171. Intriguingly, Vermes, *Christian Beginnings*, p. 56, also points to the "admiration" of the child as a unique aspect of Jesus' teaching (Matt 11:25//Luke 10:21; Matt 18:3//Mark 10:15// Luke 18:17): "This stress laid on a childlike attitude towards God is peculiar to Jesus. Neither biblical nor post-biblical Judaism make of the young an object of admiration." As Vermes further observes, even Paul appears to view adulthood as a preferable stage of life (e.g., 1 Cor 13:11; 14:20). More broadly, see Bunge, Fretheim, and Gaventa, eds., *Child in the Bible*.

172. I do not mean to suggest that this view of faith is exclusively Christian. Jewish tradition also remembers David as not only clever but little, gentle, and mild. See Bodendorfer, "David, der weise Toragelehrte," pp. 396-98. David's "littleness" thus mirrors Israel's own diminutive stature among the nations (e.g., Deut 7:7). Also like David, Israel will need to protect itself from "wild animals" once it comes into the land (Deut 7:22).

of humility and a courageous abandonment of temporal power and greed.[173] If 1 Samuel employs "bigness" as its prime metaphor for the human dilemma in which life's pragmatic circumstances are always threatening to edge God out, then perhaps Thérèse's "little way" can instead be used to articulate the positive dimension of faith made explicit in the figures of Samuel, David, Jonathan, and Abigail. Their faith is depicted as bold and inspiring, and yet simultaneously modest and vulnerable: "small as a mustard seed" (Matt 21:21-22//Mark 11:23-24). The faith of Israel also entails complete reliance upon God, just as children depend upon their parents, and in that complete reliance is perfect freedom. Not for nothing does the New Testament depict Jesus welcoming little children (Matt 18:1-5).[174] Nor should it be surprising that J. R. R. Tolkien's Christian literary vision imagines its central heroes as small of stature, as "halflings" or "hobbits."[175] As C. S. Lewis observes, Tolkien's novel depicts how the "conflict between the strongest things may come to depend on him, who is almost the weakest."[176] Or as Paul wrote in 2 Cor 1:27, "God chose what is weak in the world to shame the strong."

David's smaller stature therefore stands in sharpest contrast to the "warrior ethic" oddly admired within contemporary U.S. Christianity.[177] Garret Keizer offers a telling critique of this trend:

American Protestantism especially has often seemed to regard Christ like an ex-Marine father regarding his overly bookish son, hoping he'll bloody someone's nose just once, wishing his appeal among women has some other, earthier explanation besides his appeal to them as human beings.[178]

As a type for Christ, David radically subverts masculine stereotypes, to the discomfort of those who celebrate virility as a special mark of God's fa-

173. For an instructive economic application, see Schumacher, *Small Is Beautiful*, p. 33: "There is wisdom in smallness if only on account of the smallness and patchiness of human knowledge, which relies on experiment far more than on understanding."

174. For "littleness" as a New Testament motif, see Matt 10:40-42; 11:11, 25; 18:6, 10, 14; 25:35-36.

175. See Brown, *Christian World of* The Hobbit, pp. 156-62. On hobbits more generally, see Stanton, "Hobbits," pp. 280-82.

176. Lewis, *On Stories and Other Essays on Literature*, p. 85. Also cited in Brown, *Christian World of* The Hobbit, p. 158.

177. E.g., Weber, *Tender Warrior*; Lewis, *Raising a Modern-Day Knight*. In this context, one might also consider the phenomenon of "Christian martial arts"; e.g., Covington, *Purpose-Driven Martial Arts*.

178. Keizer, *Enigma of Anger*, p. 28. He continues by characterizing the biblical Jesus as "a man too slight to carry his own cross without assistance."

vor.[179] At the same time, just as the Samuel narrative indicts those who would equate God's favor with the manly man (as, for example, many churches do openly or covertly in pastoral searches), this narrative will not allow for the opposite stereotype either: the exclusive identification of the small and plain with God's favor. Saul was not rejected because he was big, but because the value he placed on size prevented him from rightly appraising God. Likewise David was not chosen *because* he was small or young, but because he relied on God and struggled to live faithfully for God in the world.[180] His physical stature simply helped him to "size up" God's reality more readily.

In the end, the Samuel narrative resists any technique that threatens to capture and domesticate God. Even in a Christian interpretation, the main thrust of Samuel remains stubbornly about *God*; christological interpretation is finally faithful and illuminating only insofar as it ultimately points in this direction. The domestication of God transpires in many ways, but perhaps today it occurs particularly with "strong man" stereotypes, or in the conflation of church and state, or through rote ecclesial ritualism — especially in "state" churches and "national" cathedrals. When choosing religious leaders, when making political decisions about community life, and when engaging in worship, the fundamental concern for the Christian must be one of genuine conviction and not simply precedent, procedure, or pragmatism.[181]

There are thus theological limits as well as strengths to traditional religious teachings, structures, organizations, habits, and practices. One consequence of

---

179. See, for example, Eldredge, *Wild at Heart*, p. 142 and *passim* on "the warrior-heart of Jesus." While I do appreciate Eldredge's effort to recover the adventurous spirit of the life of faith, in my judgment his caricature of masculinity fatally biases his treatment. This kind of work is nothing new; see Kingsley, *David: Five Sermons*, in which the David story is offered as a biblical warrant for what became known as "muscular Christianity." Even though Kingsley worried about how this idea might be understood, he promoted a myth of chivalry and Protestant manliness. For a fascinating treatment, see Harding, *Love of David and Jonathan*, pp. 314-29. The Samuel narrative in particular subverts rather than celebrates the cult of the warrior. In this regard it is interesting to note how David's biblical portrait has led to his feminization in visual representations over the centuries; see Osherow, *Biblical Women's Voices in Early Modern England*, pp. 111-48. "Feminized" portrayals of David (such as Donatello's famous bronze) get something exactly right about 1 Samuel: the way that David's story subverts the myth of the manly man.

180. Robert Browning also voices this aspect of the Saul narrative powerfully in his poem "Saul": "It is the weakness in strength, that I cry for!" David exclaims (line 308).

181. Cf. Silber, "Birth of Samuel and the Birth of Kingship," pp. 9-10. In traditional theological language, the point could be made that the book of Samuel rejects the idea of *ex opere operato*, namely, that a rite functions objectively apart from the holiness (or sinfulness) of the celebrant(s). This notion is roundly rejected by the Old Testament prophets as well; see Robinson, "Hebrew Sacrifice and Prophetic Symbolism," p. 137; Coleran, "Prophets and Sacrifice."

this limitation is a terrifying sense of powerlessness — which is why we resist acknowledging it and seek to overcome it through the exercise of power and control, all too eager to domesticate the things of God by "cutting them down to size." Our reflexes are always those of Saul, the Bible's consummate pragmatist. But another response to a keener awareness of our human limitations can be a renewed sense of trust in the mysterious operation of God to effect good ends:

> Our destinies are not altogether in our hands. We cannot do everything by mere force of our own will. There is something above our will, moving us and using us for purposes that are wider than our own immediate failure or success.[182]

Such is the witness of 1 Samuel, read as Christian scripture.

---

182. Davidson, "Saul's Reprobation," p. 156.

Bibliography

Abrahamson, Irving, ed. *Against Silence: The Voice and Vision of Elie Wiesel.* New York: Holocaust Library, 1985.

Ackerman, James S. "Who Can Stand before YHWH, This Holy God? A Reading of 1 Samuel 1–15." *Prooftexts* 11 (1991): 1-24.

Ackerman, Susan. *When Heroes Love: The Ambiguity of Eros in the Stories of Gilgamesh and David.* Gender, Theory, and Religion. New York: Columbia University Press, 2005.

Ackroyd, P. R. "The Succession Narrative (So-Called)." *Interp* 35 (1981): 383-96.

Adam, A. K. M., et al. *Reading Scripture with the Church: Toward a Hermeneutic for Theological Interpretation.* Grand Rapids: Baker, 2006.

Adam, Klaus-Peter. "Nocturnal Intrusions and Divine Interventions on Behalf of Judah: David's Wisdom and Saul's Tragedy in 1 Samuel 26." *VT* 59 (2009): 1-33.

———. *Saul und David in der judäischen Geschichtsschreibung: Studien zu 1 Samuel 16–2 Samuel 5.* FAT 51. Tübingen: Mohr Siebeck, 2007.

Adar, Zvi. *The Biblical Narrative.* Jerusalem: Department of Education and Culture, World Zionist Organisation, 1959.

Aejmalaeus, Anneli. "The Septuagint of 1 Samuel." Pp. 131-49 in idem, *On the Trail of the Septuagint Translators: Collected Essays.* Kampen: Kok Pharos, 1993.

Aelred of Rievaulx. *Spiritual Friendship.* Christian Classics. Edited by Dennis Billy. Translated by M. Laker. Notre Dame: Ave Maria, 2008.

Aguilar, Grace. "Hannah." Pp. 1: 254-70 in *The Women of Israel.* 2 Vols. New York: D. Appleton & Co., 1853.

Ahlström, G. W. "The Travels of the Ark: A Religio-Political Composition." *JNES* 43 (1984): 141-49.

Aichele, George. *The Control of Biblical Meaning: Canon as Semiotic Mechanism.* Harrisburg: Trinity, 2001.

Albertz, Rainer. *A History of Israelite Religion in the Old Testament Period.* OTL. 2 vols. Translated by John Bowden. Louisville: Westminster John Knox, 1994.

———. *Persönliche Frommigkeit und offizielle Religion: religionsinterner Pluralismus in Israel und Babylon.* Calwer theologische Monographien 9. Stuttgart: Calwer, 1978.

Allen, Glen O. "Structure, Symbol, and Theme in E. M. Forster's *A Passage to India.*" *Publications of the Modern Language Association of America* 70 (1955): 934-54.

Allen, R. Michael, ed. *Theological Commentary: Evangelical Perspectives.* London: T & T Clark, 2011.

Alter, Robert. *The Art of Biblical Narrative*. 2nd ed. New York: Basic Books, 2011.

———. *The David Story: A Translation with Commentary of 1 and 2 Samuel*. New York: W. W. Norton & Company, 1999.

———. "Introduction to the Old Testament." Pp. 11-35 in *The Literary Guide to the Bible*. Edited by Robert Alter and Frank Kermode. Cambridge, MA: Harvard University Press, 1987.

———. "A Literary Approach to the Bible." *Commentary* 60 (1975): 70-77.

———. "Literary Criticism and the Problem of Commentary." Pp. 131-52 in idem, *The World of Biblical Literature*. New York: Basic Books, 1992.

———. *The World of Biblical Literature*. New York: Basic Books, 1992.

Alter, Robert, and Frank Kermode, eds. *The Literary Guide to the Bible*. Cambridge, MA: Harvard University Press, 1987.

Ambrose of Milan. *Apologie de David*. Edited by Pierre Hadot. Translated by Marius Cordier. Paris: Cerf, 1977.

———. *De officiis*. Edited by Ivor J. Davidson. 2 Vols. OECS. Oxford: Oxford University Press, 2001.

Amit, Yairah. "Araunah's Threshing-Floor: A Lesson in Shaping Historical Memory." Pp. 13-23 in *Performing Memory in Biblical Narrative and Beyond*. Edited by Athalya Brenner and Frank Polak. Bible in the Modern World 25. Sheffield: Sheffield Phoenix, 2009.

———. "The Delicate Balance in the Image of Saul in the Deuteronomistic History." Pp. 71-79 in *Saul in Story and Tradition*. Edited by Carl S. Ehrlich with Marsha C. White. FAT 47. Tübingen: Mohr Siebeck, 2006.

———. "'The Glory of Israel Does Not Deceive or Change His Mind': On the Reliability of Narrator and Speakers in Biblical Narrative." *Prooftexts* 12 (1992): 201-12.

———. *In Praise of Editing in the Hebrew Bible: Collected Essays in Retrospect*. HBM 39. Translated by Betty Sigler Rozen. Sheffield: Sheffield Phoenix, 2012.

———. *Reading Biblical Narratives: Literary Criticism and the Hebrew Bible*. Translated by Yael Lotan. Minneapolis: Fortress, 2001.

———. "The Saul Polemic in the Persian Period." Pp. 647-61 in *Judah and the Judeans in the Persian Period*. Edited by Oded Lipschits and Manfred Oeming. Winona Lake: Eisenbrauns, 2006.

Anderson, Gary. "King David and the Psalms of Imprecation." *ProEccl* 15 (2006): 267-80.

Andersson, Greger. *Untamable Texts: Literary Studies and Narrative Theory in the Books of Samuel*. LHBOTS 514. New York: T & T Clark, 2009.

Andrew of St. Victor. *Commentary on Samuel and Kings*. Translated by Frans van Liere. Corpus Christianorum in Translation 3. Turnhout: Brepols, 2009.

Aphrahat. *Demonstrations*. Translated by Kuriakose Valavanolickal. 2 vols. Kottayam, India: St. Ephrem Ecumenical Resarch Institute, 2005.

Aquinas, St. Thomas. *On Kingship*. Translated by Gerald B. Phelan. Toronto: Pontifical Institute of Mediaeval Studies, 1949.

Armerding, Carl Edwin. "Were David's Sons Really Priests?" Pp. 75-86 in *Current Issues in Biblical and Patristic Interpretation: Studies in Honor of Merrill C. Tenney Presented by His Former Students*. Edited by Gerald F. Hawthorne. Grand Rapids: Eerdmans, 1975.

Arneth, Martin. "Die antiassyrische Reform Josias von Juda: Überlegungen zur Komposition und Intention von 2 Reg 23,4-15." *ZABR* 7 (2001): 189-216.

Arnold, Bill T. "The Amalekite's Report of Saul's Death: Political Intrigue or Incompatible Sources?" *JETS* 32 (1989): 289-98.

———. "The Love–Fear Antinomy in Deuteronomy 5–11." *VT* 61 (2011): 551-69.

Bibliography

————. "Necromancy and Cleromancy in 1 and 2 Samuel." *CBQ* 66 (2004): 199-213.

————. "Soul-Searching Questions About 1 Samuel 28: Samuel's Appearance at Endor and Christian Anthropology." Pp. 75-83 in *What About the Soul? Neuroscience and Christian Anthropology*. Edited by Joel B. Green. Nashville: Abingdon, 2004.

Arubas, Benny. "The Impact of Town Planning at Scythopolis on the Topography of Tel Beth-Shean: A New Understanding of Its Fortifications and Status." Pp. 48-58 in *Excavations at Tel Beth-Shean 1989-1996, Vol. 1: From the Late Bronze Age IIB to the Medieval Period*. Edited by Amihai Mazar. Jerusalem: Hebrew University and Israel Exploration Society, 2006.

Attridge, Harold W. "Pollution, Sin, Atonement, Salvation." Pp. 71-83 in *Religions of the Ancient World: A Guide*. Edited by Sarah Iles Johnson. Cambridge, MA: Harvard University Press, 2004.

Auden, W. H. "The Christian Tragic Hero: Contrasting Captain Ahab's Doom and Its Classic Greek Prototype." Pp. 143-47 in *Tragedy: Vision and Form*. Edited by Robert W. Corrigan. San Francisco: Chandler, 1965.

————. "The Quest Hero." Pp. 40-61 in *Tolkien and the Critics: Essays on J. R. R. Tolkien's The Lord of the Rings*. Edited by Neil D. Isaacs and Rose A. Zimbardo. Notre Dame: University of Notre Dame Press, 1968.

Auerbach, Eric. *Mimesis: The Representation of Reality in Western Literature*. Translated by W. R. Trask. Princeton: Princeton University Press, 1953.

Augustin, Matthias. *Der schöne Mensch im Alten Testament und im hellenistischer Judentum*. BEATAJ 3. Frankfurt: Lang, 1983.

Augustine. *Expositions on the Psalms, 121–50*. Vol. 5. Translated by Maria Boulding. Works of St. Augustine 3.20. Hyde Park, NY: New City, 2004.

Auld, A. Graeme. *I & II Samuel: A Commentary*. OTL. Louisville: Westminster John Knox, 2011.

————. "Re-Reading Samuel Historically: 'Etwas mehr Nichtwissen.'" Pp. 160-69 in *The Origin of the Ancient Israelite States*. Edited by Volkmar Fritz and P. R. Davies. JSOTSup 228. Sheffield: JSOT, 1996.

————. "The Story of David and Goliath: A Test Case for Synchrony *plus* Diachrony." Pp. 118-28 in *David and Saul im Widerstreit — Diachronie und Synchronie im Wettstreit*. Edited by Walter Dietrich. OBO 206.Göttingen: Vandenhoeck & Ruprecht, 2004.

Auld, A. Graeme, and Erik Eynikel, eds. *For and against David: Story and History in the Books of Samuel*. BETL 232. Leiden: Peeters, 2010.

Auld, A. Graeme and Craig Y. S. Ho. "The Making of David and Goliath." *JSOT* 56 (1992): 19-39.

Aurelius, Erik. "Wie David ursprünglich zu Saul kam (1 Sam 17)." Pp. 44-68 in *Vergegenwärtigung des Alten Testaments: Beiträge zur biblischen Hermeneutik; Festschrift für Rudolf Smend zum 70. Geburtstag*. Edited by Christoph Bultmann, Walter Dietrich, and Christoph Levin. Göttingen: Vandenhoeck & Ruprecht, 2003.

Avalos, Hector. *Illness and Health Care in the Ancient Near East: The Role of the Temple in Greece, Mesopotamia, and Israel*. HSM 54. Atlanta: Scholars, 1995.

————. "Is Biblical Illiteracy a Bad Thing? Reflections on Bibliolatry in the Modern Academy." *CSSR Bulletin* 38.2 (April, 2009): 47-52.

Avioz, Michael. "Could Saul Rule Forever? A New Look at 1 Samuel 13:13-14." *JHS* 5 (2005) [electronic resource].

————. "The Motif of Beauty in the Books of Samuel and Kings." *VT* 59 (2009): 341-59.

————. "The Story of Saul's Death in 1 Chronicles 10 and Its Sources." Pp. 113-19 in *Thinking*

Towards New Horizons: Collected Communications to the XIXth Congress of the International Organization for the Study of the Old Testament, Ljubljana 2007. Edited by Matthias Augstin and Herman Michael Niemann. BEATAJ 55. Frankfurt: Lang, 2008.

Avis, Paul. *Church, State and Establishment.* London: SPCK, 2001.

Azar, Michael. "The Scriptural King." *SVTQ* 50 (2006): 255-75.

Bach, Alice. "The Pleasure of Her Text." *USQR* 43 (1989): 41-58.

Baden, Joel S. *The Historical David: The Real Life of an Invented Hero.* New York: HarperCollins, 2013.

Bailey, R. C. "The Redemption of YHWH: A Literary Critical Function of the Songs of Hannah and David." *BibInt* 3 (1995): 213-31.

Bakalova, Elka. "King David as a Model for the Christian Ruler: Some Visual Sources." Pp. 93- 131 in *The Biblical Models of Power and Law: Papers of the International Conference, Bucharest, New Europe College 2005.* Edited by Ivan Biliarsky and Radu G. Paun. Rechtshistorische Reihe 366. Frankfurt: Lang, 2008.

Balthasar, Hans Urs von. *Two Sisters in the Spirit: Thérèse of Lisieux and Elizabeth of the Trinity.* San Francisco: Ignatius, 1992.

Bar, Shaul. *God's First King: The Story of Saul.* Eugene: Cascade, 2013.

Bar-Efrat, Shimon. *Das erste Buch Samuel: ein narratologisch-philologischer Kommentar.* BWANT 176. Stuttgart: Kohlhammer, 2007.

―――. *Narrative Art in the Bible.* London: T & T Clark, 2004.

―――. *Das zweite Buch Samuel: ein narratologisch-philologischer Kommentar.* BWANT 181. Stuttgart: Kohlhammer, 2009.

Bar-Ilan, M. "Scribes and Books in the Late Second Commonwealth and the Rabbinic Period." Pp. 21-37 in *Mikra': Text, Translation, Reading and Interpretation of the Hebrew Bible in Ancient Judaism and Early Christianity.* CRINT 2.1. Edited by Martin Jan Mulder. Assen: Van Gorcum, 1988.

Barber, Alex. "'I Resolved to Give an Account of Most of the Persons Mentioned in the Bible': Pierre Bayle and the Prophet David in English Biblical Culture." Pp. 231-47 in *Scripture and Scholarship in Early Modern England.* Edited by Ariel Hessayon and Nicholas Keene. Burlington: Ashgate, 2006.

Barber, Michael Patrick. "Jesus as the Davidic Temple Builder and Peter's Priestly Role in Matthew 16:16-19." *JBL* 132 (2013): 935-53.

Barr, James. *The Bible in the Modern World.* London: SCM, 1973.

―――. "Exegesis as a Theological Discipline Reconsidered and the Shadow of the Jesus of History." Pp. 11-45 in *The Hermeneutical Quest: Essays in Honor of James Luther Mays on his Sixty-Fifth Birthday.* Edited by Donald G. Miller. Allison Park, PA: Pickwick, 1986.

―――. *History and Ideology in the Old Testament.* Oxford: Oxford University Press, 2000.

―――. *Holy Scripture: Canon, Authority, Criticism.* Philadelphia: Westminster, 1983.

―――. *Old and New in Interpretation: A Study of the Two Testaments.* London: SCM, 1966.

―――. "The Symbolism of Names in the Old Testament." *BJRL* 52 (1969): 11-29.

Bartelmus, Rüdiger. "Handel and Jennens' Oratorio 'Saul': A Late Musical and Dramatic Rehabilitation of the Figure of Saul." Pp. 284-307 in *Saul in Story and Tradition* . Edited by Carol S. Ehrlich with Marsha C. White. FAT 47. Tübingen: Mohr Siebeck, 2006.

Barth, Karl. *Church Dogmatics.* Edited by G. W. Bromiley and T. F. Torrance. 14 vols. Edinburgh: T & T Clark, 1936-77.

―――. *The Epistle to the Romans.* 6th ed. Translated by E. C. Hoskyns. Oxford: Oxford University Press, 1968.

Bibliography

Barthélemy, Dominique. "La qualité du Texte Masorétique de Samuel." Pp. 1-44 in *The Hebrew and the Greek Texts of Samuel: 1980 Proceedings IOSCS Vienna*. Edited by Emanuel Tov. Jerusalem: Academon, 1980.

Barthélemy, Dominique et al., eds. *The Story of David and Goliath: Textual and Literary Criticism*. OBO 73. Fribourg: Éditions Universitaires/Göttingen: Vandenhoeck & Ruprecht, 1986.

Bartholomew, Craig G., and Michael W. Goheen. "Story and Biblical Theology." Pp. 144-71 in *Out of Egypt: Biblical Theology and Biblical Interpretation*. Edited by Craig G. Bartholomew et al. Scripture and Hermeneutics Seminar 5. Grand Rapids: Zondervan, 2004.

Bartholomew, Craig G., Colin Greene, and Karl Möller, eds. *Renewing Biblical Interpretation*. Scripture and Hermeneutics Seminar 1. Grand Rapids: Zondervan, 2000.

Bartholomew, Craig G., et al., eds. *Out of Egypt: Biblical Theology and Biblical Interpretation*. Scripture and Hermeneutics Seminar 5. Grand Rapids: Zondervan, 2004.

Barton, John. "Dating the Succession Narrative." Pp. 95-106 in *The Search for Pre-Exilic Israel: Proceedings of the Oxford Old Testament Seminar*. Edited by John Day. JSOTSup 406. London: T & T Clark, 2004.

———. *The Nature of Biblical Criticism*. Louisville: Westminster John Knox, 2007.

———. "On Biblical Commentaries." Pp. 201-14 in *The Old Testament: Canon, Literature and Theology: Collected Essays of John Barton*. Burlington: Ashgate, 2007.

———. *Oracles of God*. Oxford: Oxford University Press, 1986.

———. *Reading the Old Testament*. Philadelphia: Westminster, 1984.

———. "What Is a Book? Modern Exegesis and the Literary Conventions of Ancient Israel." Pp. 1-14 in *Intertextuality in Ugarit and Israel*. Edited by Johannes C. de Moor. OTS 40. Leiden: Brill, 1998.

Barton, Stephen C., ed. *Idolatry: False Worship in the Bible, Early Judaism, and Christianity*. London: T & T Clark, 2007.

Barzel, Hillel. "Moses: Tragedy and Sublimity." Pp. 120-40 in *Literary Interpretations of Biblical Narratives*. Edited by Kenneth R. R. Gros Louis, James S. Ackerman, and Thayer S. Warshaw. Nashville: Abingdon, 1974.

Bauck, Peter. "1 Samuel 19: David and the *teraphim*: *yhwh ʿm dwd* and the Emplotted Narrative." *SJOT* 22 (2008): 212-36.

Bautier, Robert-Henri. "Sacres et couronnements sous les Carolingiens et les premiers Capétiens: Recherches sur la genèse du sacre royal français." *Annuaire-Bulletin de la Société de l'histoire de France: Année 1987* (1989): 7-56.

Baxter, Wayne. "Healing and the 'Son of David': Matthew's Warrant." *NovT* 48 (2006): 36-50.

Bayer, Oswald. "Hermeneutical Theology." Pp. 103-20 in *Philosophical Hermeneutics and Biblical Exegesis*. Edited by Petr Pokorný and Jan Roskovec. WUNT 153. Tübingen: Mohr Siebeck, 2002.

Beale, G. K. *We Become What We Worship: A Biblical Theology of Idolatry*. Downers Grove: InterVarsity, 2008.

Beck, John A. "David and Goliath, A Story of Place: The Narrative-Geographical Shaping of 1 Samuel 17." *WTJ* 68 (2006): 321-30.

Beck, Martin. "Messiaserwartung in den Geschichtsbüchern? Bemerkungen zur Funktion des Hannaliedes (I Sam 2,1-10) in seinen diversen literarischen Kontexten (vgl. Ex 15; Dtn 32; II Sam 22)." Pp. 231-51 in *Auf dem Weg zur Endgestalt von Genesis bis II Regum: Festschrift Hans-Christoph Schmitt zum 65. Geburtstag*. Edited by Martin Beck and Ulrike Schorn. BZAW 370. Berlin: de Gruyter, 2006.

Becker, Joachim. "The Heart in the Language of the Bible." Pp. 23-31 in *Faith in Christ and the Worship of Christ.* Edited by Leo Scheffczyk. San Francisco: Ignatius, 1986.

Becker-Spörl, Silvia. *"Und Hanna Betete und Sie Sprach": literarische Untersuchungen zu 1 Samuel 1:1-10.* Tübingen: Francke, 1992.

Becking, Bob. "David Between Ideology and Evidence." Pp. 1-30 in *Between Evidence and Ideology: Essays on the History of Ancient Israel Read at the Joint Meeting of the Society for Old Testament Study and the Oud Testamentisch Werkgezelschap, Lincoln, July 2009.* OTS 59. Leiden: Brill, 2011.

Begg, C. T. "Inquire of God." *ABD* 3:417-18. 5 Vols. New York: Doubleday, 1992.

———. "King Saul's First Sin according to Josephus." *Antonianum* 74 (1999): 685-96.

———. "Seeking YHWH and the Purpose of Chronicles." *Louvain Studies* 9 (1982): 128-41.

Bellah, Robert N. "Civil Religion in America." *Daedalus* 96 (Winter, 1967): 1-21 = Pp. 168-89 in idem, *Beyond Belief: Essays on Religion in a Post-Traditional World.* New York: Harper & Row, 1970.

———. *The Broken Covenant: American Civil Religion in the Time of Trial.* 2nd ed. Chicago: University of Chicago Press, 1992.

Ben Zvi, Ehud. "The Closing Words of the Pentateuchal Books: A Clue for the Historical Status of the Book of Genesis within the Pentateuch." *BN* 62 (1992): 7-10.

———. "Looking at the Primary (Hi)story and the Prophetic Books as Literary/Theological Units within the Frame of the Early Second Temple: Some Considerations." *SJOT* 12 (1998): 26-43.

———. "On the Term Deuteronomistic in Relation to Joshua–Kings in the Persian Period." Pp. 61-71 in *Raising Up a Faithful Exegete: Essays in Honor of Richard D. Nelson.* Edited by K. L. Noll and Brooks Schramm. Winona Lake: Eisenbrauns, 2010.

———. "Once the Lamp Has Been Kindled . . . A Reconsideration of the Meaning of MT *Nîr* in 1 Kgs 11:36, 15:4; 2 Kgs 8:19, and 2 Chr 21:7." *ABR* 39 (1991): 19-30.

———. "Twelve Prophetic Books or 'The Twelve': A Few Preliminary Considerations." Pp. 125-56 in *Forming Prophetic Literature: Essays on Isaiah and the Twelve in Honor of John D. W. Watts.* Edited by Paul House and James W. Watts. JSOTSup 235. Sheffield: Sheffield Academic, 1996.

Benjamin, Walter. "The Storyteller." Pp. 83-109 in idem, *Illuminations.* Edited by Hannah Arendt. Translated by Harry Zohn. New York: Schocken, 1968.

Bentzen, Aage. *King and Messiah.* London: Lutterworth, 1955.

Bergen, Robert D. *1, 2 Samuel.* NAC 7. Nashville: Broadman & Holman, 1996.

Berger, Yitzhak. "On Patterning in the Book of Samuel: 'News of Death' and the Kingship of David." *JSOT* 35 (2011): 463-81.

Berges, Ulrich. *Die Verwerfung Sauls: eine thematische Untersuchung.* FzB 61. Würzburg: Echter Verlag, 1989.

Berlin, Adele. *Poetics and Interpretation of Biblical Narrative.* Bible and Literature Series 9. Sheffield: Almond, 1983.

———. "Point of View in Biblical Narrative." Pp. 43-82 in *A Sense of the Text: The Art of Language in the Study of the Biblical Literature.* Edited by Adele Berlin, Stephen A. Geller, and Edward L. Greenstein. JQRSup. Winona Lake: Eisenbrauns, 1982.

Berlin, Adele, Stephen A. Geller, and Edward L. Greenstein, *A Sense of the Text: The Art of Language in the Study of Biblical Literature.* JQRSup. Winona Lake: Eisenbrauns, 1982.

Berlinerblau, Jacques. "The 'Popular Religion' Paradigm in Old Testament Research: A Sociological Critique." *JSOT* 60 (1993): 3-26.

Bibliography

Bettenzoli, Giuseppe. "Samuel und das Problem des Königtums: die Tradition von Gilgal." *BZ* 30 (1986): 222-36.

———. "Samuel und Saul in geschichtlicher und theologischer Auffassung." *ZAW* 98 (1986): 338-51.

Beuken, W. A. M. "1 Samuel 28: The Prophet as 'Hammer of Witches.'" *JSOT* 6 (1978): 3-17.

Beyerlin, Walter. "Die Königscharisma bei Saul." *ZAW* 73 (1961): 186-201.

Biddle, Mark E. "Ancestral Motifs in 1 Samuel 25: Intertextuality and Characterization." *JBL* 121 (2002): 617-38.

Birch, Bruce C. "Ethical Approaches: The Story of David as Moral Tale." Pp. 369-85 in *Method Matters: Essays on the Interpretation of the Hebrew Bible in Honor of David L. Petersen.* Edited by Joel M. LeMon and Kent Harold Richards. Leiden: Brill, 2010.

———. "The First and Second Books of Samuel." *NIB* 2:947-1383. Edited by Leander E. Keck. Nashville: Abingdon, 1998.

———. *The Rise of the Israelite Monarchy: The Growth and Development of I Samuel 7–15.* SBLDS 27. Missoula: Scholars, 1976.

Black, Jonathan. "*De Civitate Dei* and the Commentaries of Gregory the Great, Isidore, Bede, and Hrabanus Maurus on the Book of Samuel." *Augustinian Studies* 15 (1984): 114-27.

Blaikie, William G. *The First Book of Samuel.* EB. New York: A. C. Armstrong and Son, 1888.

Blenkinsopp, Joseph. "Another Contribution to the Succession Narrative Debate (2 Samuel 11–20; 1 Kings 1–2)." *JSOT* 38 (2013): 35-58.

———. *David Remembered: Kingship and National Identity in Ancient Israel.* Grand Rapids: Eerdmans, 2013.

———. "Jonathan's Sacrilege: 1 Sm 14,1-46. A Study in Literary History." *CBQ* 26 (1964): 423-49.

———. *Opening the Sealed Book: Interpretations of the Book of Isaiah in Late Antiquity.* Grand Rapids: Eerdmans, 2006.

———. "The Quest of the Historical Saul." Pp. 75-99 in *No Famine in the Land: Studies in Honor of John L. McKenzie.* Edited by James W. Flanagan and Anita Weisbrod Robinson. Missoula: Scholars, 1975.

———. "Saul and the Mistress of the Spirits (1 Samuel 28.3-25)." Pp. 49-62 in *Sense and Sensitivity: Essays on Reading the Bible in Memory of Robert Carroll.* Edited by Alastair G. Hunter and Philip R. Davies. JSOTSup 348. Sheffield: Sheffield Academic, 2002.

Boccaccini, Gabriele. *Roots of Judaism: An Intellectual History, from Ezekiel to Daniel.* Grand Rapids: Eerdmans, 2002.

Bockmuehl, Markus. "The Jewish People and Their Sacred Scriptures in the Christian Bible: Response." *ScrB* 33 (2003): 15-28.

———. *Seeing the Word: Refocusing New Testament Study.* STI. Grand Rapids: Baker, 2006.

Bodendorfer, Gerhard. "David, der weise Toragelehrte: zur Funktion Davids im babylonischen Talmud." Pp. 383-99 in *Auf den Spuren der schriftgelehrten Weisen: Festschrift für Johannes Marböck anlässlich seiner Emeritierung.* Edited by Irmtraud Fischer, Ursula Rapp, and Johannes A. Schiller. BZAW 331. Berlin: de Gruyter, 2003.

Bodi, Daniel. *The Demise of the Warlord: A New Look at the David Story.* HBM 26. Sheffield: Sheffield Phoenix, 2010.

Bodi, Daniel, with Brigitte Donnet-Guez. *The Michal Affair: From Zimri-Lim to the Rabbis.* HBM 3. Sheffield: Sheffield Phoenix, 2005.

Bodner, Keith. *1 Samuel: A Narrative Commentary.* HBM 19. Sheffield: Sheffield Phoenix, 2008.

———. "Ark-Eology: Shifting Emphases in 'Ark Narrative' Scholarship." *CBR* 4 (2006): 169-97.

————. *David Observed: A King in the Eyes of His Court.* Sheffield: Sheffield Phoenix, 2005.

————. "Eliab and the Deuteronomist." *JSOT* 28 (2003): 55-71.

Boecker, Hans Jochen. *Die Beurteilung der Anfänge des Königtums in den deuteronomistischen Abschnitten des ersten Samuelisbuches.* WMANT 31. Neukirchen–Vluyn: Neukirchener, 1969.

Böhler, Dieter. "'Ecce homo!' (Joh 19, 5): ein Zitat aus dem Alten Testament." *BZ* 39 (1995): 104-8.

Boling, Robert G. "In Those Days There Was No King in Israel." Pp. 33-48 in *A Light Unto My Path: Old Testament Studies in Honor of Jacob M. Myers.* Edited by Howard N. Bream, Ralph D. Heim, and Carey A. Moore. Gettysburg Theological Studies 4. Philadelphia: Temple University Press, 1974.

Bonhoeffer, Dietrich. "Bible Study: King David, Finkenwalde, October 8–11, 1935." Pp. 870-904 in *Dietrich Bonhoeffer Works, Volume 14: Theological Education at Finkenwalde: 1935–1937.* Edited by Otto Dudzus and Jürgen Henkys. Translated by Douglas W. Scott. Minneapolis: Augsburg Fortress, 2013.

————. *Letters and Papers from Prison.* New York: Macmillan, 1971.

Booth, Wayne. *The Rhetoric of Fiction.* 2nd ed. Chicago: University of Chicago Press, 1983.

Borgman, Paul. *David, Saul, and God: Rediscovering an Ancient Story.* Oxford: Oxford University Press, 2008.

Bosworth, David. "Evaluating King David: Old Problems and Recent Scholarship." *CBQ* 68 (2006): 191-210.

Bouman, C. A. *Sacring and Crowning: The Development of the Latin Ritual for the Anointing of Kings and the Coronation of an Emperor before the Eleventh Century.* Bijdragen van het Institut voor Middeleeuwse Geschiednis der Rijks-Universiteit te Utrecht 30. Groningen: J. B. Wolters, 1957.

Bowers, Maggie Ann. *Magic(al) Realism.* The New Critical Idiom. London: Routledge, 2004.

Bowers, R. H. *The Legend of Jonah.* The Hague: Nijhoff, 1971.

Bowman, Richard C. "The Complexity of Character and the Ethics of Complexity: The Case of King David." Pp. 73-97 in *Character and Scripture: Moral Formation, Community, and Biblical Interpretation.* Edited by William P. Brown. Grand Rapids: Eerdmans, 2002.

Boyle, Marjorie O'Rourke. "The Law of the Heart: The Death of a Fool (1 Samuel 25)." *JBL* 120 (2001): 401-27.

Bradley, Ian C. *God Save the Queen: The Spiritual Dimension of the Monarchy.* London: Darton, Longman & Todd, 2002.

Breasted, James Henry. *The Development of Religion and Thought in Ancient Egypt.* London: Hodder and Stoughton, 1912.

Bremmer, Jan. "Ritual." Pp. 32-44 in *Religions of the Ancient World: A Guide.* Edited by Sarah Iles Johnson. Cambridge, MA: Harvard University Press, 2004.

Brenner, Athalya. "Rizpah [Re]Membered: 2 Samuel 1–14 and Beyond." Pp. 207-27 in *Performing Memory in Biblical Narrative and Beyond.* Edited by Athalya Brenner and Frank Polak. Bible in the Modern World 25. Sheffield: Sheffield Phoenix, 2009.

————. *Samuel and Kings.* FCB (Second Series) 7. Sheffield: Sheffield Academic, 2000.

Brenner, Athalya, and Frank Polak, eds. *Performing Memory in Biblical Narrative and Beyond.* Bible in the Modern World 25. Sheffield: Sheffield Phoenix, 2009.

Brettler, Marc Z. "Biblical Literature as Politics: The Case of Samuel." Pp. 71-92 in *Religion and Politics in the Ancient Near East.* Edited by Adele Berlin. Studies and Texts in Jewish History and Culture. University Press of Maryland, 1996.

Bibliography

———. "The Composition of 1 Samuel 1–2." *JBL* 116 (1997): 601-12.

———. *The Creation of History in Ancient Israel.* London: Routledge, 1995.

———. *God is King: Understanding an Israelite Metaphor.* JSOTSup 76. Sheffield: Sheffield Academic, 1989.

Breytenbach, Andries. "Who Is Behind the Samuel Narrative?" Pp. 50-61 in *Past, Present, Future: The Deuteronomistic History and the Prophets.* Edited by Johannes C. de Moor and Harry F. Van Rooy. OTS 44. Leiden: Brill, 2000.

Brichto, Herbert C. *Toward a Grammar of Biblical Poetics: Tales of the Prophets.* Oxford: Oxford University Press, 1992.

Briggs, Richard S. *The Virtuous Reader: Old Testament Narrative and Interpretive Virtue.* Grand Rapids: Baker, 2010.

Brooks, Phillips. *Twenty Sermons.* New York: E. P. Dutton & Co., 1890.

Brooks, Simcha Shalom. *Saul and the Monarchy: A New Look.* SOTSM. Burlington: Ashgate, 2005.

Brown, Devin. *The Christian World of* The Hobbit. Nashville: Abingdon, 2012.

Browning, Robert. *The Shorter Poems of Robert Browning.* Edited by William Clyde DeVane. New York: Crofts, 1942.

Brueggemann, Walter. "1 Samuel 1: A Sense of a Beginning." *ZAW* 102 (1990): 33-48.

———. "2 Samuel 21–24: An Appendix of Deconstruction?" *CBQ* 50 (1988): 383-97.

———. *David and His Theologian: Literary, Social, and Theological Investigations of the Early Monarchy.* Edited by K. C. Hanson. Eugene: Cascade Books, 2011.

———. *David's Truth in Israel's Imagination and Memory.* 2nd ed. Minneapolis: Fortress, 2002.

———. *First and Second Samuel.* Interpretation. Louisville: Westminster John Knox, 1990.

———. *Ichabod toward Home: The Journey of God's Glory.* Grand Rapids: Eerdmans, 2002.

———. "Narrative Coherence and Theological Intentionality in 1 Samuel 18." *CBQ* 55 (1993): 225-43.

———. "Narrative Intentionality in 1 Samuel 29." *JSOT* 43 (1989): 21-35.

———. "On Scroll-Making in Ancient Jerusalem." *BTB* 33 (2003): 5-11.

———. *Worship in Ancient Israel: An Essential Guide.* Abingdon Essential Guides. Nashville: Abingdon, 2005.

Bruner, F. D. "The How and Why of Commentary." *ThTo* 42 (1990): 399-404.

Bryson, Anna. *From Courtesy to Civility: Changing Codes of Conduct in Early Modern England.* Oxford Studies in Social History. Oxford: Oxford University Press, 1998.

Buber, Martin. "Autobiographical Fragments." Pp. 3-39 in *The Philosophy of Martin Buber.* Edited by Paul Arthur Schilpp and Maurice Freidman. Library of Living Philosophers 12. La Salle, IL: Open Court, 1967.

———. "Die Erzählung von Sauls Königswahl." *VT* 6 (1956): 113-73.

———. *Kingship of God.* 3rd ed. Translated by Richard Scheiman. London: Allen and Unwin, 1967.

———. *The Prophetic Faith.* New York: Harper & Row, 1960.

Buchanan, Colin. *Cut the Connection: Disestablishment and the Church of England.* London: Darton, Longman & Todd, 1994.

Bultmann, Rudolf. "The Significance of the Old Testament for the Christian Faith." pp. 8-35 in *The Old Testament and the Christian Faith.* Edited by Bernhard W. Anderson. New York: Harper & Row, 1963.

Bunge, Marcia, Terence E. Fretheim, and Beverly Roberts Gaventa, eds. *The Child in the Bible.* Grand Rapids: Eerdmans, 2001.

Burger, Christoph. *Jesus als Davidssohn: eine traditionsgeschichtliche Untersuchung*. FRLANT 98. Göttingen: Vandenhoeck & Ruprecht, 1970.

Busch, Eberhard. *Barth*. Abingdon Pillars of Theology. Nashville: Abingdon, 2008.

Butting, Klara. "Zwei Brote für Saul: ein Einspruch gegen die Stilisierung Sauls zur tragischen Figur." Pp. 49-59 in *Essen und Trinken in der Bibel: ein literarisches Festmahl für Rainer Kessler zum 65. Geburtstag*. Edited by Michaela Geiger. Gütersloh: Gütersloher Verlagshaus, 2009.

Cameron, Averil. *Christianity and the Rhetoric of Empire: The Development of Christian Discourse*. Berkeley: University of California Press, 1991.

Campbell, Antony F., S.J. *1 Samuel*. FOTL 7. Grand Rapids: Eerdmans, 2003.

———. *2 Samuel*. FOTL 8. Grand Rapids: Eerdmans, 2005.

———. "2 Samuel 21–24: The Enigma Factor." Pp. 347-58 in *For and against David: Story and History in the Books of Samuel*. Edited by A. Graeme Auld and Erik Eynikel. BETL 232. Leuven: Peeters, 2010.

———. *Making Sense of the Bible: Difficult Texts and Modern Faith*. Mahwah: Paulist, 2010.

———. *Of Prophets and Kings: A Late Ninth-Century Document (1 Samuel 1–2 Kings 10)*. CBQMS 17. Washington, DC: Catholic Biblical Association of America, 1986.

———. "Structure Analysis and the Art of Exegesis (1 Samuel 16:14–18:30)." Pp. 76-103 in *Problems in Biblical Theology: Essays in Honor of Rolf Knierim*. Edited by Henry T. C. Sun and Keith L. Eades with James M. Robinson and Garth I. Moller. Grand Rapids: Eerdmans, 1997.

Campenhausen, Hans Freiherr von. *The Formation of the Christian Bible*. Translated by J. A. Baker. Philadelphia: Fortress, 1972.

Carlson, R. A. *David, the Chosen King*. Translated by Eric J. Sharpe and Stanley Rudman. Stockholm: Almqvist & Wiksell, 1964.

Carlyle, Thomas. *On Heroes, Hero-Worship & the Heroic in History*. Berkeley: University of California Press, 1993.

Carmichael, Calum M. "David at the Nob Sanctuary." Pp. 201-12 in *For and against David: Story and History in the Books of Samuel*. Edited by A. Graeme Auld and Erik Eynikel. BETL 232. Leuven: Peeters, 2010.

———. *The Spirit of Biblical Law*. Athens: University of Georgia Press, 1996.

Carroll, Robert P. *From Chaos to Covenant: Prophecy in the Book of Jeremiah*. New York: Crossroad, 1981.

Carson, D. A. "Unity and Diversity in the New Testament: The Possibility of Systematic Theology." Pp. 65-96 in *Scripture and Truth*. Edited by D. A. Carson and John D. Woodbridge. Grand Rapids: Baker, 1992.

Carter, Stephen L. *Civility: Manners, Morals and the Etiquette of Democracy*. New York: Basic Books, 1998.

———. *The Culture of Disbelief: How American Law and Politics Trivialize Religious Devotion*. New York: Basic Books, 1993.

Cartledge, Tony. *1 & 2 Samuel*. Smyth & Helwys Bible Commentary. Macon: Smyth & Helwys, 2001.

———. *Vows in the Hebrew Bible and the Ancient Near East*. JSOTSup 147. Sheffield: JSOT, 1992.

Cazeaux, Jacques. *Saül, David, Salomon: La Royauté et le destin d'Israël*. LD. Paris: Cerf, 2003.

Chan, Mary. "*The Witch of Endor* and Seventeenth-Century Propaganda," *Musica Disciplina* 34 (1980): 205-14.

Bibliography

Chapman, Stephen B. "Brevard Childs as a Historical Critic: Divine Concession and the Unity of the Canon." Pp. 63-83 in *The Bible as Christian Scripture: The Work of Brevard S. Childs*. Edited by Christopher R. Seitz and Kent Harold Richards. BSNA 25. Atlanta: Society of Biblical Literature, 2013.

———. "Canon: OT." Pp. 96-109 in *The Oxford Encyclopedia of the Books of the Bible*, vol. 1. Edited by Michael Coogan. 2 vols. Oxford: Oxford University Press, 2011.

———. "The Covenant God of Israel: Joshua 8, Divine Concession, and Jesus." Pp. 63-85 in *Covenant and Election in Exilic and Post-Exilic Judaism*. Edited by Nathan MacDonald. FAT/2 79. Studies of the Sofja Kovalevska Research Group on Early Jewish Monotheism 5. Tübingen: Mohr Siebeck, 2015.

———. "Imperial Exegesis: When Caesar Interprets Scripture." Pp. 91-102 in *Anxious about Empire: Theological Essays on the New Gobal Realities*. Grand Rapids: Brazos, 2004.

———. "Interpreting the Old Testament in Baptist Life." Pp. 87-107 in *The Scholarly Vocation and the Baptist Academy: Essays on the Future of Baptist Higher Education*. Edited by Roger Ward and David P. Gushee. Macon: Mercer University Press, 2008.

———. "Joshua Son of Nun: Presentation of a Prophet." Pp. 13-26 in *Thus Says the Lord: Essays on the Former and Latter Prophets in Honor of Robert R. Wilson*. Edited by John J. Ahn and Stephen L. Cook. LHBOTS 502. New York: T & T Clark, 2009.

———. *The Law and the Prophets: A Study in Old Testament Canon Formation*. FAT 27. Tübingen: Mohr Siebeck, 2000.

———. "Martial Memory, Peaceable Vision: Divine War in the Old Testament." Pp. 47-67 in *Holy War in the Bible: Christian Morality and an Old Testament Problem*. Edited by Heath A. Thomas, Jeremy Evans, and Paul Copan. Downers Grove: IVP Academic, 2013.

———. "The Old Testament Canon and Its Authority for the Christian Church," *ExAud* 19 (2003): 125-48.

———. "The Old Testament and the Church after Christendom." *Journal of Theological Interpretation* 9 (2015): 159-83.

———. "Perpetual War: The Case of Amalek." Pp. 1-19 in *The Bible and Spirituality: Exploratory Essays in Reading Scripture Spiritually*. Edited by Andrew T. Lincoln, J. Gordon McConville, and Lloyd K. Pietersen. Eugene: Cascade, 2013.

———. "Reclaiming Inspiration for the Bible." Pp. 167-206 in *Canon and Biblical Interpretation*. Edited by Craig G. Bartholomew et al. SHS 7. Grand Rapids: Zondervan, 2006.

———. "Reading the Bible as Witness: Divine Retribution in the Old Testament." *PRS* 31 (2004): 171-90.

———. "Saul/Paul: Onomastics, Typology, and Christian Scripture." Pp. 214-43 in *The Word Leaps the Gap: Essays on Scripture and Theology in Honor of Richard B. Hays*. Edited by J. Ross Wagner, C. Kavin Rowe, and A. Katherine Grieb. Grand Rapids: Eerdmans, 2008.

———. "'A Threefold Cord is Not Quickly Broken': Interpretation by Canonical Division in Early Judaism and Christianity." Pp. 281-309 in *The Shape of the Writings*. Edited by Julius Steinberg and Timothy J. Stone, with Rachel Stone. Siphrut 16. Winona Lake: Eisenbrauns, 2015.

Chavel, Simon. "Compositry and Creativity in 2 Sam 21:1-14." *JBL* 122 (2003): 23-52.

Chazelle, Celia, and Burton Van Name Edwards, eds. *The Study of the Bible in the Carolingian Era*. Medieval Church Studies 3. Turnhout: Brepols, 2003.

Cherbonnier, Edmund La B. "Biblical Faith and the Idea of Tragedy." Pp. 23-56 in *The Tragic Vision and the Christian Faith*. Edited by Nathan A. Scott. New York: Association, 1957.

Chesebrough, David B. *Phillips Brooks: Pulpit Eloquence*. Great American Orators 30. Westport, CT: Greenwood, 2001.

Chevalier-Royet, Caroline. "Saül et David, premiers rois oints: L'interpretation de ces modeles royaux par deux exégètes Carolingiens, Raban Maur et Angélome de Luxeuil." Pp. 61-76 in *The Multiple Meaning of Scripture: The Role of Exegesis in Early-Christian and Medieval Culture*. Commentaria 2. Edited by Ineke van 't Spijker. Leiden: Brill, 2009.

Childs, Brevard S. *Biblical Theology in Crisis*. Philadelphia: Westminster, 1970.

——. "The Genre of the Biblical Commentary as Problem and Challenge." Pp. 185-92 in *Tehillah le-Moshe: Biblical and Judaic Studies in Honor of Moshe Greenberg*. Edited by Mordechai Cogan, Barry L. Eichler, and Jeffrey H. Tigay. Winona Lake: Eisenbrauns, 1997.

——. "Interpretation in Faith: The Theological Responsibility of an Old Testament Commentary." *Interp* 18 (1964): 432-49.

——. *Introduction to the Old Testament as Scripture*. Philadelphia: Fortress, 1979.

——. *Old Testament Theology in a Canonical Context*. Philadelphia: Fortress, 1985.

——. "Psalm Titles and Midrashic Exegesis." *JSS* 16 (1971): 137-50.

——. *The Struggle to Understand Isaiah as Christian Scripture*. Grand Rapids: Eerdmans, 2004.

Chisholm, Robert B. "Does God Deceive?" *Bibliotheca Sacra* 155 (1998): 11-28.

——. "The Role of Women in the Rhetorical Strategy of the Book of Judges." Pp. 34-49 in *Integrity of Heart, Skillfulness of Hands: Biblical and Leadership Studies in Honor of Donald K. Campbell*. Edited by Charles H. Dyer and Roy B. Zuck. Grand Rapids: Baker, 1994.

Chrysostom, John. *Old Testament Homilies, Volume 1: Homilies on Hannah, David and Saul*. Translated by Robert C. Hill. Brookline: Holy Cross Orthodox Press, 2003.

Ciraolo, Leda Jean, and Jonathan Seidel, eds. *Magic and Divination in the Ancient World*. Ancient Magic and Divination 2. Leiden: Brill, 2002.

Clavell, James. *Shōgun: The Epic Novel of Japan*. New York: Bantam Dell, 1976.

Clayton, Cornell W., and Richard Elgar. *Civility and Democracy in America: A Reasonable Understanding*. Pullman: Washington State University Press, 2012.

Clements, R. E. "The Deuteronomic Interpretation of the Founding of the Monarchy in 1 Sam viii." *VT* 24 (1974): 398-410.

——. *Prophecy and Tradition*. Growing Points in Theology. Atlanta: John Knox, 1975.

Clines, David J. A. "David the Man: The Construction of Masculinity." Pp. 212-43 in idem, *Interested Parties: The Ideology of Writers and Readers of the Hebrew Bible*. JSOTSup 205. Sheffield: Sheffield Academic, 1995.

——. "Story and Poem: The Old Testament as Literature and Scripture." *Interp* 34 (2001): 115-21.

Clines, David J. A., and Tamara C. Eskenazi. *Telling Queen Michal's Story: An Experiment in Comparative Interpretation*. JSOTSup 119. Sheffield: JSOT, 1991.

Cogan, Mordechai. "The Road to En-dor." Pp. 319-26 in *Pomegranates and Golden Bells: Studies in Biblical, Jewish, and Near Eastern Ritual, Law, and Literature in Honor of Jacob Milgrom*. Edited by David P. Wright, David Noel Freedman, and Avi Hurvitz. Winona Lake: Eisenbrauns, 1995.

Coggins, Richard. "A Future for the Commentary?" Pp. 163-75 in *The Open Text: New Directions for Biblical Studies?* Edited by Francis Watson. London: SCM, 1993.

——. "On Kings and Disguises." *JSOT* 50 (1991): 55-62.

——. "What Does 'Deuteronomistic' Mean?" Pp. 135-48 in *Words Remembered, Texts Re-*

Bibliography

newed: *Essays in Honour of John F. A. Sawyer*. Edited by Jon Davies, Graham Harvey, and Wilfred G. E. Watson. JSOTSup 195. Sheffield: Sheffield Academic, 1995.

Coleran, James E. "The Prophets and Sacrifice." *TS* 5 (1944): 411-38.

Collins, John J. *The Bible after Babel: Historical Criticism in a Postmodern Age*. Grand Rapids: Eerdmans, 2005.

Compton, Michael. "From Saul to Paul: Patristic Interpretation of the Names of the Apostle." Pp. 50-68 in *In Dominico Eloquio/In Lordly Eloquence: Essays on Patristic Exegesis in Honor of Robert Louis Wilken*. Edited by Paul M. Blowers et al. Grand Rapids: Eerdmans, 2002.

Conrad, Edgar W. "Heard But Not Seen: The Representation of 'Books' in the Old Testament." *JSOT* 54 (1992): 45-59.

Conrad, Joachim. "*qāṭōn*." *TDOT* 13:3-9.

————. "Die Unschuld des Tollkühnen: Überlegungen zu 1 Sam 24." Pp. 23-42 in *Ideales Königtum: Studien zu David und Salomo*. ABG 16. Edited by Rüdiger Lux. Leipzig: Evangelische Verlagsanstalt, 2005.

Conroy, Charles. *Absalom, Absalom! Narrative and Language in 2 Sam 13–20*. AnBib 81. Rome: Pontifical Biblical Institute, 2006.

Contreni, John. "Carolingian Biblical Culture." Pp. 1-23 in *Iohannes Scottus Eriugena: The Bible and Hermeneutics*. Edited by Gerd van Riel, Carlos Stell, and James McEvoy. Ancient and Medieval Philosophy 20. Louvain: University Press of Louvain, 1996.

Cook, Albert. "'Fiction' and History in Samuel and Kings." *JSOT* 36 (1986): 27-48.

Cook, Edward M. "1 Samuel xx 26–xxi 5 according to 4QSam^b." *VT* 44 (1994): 442-54.

Cook, Joan E. *Hannah's Desire, God's Design: Early Interpretations of the Story of Hannah*. JSOTSup 282. Sheffield: Sheffield Academic, 1999.

Cook, Stephen L. "The Text and Philology of 1 Samuel xii 20-1." *VT* 44 (1994): 250-54.

Cooley, Jeffrey L. "The Story of Saul's Election (1 Samuel 9–10) in the Light of Mantic Practice in Ancient Iraq." *JBL* 130 (2011): 247-61.

Cooper, Alan. "The Life and Times of King David according to the Book of Psalms." Pp. 117-32 in *The Poet and the Historian: Essays in Literary and Historical Biblical Criticism*. Edited by Richard. E. Friedman. HSM 26. Chico, CA: Scholars, 1983.

Copan, Paul. *Is God a Moral Monster? Making Sense of the Old Testament*. Grand Rapids: Baker, 2011.

Couffignal, Robert. "Le roi, le prophète et la nécromancienne: interprétation du chapitre 28 du Premier Livre de Samuel." *ZAW* 121 (2009): 19-30.

————. *Le saint roi David: la figure mythique et sa fortune*. Paris: Minard, 2003.

————. *Saül: Héros tragique de la Bible. Étude littéraire du récit de son règne d'après les Livres de Samuel (1 S IX –XXXI et 2 S I)*. Thèmes et mythes 19. Paris: Minard, 1999.

Covington, Daryl. *Purpose-Driven Martial Arts*. Blountsville, AL: Fifth Estate, 2006.

Cox, Patricia. "Origen and the Witch of Endor: Toward an Iconoclastic Typology." *AThR* 66 (1984): 137-47.

Cox, Roger. *Between Earth and Heaven: Shakespeare, Dostoyevsky, and the Meaning of Christian Tragedy*. San Francisco: Holt, Rinehart and Winston, 1969.

Craig, Kenneth M. "Rhetorical Aspects of Questions Answered with Silence in 1 Samuel 14:37 and 28:6." *CBQ* (1994): 221-39.

Creangă, Ovidiu, and Peter-Ben Smit, eds. *Biblical Masculinities Foregrounded*. HBM 62. Sheffield: Sheffield Phoenix, 2014.

Cross, Frank Moore. "The Ammonite Oppression of the Tribes of Gad and Reuben: Missing

Verses from 1 Samuel 11 Found in 4QSamuel[a]." Pp. 148-58 in *History, Historiography and Interpretation: Studies in Biblical and Cuneiform Literatures.* Edited by H. Tadmor and M. Weinfeld. Jerusalem: Magnes, 1983.

————. *Canaanite Myth and Hebrew Epic: Essays in the History of the Religion of Israel.* Cambridge, MA: Harvard University Press, 1973.

————. *From Epic to Canon: History and Literature in Ancient Israel.* Baltimore: Johns Hopkins University Press, 1998.

Cross, Frank Moore, Donald W. Parry, Richard J. Saley, and Eugene Ulrich, eds. *Qumran Cave 4.XII: 1–2 Samuel.* DJD 17. Oxford: Oxford University Press, 2005.

Crüsemann, Frank. *Der Widerstand gegen das Königtum.* WMANT 49. Neukirchen–Vluyn: Neukirchener, 1978.

Cryer, Frederick H. *Divination in Ancient Israel and its Near Eastern Environment: A Socio-Historical Investigation.* JSOTSup 142. Sheffield: Sheffield Academic, 1994.

Culler, Jonathan. "Defining Narrative Units." Pp. 123-42 in *Style and Structure in Literature: Essays in the New Stylistics.* Edited by Roger Fowler. Ithaca: Cornell University Press, 1975.

Davetian, Benet. *Civility: A Cultural History.* Toronto: University of Toronto Press, 2009.

Davidson, A. B. "Saul's Reprobation." Pp. 143-61 in idem, *The Called of God.* Edinburgh: T & T Clark, 1902.

Davies, Eryl W. "The Morally Dubious Passages of the Hebrew Bible: An Examination of Proposed Solutions." *CBR* 3 (2005): 197-228.

Davies, Graham. "The Friendship of Jonathan and David." Pp. 65-76 in *Studies on the Text and Versions of the Hebrew Bible in Honour of Robert Gordon.* Edited by Geoffrey Khan and Diana Lipton. VTSup 149. Leiden: Brill, 2012.

Davies, Philip R. "Ark or Ephod in 1 Sam 14:18," *JTS* 26 (1975): 82-87.

————. "Josiah and the Law Book." Pp. 65-77 in *Good Kings and Bad Kings: The Kingdom of Judah in the Seventh Century B.C.E.* Edited by Lester L. Grabbe. LHBOTS 393. European Seminar in Historical Methodology 5. London: T & T Clark, 2005.

————. "Son of David and Son of Saul." Pp. 123-32 in *The Fate of King David: The Past and Present of a Biblical Icon.* Edited by Tod Linafelt, Claudia V. Camp, and Timothy Beal. LHBOTS 500. New York: T. & T. Clark, 2010.

Davis, Ellen F., and Richard B. Hays, eds. *The Art of Reading Scripture.* Grand Rapids: Eerdmans, 2003.

Davis, James Calvin. *In Defense of Civility: How Religion Can Unite America on Seven Moral Issues that Divide Us.* Louisville: Westminster John Knox, 2010.

Dawn, Marva J. *A Royal "Waste" of Time: The Splendor of Worshiping God and Being Church.* Grand Rapids: Eerdmans, 1999.

Day, John. "The Canaanite Inheritance of the Israelite Monarchy." Pp. 72-90 in *King and Messiah in Israel and the Ancient Near East: Proceedings of the Oxford Old Testament Seminar.* Edited by John Day. JSOTSup 270. Sheffield: Sheffield Academic, 1998.

De Moor, Johannes C., and Harry F. Van Rooy, eds. *Past, Present, Future: The Deuteronomistic History and the Prophets.* OTS 44. Leiden: Brill, 2000.

Deist, Ferdinand. "Coincidence as a Motif of Divine Intervention in 1 Samuel 9." *OTE* 6 (1992): 7-18.

Dell, Katharine J. "Incongruity in the Story of Samuel in 1 Samuel 9–15: A Methodological Survey." Pp. 49-64 in *Studies on the Text and Versions of the Hebrew Bible in Honour of Robert Gordon.* Edited by Geoffrey Khan and Diana Lipton. VTSup 149. Leiden: Brill, 2012.

Bibliography

Desrousseaux, Louis, and Jacques Vermeylen, eds. *Figures de David à travers la Bible: XVIIe congrès de l'ACFEB, Lille, 1er–5 septembre 1997.* Paris: Cerf, 1999.

DeVries, Simon. "David's Victory over the Philistines as Saga and as Legend." *JBL* 92 (1973): 23-36.

Diamond, James A. "King David of the Sages: Rabbinic Rehabilitation or Ironic Parody?" *Prooftexts* 27 (2007): 373-426.

Dietrich, Jan. "Der Tod von eigener Hand im Alten Testament und Alten Orient: eskapistische Selbsttötungen in militärisch aussichtsloser Lage." Pp. 63-83 in *Mensch und König: Studien zur Anthropologie des Alten Testaments; Rüdiger Lux zum 60. Geburtstag.* Edited by Angelika Berlejung and Raik Heckl. Herders Biblische Studien 53. New York: Herder, 2008.

Dietrich, Walter. *1 Samuel 1–12.* BKAT 8.1. Neukirchener: Neukirchen-Vluyn, 2011.

———. *David, der Herrscher mit der Harfe.* BG 14. Leipzig: Evangelische Verlagsanstalt, 2006.

———. *David, Saul und die Propheten: das Verhältnis von Religion und Politik nach den prophetischen Überlieferung vom frühesten Königtum in Israel.* BWANT 122. Stuttgart: Kohlhammer, 1987.

———. *David und Saul im Widerstreit — Diachronie und Synchronie im Wettstreit: Beiträge zur Auslegung des ersten Samuelbuches.* OBO 206. Göttingen: Vandenhoeck & Ruprecht, 2004.

———. *The Early Monarchy in Israel: The Tenth Century B.C.E.* Biblical Encyclopedia 3. Translated by Joachim Vette. Atlanta: Society of Biblical Literature, 2007.

———. "Die Erzählung von David und Goliath in 1 Sam 17." Pp. 58-73 in idem, *Von David zu den Deuteronomisten: Studien zu den Geschichtsüberlieferungen des Alten Testaments.* BWANT 16. Stuttgart: Kohlhammer, 2002.

———. "Essen und Trinken: ein zentrales Nebenthema in den Samuelbüchern." Pp. 269-85 in *Essen und Trinken in der Bibel: ein literarisches Festmahl für Rainer Kessler zum 65. Geburtstag.* Edited by Michaela Geiger. Gütersloh: Gütersloher Verlagshaus, 2009.

———. "König David — biblisches Bild eines Herrschers im altorientalischen Kontext." Pp. 3-31 in *König David: biblische Schlüsselfigur und europäische Leitgestalt. 19. Kolloquium (2000) der Schweizerischen Akademie der Geistes- und Sozialwissenschaften.* Edited by Walter Dietrich and Hubert Herkommer. Freiburg: Universitätsverlag; Stuttgart: Kohlhammer, 2003.

———. "Martin Noth und die Zukunft des deuteronomistischen Geschichtswerkes." Pp. 181-98 in *Von David zu den Deuteronomisten: Studien zu den Geschichtsüberlieferungen des Alten Testaments.* BWANT 156. Stuttgart: Kohlhammer, 2002.

———. *Prophetie und Geschichte: eine redaktionsgeschichtliche Untersuchung zum deuteronomistischen Geschichtswerk.* FRLANT 108. Göttingen: Vandenhoeck & Ruprecht, 1972.

———. "Tendenzen neuester Forschung an den Samuelbüchern." Pp. 9-17 in *Die Samuelbücher und die Deuteronomisten.* Edited by Christa Schäfer-Lichtenberger. BWANT 188. Stuttgart: Kohlhammer, 2010.

———. *Von David zu den Deuteronomisten: Studien zu der Geschichtsüberlieferungen des Alten Testaments.* BWANT 156. Stuttgart: Kohlhammer, 2002.

———. "Von den ersten Königen Israels: Forschung an den Samuelbüchern im neuen Jahrtausend." *TRund* 77 (2012): 135-70, 263-316, 401-25 [three parts].

———. "Die zweifache Verschonung Sauls durch David (I Sam 24 und I Sam 26): zur 'diachronen Synchronisierung' zweier Erzählungen." Pp. 232-53 in *David und Saul in Widerstreit — Diachronie und Synchronie im Wettstreit: Beiträge zur Auslegung des ersten*

Samuelbuchs. Edited by Walter Dietrich. OBO 206. Göttingen: Vandenhoeck & Ruprecht, 2004.

Dietrich, Walter, and Hubert Herkommer, eds. *König David: biblische Schlüsselfigur und europäische Leitgestalt. 19. Kolloquium (2000) der Schweizerischen Akademie der Geistes- und Sozialwissenschaften.* Freiburg: Universitätsverlag; Stuttgart: Kohlhammer, 2003.

Dietrich, Walter, and Thomas Naumann. "The David-Saul Narrative." Translated by Peter T. Daniels. Pp. 276-318 in *Reconsidering Israel and Judah: Recent Studies on the Deuteronomistic History.* SBTS 8. Edited by Gary N. Knoppers and J. Gordon McConville. Winona Lake: Eisenbrauns, 2000 = Pp. 47-86 in *Die Samuelbücher.* Edited by Walter Dietrich and Thomas Naumann. EdF 287. Darmstadt: Wissenschaftliche Buchgesellschaft, 1995.

Dietrich, Walter, and Thomas Naumann, eds. *Die Samuelbücher.* EdF 287. Darmstadt: Wissenschaftliche Buchgesellschaft, 1995.

Ditchfield, Grayson. "Divine Right Theory and Its Critics in Eighteenth-Century England." Pp. 156-67 in *Biblical Interpretation: The Meanings of Scripture — Past and Present.* Edited by John M. Court. London: T & T Clark, 2003.

Dodd, C. H. *The Authority of the Bible.* Rev. ed. New York: Harper, 1958.

———. *The Bible Today.* Cambridge: Cambridge University Press, 1956.

Dohmen, Christoph, and Franz Mussner. *Nur die halbe Wahrheit? Für die Einheit der ganzen Bibel.* Freiburg: Herder, 1993.

Dohmen, Christoph, and Gunther Stemberger. *Hermeneutik der jüdischen Bibel und des Alten Testament.* Kohlhammer Studienbücher Theologie 1.2. Stuttgart: Kohlhammer, 1996.

Donne, John. *The Sermons of John Donne.* Edited by Evelyn M. Simpson and George R. Potter. 10 vols. Berkeley: University of California Press, 1953.

Donner, Herbert. *Die Verwerfung des Königs Saul.* Wiesbaden: F. Steiner, 1983.

Doody, Margaret Anne. "Infant Piety and the Infant Samuel." Pp. 103-22 in *Out of the Garden: Women Writers on the Bible.* Edited by Christina Büchmann and Celina Spiegel. New York: Fawcett Columbine, 1994.

Downey, Katherine Brown. *Perverse Midrash: Oscar Wilde, André Gide and Censorship of Biblical Drama.* New York: Continuum, 2004.

Dragga, Sam. "In the Shadow of the Judges: The Failure of Saul." *JSOT* 38 (1987): 39-46.

Driver, S. R. *Notes on the Hebrew Text and the Topography of the Books of Samuel.* 2nd ed. Oxford: Clarendon, 1912. Repr. Eugene: Wipf & Stock, 2004.

Duling, Dennis C. "The Promises to David and Their Entry into Christianity." *NTS* 20 (1973-74): 55-77.

Dumbrell, W. J. "In Those Days There Was No King in Israel; Every Man Did What Was Right in His Own Eyes: The Purpose of the Book of Judges Reconsidered." *JSOT* 25 (1983): 23-33.

Dunn, James D. G., ed. *Jews and Christians: The Parting of the Ways A. D. 70 to 135; The Second Durham-Tübingen Symposium on Earliest Christianity and Judaism (Durham, September 1989).* 2nd ed. Grand Rapids: Eerdmans, 1999.

Earl, Douglas S. "'Minimalism' and Old Testament Theological Hermeneutics: The 'David Saga' as a Test Case." *JTI* 4 (2010): 207-28.

Edelman, Diana Vikander. *King Saul in the Historiography of Judah.* JSOTSup 121. Sheffield: Sheffield Academic, 1991.

———. "Saul ben Kish in History and Tradition." Pp 142-59 in *The Origins of the Ancient Israelite States.* Edited by Volkmar Fritz and Philip R. Davies. JSOTSup 228. Sheffield: Sheffield Academic, 1996.

Bibliography

Edenburg, Cynthia. "How (Not) to Murder a King: Variations on a Theme in 1 Sam 24, 26." *SJOT* 12 (1998): 64-85.

———. "Notes on the Origin of the Biblical Tradition Regarding Achish King of Gath." *VT* 61 (2011): 34-38.

Edenburg, Cynthia, and Juha Pakkala, eds. *Is Samuel among the Deuteronomists? Current Views on the Place of Samuel in a Deuteronomistic History.* AIL 16. Atlanta: SBL, 2013.

Ehrlich, Carl S., with Marsha C. White, eds. *Saul in Story and Tradition.* FAT 47. Tübingen: Mohr Siebeck, 2006.

Ehrmann, Bart. *Lost Christianities: The Battles for Scripture and the Faiths We Never Knew.* Oxford: Oxford University Press, 2003.

Eichrodt, Walther. *Theology of the Old Testament.* OTL. 2 vols. Philadelphia: Westminster, 1961-67.

Eldredge, John. *Wild at Heart: Discovering the Secret of a Man's Soul.* Nashville: Thomas Nelson, 2001.

Eliot, T. S. "Religion and Literature." Pp. 97-106 in idem, *Selected Prose of T. S. Eliot.* Edited by Frank Kermode. London: Faber, 1975.

Elitzur, Yehudah. "David Son of Jesse: A Model for Penitents." Pp. 144-49 in *Israel and the Bible: Studies in Geography, History and Biblical Thought.* Edited by Yehudah Elitzur and Amos Frisch. Ramat Gan: Bar Ilan University Press, 1999.

Ellard, Gerald. *Ordination Anointings in the Western Church before 1000 A. D.* Academy Publications 16. Cambridge, MA: The Medieval Academy of America, 1933.

Elliott, James Keith. "Manuscripts, the Codex and the Canon." *JSNT* 63 (1996): 105-23.

Ellis, Richard J. *To the Flag: The Unlikely History of the Pledge of Allegiance.* Lawrence: University Press of Kansas, 2005.

Ellul, Jacques. *False Presence of the Kingdom.* Translated by C. Edward Hopkin. New York: Seabury, 1972.

Elman, Yaakov. "Progressive *Derash* and Retrospective *Peshat*: Nonhalakhic Considerations in Talmud Torah." Pp. 227-87 in *Modern Scholarship in the Study of Torah: Contributions and Limitations.* Edited by Shalom Carmy. Northvale, NJ: Jason Aronson, 1996.

Emmerich, Karin. *Machtverhältnisse in einer Dreiecksbeziehung: die Erzählung von Abigajil, Nabal und David in 1 Sam 25.* ATSAT 84. St. Ottilien: EOS Verlag, 2007.

Eng, Milton. *The Days of Our Lives: A Lexical Semantic Study of the Life Cycle in Biblical Israel.* LHBOTS 464. New York: T & T Clark, 2011.

Engnell, Ivan. *Studies in Divine Kingship in the Ancient Near East.* Uppsala: Almqvist & Wiksell, 1943.

Enright, Michael J. *Iona, Tara and Soissons: The Origin of the Royal Anointing Ritual.* Arbeiten zur Frühmittelalterforschung 17: Berlin: de Gruyter, 1985.

Eppstein, Victor. "Was Saul also among the Prophets?" *ZAW* 81 (1969): 287-304.

Esler, Philip F. "The Madness of Saul: A Cultural Reading of 1 Samuel 8–31." Pp. 220-62 in *Biblical Studies/Cultural Studies: The Third Sheffield Colloquium.* Edited by J. Cheryl Exum and Stephen D. Moore. JOTSup 266. Sheffield: Sheffield Academic, 1998.

———. *Sex, Wives, and Warriors: Reading Old Testament Narrative with Its Ancient Audience.* Eugene: Cascade, 2011.

Eslinger, Lyle M. *Into the Hands of the Living God.* BLS 24. Sheffield: Almond, 1989.

———. *Kingship of God in Crisis: A Close Reading of 1 Samuel 1–12.* BLS 10. Sheffield: Almond, 1985.

———. "Viewpoints and Points of View in 1 Samuel 8–12," *JSOT* 26 (1983): 61-76.

Eslinger, Lyle M., and Glen Taylor, eds. *Ascribe to the Lord: Biblical and Other Essays in Memory of Peter C. Craigie.* JSOTSup 67. Sheffield: JSOT, 1988.

Exum, J. Cheryl. "The Fate of the House of Saul." Pp. 70-95 in idem, *Tragedy and Biblical Narrative: Arrows of the Almighty.* Cambridge: Cambridge University Press, 1992.

————. *Plotted, Shot, and Painted: Cultural Representations of Biblical Women.* 2nd ed. Sheffield: Sheffield Academic, 2012.

————. "Rizpah." *Word & World* 17 (1997): 260-68.

————. *Tragedy and Biblical Narrative: Arrows of the Almighty.* Cambridge: Cambridge University Press, 1992.

Exum, J. Cheryl, and David J. A. Clines. *The New Literary Criticism and the Hebrew Bible.* Valley Forge: Trinity, 1993.

Exum, Cheryl, and J. William Whedbee. "Isaac, Samson and Saul: Reflections on the Comic and Tragic Visions." *Semeia* 32 (1984): 5-40.

Eynikel, Erik. "Das Lied der Hanna (1 Sam 2,1-11) und das Lied Davids (2 Sam 22)." Pp. 57-72 in *For and against David: Story and History in the Books of Samuel.* Edited by A. Graeme Auld and Erik Eynikel. BETL 232. Leuven: Peeters, 2010.

————. *The Reform of King Josiah and the Composition of the Deuteronomistic History.* OTS 33. Leiden: Brill, 1996.

————. "The Relation between the Eli Narratives (1 Sam. 1–4) and the Ark Narrative (1 Sam. 1–6; 2 Sam. 6:1-19)." Pp. 88-106 in *Past, Present, Future: The Deuteronomistic History and the Prophets.* Edited by Johannes C. de Moor and Harry F. Van Rooy. OTS 44. Leiden: Brill, 2000.

Fabry, Heinz-Josef. "*Lēb.*" *TDOT* 7:412-37. Edited by G. Johannes Botterweck and Helmer Ringgren. Translated by John T. Willis. Grand Rapids: Eerdmans, 1974–.

Falk, Marcia. "Reflections on Hannah's Prayer." Pp. 94-102 in *Out of the Garden: Women Writers on the Bible.* Edited by Christina Büchmann and Celina Spiegel. New York: Fawcett Columbine, 1994.

Farkasfalvy, Denis. "The Pontifical Biblical Commission's Document on Jews and Christians and their Scriptures: Attempt at an Evaluation." *Comm* 29 (2002): 715-37.

Farley, Wendy. *Tragic Vision and Divine Compassion: A Contemporary Theodicy.* Louisville: Westminster John Knox, 1990.

Feldman, Louis H. "Josephus' Portrait of Saul." Pp. 214-44 in *Saul in Story and Tradition.* Edited by Carl. S. Ehrlich with Marsha C. White. FAT 47. Tübingen: Mohr Siebeck, 2006.

Fenton, Terry L. "Deuteronomistic Advocacy of the *nabi*': 1 Samuel ix 9 and Questions of Israelite Prophecy." *VT* 47 (1997): 23-42.

Fentress-Williams, Judy. *"What Has Happened to the Son of Kish?" A Dialogic Reading of the Saul Narrative in 1 Samuel.* Ph.D. dissertation. Yale University, 1999.

Fewell, Danna Nolan, and David M. Gunn. *Gender, Power, and Promise: The Subject of the Bible's First Story.* Nashville: Abingdon, 1993.

Fiddes, Paul S. "Prophecy, Corporate Personality, and Suffering: Some Themes and Methods in Baptist Scholarship." Pp. 72-98 in *The "Plainly Revealed" Word of God? Baptist Hermeneutics in Theory and Practice.* Edited by Helen Dare and Simon Woodman. Macon: Mercer University Press, 2011.

Fields, Weston W. "The Motif of 'Night as Danger' Associated with Three Biblical Destruction Narratives." Pp. 17-32 in *"Sha'arei Talmon": Studies in the Bible, Qumran, and the Ancient Near East Presented to Shemaryahu Talmon.* Edited by Michael A. Fishbane, Emanuel Tov, and Weston W. Fields. Winona Lake: Eisenbrauns, 1992.

Bibliography

Figgis, John Neville. *The Divine Right of Kings*. New York: Harper, 1965.

Fincke, Andrew. *The Samuel Scroll from Qumran: 4QSam^a Restored and Compared to the Septuagint and 4QSam^c*. STDJ 43. Leiden: Brill, 2001.

Finkelstein, Israel, and Neil Asher Silberman. *David and Solomon: In Search of the Bible's Sacred Kings and the Roots of the Western Tradition*. New York: Free Press, 2006.

Finsterbusch, Karin, and Armin Lange, eds. *What Is Bible?* CBET 67. Leuven: Peeters, 2012.

Firth, David G. *1 & 2 Samuel*. AOTC 8. Nottingham: Apollos, 2009.

————. *1 and 2 Samuel: A Kingdom Comes*. Phoenix Guides to the Old Testament 9. Sheffield: Sheffield Phoenix, 2013.

————. "The Accession Narrative (1 Samuel 27–2 Samuel 1)." *TynBul* 58 (2007): 61-81.

————. "'Is Saul Also among the Prophets?' Saul's Prophecy in 1 Samuel 19:23." Pp. 294-305 in *Presence, Power, and Promise: The Role of the Spirit of God in the Old Testament*. Edited by David G. Firth and Paul D. Wegner. Downers Grove: IVP Academic 2011.

————. "Parallelismus Membrorum in Prose Narrative: The Function of Repetition in 1 Samuel 5–6." *OTE* 15 (2002): 647-56.

————. "'Play it again, Sam': The Poetics of Narrative Repetition in 1 Samuel 1–7." *TynBul* 56 (2005): 1-17.

————. "Shining the Lamp: The Rhetoric of 2 Samuel 5–24." *TynBul* 52 (2001): 203-24.

————. "'That the World Might Know': Narrative Poetics in 1 Samuel 16–17." Pp. 20-32 in *Text and Task: Scripture and Mission*. Edited by Michael Parsons. Milton Keynes: Paternoster, 2005.

Fischer, Alexander A. "Die Saul-Überlieferung im deuteronomistischen Samuelbuch (am Beispiel von I Samuel 9–10)." Pp. 163-81 in *Die deuteronomistischen Geschichtswerke: redaktions- und religionsgeschichtliche Perspektiven zur "Deuteronomismus"-Diskussion in Tora und Vorderen Propheten*. Edited by Markus Witte et al. BZAW 365. Berlin: de Gruyter, 2006.

————. *Von Hebron nach Jerusalem: eine redaktionsgeschichtliche Studie zur Erzählung von König David in II Sam 1–5*. BZAW 335. Berlin: de Gruyter, 2004.

Fischer, Irmtraud. "Abigajil: Weisheit und Prophetie in einer Person vereint." Pp. 45-61 in *Auf den Spuren der schriftgelehrten Weisen: Festschrift für Johannes Marböck anlässlich seiner Emeritierung*. Edited by Irmtraud Fischer, Ursula Rapp, and Johannes Schiller. BZAW 331. Berlin: de Gruyter, 2003.

Fishbane, Michael. "1 Samuel 3: Historical Narrative and Narrative Poetics." Pp. 191-203 in *Literary Interpretations of Biblical Narratives, Volume 2*. Edited by Kenneth R. R. Gros Louis, James S. Ackerman, and Thayer S. Warshaw. Nashville: Abingdon, 1982.

————. *Haftarot: The Traditional Hebrew Text with the New JPS Translation*. Philadelphia: JPS, 2002.

Flanagan, James W. "Court History or Succession Document? A Study of 2 Samuel 9–20 and 1 Kings 1–2." *JBL* 9 (1972): 172-81.

Fleming, Daniel E. "The Biblical Tradition of Anointing Priests." *JBL* 117 (1998): 401-14.

Flint, Peter W. "Noncanonical Writings in the Dead Sea Scrolls: Apocrypha, Other Previously Known Writings, Pseudepigrapha." Pp. 80-126 in *The Bible at Qumran: Text, Shape, and Interpretation*. SDSSRL. Edited by Peter W. Flint with Tae Hun Kim. Grand Rapids: Eerdmans, 2001.

Flynn, Shawn W. "The *teraphim* in Light of Mesopotamian and Egyptian Evidence." *CBQ* 74 (2012): 694-711.

Fohrer, Georg. *History of Israelite Religion*. Translated by David E. Green. Nashville: Abingdon, 1973.

Fokkelman, Jan P. *Narrative Art and Poetry in the Books of Samuel, Vol. II: The Crossing Fates (I Sam. 13–31 and II Sam. 1)*. SSN 23. Assen: Van Gorcum, 1986.

———. *Narrative Art and Poetry in the Books of Samuel, Vol. III: Throne and City (II Sam. 2–8 and 21–24)*. SSN 27. Assen: Van Gorcum, 1990.

———. *Narrative Art and Poetry in the Books of Samuel, Vol. IV: Vow and Desire (I Sam. 1–12)*. SSN 31. Assen: Van Gorcum, 1993.

———. *Reading Biblical Narrative: An Introductory Guide*. Translated by Ineke Smit. Louisville: Westminster John Knox, 1999.

———. "Structural Reading on the Fracture between Synchrony and Diachrony." *JEOL* 30 (1987–88): 123-36.

Ford, David F., and Graham Stanton, eds. *Reading Texts, Seeking Wisdom: Scripture and Theology*. Grand Rapids: Eerdmans, 2003.

Foresti, Fabrizio. *The Rejection of Saul in the Perspective of the Deuteronomistic School: A Study of 1 Sm 15 and Related Texts*. Studia theologica-Teresianum 5. Rome: Edizioni del Teresianum, 1984.

Forster, E. M. *Aspects of the Novel and Related Writings*. London: Edward Arnold, 1974.

———. *A Passage to India*. London: Arnold, 1978.

Fosdick, Harry Emerson. *A Guide to Understanding the Bible: The Development of Ideas within the Old and New Testaments*. New York: Harper & Brothers, 1938.

Fowl, Stephen E. *Engaging Scripture: A Model for Theological Education*. Challenges in Contemporary Theology. Oxford: Blackwell, 1998.

Fowler, Mervyn D. "The Meaning of *lipnê* YHWH in the Old Testament." *ZAW* 99 (1987): 384-90.

Franke, John R. *Joshua, Judges, Ruth, 1–2 Samuel*. ACCS. Downers Grove: InterVarsity, 2005.

Frankfort, Henri. *Kingship and the Gods: A Study of Ancient Near Eastern Religion as the Integration of Society and Nature*. Chicago: University of Chicago Press, 1978.

Franklin, John Curtis. "Lyre Gods of the Bronze Age: Musical Koine." *JANER* 6 (2006): 39-70.

Frei, Hans W. *The Eclipse of Biblical Narrative*. New Haven: Yale University Press, 1974.

Fretheim, Terence E. "Divine Foreknowledge, Divine Constancy, and the Rejection of Saul's Kingship." *CBQ* 47 (1985): 595-602.

Fried, Lisbeth S. "The High Places (*Bāmôt*) and the Reforms of Hezekiah and Josiah: An Archaeological Investigation." *JAOS* 122 (2002): 437-65.

Frisch, Amos. "'For I Feared the People, and I Yielded to Them' (1 Sam 15,24) — Is Saul's Guilt Attenuated or Intensified?" *ZAW* 108 (1996): 98-104.

Froehlich, Karlfried. "Bibelkommentar — zur Krise einer Gattung." *ZTK* 84 (1987): 465-92.

Frohlich, Mary, ed. *St. Thérèse of Lisieux: Essential Writings*. Maryknoll, NY: Orbis, 2003.

Frolov, Serge. "'Certain Men' in Judges and Samuel: A Rejoinder to Mark Leuchter." *CBQ* 73 (2011): 251-64.

———. "The Semiotics of Covert Action in 1 Samuel 9–10." *JSOT* 31 (2007): 429-50.

———. *The Turn of the Cycle: 1 Samuel 1–8 in Synchronic and Diachronic Perspectives*. BZAW 342. Berlin: de Gruyter, 2004.

Frontain, Raymond-Jean, and Jan Wojcik, eds. *The David Myth in Western Literature*. West Lafayette: Purdue University Press, 1980.

Frye, Northrop. *The Anatomy of Criticism: Four Essays*. Toronto: University of Toronto Press, 2007.

Bibliography

————. *The Great Code: The Bible and Literature.* New York: Harcourt Brace Jovanovich, 1982.

Gadamer, Hans-Georg. "Aesthetics and Hermeneutics." Pp. 95-104 in idem, *Philosophical Hermeneutics.* Translated by David E. Linge. Berkeley: University of California Press, 1976.

Galling, Kurt. "Goliath und seine Rüstung." Pp. 150-69 in *Volume du Congrès: Genève 1965.* VTSup 15. Leiden: Brill, 1966.

Galpaz-Feller, Pnina. "David and the Messenger — Different Ends, Similar Means in 2 Samuel 1." *VT* 59 (2009): 199-210.

Gamble, Harry Y. *Books and Readers in the Early Church: A History of the Early Church: A History of Early Christian Texts.* New Haven: Yale University Press, 1995.

Garbini, Giovanni. *Myth and History in the Bible.* Translated by Chiara Peri. JSOTSup 362. London: Sheffield Academic, 2003.

García-Treto, Francisco O. "'A Mother's Paean, A Warrior's Dirge': Reflections on the Use of Poetic Inclusions in the Books of Samuel." *Shofar* 11 (1993): 51-64.

Garsiel, Moshe. "The Book of Samuel: Its Composition, Structure and Significance as a Historiographical Source." *JHS* 10 (2010) [electronic resource].

————. "David's Elite Warriors and Their Exploits in the Books of Samuel and Chronicles." *JHS* 11 (2011) [electronic resource].

————. *The First Book of Samuel: A Literary Study of Comparative Structures, Analogies and Parallels.* Ramat-Gan: Revivum, 1985.

————. "The Valley of Elah Battle and the Duel of David with Goliath: Between History and Artistic Theological Historiography." Pp. 391-426 in *Homeland and Exile: Biblical and Ancient Near Eastern Studies in Honour of Bustenay Oded.* Leiden: Brill, 2009.

————. "Wit, Words, and a Woman: 1 Samuel 25." Pp. 161-68 in *On Humour and the Comic in the Hebrew Bible.* Edited by Yehuda T. Radday and Athalya Brenner. BLS 23. JSOTSup 92. Sheffield: Almond, 1990. Pp. 161-68.

Gebrandt, Gerald Eddie. *Kingship According to the Deuteronomistic History.* SBLDS 87. Atlanta: Scholars, 1986.

Geertz, Clifford. *The Interpretation of Cultures.* New York: Basic Books, 1973.

Gehrig, Gail. *American Civil Religion: An Assessment.* Storrs, CT: Society for the Scientific Study of Religion, 1981.

Gelander, Shamai. *David and His God: Religious Ideas as Reflected in Biblical Historiography and Literature.* Translated by Ruth Debel. Jerusalem Biblical Studies 5. Jerusalem: Simor, 1991.

Gelston, Anthony. "The Repentance of God." Pp. 453-62 in *On Stone and Scrolls: Essays in Honour of Graham Ivor Davies.* Edited by James K. Aitken, Katharine J. Dell and Brian A. Mastin. BZAW 420. Berlin: de Gruyter, 2011.

Genette, Gérard. *The Work of Art: Immanence and Transcendence.* Translated by G. M. Goshgarian. Ithaca: Cornell University Press, 1997.

Gentile, Emilio. *Politics as Religion.* Translated by George Staunton. Princeton: Princeton University Press, 2006.

Geoffrey of Monmouth. *The History of the Kings of Britain.* Translated by Lewis Thorpe. London: Penguin, 1966.

George, Mark K. "Constructing Identity in 1 Samuel 17." *BibInt* 7 (1999): 389-412.

————. "Yhwh's Own Heart." *CBQ* 64 (2002): 442-59.

Gerdmar, Anders. *Roots of Theological Anti-Semitism: German Biblical Interpretation and the*

Jews, from Herder and Semler to Kittel and Bultmann. Studies in Jewish History and Culture 20. Leiden: Brill, 2009.

Giercke-Ungermann, Annett. *Die Niederlage im Sieg: eine synchrone und diachrone Untersuchung der Erzählung von 1 Samuel 15.* ETS 97. Wurzburg: Echter Verlag, 2010.

―――. "Vom Griff nach dem Obergewand zum Entzug der Königsherrschaft: Überlegungen zu 1 Sam 15,27-29." *BZ* 55 (2011): 75-86.

Gilmour, Rachelle. *Representing the Past: A Literary Analysis of Narrative Historiography in the Book of Samuel.* VTSup 143. Leiden: Brill, 2011.

―――. "Suspense and Anticipation in 1 Samuel 9:1-14," *JHS* (2009) [electronic resource].

Gitay, Yehoshua. "Reflections on the Poetics of the Samuel Narrative: The Question of the Ark Narrative." *CBQ* 54 (1992): 221-30.

Gladwell, Malcom. *David and Goliath: Underdogs, Misfits, and the Art of Battling Giants.* New York: Back Bay, 2013.

Gnuse, Robert K. *The Dream Theophany of Samuel: Its Structure in Relation to Ancient Near Eastern Dreams and Its Theological Significance.* Lanham, MD: University Press of America, 1984.

―――. "A Reconsideration of the Form-Critical Structure in I Samuel 3: An Ancient Near Eastern Dream Theophany." *ZAW* 94 (1982): 379-90.

―――. *No Tolerance for Tyrants: The Biblical Assault on Kings and Kingship.* Collegeville: Liturgical, 2011.

Godman, Peter. *Poetry of the Carolingian Renaissance.* Norman: University of Oklahoma Press, 1985.

Goldingay, John. *Old Testament Theology: Volume 3, Israel's Life.* Downers Grove: IVP Academic, 2009.

Good, Edwin M. "Saul: The Tragedy of Greatness." Pp. 56-80 in *Irony in the Old Testament.* BLS 3. Sheffield: Almond, 1981.

Gooding, David W. "An Approach to the Literary and Textual Problems in the David-Goliath Story: 1 Samuel 16-18." Pp. 55-86 in *The Story of David and Goliath: Textual and Literary Criticism, Papers of a Joint Research Venture.* Edited by Dominique Barthélemy et al. OBO 73. Göttingen: Vandenhoeck & Ruprecht, 1986.

Gordis, Robert. "Observations on Problems and Methods in Biblical Research: Writing a Commentary on Job." *PAAJR* 41 (1973): 105-35.

Gordon, Bruce. "God Killed Saul: Heinrich Bullinger and Jacob Ruef on the Power of the Devil." Pp. 155-79 in *Werewolves, Witches, and Wandering Spirits: Traditional Belief and Folklore in Early Modern Europe.* Edited by Kathryn A. Edwards. Kirksville, MO: Truman State University Press, 2002.

Gordon, Robert P. *I & II Samuel: A Commentary.* Library of Biblical Interpretation. Grand Rapids: Zondervan, 1986.

―――. *1 & 2 Samuel.* OTG. Sheffield: JSOT, 1984.

―――. "David's Rise and Saul's Demise: Narrative Analogy in 1 Samuel 24-26." *TynBul* 31 (1980): 37-64 = Pp. 319-39 in *Reconsidering Israel and Judah: Recent Studies on the Deuteronomistic History.* SBTS 8. Edited by Gary N. Knoppers and J. Gordon McConville. Winona Lake: Eisenbrauns, 2000.

―――. "Who Made the Kingmaker? Reflections on Samuel and the Institution of the Monarchy." Pp 255-69 in *Faith, Tradition, and History: Old Testament Historiography in Its Near Eastern Context.* Edited by Alan R. Millard, James K. Hoffmeier, and David W. Baker. Winona Lake: Eisenbrauns, 1994.

Bibliography

———. "In Search of David: The David Tradition in Recent Study." Pp. 285-98 in *Faith, Tradition and History: Old Testament Historiography in its Ancient Near Eastern Context*. Edited by Alan R. Millard, James K. Hoffmeier, and David W. Baker. Winona Lake: Eisenbrauns, 1994. Pp. 285-98.

Gorman, Michael. *Elements of Biblical Exegesis: A Basic Guide for Students and Ministers*. 2nd ed. Peabody, MA: Hendrickson, 2009.

Gosselin, Edward A. *The King's Progress to Jerusalem: Some Interpretations of David during the Reformation Period and their Patristic and Medieval Background*. Humanitas civilitas 2. Malibu: Undena Publications 1976.

Gottlieb, Isaac B. "*Sof Davar*: Biblical Endings." *Prooftexts* 11 (1991): 213-24.

Grabbe, Lester L. "'The Comfortable Theory,' 'Maximal Conservatism' and Neo-Fundamentalism Revisited." Pp. 17-93 in *Sense and Sensitivity: Essays on Reading the Bible in Memory of Robert Carroll*. Edited by Alastair G. Hunter and Philip R. Davies. JSOTSup 348. Sheffield: Sheffield Academic, 2002.

———. *Good Kings and Bad Kings*. LHBOTS 393. London: T & T Clark, 2005.

Grabher, Gudrun M., and Ulrike Jessner, eds. *Semantics of Silences in Linguistics and Literature*. Anglistische Forschungen 244. Heidelberg: C. Winter, 1996.

Green, Adam. *King Saul: The True History of the First Messiah*. Cambridge: Lutterworth, 2007.

Green, Barbara. "Enacting Imaginatively the Unthinkable: 1 Samuel 25 and the Story of Saul." *BibInt* 11 (2003): 1-23.

———. *How Are the Mighty Fallen? A Dialogical Study of King Saul in 1 Samuel*. JSOTSup 365. Sheffield: Sheffield Academic, 2003.

———. *King Saul's Asking*. Interfaces. Collegeville: Liturgical, 2003.

Green, Joel B. "Commentary." Pp. 123-27 in *DTIB*. Edited by Kevin J. Vanhoozer. Grand Rapids: Baker, 2005.

———. *Practicing Theological Interpretation: Engaging Biblical Texts for Faith and Formation*. Grand Rapids: Baker, 2011.

Greenberg, Moshe. *Biblical Prose Prayer*. Berkeley: University of California Press, 1983.

———. "To Whom and for What Should a Bible Commentator Be Responsible?" Pp. 235-43 in idem, *Studies in the Bible and Jewish Thought*. Philadelphia: Jewish Publication Society, 1995.

Greenspoon, Leonard J. "The Use and Abuse of the Term 'LXX' and Related Terminology in Recent Scholarship." *BIOSCS* 20 (1987): 21-29.

Greenwood, Kyle R. "Labor Pains: The Relationship between David's Census and *Corvée* Labor." *BBR* 20 (2010): 467-78.

Greer, Rowan A., and Margaret M. Mitchell, eds. *The "Belly-Myther" of Endor: Interpretations of 1 Kingdoms 28 in the Early Church*. SBLWGRW 16. Atlanta: Society of Biblical Literature, 2007.

Grønbaek, Jakob H. *Die Geschichte vom Aufstieg Davids (1. Sam. 15 – 2. Sam. 5): Tradition und Komposition*. ATD 10. Copenhagen: Prostant apud Munksgaard, 1971.

Gros Louis, Kenneth R. R. "The Difficulty of Ruling Well: King David of Israel." *Semeia* 8 (1977): 15-33.

Gros Louis, Kenneth R. R., ed. *Literary Interpretations of Biblical Narratives*. 2 vols. Nashville: Abingdon, 1974, 1982.

Gros Louis, Kenneth R. R., James S. Ackerman, and Thayer S. Warshaw, eds. *Literary Interpretations of Biblical Narratives*. Nashville: Abingdon, 1974.

Grottanelli, Cristiano. *Kings and Prophets: Monarchic Power, Inspired Leadership, and Sacred Text in Biblical Narrative*. Oxford: Oxford University Press, 1999.

Guinness, Os. *The Case for Civility and Why Our Future Depends on It*. New York: HarperOne, 2008.

Gunn, David M. *The Fate of King Saul: An Interpretation of a Biblical Story*. JSOTSup 14. Sheffield: JSOT, 1980.

———. "Hebrew Narrative." Pp. 223-52 in *Text in Context: Essays by Members of the Society for Old Testament Study*. Edited by A. D. H. Mayes. Oxford: Oxford University Press, 2000.

———. "In Security: The David of Biblical Narrative." Pp. 133-51 in *Signs and Wonders: Biblical Texts in Literary Focus*. Edited by J. Cheryl Exum. SBLSemS. Decatur: Scholars, 1989.

———. "A Man Given Over to Trouble: The Story of King Saul." Pp. 89-112 in *Images of Man and God: Old Testament Short Stories in Literary Focus*. BLS 1. Edited by Burke O. Long. Sheffield: Almond, 1981.

———. "New Directions in the Study of Biblical Hebrew Narrative." *JSOT* 39 (1987): 65-75.

———. "Reading Right: Reliable and Omniscient Narrator, Omniscient God, and Foolproof Composition in the Hebrew Bible." Pp. 53-64 in *The Bible in Three Dimensions*. Edited by David J. A. Clines, Stephen E. Fowl, and Stanley E. Porter. JSOTSup 87. Sheffield: JSOT, 1990.

———. *The Story of King David: Genre and Interpretation*. JSOTSup 6. Sheffield: JSOT, 1978. Repr. 1989.

Gunn, David M., ed. *Narrative and Novella in Samuel: Studies by Hugo Gressmann and Other Scholars 1906–1923*. JSOTSup 116. Sheffield: Almond, 1991.

Gutteridge, Richard. *Open Thy Mouth for the Dumb! The German Evangelical Church and the Jews 1879–1950*. Oxford: Blackwell, 1976.

Hagan, Kenneth. "What Did the Term *Commentarius* Mean to Sixteenth-century Theologians?" Pp. 13-38 in *Théorie et pratique de l'exégèse. Actes du troisième colloque international sur l'histoire de l'exégèse biblique au XVIᵉ siècle*. Etudes de philology et d'histoire 43. Edited by Irena Backus and Francis Higman. Geneva: Droz, 1990.

Hagan, Harry. "Deception as Motif and Theme in 2 Sm 9–20; 1 Kgs 1–2." *Bib* 60 (1979): 301-26.

Hahn, Scott W. *The Kingdom of God as Liturgical Empire: A Theological Commentary on 1–2 Chronicles*. Grand Rapids: Baker, 2012.

Hall, John A. *The Importance of Being Civil: The Struggle for Political Decency*. Princeton: Princeton University Press, 2013.

Hall, Joseph. *Contemplations on the Historical Passages of the Old and New Testaments*. London: T. Nelson and Sons, 1860.

Hall, Sarah Lebhard. *Conquering Character: The Characterization of Joshua in Joshua 1–11*. LHBOTS 512. New York: T & T Clark, 2010.

Hall, Stuart G. "In the Beginning was the Codex: The Early Church and Its Revolutionary Books." Pp. 1-10 in *The Church and the Book: Papers Read at the 2000 Summer Meeting and the 2001 Winter Meeting of the Ecclesiastical History Society*. Edited by R. N. Swanson. Studies in Church History 38. Rochester: Boydell and Brewer, 2004.

Halliburton, John. "Anointing in the Early Church." Pp. 77-91 in *The Oil of Gladness: Anointing in the Christian Tradition*. Edited by Martin Dudley and Geoffrey Rowell. Collegeville: Liturgical, 1993.

Hallie, Philip. *Lest Innocent Blood Be Shed: The Story of the Village of Le Chambon and How Goodness Happened There*. New York: HarperCollins, 1994.

Hallo, William W. "The First Purim." *BA* 46 (1983): 19-26.

Halpern, Baruch. *David's Secret Demons: Messiah, Murderer, Traitor, King.* Grand Rapids: Eerdmans, 2001.

Hamilton, James M. "The Typology of David's Rise to Power: Messianic Patterns in the Book of Samuel." *Southern Baptist Journal of Theology* 16 (2012): 4-25.

Hamilton, Mark W. *The Body Royal: The Social Poetics of Kingship in Ancient Israel.* BibInt 78. Leiden: Brill, 2005.

———. "The Creation of Saul's Royal Body: Reflections on 1 Samuel 8–10." Pp. 139-55 in *Saul in Story and Tradition.* Edited by Carl S. Ehrlich with Marsha C. White. FAT 47. Tübingen: Mohr Siebeck, 2006. Pp. 139-55.

Hamori, Esther. "The Prophet and the Necromancer: Women's Divination for Kings." *JBL* 132 (2013): 827-43.

Handy, Lowell K. "Historical Probability and the Narrative of Josiah's Reform in 2 Kings." Pp. 252-75 in *The Pitcher is Broken: Memorial Essays for Gösta W. Ahlström.* Edited by Steven W. Holloway and Lowell K. Handy. JSOTSup 190. Sheffield: Sheffield Academic, 1995.

Hardmeier, Christof. "König Joschija in der Klimax des DtrG (2 Reg 22f.) und das vordtr Dokument einer Kultreform am Residenzort (23,4-15*)." Pp. 81-145 in *Erzählte Geschichte: Beiträge zur narrativen Kultur im alten Israel.* Edited by Rüdiger Lux. BTS 40. Neukirchen–Vluyn: Neukirchener, 2000.

Hanson, Paul D. "The Song of Heshbon and David's *Nîr.*" *HTR* 61 (1968): 297-320.

Haran, Menahem. "Archives, Libraries, and the Order of the Biblical Books." *JANES* 22 (1993): 51-61.

———. "Book-Scrolls in Israel in Pre-Exilic Times." *JJS* 33 (1982): 161-73.

———. "Book-Scrolls at the Beginning of the Second Temple Period: The Transition from Papyrus to Skins." *HUCA* 54 (1983): 111-22.

———. "Book-Size and the Thematic Cycles in the Pentateuch." Pp. 165-76 in *Die hebräische Bibel und ihre zweifache Nachgeschichte: Festschrift für Rolf Rendtorff zum 65. Geburtstag.* Edited by Erhard Blum, Christian Macholz, and Ekkehard W. Stegemann. Neukirchen–Vluyn: Neukirchener, 1990.

———. "The Books of the Chronicles 'of the Kings of Judah' and 'of the Kings of Israel': What Sort of Books Were They?" *VT* 49 (1999): 156-64.

———. "Codex, *Pinax* and Writing Slat." *Scripta Classica Israelica* 15 (1996): 212-22.

———. *Temple and Temple Service in Ancient Israel.* Oxford: Clarendon, 1978.

Harden, Jamie M. *Professional Civility: Communicative Virtue at Work.* New York: Lang, 2013.

Harding, James E. *The Love of David and Jonathan: Ideology, Text, Reception.* Bible World. Sheffield: Equinox, 2013.

Harnack, Adolf von. "Appendix 2." Pp. 169-83 in idem, *The Origin of the New Testament and the Most Important Consequences of the New Creation.* Translated by J. R. Wilkinson. New Testament Studies 6. London: Williams & Norgate, 1925; repr. Eugene: Wipf & Stock, 2004.

———. *Bible Reading in the Early Church.* Translated by J. R. Wilkinson. London: Williams & Norgate, 1912. Repr. Eugene: Wipf & Stock, 2005.

———. *Marcion: The Gospel of the Alien God.* 2nd ed. Translated by J. E. Steely and L. D. Bierma. Durham, NC: Labyrinth, 1990.

Harrelson, Walter. "Creative Spirit in the Old Testament: A Study of the Last Words of David (2 Sam. 23. 1-7)." Pp. 127-33 in *Sin, Salvation, and the Spirit.* Edited by D. Durkin. Collegeville: Liturgical, 1979.

Harrington, Daniel J. *How Do Catholics Read the Bible?* Come and See Series. Lanham, MD: Sheed & Ward, 2005.

Harrington, Daniel J., and Anthony J. Saldarini. *Targum Jonathan of the Former Prophets: Introduction, Translation and Notes.* The Aramaic Bible 10. Edinburgh: T & T Clark, 1987.

Harrison, Timothy P., and James F. Osborne. "Building XVI and the Neo-Assyrian Sacred Precinct at Tell Tayinat." *JCS* 64 (2012): 125-43.

Harvey, Graham. "The Suffering of Witches and Children: Uses of the Witchcraft Passages in the Bible." Pp. 113-34 in *Words Remembered, Texts Renewed: Essays in Honour of John F. A. Sawyer.* Edited by Jon Davies, Graham Harvey and Wilfred G. E. Watson. JSOTSup 195. Sheffield: Sheffield Academic, 1995.

Hauerwas, Stanley, and William H. Willimon. *Resident Aliens: Life in the Christian Colony.* Exp. 25th anniversary ed. Nashville: Abingdon, 2014.

Hawk, L. Daniel. "Saul's Altar." *CBQ* 72 (2010): 678-87.

Hawkins, Ralph K. "The First Glimpse of Saul and His Subsequent Transformation." *BBR* 22 (2012): 353-62.

Hays, Richard B. *The Moral Vision of the New Testament: Community, Cross, New Creation.* San Francisco: HarperCollins, 1996.

Heacock, Anthony. *Jonathan Loved David: Manly Love in the Bible and the Hermeneutics of Sex.* Bible in the Modern World 22. Sheffield: Sheffield Phoenix, 2011.

Heither, Theresia. *Biblische Gestalten bei den Kirchenvätern: David.* Munster: Aschendorff, 2012.

Helfgot, Nathaniel. "Amalek: Ethics, Values and Halakhic Development." Pp. 79-94 in *The Tanakh Companion to the Book of Samuel.* Edited by Nathaniel Helfgot. Yeshivat Chovevei Torah Rabbinical School. Teaneck, NJ: Ben Yehuda, 2006.

Helfgot, Nathaniel, ed. *The Tanakh Companion to the Book of Samuel.* Yeshivat Chovevei Torah Rabbinical School. Teaneck, NJ: Ben Yehuda, 2006.

Heller, Roy L. *Power, Politics, and Prophecy: The Character of Samuel and the Deuteronomistic Evaluation of Prophecy.* LHBOTS 440. New York: T & T Clark, 2006.

Hendel, Ronald. "Plural Texts and Literary Criticism: For Instance, 1 Samuel 17." *Textus* 23 (2007): 97-114.

Hentschel, Georg. "Die Hinrichtung der Nachkommen Sauls (2 Sam 21,1-14)." Pp. 93-116 in *Nachdenken über Israel, Bibel und Theologie: Festschrift Klaus-Dietrich Schunck.* Edited by Hermann Michael Niemann. BEATAJ 37. Frankfurt: Lang, 1994.

———. "Saul und das deuteronomistische Geschichswerk: die Kritik an Saul und die Abkehr von der Monarchie." Pp. 207-24 in *Das deuteronomistische Geschichtswerk.* Edited by Hermann-Josef Stipp. Österreichische biblische Studien 39. Frankfurt: Lang, 2011.

———. *Saul: Schuld, Reue und Tragik eines "Gesalbten."* BG 7. Leipzig: Evangelische Verlagsanstalt, 2003.

Herbst, Susan. *Rude Democracy: Civility and Uncivility in American Politics.* Philadelphia: Temple University Press, 2010.

Heringer, Seth. "The Practice of Theological Commentary," *JTI* 4 (2010): 127-37.

Herkommer, Hubert. "Typus Christi – Typus Regis: König David als politische Legitimationsfigur." Pp. 383-436 in *König David — biblische Schlüsselfigur und europäische Leitgestalt.* Edited by Walter Dietrich and Hubert Herkommer. Freiburg: Universitätsverlag, 2003.

Hertzberg, Hans Wilhelm. *I & II Samuel: A Commentary.* OTL. Translated by J. S. Bowden. Philadelphia: Westminster, 1969.

Herzfeld, Shmuel. "David and Batsheva: Echoes of Saul and the Gift of Forgiveness (II Samuel

11–12)." Pp. 227-52 in *Tanakh Companion to the Book of Samuel*. Edited by Nathaniel Helfgot. Teaneck, NJ: Ben Yehuda, 2006.

Heym, Stefan. *The King David Report*. New York: Putnam, 1973.

Hill, Robert C. "Chrysostom's Homilies on David and Saul." *SVTQ* 44 (2000): 123-41.

Hobbs, R. Gerald. "Bucer's Use of King David as Mirror of the Christian Prince." *Reformation and Renaissance Review* 5 (2003): 102-28.

Hobbs, T. Raymond. "Reflections on Honor, Shame, and Covenant Relations." *JBL* 116 (1997): 501-03.

Hoffmann, H.-D. *Reform und Reformen: Untersuchung zu einem Grundthema der deuteronomistischen Geschichtsschreibung*. ATANT 66. Zurich: Theologischer Verlag, 1980.

Holcomb, Justin S., ed. *Christian Theologies of Scripture*. New York: New York University Press, 2006.

Hollenstein, Helmut. "Literarkritische Erwägungen zum Bericht über die Reformmassnahmen Josias 2 Kön. 23,4ff." *VT* 27 (1977): 321-36.

Holzer, Vincent. "Karl Rahner, Hans Urs von Balthasar, and Twentieth-Century Catholic Currents on the Trinity." Pp. 314-27 in *The Oxford Handbook of the Trinity*. Edited by Gilles Emery and Matthew Levering. Oxford: Oxford University Press, 2011.

Hooke, S. H., ed. *Myth, Ritual and Kingship: Essays on the Theory and Practice of Kingship in the Ancient Near East and in Israel*. Oxford: Clarendon, 1958.

Horner, Tom. *Jonathan Loved David: Homosexuality in Biblical Times*. Philadelphia: Westminster, 1978.

Horowitz, Wayne, and Victor A. Hurowitz. "Urim and Thummim in Light of a Psephomancy Ritual from Assur (LKA 137)." *JANES* 21 (1992): 95-115.

Hossfeld, Frank-Lothar. "Die Aufwertung Hannas durch ihren Lobgesang: 1 Sam 2,1-10." Pp. 246-58 in *"Gott bin ich, kein Mann": Beiträge zur Hermeneutik der biblischen Gottesrede; Festschrift für Helen Schüngel-Straumann zum 65. Geburtstag*. Edited by Ilona Riedel-Spangenberger and Erich Zenger. Paderborn: Schöningh, 2005.

————. "David als exemplarischer Mensch: literarische Biographie und Anthropologie am Beispiel Davids." Pp. 243-55 in *Biblische Anthropologie: neue Einsichten aus dem Alten Testament*. Edited by Christian Frevel. QD 237. Freiburg: Herder, 2010.

Hourihane, Colum, ed. *King David in the Index of Christian Art*. Index of Art Resources 2. Princeton: Princeton University Press, 2002.

Houtman, Cornelis. "The Urim and Thummim: A New Suggestion." *VT* 40 (1990): 229-32.

Hoyle, James. "The Weapons of God in Samuel." *This World* 7 (1984): 118-34.

Huber, Konrad. "Die Könige Israels: Saul, David und Salomo." Pp. 161-83 in *Alttestamentliche Gestalten im Neuen Testament: Beiträge zur Biblischen Theologie*. Edited by Markus Öhler. Darmstadt: Wissenschaftliche Buchgesellschaft, 1999.

Hubmaier, Balthasar. "On the Sword." Pp. 181-209 in *The Radical Reformation*. Edited by Michael G. Taylor. Cambridge Texts in the History of Political Thought. Cambridge: Cambridge University Press, 1991.

Huffmon, Herbert G. "Priestly Divination in Israel." Pp. 355-58 in *The Word of the Lord Shall Go Forth: Essays in Honor of David Noel Freedman in Celebration of His Sixtieth Birthday*. Edited by Carol L. Meyers and Michael O'Connor. ASOR Special Volumes Series 1. Winona Lake: Eisenbrauns, 1983.

Hugo, Philippe. "Text History of the Books of Samuel: An Assessment of Recent Rearch." Pp. 1-19 in *Archaeology of the Books of Samuel: The Entangling of the Textual and Literary History*. Edited by Philippe Hugo and Adrian Schenker. VTSup 132. Leiden: Brill, 2010.

Hugo, Philippe, and Adrian Schenker, eds. *Archaeology of the Books of Samuel: The Entangling of the Textual and Literary History.* VTSup 132. Leiden: Brill, 2010.

Humphreys, W. Lee. "From Tragic Hero to Villain: A Study of the Figure of Saul and the Development of 1 Samuel," *JSOT* 22 (1982): 95-117.

―――. "The Rise and Fall of King Saul: A Study of an Ancient Narrative Stratum in 1 Samuel," *JSOT* 18 (1980): 74-90.

―――. "The Tragedy of King Saul: A Study in the Structure of 1 Samuel 9–31." *JSOT* 6 (1978): 18-27.

―――. *The Tragic Vision and the Hebrew Tradition.* OBT 18. Philadelphia: Fortress, 1985.

Hurowitz, Victor. "True Light on the Urim and Thummim," *JQR* 88 (1998): 263-74.

Hurvitz, Avi. "The Origins and Development of the Expression *megillat sefer*: A Study in the History of Writing-Related Terminology in Biblical Times." Pp. *37-46* (Hebrew) in *Texts, Temples, and Traditions: A Tribute to Menahem Haran.* Edited by Michael V. Fox et al. Winona Lake: Eisenbrauns, 1996.

Hütter, Reinhard. "'In': Some Incipient Reflections on *The Jewish People and Their Sacred Scriptures in the Christian Bible*." *ProEccl* 13 (2004): 13-24.

Hutzli, Jürg. *Die Erzählung von Hanna und Samuel: textkritische und literarische Analyse von 1. Samuel 1–2 unter Berücksichtigung des Kontexts.* ATANT 89. Zurich: Theologischer Verlag, 2007.

Iser, Wolfgang. *The Act of Reading: A Theory of Aesthetic Response.* Baltimore: Johns Hopkins University Press, 1978.

Ishida, Tomoo. *History and Historical Writing in Ancient Israel: Studies in Biblical Historiography.* SHANE 16. Leiden: Brill, 1999.

―――. *The Royal Dynasties in Ancient Israel: A Study on the Formation and Development of Royal-Dynastic Ideology.* BZAW 142. Berlin: de Gruyter, 1977.

Isser, Stanley. *The Sword of Goliath: David in Heroic Literature.* Studies in Biblical Literature 6. Atlanta: Society of Biblical Literature, 2003.

Iwry, Samuel. "New Evidence for Belomancy in Ancient Palestine and Phoenicia." *JAOS* 81 (1961): 27-32.

Jacob, Edmund. *Theology of the Old Testament.* London: Hodder and Stoughton, 1958.

Jacobs, Jonathan. "The Role of the Secondary Characters in the Story of the Anointing of Saul (I Samuel ix–x)." *VT* 58 (2008): 495-509.

Jacobsen, Thorkild. *The Treasures of Darkness: A History of Mesopotamian Religion.* New Haven: Yale University Press, 1976.

Jankulak, Karen. *Geoffrey of Monmouth.* Cardiff: University of Wales Press, 2010.

Janowski, Bernd. "The One God of the Two Testaments: Basic Questions of a Biblical Theology." *ThTo* 7 (2000): 297-324.

Janzen, David. "The Sacrifices of Saul Thoroughly Examined: An Essay in Honor of James Franklin Armstrong." *PSB* 26 (2005): 136-43.

Japhet, Sara. *I & II Chronicles: A Commentary.* OTL. Louisville: Westminster John Knox, 1993.

Jeffers, Ann. *Magic and Divination in Ancient Palestine and Syria.* SHANE 8. Leiden: Brill, 1996.

Jenkins, Philip. *The New Faces of Christianity: Believing the Bible in the Global South.* Oxford: Oxford University Press, 2006.

Jenni, Ernst. *Die hebräischen Präpositionen.* 2 Vols. Stuttgart: Kohlhammer, 1992.

Jenni, Ernst, and Claus Westermann. *Theological Lexicon of the Old Testament.* Translated by Mark E. Biddle. 2 Vols. Peabody, MA: Hendrickson, 1997.

Jensen, David H. *1 & 2 Samuel.* Belief. Louisville: Westminster John Knox, 2015.

Bibliography

Jensen, Hans Jørgen Lundager. "The Fall of the King." *SJOT* 1 (1991): 121-47.

Jenson, Robert W. "Scripture's Authority in the Church." Pp. 27-37 in *The Art of Reading Scripture*. Edited by Ellen F. Davis and Richard B. Hays. Grand Rapids: Eerdmans, 2003.

Jipp, Joshua W. "Luke's Scriptural Suffering Messiah: A Search for Precedent, a Search for Identity." *CBQ* 72 (2010): 255-74.

Jobling, David. *1 Samuel*. Berit Olam. Collegeville: Liturgical, 1998.

———. "Saul's Fall and Jonathan's Rise: Tradition and Redaction in 1 Sam 14:1-46." *JBL* 95 (1976): 367-76.

———. "What, If Anything, Is 1 Samuel?" *SJOT* 7 (1993): 17-31.

Johnson, Aubrey R. *Sacral Kingship in Ancient Israel.* 2nd ed. Cardiff: University of Wales Press, 1967.

Johnson, Benjamin M. "David Then and Now: Double-Voiced Discourse in 1 Samuel 16:14-23." *JSOT* 38 (2013): 201-15.

———. "The Heart of YHWH's Chosen One in 1 Samuel." *JBL* 131 (2012): 455-66.

———. "Reconsidering 4QSam^a and the Textual Support for the Long and Short Versions of the David and Goliath Story." *VT* 62 (2012): 534-49.

Johnson, Luke Timothy. "Imagining the World Scripture Imagines." Pp. 3-18 in *Theology and Scriptural Imagination*. Edited by L. Gregory Jones and James J. Buckley. Directions in Modern Theology. Oxford: Blackwell, 1998.

Johnson, Sarah Iles, ed. *Religions of the Ancient World: A Guide.* Harvard University Press Reference Library. Cambridge, MA: Harvard University Press, 2004.

Johnson, Vernon, ed. *Spiritual Childhood: The Spirituality of St. Thérèse of Lisieux.* 3rd ed. San Francisco: Ignatius, 2001.

Johnson, Vivian L. *David in Distress: His Portrait Through the Historical Psalms.* LHBOTS 505. New York: T & T Clark, 2009.

Jones, D. Martyn Lloyd. "When the Gods Fall." Pp. 58-71 in *Old Testament Evangelistic Sermons.* Edinburgh: Banner of Truth, 1995.

Jonge, Marinus de. "Jesus, Son of David and Son of God." Pp. 95-104 in *Intertextuality in Biblical Writings: Essays in Honour of Bas van Iersel.* Edited by Sipke Draisma. Kampen: Kok, 1989.

Joosten, Jan. "Workshop: Meaning and Use of the Tenses in 1 Samuel 1." Pp. 72-83 in *Narrative Syntax and the Hebrew Bible: Papers of the Tilburg Conference 1996.* Edited by Ellen van Wolde. BibInt 29. Leiden: Brill, 1997.

Josipovici, Gabriel. "David and Tears." Pp. 191-209 in *The Book of God: A Response to the Bible.* New Haven: Yale University Press, 1988.

Jüngel, Eberhard. *God's Being Is in Becoming: The Trinitarian Being of God in the Theology of Karl Barth.* Grand Rapids: Eerdmans, 2001.

———. "Das Verhältnis von 'ökonomischer' und 'immanenter' Theologie." *ZTK* 72 (1975): 353-64.

Kaiser, Otto. "David und Jonathan: Tradition, Redaktion und Geschichte in 1 Sam 16-20: ein Versuch." *ETL* 66 (1990): 281-96.

———. "Der historische und der biblische König Saul (Teil I)." *ZAW* 122 (2010): 520-45.

———. "Der historische und der biblische König Saul (Teil II)." *ZAW* 123 (2011): 1-14.

Kallai, Zecharia. "Samuel in Qumran: Expansion of a Historiographical Pattern (4QSam^a)." *RB* 103 (1996): 581-91.

Kammerer, Stefan. "Die mißratenen Söhne Samuels." *BN* 88 (1997): 75-88.

Kang, Sa-Moon. *Divine War in the Old Testament and in the Ancient Near East.* BZAW 177. Berlin: de Gruyter, 1989.

Kantorowicz, Ernst. *The King's Two Bodies: A Study in Medieval Political Theology.* Princeton: Princeton University Press, 1957.

————. *Laudes regiae: A Study in Liturgical Acclamations and Medieval Ruler Worship.* Berkeley: University of California Press, 1958.

Kaplan, Jonathan. "1 Samuel 8:11-18 as 'A Mirror for Princes.'" *JBL* 131 (2012): 625-42.

Karrer, Martin. "Von David zu Christus." Pp. 327-65 in *König David — biblische Schlüsselfigur und europäische Leitgestalt.* Edited by Walter Dietrich and Hubert Herkommer. Freiburg: Universitätsverlag, 2003.

Kaufmann, Walter. *Tragedy and Philosophy.* Princeton: Princeton University Press, 1968.

Kaufmann, Yehezkel. *The Religion of Israel, from Its Beginnings to the Babylonian Exile.* Translated and abridged by Moshe Greenberg. Chicago: University of Chicago Press, 1960.

Kauhanen, Tuukka. *The Proto-Lucianic Problem in 1 Samuel.* De Septuaginta investigationes 3. Göttingen: Vandenhoeck & Ruprecht, 2012.

Keble, John. "The Man after God's Own Heart." Pp. 150-65 in *Sermons for the Sundays after Trinity, Part 1: Sunday I-XII.* London: Walter Smith, 1885.

Keel, Othmar, and Christoph Uehlinger. *Gods, Goddesses, and Images of God in Ancient Israel.* Minneapolis: Fortress, 1998.

Keizer, Garret. *The Enigma of Anger: Essays on a Sometimes Deadly Sin.* San Francisco: Jossey-Bass, 2002.

Kellenberger, Edgar. "David als Lehrer der nachexilischen Gemeinde: Überlegungen zu 1 Sam 17,46f." Pp. 175-83 in *"Sieben Augen auf einem Stein" (Sach 3,9): Studien zur Literatur des Zweiten Tempels: Festschrift für Ina Willi-Plein zum 65. Geburtstag.* Edited by Friedhelm Hartenstein and Michael Pietsch. Neukirchen-Vluyn: Neukirchener, 2007.

Kelly, Brian E. "David's Disqualification in 1 Chronicles 22:8: A Response to Piet B. Dirksen." *JSOT* 80 (1998): 53-61.

Kelley, George Armstrong. *Politics and Religious Consciousness in America.* New Brunswick: Transaction, 2005.

Kent, Grenville J. R. *Say It Again Sam: A Literary and Filmic Study of Narrative Repetitions in 1 Samuel 28.* Cambridge: Lutterworth, 2011.

Kenyon, Frederic George. *Books and Readers in Ancient Greece and Rome.* Oxford: Clarendon, 1951.

Keren, Orly. "David and Jonathan: A Case of Unconditional Love?" *JSOT* 37 (2012): 3-23.

Kereszty, Roch. "The Jewish–Christian Dialogue and the Pontifical Biblical Commission's Document on 'The Jewish People and Their Sacred Scriptures in the Christian Bible.'" *Comm* 29 (2002): 738-45.

Kermode, Frank. *The Sense of an Ending: Studies in the Theory of Fiction.* Oxford: Oxford University Press, 1967.

Kessler, John. "Sexuality and Politics: The Motif of the Displaced Husband in the Books of Samuel." *CBQ* 62 (2000): 409-23.

Kessler, Martin. "Narrative Technique in 1 Sm 16,1-13." *CBQ* 32 (1970): 543-54.

Kessler, Rainer. *Samuel: Priester und Richter, Königsmacher und Prophet.* BG 18. Leipzig: Evangelische Verlagsanstalt, 2008.

Keys, Gillian. *The Wages of Sin: A Reappraisal of the "Succession Narrative."* JSOTSup 221. Sheffield: Sheffield Academic, 1996.

Khan, Geoffrey, and Diana Lipton, eds. *Studies on the Text and Versions of the Hebrew Bible in Honour of Robert Gordon.* VTSup 149. Leiden: Brill, 2012.

Bibliography

Kierkegaard, Søren. *Practice in Christianity*. Edited by Howard V. Hong and Edna H. Hong. Princeton: Princeton University Press, 1991.

Kim, Jeong Bong, and Dirk J. Human. "Nagid: A Re-examination in the Light of the Royal Ideology in the Ancient Near East." *Hervormde teologiese studies* 64 (2008): 1475-97.

Kim, Koowon. *Incubation as a Type-Scene in the 'Aqhatu, Kirta, and Hannah Stories: A Form-Critical and Narratological Study of KTU 1.14 I–1.15 III, 1.17 I–II, and 1 Samuel 1:1–2.11*. VTSup 145. Leiden: Brill, 2011.

Kim, Uriah Y. *Identity and Loyalty in the David Story: A Postcolonial Reading*. HBM 22. Sheffield: Sheffield Phoenix, 2008.

Kinneson, Philip D. *Selling Out the Church: The Dangers of Church Marketing*. Nashville: Abingdon, 1997.

King, J. N. "Henry VIII as David: The King's Image and Reformation Politics." Pp. 78-92 in *Rethinking the Henrician Era: Essays on Early Tudor Texts and Contexts*. Edited by Peter C. Herman. Urbana: University of Illinois Press, 1994.

Kingsbury, Jack Dean. *Matthew: Structure, Christology, Kingdom*. Philadelphia: Fortress, 1975.

————. "The Title 'Son of David' in Matthew's Gospel." *JBL* 95 (1976): 591-602.

Kingsley, Charles. *David: Five Sermons*. 2nd ed. London: Macmillan, 1874.

Kipling, Rudyard. *Collected Works*. New York: Doubleday, 1941.

Kirova, Milena. "Knowledge, Information and Power in the 'Biblical' Sense: The Story of King Saul." *Bible & Critical Theory* 7 (2011) [electronic resource].

————. "When Real Men Cry: The Symbolism of Weeping in the Torah and the Deuteronomistic History." Pp. 35-50 in *Biblical Masculinities Foregrounded*. HBM 62. Sheffield: Sheffield Academic, 2014.

Kitz, Anne Marie. "The Hebrew Terminology of Lot Casting and Its Ancient Near Eastern Context." *CBQ* 62 (2000): 207-14.

Kleer, Martin. *"Der liebliche Sänger der Psalmen Israels": Untersuchungen zu David als Dichter und Beter der Psalmen*. BBB 108. Bodenheim: Philo, 1996.

Klein, Johannes. "1 Sam 18 — Spiel mit den Leerstellen." Pp. 108-15 in *Die Samuelbücher und die Deuteronomisten*. Edited by Christa Schäfer-Lichtenberger. BWANT 188. Stuttgart: Kohlhammer, 2010.

————. *David versus Saul: ein Beitrag zum Erzählsystem der Samuelbücher*. BWANT 158. Stuttgart: Kohlhammer, 2002.

————. "Davids Flucht zu den Philistern (1 Sam XXVII–XXIX)." *VT* 55 (2005): 176-84.

Klein, Ralph. W. *1 Samuel*. WBC 10. 2nd ed. Nashville: Thomas Nelson, 2008.

Klein, Renate, and Johannes Klein. "ויהי כמחריש" (1 Sam 10,27): Plädoyer für eine neue Diskussion eines alten Problems der alttestamentlichen Auslegung." Pp. 185-92 in *"Sieben Augen auf einem Stein" (Sach 3,9): Studien zur Literatur des Zweiten Tempels: Festschrift für Ina Willi-Plein zum 65. Geburtstag*. Edited by Friedhelm Hartenstein and Michael Pietsch. Neukirchen–Vluyn: Neukirchener, 2007.

Klein, William W., Craig L. Blomberg, and Robert L. Hubbard, Jr. *Introduction to Biblical Interpretation*. Dallas: Word, 1993.

Kleiner, Michael. *Saul in En-Dor — Wahrsagung oder Totenbeschwörung? Eine synchrone und diachrone Untersuchung zu 1 Sam 28*. ETS 66. Leipzig: Benno, 1995.

Kleinheyer, Bruno. *Die Priesterweihe im römischen Ritus: eine liturgiehistorische Studie*. Trier: Paulinus, 1962.

Klement, Herbert. H. *II Samuel 21–24: Context, Structure and Meaning in the Samuel Conclusion*. European University Studies 23. Theology 682. Frankfurt: Lang, 2000.

Klingbeil, Martin. *Yahweh Fighting from Heaven: God as Warrior and as God of Heaven in the Hebrew Psalter and Ancient Near Eastern Iconography.* OBO 169. Göttingen: Vandenhoeck & Ruprecht, 1999.

Knapp, Andrew. *Royal Apologetic in the Ancient Near East.* WAWSup 4. Atlanta: SBL, 2015.

Knauf, Ernst Axel. "Does 'Deuteronomistic Historiography' (DtrH) Exist?" Pp. 388-98 in *Israel Constructs Its History: Deuteronomistic Historiography in Recent Research.* Edited by Albert de Pury, Thomas Römer, and Jean-Daniel Macchi. JSOTSup 306. Sheffield: Sheffield Academic, 2000.

Knight, Douglas A. "Deuteronomy and the Deuteronomists." Pp. 61-79 in *Old Testament Interpretation: Past, Present, and Future.* Edited by James Luther Mays, David L. Petersen and Kent Harold Richards. Nashville: Abingdon, 1995.

———. "Political Rights and Powers in Monarchic Israel." *Semeia* 66 (1994): 93-117.

Knohl, Israel. *The Sanctuary of Silence: The Priestly Torah and the Holiness School.* Minneapolis: Fortress, 1994.

Knoppers, Gary N. "The Deuteronomist and the Deuteronomic Law of the King: A Reexamination of a Relationship." *ZAW* 108 (1996): 329-46.

———. "Images of David in Early Judaism: David as Repentant Sinner in Chronicles." *Bib* 76 (1995): 449-70.

———. "Is There a Future for the Deuteronomistic History?" Pp. 119-34 in *The Future of the Deuteronomistic History.* Edited by Thomas Römer. BETL 147. Leuven: University Press, 2000.

———. "Israel's First King and 'The Kingdom of YHWH in the Hands of the Sons of David': The Place of the Saulide Monarchy in the Chronicler's Historiography." Pp. 187-213 in *Saul in Story and Tradition.* Edited by Carl S. Ehrlich with Marsha C. White. FAT 47. Tübingen: Mohr Siebeck, 2006.

Knoppers, Gary N., and J. Gordon McConville, eds. *Reconsidering Israel and Judah: Recent Studies on the Deuteronomistic History.* SBTS 8. Winona Lake: Eisenbrauns, 2000.

Koch, Christoph. "Bundestheologie und autoritativer Text im Deuteronomium: das Tafelmotiv in Deuteronomium 5.9-10 vor dem Hintergrund altorientalischer Vertragspraxis." Pp. 29-47 in *Covenant and Election in Exilic and Post-Exilic Judaism.* Edited by Nathan MacDonald. FAT/2 79. Studies of the Sofja Kovalevska Research Group on Early Jewish Monotheism 5. Tübingen: Mohr Siebeck, 2015.

Koch, Klaus. "Der doppelter Ausgang des Alten Testaments in Judentum und Christentum." *Jahrbuch für Biblische Theologie* 6 (1991): 215-42.

———. *The Growth of the Biblical Tradition: The Form-Critical Method.* Translated by S. M. Cupitt. New York: Scribner's Sons, 1969.

Kofoed, Jens Bruun. "Saul and Cultural Memory." *SJOT* 25 (2011): 124-50.

———. *Text and History: Historiography and the Study of the Biblical Text.* Winona Lake: Eisenbrauns, 2005.

Kooij, Arie van der. "The Story of David and Goliath: The Early History of Its Text." *ETL* 68 (1992): 118-31.

Koskie, Steven J. "Seeking Comment: The Commentary and the Bible as Christian Scripture." *JTI* 1 (2007): 237-49.

Kratz, Reinhard G. *The Composition of the Narrative Books of the Old Testament.* Translated by John Bowden. New York: T & T Clark, 2005.

Kreiner, Armin. "Die Relevanz der Wahrheitsfrage für die Schriftauslegung." Pp. 46-64 in

Bibliography

Theologie als gegenwärtige Schriftauslegung. Edited by Eberhard Jüngel. ZTKB 9. Tübingen: Mohr Siebeck, 1995.

Krook, Dorothea. *Elements of Tragedy*. New Haven: Yale University Press, 1969.

Krüger, Thomas. "Theoretische und methodische Probleme der Geschichte des alten Israel in der neueren Diskussion." *VF* 53 (2008): 4-22.

Kucová, Lydie. "Obeisance in the Biblical Stories of David." Pp. 241-60 in *Reflection and Refraction: Studies in Biblical Historiography in Honour of A. Graeme Auld*. Edited by Robert Rezetko, Timothy Lim, and W. Brian Aucker. VTSup 113. Leiden: Brill, 2007.

Kuhrt, Amélie. "Usurpation, Conquest and Ceremonial: From Babylon to Persia." Pp. 20-55 in *Rituals of Royalty: Power and Ceremonial in Traditional Societies*. Edited by David Cannadine and Simon Price. Cambridge: Cambridge University Press, 1987.

Kunz, Andreas. *Die Frauen und der König David: Studien zur Figuration von Frauen in den Davidserzählungen*. ABG 8. Leipzig: Evangelische Verlagsanstalt, 2004.

Kuske, Martin. *The Old Testament as the Book of Christ: An Appraisal of Bonhoeffer's Interpretation*. Philadelphia: Westminster John Knox, 1976.

Kutler, Laurence B. "Features of the Battle Challenge in Biblical Hebrew, Akkadian and Ugaritic." *UF* 19 (1987): 95-99.

Kutsch, Ernst. *Salbung als Rechtsakt im Alten Testament und im Alten Orient*. BZAW 87. Berlin: Töpelmann, 1963.

Kuyumdzhieva, Margarita. "David Rex Penitent: Some Notes on the Interpretation of King David in Byzantine and Post-Byzantine Art." Pp. 133-51 in *The Biblical Models of Power and Law: Papers of the International Conference, Bucharest, New Europe College 2005*. Edited by Ivan Biliarsky and Radu G. Paun. Rechtshistorische Reihe 366. Frankfurt: Lang, 2008.

Laato, Antti. *A Star is Rising: The Historical Development of the Old Testament Royal Ideology and the Rise of the Jewish Messianic Expectations*. University of South Florida International Studies in Formative Christianity and Judaism. Atlanta: Scholars, 1997.

Laistner, M. L. W. "Some Early Medieval Commentaries on the Old Testament." Pp. 181-201 in *The Intellectual Heritage of the Early Middle Ages*. Edited by Chester G. Starr. Ithaca: Cornell University Press, 1957.

Lamb, David. *Righteous Jehu and His Evil Heirs: The Deuteronomist's Negative Perspective on Dynastic Succession*. OTM 10. Oxford: Oxford University Press, 2007.

Lambert, W. G. "Kingship in Ancient Mesopotamia." Pp. 55-70 in *King and Messiah in Ancient Israel and the Ancient Near East: Proceedings of the Oxford Old Testament Seminar*. Edited by John Day. JSOTSup 270. Sheffield: Sheffield Academic, 1998.

Lampe, G. W. H. "The Bible since the Rise of Critical Study." Pp. 125-44 in *The Church's Use of the Bible*. Edited by D. E. Nineham. London: SPCK, 1963.

Lanfranchi, Giovanni, and Robert Bollinger, eds. *Concepts of Kingship in Antiquity: Proceedings of the European Science Foundation Exploratory Workshop held in Padova, November 28th–December 1st 2007*. History of the Ancient Near East Monographs 11. Padua: Sargon, 2010.

Lang, Bernhard. *The Hebrew God: Portrait of an Ancient Deity*. New Haven: Yale University Press, 2002.

Lapsley, Jacqueline E. "Feeling Our Way: Love for God in Deuteronomy." *CBQ* 65 (2003): 350-69.

Lasine, Stuart. *Knowing Kings: Knowledge, Power, and Narcissism in the Hebrew Bible*. Atlanta: Society of Biblical Literature, 2001.

Lauinger, Jacob. "Esarhaddon's Succession Treaty at Tell Tayinat: Text and Commentary." *JCS* 64 (2012): 87-123.

Launderville, Dale. *Piety and Politics: The Dynamics of Royal Authority in Homeric Greece, Biblical Israel, and Old Babylonian Mesopotamia.* Grand Rapids: Eerdmans, 2003.

Lawton, Robert B. "1 Samuel 18: David, Merob, and Michal." *CBQ* 51 (1989): 423-25.

—————. "Saul, Jonathan and the 'Son of Jesse.'" *JSOT* 58 (1993): 35-46.

Leeb, Carolyn S. *Away from the Father's House: The Social Location of* na'ar *and* na'arah *in Ancient Israel.* JSOTSup 301. Sheffield: Sheffield Academic, 2000.

Lefebvre, Philippe. *Livres de Samuel et récits de résurrection: Le messie ressuscité "selon les Écritures."* LD. Paris: Cerf, 2004.

Leithart, Peter J. *A Son to Me: An Exposition of 1 & 2 Samuel.* Moscow, ID: Canon, 2003.

Lemche, Niels Peter. "Did a Reform Like Josiah's Happen?" Pp. 11-19 in *The Historian and the Bible: Essays in Honour of Lester L. Grabbe.* Edited by Philip R. Davies and Diana V. Edelman. New York: T & T Clark, 2010.

Leneman, Helen. *Love, Lust and Lunacy: The Stories of Saul and David in Music.* Bible in the Modern World 29. Sheffield: Sheffield Phoenix, 2010.

Leuchter, Mark. *Josiah's Reform and Jeremiah's Scroll: Historical Calamity and Prophetic Response.* HBM 6. Sheffield: Sheffield Phoenix, 2006.

—————. "A King Like All the Nations: The Composition of I Samuel 8,11-18." *ZAW* 117 (2005): 543-58.

—————. "'Now There Was a [Certain] Man': Compositional Chronology in Judges–1 Samuel." *CBQ* 69 (2007): 429-39.

—————. *Samuel and the Shaping of Tradition.* Oxford: Oxford University Press, 2013.

—————. "Samuel, Saul, and the Deuteronomistic Categories of History." Pp. 101-10 in *From Babel to Babylon: Essays on Biblical History and Literature in Honour of Brian Peckham.* Edited by Joyce Rilett Wood, John E. Harvey, and Mark Leuchter. LHBOTS 455. New York: T & T Clark, 2006.

Levenson, Jon D. "1 Samuel 25 as Literature and History." *CBQ* 40 (1978): 11-28.

—————. "Is There a Counterpart in the Hebrew Bible to New Testament Antisemitism?" *JES* 22 (1985): 242-60.

—————. "A Technical Meaning for *n'm* in the Hebrew Bible." *VT* 35 (1985): 61-67.

Levine, Amy-Jill. *The Misunderstood Jew: The Church and the Scandal of the Jewish Jesus.* San Francisco: HarperCollins, 2006.

Levine, Baruch. "*Lpny YHWH*: Phenomenology of the Open-Air Altar in Biblical Israel." Pp. 196-205 in *Biblical Archaeology Today: Proceedings of the Second International Congress on Biblical Archaeology.* Edited by Avraham Biran and Joseph Aviram. Jerusalem: Israel Exploration Society, 1993.

Levinson, Bernard M. *Deuteronomy and the Hermeneutics of Legal Innovation.* Oxford: Oxford University Press, 1998.

—————. "The Reconceptualization of Kingship in Deuteronomy and the Deuteronomistic History's Transformation of Torah." *VT* 51 (2001): 511-34.

Levinson, Bernard M., and Jeffrey Stackert. "Between the Covenant Code and Esarhaddon's Succession Treaty: Deuteronomy 13 and the Composition of Deuteronomy." *JAJ* 3 (2012): 123-40.

Levinson, Deirdre. "The Psychopathology of King Saul." Pp. 123-41 in *Out of the Garden: Women Writers on the Bible.* Edited by Christina Büchmann and Celina Spiegel. New York: Fawcett Columbine, 1994.

Bibliography

Levy, Bryna Jocheved. *Waiting for Rain: Reflections at the Turning of the Year.* Philadelphia: JPS, 2008.

Lewis, C. S. *The Literary Impact of the Authorized Version.* Rev. ed. Facet Books; Biblical Series 4. Philadelphia: Fortress, 1967.

———. *On Stories and Other Essays on Literature.* New York: Harvest, 1982.

———. *Reflections on the Psalms.* Glasgow: Collins, 1961.

Lewis, Robert. *Raising a Modern-Day Knight: A Father's Role in Guilding His Son to Authentic Manhood.* 2nd ed. Carol Stream, IL: Tyndale House, 2007.

Lewis, Theodore J. "The Textual History of the Song of Hannah: 1 Samuel II 1-10." *VT* 44 (1994): 18-46.

Liere, Frans van. "The Literal Sense of the Books of Samuel and Kings; From Andrew of St Victor to Nicholas of Lyra." Pp. 59-81 in *Nicholas of Lyra: The Sense of Scripture.* Edited by Philip D. W. Krey and Lesley Smith. Leiden: Brill, 2000.

Linafelt, Tod. "Private Poetry and Public Eloquence in 2 Samuel 1:17-27: Hearing and Over-hearing David's Lament for Jonathan and Saul." *JR* 88 (2008): 497-526.

———. "Taking Women in Samuel." Pp. 99-113 in *Reading between Texts: Intertextuality and the Hebrew Bible.* Literary Currents in Biblical Interpretation. Edited by Dana Nolan Fewell. Louisville: Westminster John Knox, 1992.

Linafelt, Tod, Claudia V. Camp, and Timothy Beal, eds. *The Fate of King David: The Past and Present of a Biblical Icon.* LHBOTS 500. New York: T & T Clark, 2010.

Lind, Millard. *Yahweh Is a Warrior: The Theology of Warfare in Ancient Israel.* Scottdale, PA: Herald, 1980.

Lindbeck, George. "Scripture, Consensus and Community." Pp. 71-101 in *Biblical Interpretation in Crisis: The Ratzinger Conference on Bible and Church.* Edited by Richard John Neuhaus. Grand Rapids: Eerdmans, 1989.

Lindblom, Johannes. "Lot-Casting in the Old Testament." *VT* 12 (1962): 164-78.

Lipiński, Edward. "'Leadership': The Roots DGR and NGD in Aramaic." Pp. 509-14 in *"Und Mose schrieb dieses Lied auf": Studien zum Alten Testament und zum alten Orient; Festschrift für Oswald Loretz zur Vollendung seines 70. Lebensjahres mit Beiträgen von Freunden, Schülern und Kollegen.* Edited by Manfred Dietrich and Ingo Kottsieper. AOAT 250. Munster: Ugarit-Verlag, 1998.

Liss, Hanna. "The Innocent King: Saul in Rabbinic Exegesis." Pp. 245-60 in *Saul in Story and Tradition.* Edited by Carl S. Ehrlich with Marsha C. White. FAT 47. Tübingen: Mohr Siebeck, 2006.

Livy. *The Early History of Rome.* Penguin Classics. Translated by Aubrey de Sélincout. Harmondsworth: Penguin, 1971.

Lloyd-Jones, D. Martyn. "When the Gods Fall." Pp. 58-71 in idem, *Old Testament Evangelistic Sermons.* Edinburgh: Banner of Truth, 1995.

Lohfink, Norbert. "The Cult Reform of Josiah of Judah: 2 Kings 22–23 as a Source for the History of Israelite Religion." Pp. 459-75 in *Ancient Israelite Religion: Essays in Honor of Frank Moore Cross.* Edited by Patrick D. Miller, Jr., Paul D. Hanson, and S. Dean McBride. Philadelphia: Fortress, 1987.

———. "Opfer und Säkularisierung im Deuteronomium." Pp. 15-43 in *Studien zu Opfer und Kult im Alten Testament.* Edited by Adrian Schenker. FAT 3. Tübingen: Mohr Siebeck, 1992.

———. "Was There a Deuteronomistic Movement?" Pp. 36-66 in *Those Elusive Deuterono-*

mists: *The Phenomenon of Pan-Deuteronomism*. Edited by Linda S. Schearing and Steven L. McKenzie. JSOTSup 268. Sheffield: Sheffield Academic, 1999.

———. "Zur neuesten Diskussion über 2 Kön 22–23." Pp. 179-207 in idem, *Studien zum Deuteronomium und zur deuteronomistischen Literatur* II. SBAB. Stuttgart: Katholisches Bibelwerk, 1991.

Long, Burke O. "The Effect of Divination upon Israelite Literature." *JBL* 92 (1973): 489-97.

———. "Framing Repetitions in Biblical Historiography." *JBL* 106 (1987): 385-99.

Long, Gary. "The Written Story: Toward Understanding Text as Representation and Function." *VT* 49 (1999): 165-85.

Long, V. Philips. *The Art of Biblical History*. Grand Rapids: Zondervan, 1994.

———. "How Did Saul Become King? Literary Reading and Historical Reconstruction." Pp. 271-84 in *Faith, Tradition, and History: Old Testament Historiography in Its Near Eastern Context*. Edited by A. R. Millard, James K. Hoffmeier, and David W. Baker. Winona Lake: Eisenbrauns, 1994.

———. *The Reign and Rejection of King Saul: A Case for Literary and Theological Coherence*. SBLDS 118. Atlanta: Scholars, 1989.

———. "Scenic, Succinct, Subtle: An Introduction to the Literary Artistry of 1 and 2 Samuel." *Presbyterion* 19 (1993): 32-47.

Long, V. Philips, ed. *Israel's Past in Present Research: Essays on Ancient Israelite Historiography*. SBTS 7. Winona Lake: Eisenbrauns, 1999.

Longman, Tremper, III, and Daniel G. Reid. *God Is a Warrior*. Studies in Old Testament Biblical Theology. Grand Rapids: Zondervan, 1995.

Lorberbaum, Yair. *Disempowered King: Monarchy in Classical Jewish Literature*. New York: Continuum, 2010.

Loretz, Oswald. "Die Teraphim als 'Ahnen-Götter-Figur(in)en' im Lichte der Texte aus Nuzi, Emar und Ugarit." *UF* 24 (1992): 133-78.

Lott, M. Ray. *Police on Screen: Hollywood Cops, Detectives, Marshals and Rangers*. Jefferson, NC: McFarland and Co., 2006.

Lozovyy, Joseph. *Saul, Doeg, Nabal, and the "Son of Jesse": Readings in 1 Samuel 16–25*. LHBOTS 497. New York: T & T Clark, 2009.

Ludwig, Claudia. "David – Christus – Basileus: Erwartungen an eine Herrschergestalt." Pp. 367-82 in *König David — biblische Schlüsselfigur und europäische Leitgestalt*. Edited by Walter Dietrich and Hubert Herkommer. Freiburg: Universitätsverlag, 2003.

Lüthi, Walter. *Das erste Buch Samuel, ausgelegt für die Gemeinde*. Basel: Friedrich Reinhardt, 1964.

Lust, Johan. "The Story of David and Goliath in Hebrew and in Greek." Pp. 5-18 in *The Story of David and Goliath: Textual and Literary Criticism, Papers of a Joint Research Venture*. Edited by Dominique Barthélemy et al. OBO 73. Göttingen: Vandenhoeck & Ruprecht, 1986.

Mabee, Charles. "Judicial Instrumentality in the Ahimelech Story." Pp. 17-32 in *Early Jewish and Christian Exegesis: Studies in Memory of William H. Brownlee*. Edited by Craig A. Evans and William Franklin Stinespring. Atlanta: Scholars, 1987.

MacDonald, John. "The Status and Role of the *Na'ar* in Israelite Society." *JNES* 35 (1976): 147-70.

MacDonald, Nathan. *Deuteronomy and the Meaning of "Monotheism"*. FAT/2 1. 2nd ed. Tübingen: Mohr Siebeck, 2012.

———. *Not Bread Alone: The Uses of Food in the Old Testament*. Oxford: Oxford University Press, 2008.

Bibliography

————. *What Did the Ancient Israelites Eat? Diet in Biblical Times*. Grand Rapids: Eerdmans, 2008.

Măcelaru, Marcel V. "Saul in the Company of Men: (De)constructing Masculinity in 1 Samuel 9–31." Pp. 51-68 in *Biblical Masculinities Foregrounded*. Edited by Ovidiu Creangă and Peter-Ben Smit. HBM 62. Sheffield: Sheffield Phoenix, 2014.

Machinist, Peter. "Hosea and the Ambiguity of Kingship in Ancient Israel." Pp. 153-81 in *Constituting the Community: Studies on the Polity of Ancient Israel in Honor of S. Dean McBride Jr.* Edited by John T. Strong and Steven S. Tuell. Winona Lake: Eisenbrauns, 2005.

MacWilliam, Stuart. "Ideologies of Male Beauty and the Hebrew Bible." *BibInt* 17 (2009): 265-87.

Madl, Helmut. "Die Gottesbefragung mit dem Verb *ša'al.*" Pp. 37-50 in *Bausteine Biblischer Theologie: Festschrift G. J. Botterweck*. Edited by Heinz-Josef Fabry. BBB 50. Cologne: Hanstein, 1977.

Maeir, Aren M. "A New Interpretation of the Term *'opalim* (עפלים) in the Light of Recent Archaeological Finds from Philistia." *JSOT* 32 (2007): 23-40.

Maffesoli, Michel. "The Return of the Tragic in Postmodern Societies." Pp. 319-36 in *Rethinking Tragedy*. Edited by Rita Felski. Baltimore: Johns Hopkins University Press, 2008.

Magennis, Feidhlimidh T. *First and Second Samuel*. New Collegeville Bible Commentary 8. Collegeville: Liturgical, 2012.

Magonet, Jonathan. *A Rabbi Reads the Bible*. 2nd ed. London: SCM, 2004.

Manuel, Frank E. *The Broken Staff: Judaism through Christian Eyes*. Cambridge, MA: Harvard University Press, 1992.

March, Daniel. *Night Scenes in the Bible*. Philadelphia: Zeigler, McCurdy and Co., 1869.

Marvin, Carolyn, and David W. Ingle. *Blood Sacrifice and the Nation: Totem Rituals and the American Flag*. Cambridge: Cambridge University Press, 1999.

Mathisen, James A. "Twenty Years after Bellah: Whatever Happened to American Civil Religion?" *Sociological Analysis* 50 (1989): 129-46.

Mathys, Hans-Peter. "Anmerkungen zu 2 Sam 24." Pp. 229-46 in *"Sieben Augen auf einem Stein" (Sach 3,9): Studien zur Literatur des Zweiten Tempels; Festschrift für Ina Willi-Plein zum 65. Geburtstag*. Edited by Friedhelm Hartenstein and Michael Pietsch. Neukirchen–Vluyn: Neukirchener, 2007.

————. *Dichter und Beter: Theologen aus spätalttestamentlicher Zeit*. OBO 132. Göttingen: Vandenhoeck & Ruprecht, 1994.

Mays, James Luther. "The David of the Psalms." *Interp* 40 (1986): 143-55.

Mazar, Amihai. "Was King Saul Impaled on the Wall of Beth Shean?" *BAR* 38 (Mar–Apr 2012): 34-41, 70-71.

McAleese, Killian. "Danger at the King's Table: Insult and Family Conflict at Saul's New Moon Fest." Pp. 24-38 in *Text, Theology, and Trowel: New Investigations in the Biblical World*. Edited by Lidia D. Matassa and Jason M. Silverman. Eugene: Pickwick, 2011.

McCarter, P. Kyle, Jr. *I Samuel: A New Translation with Introduction and Commentary*. AB 8. Garden City, NY: Doubleday, 1980.

————. *II Samuel: A New Translation with Introduction and Commentary*. AB 9. Garden City, NY: Doubleday, 1984.

————. "The Apology of David." *JBL* 99 (1980): 489-504.

————. "The Historical David." *Interp* 40 (1986): 117-29.

McCarthy, Dennis. "II Samuel 7 and the Structure of the Deuteronomistic History." *JBL* 84 (1965): 131-38.

————. "The Inauguration of the Monarchy in Israel: A Form-Critical Study of 1 Sam 8–12." *Interp* 27 (1973): 401-12.

McConville, J. Gordon. *God and Earthly Power: An Old Testament Political Theology.* LHBOTS 454. New York: T & T Clark, 2006.

————. "Priesthood in Joshua to Kings." *VT* 49 (1999): 73-87.

McDonald, Lee Martin. *The Biblical Canon: Its Origin, Transmission, and Authority.* 3rd ed. Peabody, MA: Hendrickson, 2007.

McGlasson, Paul. *Invitation to Dogmatic Theology.* Grand Rapids: Brazos, 2006.

McGinnis, Claire Mathews. "Swimming with the Divine Tide: An Ignatian Reading of 1 Samuel." Pp. 240-70 in *Theological Exegesis: Essays in Honor of Brevard S. Childs.* Edited by Christopher Seitz and Kathryn Greene-McCreight. Grand Rapids: Eerdmans, 1999.

McKenzie, Steven L. "David's Enemies." Pp. 33-49 in *König David: biblische Schlüsselfigur und europäische Leitgestalt. 19. Kolloquium (2000) der Schweizerischen Akademie der Geistes- und Sozialwissenschaften.* Edited by Walter Dietrich and Hubert Herkommer. Freiburg: Universitätsverlag; Stuttgart: Kohlhammer, 2003.

————. "Elaborated Evidence for the Priority of 1 Samuel 26." *JBL* 129 (2010): 437-44.

————. *King David: A Biography.* Oxford: Oxford University Press, 2000.

————. "Saul in the Deuteronomistic History." Pp. 59-70 in *Saul in Story and Tradition.* Edited by Carl S. Ehrlich with Marsha C. White. FAT 47. Tübingen: Mohr Siebeck, 2006. Pp. 59-70.

————. "The Trouble with Kingship." Pp. 286-314 in *Israel Constructs Its History: Deuteronomistic History in Recent Research.* Edited by Albert de Pury, Thomas Römer, and Jean-Daniel Macchi. JSOTSup 306. Sheffield: Sheffield Academic, 2000.

McKenzie, Steven L., and M. Patrick Graham, eds. *The History of Israel's Traditions: The Heritage of Martin Noth.* JSOTSup 182. Sheffield: Sheffield Academic, 1994.

Meier, Samuel A. "The Sword: From Saul to David." Pp. 156-74 in *Saul in Story and Tradition.* Edited by Carl S. Ehrlich with Marsha C. White. FAT 47. Tübingen: Mohr Siebeck, 2006.

Mettinger, Tryggve N. D. *King and Messiah: The Civil and Sacral Legitimation of the Israelite Kings.* ConBOT 8. Lund: Gleerup, 1976.

Metzger, Hans-Dieter. "David und Saul in Staats- und Widerstandslehren der Frühen Neuzeit." Pp. 437-84 in *König David — biblische Schlüsselfigur und europäische Leitgestalt.* Edited by Walter Dietrich and Hubert Herkommer. Freiburg: Universitätsverlag, 2003.

Meyers, Carol. "David as Temple Builder." Pp. 357-76 in *Ancient Israelite Religion: Essays in Honor of Frank Moore Cross.* Edited by Patrick D. Miller, Jr., Paul D. Hanson, and S. Dean McBride. Philadelphia: Fortress, 1987.

————. "The Hannah Narrative in Feminist Perspective." Pp. 117-26 in *"Go to the Land I Will Show You": Studies in Honor of Dwight W. Young.* Edited by Joseph E. Coleson and Victor H. Matthews. Winona Lake: Eisenbrauns, 1996.

Meyers, Eric M. "The Torah Shrine in the Ancient Synagogue." *JSQ* 4 (1997): 303-38.

Michael, Matthew. "The Prophet, the Witch and the Ghost: Understanding the Parody of Saul as a 'Prophet' and the Purpose of Endor in the Deuteronomistic History." *JSOT* 38 (2014): 315-46.

Milgrom, Jacob. "The Alleged 'Demythologization and Secularization' in Deuteronomy." *IEJ* 23 (1973): 156-61.

————. *Leviticus 1–16.* AB 3. Garden City: Doubleday, 1991.

————. *Numbers: The Traditional Hebrew Text with the New JPS Translation.* Philadelphia: JPS, 1990.

Bibliography

Millard, Alan R. "Are There Anachronisms in the Books of Samuel?" Pp. 39-48 in *Studies on the Text and Versions of the Hebrew Bible in Honour of Robert Gordon*. Edited by Geoffrey Khan and Diana Lipton. VTSup 149. Leiden: Brill, 2012.

————. "The Armor of Goliath." Pp. 337-43 in *Exploring the* Longue Durée: *Essays in Honor of Lawrence E. Stager*. Edited by J. David Schloen. Winona Lake: Eisenbrauns, 2000.

————. "Authors, Books, and Readers in the Ancient World." Pp. 544-64 in *The Oxford Handbook of Biblical Studies* Edited by J. W. Rogerson and Judith M. Lieu. Oxford: Oxford University Press, 2006.

————. *Reading and Writing in the Time of Jesus*. New York: New York University Press, 2000.

Millard, Alan R., James K. Hoffmeier, and David W. Baker. *Faith, Tradition, and History: Old Testament Historiography in Its Near Eastern Context*. Winona Lake: Eisenbrauns, 1994.

Miller, Dean A. *The Epic Hero*. Baltimore: Johns Hopkins University Press, 2000.

Miller, Eric P. "The Political Significance of Christ's Kingship in the Biblical Exegesis of Hrabanus Maurus and Angelomus of Luxeuil." Pp. 193-213 in *Biblical Studies in the Early Middle Ages*. Edited by Claudio Leonardi and Giovanni Orlandi. Florence: SISMEL, 2005.

Minear, Paul S. *I Pledge Allegiance: Patriotism and the Bible*. Philadelphia: Geneva, 1975.

Miscall, Peter D. *1 Samuel: A Literary Reading*. ISBL. Bloomington: Indiana University Press, 1986.

————. *The Workings of Biblical Narrative*. SBLSemS. Philadelphia: Fortress; Chico, CA: Scholars, 1983.

Miura, Yuzuru. *David in Luke–Acts: His Portrayal in the Light of Early Judaism*. WUNT 2/232. Tübingen: Mohr Siebeck, 2007.

Moberly, R. W. L. "By Stone and Sling: 1 Samuel 17:50 and the Problem of Misreading David's Victory over Goliath." Pp. 329-42 in *On Stone and Scrolls: Essays in Honour of Graham Ivor Davies*. Edited by James K. Aitken, Katharine J. Dell, and Brian A. Mastin. BZAW 420. Berlin: de Gruyter, 2011.

————. "'God Is Not a Human that He Should Repent' (Numbers 23:19 and 1 Samuel 15:29)." Pp. 112-23 in *God in the Fray: A Tribute to Walter Brueggemann*. Edited by Tod Linafelt and Timothy K. Beal. Minneapolis: Fortress, 1998.

————. "'Interpret the Bible like Any Other Book'? Requiem for an Axiom." *JTI* 4 (2010): 91-110.

————. "To Hear the Master's Voice: Revelation and Spiritual Discernment in the Call of Samuel." *SJT* 48 (1995): 443-68.

————. "What Is Theological Commentary? An Old Testament Perspective." Pp. 172-86 in *Theological Commentary: An Evangelical Perspective*. Edited by R. Michael Allen. London: T & T Clark, 2011.

Mobley, Gregory. *The Empty Men: The Heroic Tradition of Ancient Israel*. ABRL. New York: Doubleday, 2005.

————. "Glimpses of the Heroic Saul." Pp. 80-87 in *Saul in Story and Tradition*. Edited by Carl S. Ehrlich with Marsha C. White. FAT 47. Tübingen: Mohr Siebeck, 2006.

Moenikes, Ansgar. *Die grundsätzliche Ablehnung des Königtums in der Hebräischen Bibel*. BBB 99. Weinheim: Beltz Athenäum, 1995.

Mommer, Peter. "Ist auch Saul unter den Propheten? Ein Beitrag zu 1 Sam 19:18-24." *BN* 38 (1987): 53-61.

————. *Samuel: Geschichte und Überlieferung*. WMANT 65. Neukirchen–Vluyn: Neukirchener, 1991.

Monroe, Lauren A. S. *Josiah's Reform and the Dynamics of Defilement: Israelite Rites of Violence and the Making of a Biblical Text.* Oxford: Oxford University Press, 2011.

Moor, Johannes C. de, and Harry F. Van Rooy, eds. *Past, Present, Future: The Deuteronomistic History and the Prophets.* OTS 44. Leiden: Brill, 2000.

Moore, Stephen P., and Yvonne Sherwood. *The Invention of a Biblical Scholar: A Critical Manifesto.* Minneapolis: Fortress, 2011.

Moran, Jo Ann Hoeppner. "E. M. Forster's *A Passage to India*: What Really Happened in the Caves." *Modern Fiction Studies* 34 (1988): 596-604.

Moran, William L. "The Ancient Near Eastern Background of the Love of God in Deuteronomy." *CBQ* 25 (1963): 77-87.

Morenz, Ludwig, and Stefan Schorch, eds. *Was ist ein Text? Alttestamentliche, ägyptologische und altorientalische Perspektiven.* BZAW 362. Berlin: de Gruyter, 2007.

Morgan, G. Campbell. "Playing the Fool." In idem, *The Westminster Pulpit.* 10 Vols. Westwood, NJ: Fleming H. Revell, 1954. 9:9-22.

Morrison, Craig E. *2 Samuel.* Berit Olam. Collegeville: Liturgical, 2013.

⸻. *The Character of the Syriac Version of the First Book of Samuel.* Monographs of the Peshitta Institute Leiden 11. Leiden: Brill, 2001.

Mosis, Rudolf. *Welterfahrung und Gottesglaube: drei Erzählungen aus dem Alten Testament.* Würzburg: Echter, 2004.

Mouw, Richard J. *Uncommon Decency: Christian Civility in an Uncivil World.* 2nd ed. Downers Grove: InterVarsity, 2010.

Mower, Deborah S., and Wade L. Robison, eds. *Civility in Politics and Education.* Routledge Studies in Contemporary Philosophy 31. New York: Routledge, 2012.

Mowinckel, Sigmund. *The Spirit and the Word: Prophecy and Tradition in Ancient Israel.* Edited by K. C. Hanson. Minneapolis: Augsburg Fortress, 2002.

Mrázek, Jiří. "Messiah, the Healer of the Sick: A Study of Jesus as the Son of David in the Gospel of Matthew." *TLZ* 133 (2008): 381-83.

Müller, Møgens. *The First Bible of the Church: A Plea for the Septuagint.* Copenhagen International Seminar 1. Sheffield: Sheffield Academic, 1996.

Müllner, Ilse. "Die Samuelbücher: Frauen im Zentrum der Geschichte Israels." Pp. 114-29 in *Kompendium Feministische Bibelausleung.* Edited by Luise Schottroff and Marie-Theres Wacker. 2nd ed. Gütersloh: Gütersloher Verlagshaus, 1999.

Murphy, Francesca Aran. *1 Samuel.* Brazos Theological Commentary on the Bible. Grand Rapids: Brazos, 2010.

Murray, Donald. *Divine Prerogative and Royal Pretension: Pragmatics, Poetics and Polemics in a Narrative Sequence about David (2 Samuel 5.17–7.29).* JSOTSup 264. Sheffield: Sheffield Academic, 1998.

Na'aman, Nadav. "The Pre-Deuteronomistic Story of King Saul and Its Historical Significance." *CBQ* 54 (1992): 638-58.

⸻. "Sources and Composition in the History of David." Pp. 170-86 in *The Origins of the Ancient Israelite States.* Edited by Volkmar Fritz and Philip R. Davies. JSOTSup 228. Sheffield: Sheffield Academic, 1996.

Nahkola, Aulikki. *Double Narratives in the Old Testament: The Foundations of Method in Biblical Criticism.* BZAW 290. Berlin: de Gruyter, 2001.

Naiden, F. S. "Rejected Sacrifices in Greek and Hebrew Religion." *JANER* 6 (2006): 189-223.

Naiditch, P. G. *A. E. Housman at University College, London: The Election of 1892.* Leiden: Brill, 1988.

Bibliography

Naumann, Thomas. "David und die Liebe." Pp. 51-38 in *König David: biblische Schlüsselfigur und europäische Leitgestalt. 19. Kolloquium (2000) der Schweizerischen Akademie der Geistes- und Sozialwissenschaften*. Edited by Walter Dietrich and Hubert Herkommer. Freiburg: Universitätsverlag; Stuttgart: Kohlhammer, 2003.

Negev, Avraham, and Shimon Gibson, eds. *The Archaeological Encyclopedia of the Holy Land*. New York: Continuum, 2001.

Nelson, Janet L. "The Lord's Anointed and the People's Choice: Carolingian Royal Ritual." Pp. 137-80 in *Rituals of Royalty: Power and Ceremonial in Traditional Societies*. Edited by David Cannadine and Simon Price. Cambridge: Cambridge University Press, 1987.

Nelson, Richard D. "*Ḥerem* and the Deuteronomic Social Conscience." Pp. 39-54 in *Deuteronomy and Deuteronomic Literature: Festschrift C. H. W. Brekelmans*. BETL 133. Edited by M. Vervenne and J. Lust. Leuven: Leuven University Press, 1997. Pp. 39-54.

———. "The Role of the Priesthood in the Deuteronomistic History." Pp. 132-47 in *Congress Volume: Leuven 1989*. Edited by J. A. Emerton. VTSup 43. Leiden: Brill, 1991.

Nentel, Jochen. *Trägerschaft und Intentionen des deuteronomistischen Geschichtswerks: Untersuchungen zu den Reflexionsreden Jos 1; 23; 24; 1Sam 12 und 1Kön 8*. BZAW 297. Berlin: de Gruyter, 2000.

Neuhaus, Richard John. *The Naked Public Square: Religion and Democracy in America*. Grand Rapids: Eerdmans, 1984.

Newkirk, Thomas. *The Art of Slow Reading: Six Time-Honored Practices for Engagement*. Portsmouth, NH: Heinemann, 2011.

Newman, Amy. "The Death of Judaism in German Protestant Thought from Luther to Hegel." *JAAR* 61 (1993): 455-84.

Newman, John Henry. *Parochial and Plain Sermons*. San Francisco: Ignatius, 1987.

Nicol, George G. "David, Abigail and Bathsheba, Nabal and Uriah: Transformations within a Triangle." *SJOT* 12 (1998): 130-45.

Nicholson, Ernest W. *God and His People: Covenant and Theology in the Old Testament*. Oxford: Clarendon, 1986.

Nicholson, Sarah. "Catching the Poetic Eye: Saul Reconceived in Modern Literature." Pp. 284-333 in *Saul in Story and Tradition*. Edited by Carl S. Ehrlich with Marsha C. White. FAT 47. Tübingen: Mohr Siebeck, 2006.

———. *Three Faces of Saul: An Intertextual Approach to Biblical Tragedy*. JSOTSup 339. Sheffield: Sheffield Academic, 2002.

Niebuhr, Reinhold. *Beyond Tragedy: Essays on the Christian Interpretation of History*. New York: Scribner's Sons, 1937.

———. "Christianity and Tragedy." Pp. 155-69 in idem, *Beyond Tragedy: Essays on the Christian Interpretation of History*. New York: Charles Scribner's Sons, 1941.

Niehr, Herbert. "Die Reform des Joschija: methodische, historische und religionsgeschichtliche Aspekte." Pp. 33-55 in *Jeremia und die "deuteronomistische Bewegung."* Edited by Walter Gross. BBB 98. Weinheim: Beltz Athenäum, 1995.

Nielson, Fleming A. J. *The Tragedy in History: Herodotus and the Deuteronomistic History*. JSOTSup 251. Sheffield: Sheffield Academic, 1997.

Nigosian, Solomon. *Magic and Divination in the Old Testament*. Brighton: Sussex Academic, 2008.

Nihan, Christophe. "Saul among the Prophets (1 Sam 10:10-12 and 19:18-24): The Reworking of Saul's Figure in the Context of the Debate on 'Charismatic Prophecy' in the Persian

Era." Pp. 88-118 in *Saul in Story and Tradition*. Edited by Carl S. Ehrlich with Marsha C. White. FAT 47. Tübingen: Mohr Siebeck, 2006.

Nissinen, Marti. "Die Liebe von David und Jonathan als Frage der modernen Exegese." *Bib* 80 (1999): 250-63.

Nitsche, Stefan Ark. *David gegen Goliath: die Geschichte der Geschichten einer Geschichte, zur fächerübergreifenden Rezeption einer biblischen Story*. ATM 4. Munich: Lit, 1998.

Nogalski, James. "Reading David in the Psalter: A Study in Liturgical Hermeneutics." *HBT* 23 (2001): 168-91.

Noll, K. L. "Deuteronomistic History or Deuteronomic Debate? (A Thought Experiment)." *JSOT* 31 (2007): 311-45.

————. *The Faces of David*. JSOTSup 242. Sheffield: Sheffield Academic, 1997.

Noll, Mark A., Nathan O. Hatch, and George M. Marsden, *The Search for Christian America*. Westchester, IL: Crossway, 1983.

Nolland, John. "The Purpose and Value of Commentaries." *JSNT* 29 (2007): 305-11.

North, Christopher. "The Religious Aspects of Hebrew Kingship." *ZAW* 50 (1932): 8-38.

Norton, David. *A History of the Bible as Literature*. 2 vols. Cambridge: Cambridge University Press, 1993.

Noth, Martin. *The Deuteronomistic History*. JSOTSup 15. Translated by J. Doull et al. Sheffield: JSOT, 1981.

Novak, David. "What Does Edith Stein Mean for Jews?" Pp. 146-66 in idem, *Talking with Christians: Musings of a Jewish Theologian*. Radical Traditions. Grand Rapids: Eerdmans, 2005.

O'Connor, Michael P. "War and Rebel Chants in the Former Prophets." Pp. 322-37 in *Fortunate the Eyes That See: Essays in Honor of David Noel Freedman in Celebration of His Seventieth Birthday*. Edited by Astrid B. Beck et al. Grand Rapids: Eerdmans, 1995.

O'Donovan, Oliver. *The Desire of Nations: Rediscovering the Roots of Political Theology*. Cambridge: Cambridge University Press, 1996.

O'Kane, Martin. "The Biblical King David and His Artistic and Literary Afterlives." *BibInt* 6 (1998): 313-47.

Oakley, Francis. *Kingship: The Politics of Enchantment*. Malden, MA: Blackwell, 2006.

Oakman, Douglas. "Biblical Hermeneutics — Marcion's Truth and a Developmental Perspective." Pp. 267-83 in *Ancient Israel: The Old Testament in Its Social Context*. Edited by Philip F. Esler. Minneapolis: Fortress, 2006.

Oesterley, W. O. E., and Theodore H. Robinson. *Hebrew Religion: Its Origin and Development*. New York: Macmillan, 1930.

Öhler, Markus, ed. *Alttestamentliche Gestalten im Neuen Testament: Beiträge zur Biblischen Theologie*. Darmstadt: Wissenschaftliche Buchgesellschaft, 1999.

Oiry, Béatrice. "Raconter le simultané: entre contraintes narratives et manipulations stratégiques; le exemple de 1 S 27–2 S 1." Pp. 381-96 in *L'intrigue dans le récit biblique: quatrième colloque international du RRENAB, Université Laval, Quebec, 29 Mai – 1ᵉʳ Juin 2008*. Edited by Anne Pasquier, Daniel Marguerat, and André Wénin. BETL 237. Leuven: Peeters, 2010.

Ollenburger, Ben C. "What Krister Stendahl 'Meant': A Normative Critique of 'Descriptive Biblical Theology.'" *HBT* 8 (1996): 61-98.

Olmo Lete, Gregorio del. "David's Farewell Oracle (2 Samuel xxiii 1-7): A Literary Analysis." *VT* 34 (1984): 414-37.

————. "Royal Aspects of the Ugaritic Cult." Pp. 51-66 in *Ritual and Sacrifice in the Ancient Near East: Proceedings of the International Conference organized by the Katholieke Uni-*

Bibliography

versiteit Leuven from the 17th to the 20th of April 1991. Orientalia Lovaniensia Analecta 55. Edited by Jan Quaegebeur. Leuven: Peeters, 1993.

Olson, Dennis T. "Buber, Kingship, and the Book of Judges: A Study of Judges 6–9 and 17–21." Pp. 209-21 in *David and Zion; Biblical Studies in Honor of J. J. M. Roberts.* Edited by Bernard F. Batto and Kathryn L. Roberts. Winona Lake: Eisenbrauns, 2004.

———. "Rediscovering Lost Treasure: Forgotten Preaching Texts of the Old Testament." *Journal for Preachers* 13 (1990): 2-10.

Olyan, Saul M. "Honor, Shame, and Covenant Relations in Ancient Israel and Its Environment." *JBL* 115 (1996): 201-18.

———. "'Surpassing the Love of Women': Another Look at 2 Samuel 1:26 and the Relationship of David and Jonathan." Pp. 7-16 in *Authorizing Marriage? Canon, Tradition, and Critique in the Blessing of Same-Sex Unions.* Edited by M. D. Jordan, M. T. Sweeney, and D. M. Mellott. Princeton University Press, 2006.

Orelli, Conrad von. *The Old Testament Prophecy of the Consummation of God's Kingdom, Traced in Its Historical Development.* Translated by J. S. Banks. Clark's Foreign Theological Library, New Series 22. Edinburgh: T & T Clark, 1885.

Osherow, Michele. *Biblical Women's Voices in Early Modern England.* Women and Gender in the Early Modern World. Burlington: Ashgate, 2009.

Otto, Eckart. "Tora und Charisma: Legitimation und Delegitimation des Königtums in 1 Samuel 8 – 2 Samuel 1 im Spiegel neuerer Literatur." *ZABR* 12 (2006): 225-44.

———. "Treueid und Gesetz: die Ursprünge des Deuteronomiums im Horizont neuassyrischen Vertragsrechts." *ZABR* 2 (1996): 1-52.

Ozick, Cynthia, "Hannah and Elkanah: Torah as the Matrix for Feminism." Pp. 88-93 in *Out of the Garden: Women Writers on the Bible.* Edited by Christina Büchmann and Celina Spiegel. New York: Fawcett Columbine, 1994.

Packer, James I. "An Evangelical View of Progressive Revelation." Pp. 143-58 in *Evangelical Roots.* Edited by Kenneth S. Kanzler. Nashville: Thomas Nelson, 1978.

Padgett, Alan G. and Patrick R. Kiefert, eds. *But Is It All True? The Bible and the Question of Truth.* Grand Rapids: Eerdmans, 2006.

Page, Hugh R. "The Dynamics of Scripturalization: The Ancient Near East." Pp. 55-61 in *Theorizing Scriptures: New Critical Orientations to a Cultural Phenomenon.* Edited by Vincent L. Wimbush. New Brunswick: Rutgers University Press, 2008.

Parker, Simon B. "Possession, Trance and Prophecy in Pre-exilic Israel. *VT* 28 (1978): 271-85.

———. "The Vow in Ugaritic and Israelite Narrative Literature." *UF* 11 (1979): 693-700.

Parks, Lewis A., and Bruce C. Birch, *Ducking Spears, Dancing Madly: A Biblical Model of Church Leadership.* Nashville: Abingdon, 2004.

Parry, Donald. W. "The Challenge of 4QSam^a and the Canon." Pp. 219-39 in *The Hebrew Bible and Qumran.* Edited by James H. Charlesworth. N. Richland Hills, TX: BIBAL, 2000.

———. "Hannah in the Presence of the Lord." Pp. 53-73 in *Archaeology of the Books of Samuel: The Entangling of the Textual and Literary History.* Edited by Philippe Hugo and Adrian Schenker. VTSup 132. Leiden: Brill, 2010.

———. "Unique Readings in 4QSam^a." Pp. 209-19 in *The Bible as Book: The Hebrew Bible and the Judaean Desert Discoveries.* Edited by Edward D. Herbert and Emanuel Tov. London: British Library, 2002.

Patrick, Dale. *Old Testament Law.* Atlanta: John Knox, 1985.

Paul, S. M. "1 Samuel 9,7: An Interview Fee." *Bib* 59 (1978): 542-44.

Pawlikowsky, John T. *The Challenge of the Holocaust for Christian Theology*. New York: Anti-Defamation League of B'nai B'rith, 1978.

Payne, D. F. "Estimates of the Character of David." *IBS* 6 (1984): 54-70.

Peckham, Brian. "The Deuteronomistic History of Saul." *ZAW* 97 (1985): 190-209.

Peetz, Melanie. *Abigajil, die Prophetin — mit Klugheit und Schönheit für Gewaltverzicht: eine exegetische Untersuchung zu 1 Sam 25*. FzB 116. Würzburg: Echter, 2008.

Peleg, Yaron. "Love at First Sight? David, Jonathan, and the Biblical Politics of Gender." *JSOT* 30 (2005): 171-189.

Pelland, G. "La figura di Samuele nella tradizione cristiana antica." Pp. 127-57 in *Samuele tra politica e fede: Atti del Seminario invernale, Sorrento, 17-20 febraio 1994*. Florence: Biblia, 1995.

Penchansky, David. *What Rough Beast? Images of God in the Hebrew Bible*. Louisville: Westminster John Knox, 1999.

Perdue, Leo G. "Is There Anyone Left of the House of Saul? Ambiguity and the Characterization of David in the Succession Narrative." *JSOT* 30 (1984): 67-84.

Petersen, David L. "Portraits of David Canonical and Otherwise." *Interp* 40 (1986): 130-42.

Peterson, Eugene H. *First and Second Samuel*. Westminster Bible Companion. Louisville: Westminster John Knox, 1999.

————. *Leap Over a Wall: Earthy Spirituality for Everyday Christians*. San Francisco: HarperCollins, 1997.

Pietersma, Albert, and Benjamin G. Wright, eds. *A New English Translation of the Septuagint*. Oxford: Oxford University Press, 2007.

Pinksy, Robert. *The Life of David*. Jewish Encounters. New York: Schocken, 2005.

Pisano, Stephen. *Additions or Omissions in the Books of Samuel: The Significant Pluses and Minuses in the Massoretic, LXX and Qumran Texts*. OBO 57. Göttingen: Vandenhoeck & Ruprecht, 1984.

Placher, William C. *The Triune God: An Essay in Postliberal Theology*. Louisville: Westminster John Knox, 2007.

Polykala, Kenneth. "Images of David in Early Judaism." Pp. 1.33-46 in *Of Scribes and Sages: Early Jewish Interpretation and Transmission of Scripture*. Edited by Craig A. Evans. 2 Vols. LSTS 50, 51. London: T & T Clark, 2004.

Polzin, Robert. "1 Samuel: Biblical Studies and the Humanities." *Religious Studies Review* 15.4 (October, 1989): 297-306.

————. *David and the Deuteronomist: A Literary Study of the Deuteronomic History; Part Three: 2 Samuel*. ISBL. Bloomington: Indiana University Press, 1993.

————. "On Taking Renewal Seriously: 1 Sam 11:1-15." Pp. 493-507 in *Ascribe to the Lord: Biblical and Other Essays in Memory of Peter C. Craigie*. Edited by Lyle M. Eslinger and Glen Taylor. JSOTSup 67. Sheffield: JSOT, 1988.

————. *Samuel and the Deuteronomist: A Literary Study of the Deuteronomic History; Part Two: 1 Samuel*. ISBL. Bloomington: Indiana University Press, 1989.

Porter, J. R. "Ancient Israel." Pp. 191-214 in *Oracles and Divination*. Edited by Michael Loewe and Carmen Blacker. Boulder: Shambhala, 1981.

Preston, Thomas R. "The Heroism of King Saul: Patterns of Meaning in the Narrative of Early Kingship." *JSOT* 24 (1982): 27-46.

Prothero, Stephen. *Religious Literacy: What Every American Needs to Know and Doesn't*. San Francisco: HarperCollins, 2007.

Bibliography

Prouser, Ora Horn. "Suited to the Throne: The Symbolic Use of Clothing in the David and Saul Narratives." *JSOT* 71 (1996): 27-37.

Provan, Iain W. *Hezekiah and the Book of Kings.* BZAW 172. Berlin: de Gruyter, 1988.

Pseudo-Jerome. *Quaestiones on the Book of Samuel.* Edited by Avrom Saltman. Studia Post-Biblica 26. Leiden: Brill, 1975.

Pury, Albert de, and Thomas Römer, eds. *Die sogenannte Thronfolgegeschichte Davids: neue Einsichten und Anfragen.* OBO 176. Göttingen: Vandenhoeck & Ruprecht, 2000.

Rabinowitz, Peter. "Reading Beginnings and Endings." Pp. 300-17 in *Narrative Dynamics: Essays on Time, Plot, Closure, and Frames.* Edited by Brian Richardson. Columbus: Ohio State University Press, 2002.

Rad, Gerhard von. *Holy War in Ancient Israel.* Translated by Marva J. Dawn. Grand Rapids: Eerdmans, 1991.

—————. *The Message of the Prophets.* New York: Harper & Row, 1967.

—————. *Old Testament Theology.* 2 vols. Translated by D. M. G. Stalker. New York: Harper & Row, 1962.

—————. *Studies in Deuteronomy.* SBT. Translated by David Stalker. London: SCM, 1953.

Rahner, Karl. *The Trinity.* Translated by J. Donceel. New York: Crossroad, 1999.

Ramsey, George W. *The Quest for the Historical Israel.* Atlanta: John Knox, 1981.

Ramond, Sophie. *Leçon de non-violence pour David: une analyse narrative et littéraire de 1 Samuel 24-26.* Lire la Bible 146. Paris: Cerf, 2007.

Raphael, Rebecca. "Madly Disobedient: The Representation of Madness in Handel's Oratorio *Saul.*" *PRS* 34 (2007) : 7-21.

Rapp, Claudia. "Comparison, Paradigm and the Case of Moses in Panegyric and Hagiography." Pp. 277-98 in *The Propaganda of Power: The Role of Panegyric in Late Antiquity.* Edited by Mary Whitby. Leiden: Brill, 1998.

—————. "Old Testament Models for Emperors in Early Byzantium." Pp. 175-97 in *The Old Testament in Byzantium.* Edited by Paul Magdalino and Robert Nelson. Dumbarton Oaks Byzantine Symposia and Colloquia. Washington, DC: Dumbarton Oaks Research Library and Collection, 2010.

Redford, Donald B. *Egypt, Canaan and Israel in Ancient Times.* Princeton: Princeton University Press, 1992.

Reemts, Christiana. *Samuel: mit Texten und deutscher Übersetzung von Origenes 1. und 5. Samuelhomilie und Ambrosiaster, Quaestio 27 und 46.* Biblische Gestalten bei den Kirchenvätern. Münster: Aschendorff, 2009.

Regev, Eyal. "Priestly Dynamic Holiness and Deuteronomic Static Holiness." *VT* 51 (2001): 243-61.

Reid, J. K. S. *The Authority of Scripture: A Study of the Reformation and Post-Reformation Understanding of the Bible.* London: Methuen & Co., 1957.

Reimer, David J. "An Overlooked Term in Old Testament Theology — Perhaps." Pp. 325-46 in *Covenant as Context: Essays in Honour of E. W. Nicholson.* Edited by A. D. H. Mayes and R. B. Salters. Oxford: Oxford University Press, 2003.

Reindl, Joseph. *Das Angesicht Gottes im Sprachgebrauch des Alten Testaments.* ETS 25. Leipzig: St. Benno, 1970.

Reinhartz, Adele. "Anonymity and Character in the Books of Samuel." *Semeia* 63 (1993): 117-41.

—————. *"Why Ask My Name?" Anonymity and Identity in Biblical Narrative.* Oxford: Oxford University Press, 1998.

Reis, Pamela Tamarkin. "Collusion at Nob: A New Reading of 1 Samuel 21–22." *JSOT* 61 (1994): 59-73.

———. *Reading the Lines: A Fresh Look at the Hebrew Bible.* Peabody, MA: Hendrickson, 2002.

Rendtorff, Rolf. "The Birth of the Deliverer: 'The Childhood of Samuel' Story in Its Literary Framework." Pp. 135-45 in idem, *Canon and Theology: Overtures to an Old Testament Theology.* Minneapolis: Fortress, 1993.

———. *The Problem of the Process of Transmission in the Pentateuch.* JSOTSup 89. Sheffield: JSOT, 1990.

———. "The Psalms of David: David in the Psalms." Pp. 53-64 in *The Book of Psalms: Composition and Reception.* Edited by Peter W. Flint and Patrick D. Miller, Jr. VTSup 99. Leiden: Brill, 2005.

———. "Samuel the Prophet: A Link between Moses and the Kings." Pp. 27-36 in *The Quest for Context and Meaning: Studies in Biblical Intertextuality in Honor of James A. Sanders.* Edited by Craig A. Evans and Shemaryahu Talmon. Leiden: Brill, 1997.

Richardson, Alan. "The Rise of Modern Biblical Scholarship and Recent Discussion of the Authority of the Bible." Pp. 294-338 in *The Cambridge History of the Bible: Vol. 3, The West from the Reformation to the Present Day.* Edited by S. L. Greenslade. Cambridge: Cambridge University Press, 1963.

Richey, Russell E., and Donald G. Jones, eds. *American Civil Religion.* New York: Harper & Row, 1974.

Richter, Sandra L. *The Deuteronomistic History and the Name Theology:* l^e šakkēn $š^e$mô šām *in the Bible and the Ancient Near East.* BZAW 318. Berlin: de Gruyter, 2002.

Ricoeur, Paul. "The Canon between the Text and the Community." Pp. 7-26 in *Philosophical Hermeneutics and Biblical Exegesis.* Edited by Petr Pokorný and Jan Roskovec. WUNT 153. Tübingen: Mohr Siebeck, 2002.

———. *Essays on Biblical Interpretation.* Edited by Lewis S. Mudge. Philadelphia: Fortress, 1980.

———. "The Hermeneutical Function of Distanciation." Pp. 131-44 in idem, *Hermeneutics and the Human Sciences.* Edited by John B. Thompson. Cambridge: Cambridge University Press, 1981.

———. *Hermeneutics and the Human Sciences.* Edited by John B. Thompson. Cambridge: Cambridge University Press, 1981.

———. "What is a Text? Explanation and Interpretation." Pp. 233-46 in *Hermeneutical Inquiry: Volume I, The Interpretation of Texts.* Edited by David E. Klemm. AARSR. Atlanta: Scholars, 1986.

Riede, Peter. "David und der Floh: Tiere und Tervergleiche in den Samuelbüchern." *BN* 77 (1995): 86-117.

Roberts, J. J. M. "In Defense of the Monarchy: The Contribution of Israelite Kingship to Biblical Theology." Pp. 377-96 in *Ancient Israelite Religion: Essays in Honor of Frank Moore Cross.* Edited by Patrick D. Miller, Jr., Paul D. Hanson, and S. Dean McBride. Philadelphia: Fortress, 1987.

———. "The Legal Basis for Saul's Slaughter of the Priests of Nob (1 Samuel 21–22)." *JNSL* 25 (1999): 21-29.

Robinson, Bernard P. *Israel's Mysterious God: An Analysis of Some Old Testament Narratives.* Newcastle upon Tyne: Grevatt and Grevatt, 1986.

Robinson, Gnana. *Let Us Be Like the Nations: A Commentary on the Books of 1 and 2 Samuel.* International Theological Commentary. Grand Rapids: Eerdmans, 1993.

Bibliography

Robinson, H. Wheeler. "Hebrew Sacrifice and Prophetic Symbolism." *JTS* 43 (1942): 131-39.

———. "Prophetic Symbolism." Pp. 1-17 in *Old Testament Essays: Papers Read before the Society for Old Testament Study at its Eighteenth Meeting, Held at Keble College, Oxford, September 27th to 30th, 1927.* Edited by T. H. Robinson. London: C. Griffiths, 1927.

Rofé, Alexander. "4QMidrash Samuel? — Observations Concerning the Character of 4QSam^a." *Textus* 19 (1998): 63-74.

———. "The Acts of Nahash according to 4QSam^a." *IEJ* 32 (1982): 129-33.

———. "The Battle of David and Goliath." Pp. 117-51 in *Judaic Perspectives on Ancient Israel.* Edited by J. Neusner. Philadelphia: Fortress, 1987.

Rogerson, John W. "Die Bibel lesen wie jedes andere Buch? Auseinandersetzungen um die Autorität der Bibel vom 18. Jahrhundert an bis heute." Pp. 211-34 in *Biblischer Text und theologische Theoriebildung.* Edited by Stephen Chapman, Christine Helmer, and Christof Landmesser. BTS 44. Neukirchen–Vluyn: Neukirchener, 2001.

———. "Progressive Revelation: Its History and Value as a Key to Old Testament Interpretation." *Epworth Review* 9 (1982): 73-86.

Römer, Thomas C. *The So-Called Deuteronomistic History: A Sociological, Historical and Literary Introduction.* New York: T & T Clark, 2005.

———. "Transformations in Deuteronomistic Biblical Historiography: On 'Book-Finding' and Other Literary Strategies." *ZAW* 109 (1997): 1-11.

Römer, Thomas C., and Albert de Pury. "Deuteronomistic Historiography (DH): History of Research and Debated Issues." Pp. 24-141 in *Israel Constructs its History: Deuteronomistic Historiography in Recent Research.* Edited by Albert de Pury, Thomas Römer, and Jean-Daniel Macchi. JSOTSup 306. Sheffield: Sheffield Academic, 2000.

Römer, Thomas and Jan Rückl. "Jesus, Son of Joseph and Son of David, in the Gospels." Pp. 65-81 in *The Torah in the New Testament: Papers Delivered at the Manchester–Lausanne Seminar of June 2008.* Edited by Michael Tait and Peter Oakes. London: T & T Clark, 2009.

Rooke, Deborah W. "Kingship as Priesthood: The Relationship between the High Priesthood and the Monarchy." Pp. 187-208 in *King and Messiah in Israel and the Ancient Near East: Proceedings of the Oxford Old Testament Seminar.* Edited by John Day. JSOTSup 270. Sheffield Academic, 1998.

———. *Zadok's Heirs: The Role and Development of the High Priesthood in Ancient Israel.* OTM. Oxford: Oxford University Press, 2012.

Rooy, Harry F. van. "Prophetic Utterances in Narrative Texts, with Reference to 1 Samuel 2:27-36." *OTE* 3 (1990): 203-18.

Rose, Ashley S. "The 'Principles' of Divine Election: Wisdom in 1 Samuel 16." Pp. 43-67 in *Rhetorical Criticism: Essays in Honor of James Muilenburg.* Edited by Jared J. Jackson and Martin Kessler. Pittsburgh Theological Monograph Series 1. Pittsburgh: Pickwick, 1974.

Rösel, H. N. "Does a Comprehensive 'Leitmotiv' Exist in the Deuteronomistic History?" Pp. 195-211 in *The Future of the Detueronomistic History.* Edited by Thomas Römer. BETL 147. Leuven: Leuven University Press, 2000.

Rosenberg, A. J., ed. *Samuel I: A New English Translation of the Text and Rashi, with a Commentary Digest.* New York: Judaica, 1988.

Rosenberg, Joel. "1 and 2 Samuel." Pp. 122-45 in *The Literary Guide to the Bible.* Edited by Robert Alter and Frank Kermode. Cambridge, MA: Harvard University Press, 1987.

Rosenzweig, Franz. *The Star of Redemption.* Translated by Barbara E. Galli. Madison: University of Wisconsin Press, 2005.

Rost, Leonhard. "Die Überlieferung von der Thronnachfolge Davids." Pp. 119-253 in idem, *Das kleine Credo und andere Studien zum Alten Testament*. Heidelberg: Quelle & Meyer, 1965.

Rowe, C. Kavin, and Richard B. Hays. "What Is a Theological Commentary?" *ProEccl* 16 (2007): 26-32.

Rowe, Jonathan Y. *Michal's Moral Dilemma: A Literary, Anthropological and Ethical Interpretation*. LHBOTS 533. New York: T & T Clark, 2011.

Rowley, H. H. *The Missionary Messsage of the Old Testament*. London: Carey, 1945.

————. *Worship in Ancient Israel*. London: SPCK, 1967.

Rudman, Dominic. "The Commissioning Stories of Saul and David as Theological Allegory." *VT* 50 (2000): 519-30.

Rudnig, Thilo Alexander. *Davids Thron: redaktionskritische Studien zur "Geschichte von Thronnachfolge Davids."* BZAW 358. Berlin: de Gruyter, 2006.

Rüterswörden, Udo. "Die Liebe zu Gott im Deuteronomium." Pp. 229-38 in *Die Deuteronomistichen Geschichtswerke: redaktions- und religionsgeschichtliche Perspektiven zur "Deuteronomismus" — Diskussion in Tora und Vorderen Propheten*. BZAW 365. Edited by Markus Witte et al. Berlin: de Gruyter, 2006.

————. *Martin Noth — aus der Sicht der heutigen Forschung*. BTS 58. Neukirchen–Vluyn: Neukirchener, 2004.

Ryken, Leland. *Windows to the World: Literature in Christian Perspective*. Eugene: Wipf & Stock, 2000.

————. *Words of Delight: A Literary Introduction to the Bible*. Grand Rapids: Baker, 1987.

Sanders, E. P. *Jesus and Judaism*. Philadelphia: Fortress, 1985.

————. *Paul and Palestinian Judaism: A Comparison of Patterns of Religion*. Philadelphia: Fortress, 1977.

Sandmel, Samuel. "The Haggadah within Scripture." *JBL* 80 (1961): 105-22.

Sands, Kathleen. *Escape from Paradise: Evil and Tragedy in Feminist Theology*. Minneapolis: Fortress, 1994.

Sasson, Jack M. "The Eyes of Eli: An Essay in Motif Accretion." Pp. 171-90 in *Inspired Speech: Prophecy in the Ancient Near East; Essays in Honor of Herbert B. Huffmon*. Edited by John Kaltner and Louis Stulman. London: T & T Clark, 2004.

Satterthwaite, Philip E. "David in the Books of Samuel: A Messianic Hope?" Pp. 41-65 in *The Lord's Anointed: Interpretation of Old Testament Messianic Texts*. Edited by Philip E. Satterthwaite, Richard S. Hess, and Gordon J. Wenham. Tyndale House Studies. Carlisle: Paternoster, 1995.

————. "'No King in Israel': Narrative Criticism and Judges 17–21." *TynBul* 49 (1993): 75-88.

Schäfer, Rolf. *Die Bibelauslegung in der Geschichte der Kirche*. Studienbücher Theologie: Kirchen- und Dogmengeschichte. Gütersloh: Mohn, 1980.

Schäfer-Lichtenberger, Christa, ed. *Die Samuelbücher und die Deuteronomisten*. BWANT 188. Stuttgart: Kohlhammer, 2010.

————. "Überlegungen zum Aufbau und zur Entstehung der Samuelbücher." Pp. 103-16 in *"Basel und Babel": Collected Communications to the XVIIth Congress of the International Organization for the Study of the Old Testament, Basel 2001*. Edited by Matthias Augustin and Hermann Michael Niemann. BEATAJ 51. Frankfurt: Lang, 2004.

Scheffler, Eben. "Saving Saul from the Deuteronomist." Pp. 263-71 in *Past, Present, Future: The Deuteronomistic History and the Prophets*. Edited by Johannes C. de Moor and Harry F. Van Rooy. OTS 44. Leiden: Brill, 2000.

Bibliography

Schenker, Adrian. *Der Mächtige im Schmelzofen des Mitleids: eine Interpretation von 2 Sam 24.* OBO 42. Göttingen: Vandenhoeck & Ruprecht, 1982.

Schicklberger, Franz. *Die Ladeerzählung des ersten Samuel-Buches: eine literaturwissenschaftliche und theologiegeschichtliche Untersuchung.* FzB 7. Würzburg: Echter, 1973.

Schiffman, Lawrence H. "'Memory and Manuscript': Books, Scrolls, and the Tradition of the Qumran Texts." Pp. 133-50 in *New Perspectives on Old Texts: Proceedings of the Tenth International Symposium of the Orion Center for the Study of the Dead Sea Scrolls and Associated Literature, 9–11 January, 2005.* Edited by Esther G. Chazon and Betsy Halpern-Amaru, with Ruth A. Clements. STDJ. Leiden: Brill, 2010.

Schipper, Jeremy. "Disabling Israelite Leadership: 2 Samuel 6:23 and Other Images of Disability in the Deuteronomistic History." Pp. 103-13 in *This Abled Body: Rethinking Disabilities in Biblical Studies.* Edited by Hector Avalos, Sarah J. Melcher, and Jeremy Schipper. SBLSemS 55. Atlanta: Society of Biblical Literature, 2007.

Schmid, Hans Heinrich. *Altorientalische Welt in der alttestamentlichen Theologie.* Zurich: Theologischer Verlag, 1974.

———. *Gerechtigkeit als Weltordnung: Hintergrund und Geschichte des alttestamentlichen Gerechtigkeitsbegriffes.* Beiträge zur historischen Theologie 40. Tübingen: Mohr Siebeck, 1968.

Schmidt, Brian B. "The 'Witch' of En-Dor." Pp. 111-29 in *Ancient Magic and Ritual Power.* Edited by Marvin Meyer and Paul Mirecki. Religions in the Graeco-Roman World 129. Leiden: Brill, 1995.

Schmidt, Ludwig. *Menschlicher Erfolg und Jahwes Initiative: Studien zu Tradition, Interpretation und Historie in Überlieferungen von Gideon, Saul und David.* WMANT 38. Neukirchen–Vluyn: Neukirchener, 1970.

Schmidt, Werner H. *Königtum Gottes in Ugarit und Israel: zur Herkunft der Königsprädikation Jahwes.* BZAW 80. Berlin: Töpelmann, 1961.

———. *Old Testament Introduction.* 2nd ed. Berlin: de Gruyter, 1999.

Schökel, Luis Alonso. "Narrative Art in Joshua–Judges–Samuel–Kings." Pp. 255-78 in *Israel's Past in Present Research: Essays on Ancient Israelite Historiography.* Edited by V. Philips Long. SBTS 7. Winona Lake: Eisenbrauns, 1999. Pp. 255-78.

Schramm, Percy Ernest. "Das Alte und das Neue Testament in der Stattslehre und Staatssymbolik das Mittelalters." Pp. 229-55 in *La Bibbia nell' Alto Medioevo: 26 Aprile – 2 Maggio 1962.* Spoleto: Presso la Sede del Centro, 1963.

———. *Kaiser, Könige und Päpste: Gesammelte Aufsätze zur Geschichte des Mittelalters.* 4 vols. in 5. Stuttgart: Anton Hiersemann, 1968.

Schroer, Silvia. *Die Samuelbücher.* Neuer Stuttgarter Kommentar — Altes Testament. Stuttgart: Katholisches Bibelwerk, 1992.

Schroer, Silvia, and Thomas Staubli. "Saul, David and Jonathan: The Story of a Triangle? A Contribution to the Issue of Homosexuality in the First Testament." Pp. 22-36 in *Samuel and Kings.* Edited by Althalya Brenner. FCB, Second Series 7. Sheffield: Sheffield Academic, 2000.

Schulz, Alfons. "Narrative Art in the Books of Samuel." Pp. 119-70 in idem, *Narrative and Novella in Samuel.* Edited by David M. Gunn. Sheffield: Almond, 1991.

Schumacher, E. F. *Small is Beautiful: Economics as if People Mattered.* New York: Harper & Row, 1973.

Schwáb, Zoltán. "Mind the Gap: The Impact of Wolfgang Iser's Reader-Response Criticism on Biblical Studies — A Critical Assessment." *Literature and Theology* 17 (2003): 170-81.

Scott, David. "Tragedy's Time: Postemancipation Futures Past and Present." Pp. 199-217 in *Rethinking Tragedy*. Edited by Rita Felski. Baltimore: Johns Hopkins University Press, 2008.

Seebass, Horst. *David, Saul und das Wesen des biblischen Glaubens*. Neukirchen–Vluyn: Neukirchener, 1980.

Seidl, Theodor. "David statt Saul: göttliche Legitimation und menschliche Kompetenz des Königs als Motive der Redaktion von 1 Sam 16–18." *ZAW* 98 (1986): 39-55.

Sellars, Dawn Maria. "An Obedient Servant? The Reign of King Saul (1 Samuel 13–15) Reassessed." *JSOT* 35 (2011): 317-38.

Sewall, R. B. *The Vision of Tragedy*. New Haven: Yale University Press, 1959.

Shaffer, Peter. *Amadeus*. New York: French, 1981.

Shapira, Amnon. "'In Those Days There Was No King in Israel; Everyone Did as He Pleased': Was There Really Anarchy?" Pp. 125-41 in *Proceedings of the Twelfth World Congress of Jewish Studies, July 29–Aug 5, 1997*. Edited by Ron Margolin. Jerusalem: World Union of Jewish Studies, 1999.

Shaviv, Shemuel. "Nābî' and Nāgîd in 1 Samuel ix 1–x 16." *VT* 34 (1984): 108-13.

Shemesh, Yael. "David in the Service of King Achish of Gath: Renegade to His People or a Fifth Column in the Philistine Army?" *VT* 57 (2007): 73-90.

———. "Measure for Measure in the David Stories." *SJOT* 17 (2003): 89-109.

———. "Suicide in the Bible." *JBQ* 37 (2009): 157-68.

Sheppard, Gerald T. "The Book of Isaiah: Competing Structures according to a Late Modern Description of Its Shape and Scope." Pp. 549-82 in *Society of Biblical Literature 1992 Seminar Papers*. Edited by Eugene H. Loving. Atlanta: Scholars, 1992.

———. *Wisdom as a Hermeneutical Construct*. BZAW 151. Berlin: de Gruyter, 1980.

Shields, Mary. "A Feast Fit for a King: Food and Drink in the Abigail Story." Pp. 38-54 in *The Fate of King David: The Past and Present of a Biblical Icon*. Edited by Tod Linafelt, Claudia V. Camp, and Timothy Beal. LHBOTS 500. New York: T & T Clark, 2010.

Short, J. Randall. *The Surprising Election and Confirmation of King David*. HTS 63. Cambridge, MA: Harvard University Press, 2010.

Siegele-Wenschkewitz, Leonore, ed. *Christlicher Antijudaismus und Antisemitismus: theologische und kirchliche Programme Deutscher Christen*. Arnoldshainer Texte 85. Frankfurt: Haag & Herchen, 1994.

Silber, David. "Anarchy and Monarchy Part One: Samuel the Prophet King (1 Samuel 8–13)." Pp. 37-54 in *Tanakh Companion to the Book of Samuel*. Edited by Nathaniel Helfgot. Teaneck, NJ: Ben Yehuda, 2006.

———. "The Birth of Samuel and the Birth of Kingship (1 Sam 1:1–2:10)." Pp. 1-22 in *Tanakh Companion to the Book of Samuel*. Edited by Nathaniel Helfgot. Teaneck, NJ: Ben Yehuda, 2006.

Simon, László T. *Identity and Identification: An Exegetical and Theological Study of 2 Samuel 21–24*. Tesi Gregoriana Serie Theologia 64. Rome: Gregorian University Press, 2000.

Simon, Uriel. "1 Samuel 28:3-25: The Stern Prophet and the Kind Witch." Pp. 281-87 in *Wünschet Jerusalem Frieden: Collected Communications to the XIIth Congress of the International Organization for the Study of the Old Testament, Jerusalem 1986*. Edited by Mattias Augustin and Klaus-Dietrich Schunck. BEATAJ 13. Frankfurt: Lang, 1988.

———. "Minor Characters in Biblical Narrative." *JSOT* 46 (1990): 11-19.

———. "Saul at Endor." Pp. 73-92 in idem, *Reading Prophetic Narratives*. ISBL. Bloomington: Indiana University Press, 1997.

Bibliography

Ska, Jean-Louis. *"Our Fathers Have Told Us": Introduction to the Analysis of Hebrew Narrative.* SubBi 13. Rome: Pontifical Biblical Institute, 2000.

Skinner, John. *Prophecy and Religion.* Cambridge: Cambridge University Press, 1922.

Smelik, Klaas A. D. "The Ark Narrative Reconsidered." Pp. 128-44 in *New Avenues in the Study of the Old Testament.* Edited by A. S. van der Woude. OTS 25. Leiden: Brill, 1989.

———. *Converting the Past: Studies in Ancient Israelite and Moabite Historiography.* OTS 28. Leiden: Brill, 1992.

———. "The Witch of Endor: 1 Samuel 28 in Rabbinic and Christian Exegesis Till 800 A. D." *VigChr* 33 (1977): 160-79.

Smith, Barbara Hernstein. *Poetic Closure: A Study of How Poems End.* Chicago: University of Chicago Press, 1968.

Smith, Duane E. "'Pisser against a Wall': Echo of Divination in Biblical Hebrew." *CBQ* 72 (2010): 699-717.

Smith, Henry Preserved. *A Critical and Exegetical Commentary on the Books of Samuel.* ICC 9. Edinburgh: T & T Clark, 1899.

Smith, J. M. P. "The Character of David," *JBL* 52 (1933): 1-11.

Smith, Wilfred Cantwell. *What Is Scripture?* Minneapolis: Fortress, 1993.

Smith, William Robertson. *Religion of the Semites.* Edited by Robert A. Segal. Repr. New Brunswick: Transaction, 2002.

Smith-Christopher, Daniel L. "Gideon at Thermopylae? On the Militarization of Miracle in Biblical Narrative and 'Battle Maps.'" Pp. 197-212 in *Writing and Reading War: Rhetoric, Gender, and Ethics in Biblical and Modern Contexts.* Edited by Brad E. Kelle and Frank Ritchel Ames. Atlanta: Society of Biblical Literature, 2008.

Smolar, Leivy, and Moses Aberbach. *Studies in Targum Jonathan to the Prophets and Targum Jonathan to the Prophets, by Pinkohs Churgin.* New York: KTAV; Baltimore: Baltimore Hebrew College, 1983.

Soden, Wolfram von. *Herrscher im alten Orient.* Berlin: Springer, 1954.

Solomon, Nathan. "David and Jonathan in Iraq." Pp. 21-32 in *Probing the Frontiers of Biblical Studies.* Edited by J. Harold Ellens and John T. Greene. PTMS 111. Eugene: Pickwick, 2009.

Soloveitchik, Joseph Dov. *Worship of the Heart: Essays on Jewish Prayer.* Edited by Shalom Carmy. New York: Toras Horav Foundation, 2003.

Somerset, FitzRoy Richard, Lord Raglan. *The Hero: A Study in Tradition, Myth, and Drama.* The Thinker's Library 133. London: Watts and Co., 1936.

Sommer, Benjamin D. "The Scroll of Isaiah as Jewish Scripture, Or, Why Jews Don't Read Books." Pp. 225-42 in *Society of Biblical Literature 1996 Seminar Papers.* Atlanta: Scholars, 1996. Pp. 225-42.

Sommer, Benjamin D., ed. *Jewish Concepts of Scripture: A Comparative Introduction.* New York: New York University Press, 2012.

Soulen, R. Kendall. *The God of Israel and Christian Theology.* Minneapolis: Fortress, 1996.

Sparks, Kenton L. *God's Word in Human Words: An Evangelical Appropriation of Critical Biblical Scholarship.* Grand Rapids: Baker, 2008.

Spieckermann, Hermann. "Das neue Bild der Religionsgeschichte Israels: eine Herausfordering der Theologie?" *ZTK* 105 (2008): 259-80.

Spina, Frank Anthony. "Eli's Seat: The Transition from Priest to Prophet in 1 Samuel 1-4." *JSOT* 62 (1994): 67-75.

———. "Moses and Joshua: Servants of the Lord as Purveyors of the Word." Pp. 65-92 in

Go Figure! Figuration in Biblical Interpretation. Edited by Stanley D. Walters. PTMS 81. Eugene: Pickwick, 2008.

―――. "A Prophet's 'Pregnant Pause': Samuel's Silence in the Ark Narrative (1 Samuel 4:1–7:2)." *HBT* 13 (1991): 59-73.

Staalduine-Sulman, Eveline van. *The Targum of Samuel.* SAIS 1. Leiden: Brill, 2002.

Stähli, Hans Peter. *Knabe – Jüngling – Knecht: Untersuchungen zum Begriff* נער *im Alten Testament.* BBET 7. Frankfurt: Lang, 1978.

Stansell, Gary. "Honor and Shame in the David Narratives." Pp. 94-114 in *Was ist der Mensch? Beiträge zur Anthropologie des Alten Testaments; Hans Walter Wolff zum 80. Geburtstag.* Edited by Frank Crüsemann, Christof Hardmeier, and Rainer Kessler. Munich: Kaiser, 1992.

―――. "'You've Got a Friend': Friendship in the House of Saul." Pp. 210-27 in *Where the Wild Ox Roams: Biblical Essays in Honour of Norman C. Habel.* Edited by Alan H. Cadwallader with Peter L. Trudinger. Sheffield: Sheffield Phoenix, 2012.

Stanton, Michael N. "Hobbits." Pp. 280-82 in *J. R. R. Tolkien Encyclopedia: Scholarship and Critical Assessment.* Edited by Michael D. C. Drout. London: Routledge, 2007.

Stark, Thom. *The Human Faces of God: What Scripture Reveals When It Gets God Wrong (and Why Inerrancy Tries to Hide It).* Eugene: Wipf & Stock, 2011.

Steger, Hugo. *David Rex et Propheta: König David als vorbildliche Verkörperung des Herrschers und Dichters im Mittelalter, nach Bilddarstellungen des 8.–12. Jahrhunderts.* EBSK 6. Nuremberg: Hans Carl, 1961.

Stein, Peter. "'Und man berichtete Saul . . .': Text- und literarkritische Untersuchungen zu 1 Samuelis 24 und 25." *BN* 90 (1997): 46-66.

Steinberg, Julius, and Timothy J. Stone, with Rachel Stone, eds. *The Shape of the Writings.* Siphrut 16. Winona Lake: Eisenbrauns, 2015.

Steiner, George. *The Death of Tragedy.* New York: Knopf, 1961.

―――. "The Good Books." *The New Yorker* (January 11, 1988): 94-98 = *Religion & Intellectual Life* 6 (2006): 9-16.

Steinmetz, David. "Uncovering a Second Narrative: Detective Fiction and the Construction of Historical Method." Pp. 54-65 in *The Art of Reading Scripture.* Edited by Ellen F. Davis and Richard B. Hays. Grand Rapids: Eerdmans, 2003.

Steins, Georg. "Geschichte, die im Rahmen bleibt: kanonische Beobachtungen an 1 Sam 2 und 2 Sam 22f." Pp. 198-211 in *Der Bibelkanon in der Bibelauslegung: Methodenreflexionen und Beispielexegesen.* Edited by Egbert Ballhorn and Georg Steins. Stuttgart: Kohlhammer, 2007.

Stendahl, Krister. "Biblical Theology, Contemporary." *IDB* 1:418-32. Edited by George Arthur Buttrick. 4 Vols. Nashville: Abingdon, 1962.

Stern, Philip D. "1 Samuel 15: Towards an Ancient View of the War-Ḥerem." *UF* 21 (1989): 413-20.

―――. *The Biblical Ḥerem: A Window on Israel's Religious Experience.* BJS 211. Atlanta: Scholars, 1991.

Sternberg, Meir. "The Bible's Art of Persuasion: Ideology, Rhetoric, and Poetics in Saul's Fall." *HUCA* 54 (1983): 45-82.

―――. *The Poetics of Biblical Narrative: Ideological Literature and the Drama of Reading.* ISBL. Bloomington: Indiana University Press, 1985.

―――. "Telling in Time (III): Chronology, Estrangement, and Stories of Literary History." *Poetics Today* 27 (2006): 125-235.

————. "Time and Space in Biblical (Hi)story Telling: The Grand Chronology." Pp. 81-145 in *The Book and the Text: The Bible and Literary Theory*. Edited by Regina M. Schwartz. Cambridge, MA: Blackwell, 1990.

Steussy, Marti J. *David: Biblical Portraits of Power*. Studies on Personalities of the Old Testament. Columbia: University of South Carolina Press, 1999.

————. "The Problematic God of Samuel." Pp. 127-61 in *Shall Not the Judge of All the Earth Do What is Right? Studies on the Nature of God in Tribute to James L. Crenshaw*. Edited by David L. Penchansky and Paul L. Redditt. Winona Lake: Eisenbrauns, 2000.

————. *Samuel and His God*. Studies on Personalities of the Old Testament. Columbia: University of South Carolina Press, 2010.

Stevenson, Robert Louis. *The Works of Robert Louis Stevenson*. 25 vols. Edited by Andrew Lang. Swanston Edition. London: Chatto & Windus, 1912.

Stipp, Hermann-Josef, ed., *Das deuteronomistische Geschichtswerk*. Österreichische biblische Studien 39. Frankfurt: Lang, 2011.

Stoebe, Hans-Joachim. "David und Mikal: Überlegungen zur Jugendgeschichte Davids." Pp. 224-43 in *Von Ugarit nach Qumran: Beiträge zur alttestamentlichen und altorientalischen Forschung. Festschrift für O. Eissfeldt*. BZAW 77. Edited by Johannes Hempel and Leonhard Rost. Berlin: Töpelmann, 1958 = Pp. 91-110 in *Geschichte, Schicksal, Schuld und Glaube*. Athenäums Monografien, Theologie 72. Frankfurt: Athenäum, 1989.

————. *Das erste Buch Samuelis*. KAT 8. Gütersloh: Mohn, 1973.

————. "Gedanken zur Heldensage in den Samuelbüchern." Pp. 208-18 in *Das ferne und das nahe Wort: Festschrift Leonhard Rost*. BZAW 105. Edited by Fritz Maass. Berlin: de Gruyter, 1967.

————. "Überlegungen zur Exegese historischer Texte: dargestellt an den Samuelisbüchern." *TZ* 45 (1989): 290-314.

Stone, Ken. "1 and 2 Samuel." Pp. 195-221 in *The Queer Bible Commentary*. Edited by Deryn Guest et al. London: SCM, 2006.

Stoneman, Richard, ed. *Alexander the Great: A Life of the Conqueror*. London: Taurus, 2012.

Stott, Katherine. "Herodotus and the Old Testament: A Comparative Reading of the Ascendancy Stories of King Cyrus and David." *SJOT* 16 (2002): 52-78.

Stout, Janis P. *Strategies of Reticence: Silence and Meaning in the Works of Jane Austen, Willa Cather, Katherine Anne Porter, and Joan Didion*. Charlottesville: University Press of Virginia, 1990.

Stout, Jeffrey. "What is the Meaning of a Text?" *New Literary History* 14 (1982): 1-12.

Stroup, G. W. "A Bibliographical Critique." *ThTo* 32 (1975): 133-43.

Sturdy, John. "The Original Meaning of 'Is Saul also among the Prophets?' (1 Samuel X 11, 12, XIX 24)." *VT* 20 (1970): 206-13.

Swanson, R. N. *The Church and the Book: Papers Read at the 2000 Summer Meeting and the 2001 Winter Meeting of the Ecclesiastical History Society*. Rochester: Boydell and Brewer, 2004.

Sypeck, Jeff. *Becoming Charlemagne: Europe, Baghdad, and the Empires of A.D. 800*. New York: HarperCollins, 2007.

Tadmor, H., and M. Weinfeld, eds. *History, Historiography and Interpretation: Studies in Biblical and Cuneiform Literatures*. Jerusalem: Magnes, 1983.

Thelle, Rannfrid I. *Ask God: Divine Consultation in the Literature of the Hebrew Bible*. Beiträge zur biblischen Exegese und Theologie 30. Frankfurt: Lang, 2002.

Theobald, Gerd. "Von der Biblischen Theologie zur Buch-Theologie: das Hiobbuch als Vorspiel zu einer christlichen Hermeneutik." *NZSTR* 35 (1993): 276-302.

Thiel, Winfred. "Martin Noths Arbeit am Deuteronomistischen Geschichtswerk." Pp. 223-34 in *Kontexte: biografische und forschungsgeschichtliche Schnittpunkte der alttestamentlichen Wissenschaft; Festschrift für Hans Jochen Boecker zum 80. Geburtstag*. Edited by Kurt Erlemann, Dieter Vieweger, and Thomas Wagner. Neukirchen–Vluyn: Neukirchener, 2008.

Thiemann, Ronald. "Response to George Lindbeck." *ThTo* 43 (1986): 377-82.

Thompson, J. A. "The Significance of the Verb *Love* in the David-Jonathan Narratives in 1 Samuel." *VT* 24 (1975): 334-38.

Tollington, Janet. "The Ethics of Warfare and the Holy War Tradition in the Book of Judges." Pp. 71-87 in *Ethical and Unethical in the Old Testament: God and Humans in Dialogue*. Edited by Katharine J. Dell. LHBOTS 528. New York: T & T Clark, 2000.

Tompkins, Jane. *West of Everything: The Inner Life of Westerns*. Oxford: Oxford University Press, 1992.

Toorn, Karel van der. *Family Religion in Babylonia, Syria and Israel*. SHANE 7. Leiden: Brill, 1996.

———. "The Nature of the Biblical Teraphim in the Light of the Cuneiform Evidence." *CBQ* 52 (1990): 203-22.

———. "Saul and the Rise of Israelite State Religion." *VT* 43 (1993): 519-42.

Torgovnick, Marianna. *Closure in the Novel*. Princeton: Princeton University Press, 1981.

Tosato, Angelo. "La Colpa di Saul (1 Sam 15,22-23)." *Bib* 59 (1978): 251-59.

Tov, Emanuel. "The Composition of 1 Samuel 16–18 in the Light of the Septuagint Version." Pp. 97-130 in *Empirical Models for Biblical Criticism*. Edited by J. H. Tigay. Philadelphia: University of Pennsylvania Press, 1985.

———. "The Nature of Large-Scale Differences between the LXX and MT S T V, Compared with Similar Evidence from Qumran and the SP and with Reference to the Original Shape of the Bible." Pp. 121-44 in *The Earliest Text of the Hebrew Bible: The Relation between the Masoretic Text and the Hebrew Base of the Septuagint Reconsidered*. Edited by Adrian Schenker. SBLSCS 52. Leiden: Brill, 2003.

———. "Scribal Practices and Physical Aspects of the Dead Sea Scrolls." Pp. 9-33 in *The Bible as Book: The Manuscript Tradition*. Edited by John L. Sharpe III and Kimberly van Kampen. London: The British Library, 1998.

———. "Scribal Practices Reflected in the Documents from the Judean Desert and in the Rabbinic Literature: A Comparative Study." Pp. 383-403 in *Texts, Temples, and Traditions: A Tribute to Menahem Haran*. Edited by Michael V. Fox et al. Winona Lake: Eisenbrauns, 1996.

Trebolle Barrera, Julio C. "Origins of a Tripartite Old Testament Canon." Pp. 128-45 in *The Canon Debate*. Edited by Lee Martin McDonald and James A. Sanders. Peabody, MA: Hendrikson, 2002.

———. "The Story of David and Goliath (1 Sam 17–18): Textual Variants and Literary Composition." *BIOSCS* 23 (1990): 16-30.

Treier, Daniel. "Biblical Theology and/or Theological Interpretation of Scripture? Defining the Relationship." *SJT* 61 (2008): 16-31.

———. *Introducing Theological Interpretation of Scripture: Recovering a Christian Practice*. Grand Rapids: Baker, 2008.

Trible, Phyllis. *Texts of Terror: Literary-Feminist Readings of Biblical Narratives*. OBT. Philadelphia: Fortress, 1984.

Tropper, Josef. *Nekromantie: Totenbefragung im Alten Orient und im Alten Testament*. AOAT 223. Neukirchen–Vluyn: Neukirchener, 1989.

Bibliography

Tsevat, M. "Was Samuel a Nazirite?" Pp. 199-204 in *"Sha'arei Talmon": Studies in the Bible, Qumran, and the Ancient Near East Presented to Shemaryahu Talmon*. Edited by Michael Fishbane and Emanuel Tov. Winona Lake: Eisenbrauns, 1992.

Tsumura, David Toshio. *The First Book of Samuel*. NICOT. Grand Rapids: Eerdmans, 2007.

Tudor-Craig, Pamela. "Henry VIII and King David." Pp. 183-205 in *Early Tudor England: Proceedings of the 1987 Harlaxton Symposium*. Edited by Daniel Williams. Woodbridge: Boydell, 1989.

Uehlinger, Christoph. "Was There a Cult Reform Under King Josiah? The Case for a Well-grounded Minimum." Pp. 270-316 in *Good Kings and Bad Kings: The Kingdom of Judah in the Seventh Century BCE*. Edited by Lester L. Grabbe. LHBOTS 393. New York: T & T Clark, 2005.

Ullmann, Walter. "The Bible and Principles of Government in the Middle Ages." Pp. 181-227 in *La Bibbia nell'alto Medioevo: 26 Aprile–2 Maggio 1962*. Spoleto: Centro italiano di studi sull'alto Medioevo, 1963.

———. *The Carolingian Renaissance and the Idea of Kingship*. London: Methuen, 1969.

Ulrich, Eugene. "From Literature to Scripture: Reflections on the Growth of a Text's Authoritativeness." *DSD* 10 (2003): 3-25.

———. "A Qualitative Assessment of the Textual Profile of 4QSam^a." Pp. 147-61 in *Flores Florentino: Dead Sea Scrolls and Other Early Jewish Studies in Honour of Florentino García Martínez*. Edited by Anthony Hilhorst, Emile Puech, and Eibert Tigchelaar. JSJSup 122. Leiden: Brill, 2007.

———. *The Qumran Text of Samuel and Josephus*. HSM 19. Missoula: Scholars, 1978.

Urbach, Ephraim E. *The Sages: Their Concepts and Beliefs*. Translated by Israel Abrahams. Cambridge, MA: Harvard University Press, 1979.

Uspensky, Boris. *A Poetics of Composition: The Structure of the Artistic Text and Typology of a Compositional Form*. Translated by Valentina Zavarin and Susan Wittig. Berkeley: University of California Press, 1973.

Van Dam, Cornelis. *The Urim and Thummim: A Means of Revelation in Ancient Israel*. Winona Lake: Eisenbrauns, 1997.

VanderKam, James C. "Davidic Complicity in the Deaths of Abner and Eshbaal: A Historical and Redactional Study." *JBL* 99 (1980): 521-39.

———. *The Dead Sea Scrolls and the Bible*. Grand Rapids: Eerdmans, 2012.

———. *From Joshua to Caiaphas: High Priests after the Exile*. Minneapolis: Fortress, 2004.

VanGemeren, Willem. *The Progress of Redemption: The Story of Salvation from Creation to the New Jerusalem*. Grand Rapids: Baker Books, 1988.

Vannoy, J. Robert. *Covenant Renewal at Gilgal: A Study of 1 Samuel 11:14–12:25*. Cherry Hill, NJ: Mack Publishing Co., 1978.

Van Seters, John. *The Biblical Saga of King David*. Winona Lake: Eisenbrauns, 2009.

———. *In Search of History: Historiography in the Ancient World and the Origins of Biblical History*. New Haven: Yale University Press, 1983.

———. "Two Stories of David Sparing Saul's Life in 1 Samuel 24 and 26: A Question of Priority." *SJOT* 25 (2011): 93-104.

Van Sickle, John. "The Book-Roll and Some Conventions of the Poetic Books." *Arethusa* 13 (1980): 5-42.

Van Wijk-Bos, Johanna W. H. *Reading Samuel: A Literary and Theological Commentary*. Macon: Smyth & Helwys, 2011.

Vattioni, Francesco. "La necromanzia nell'Antico Testamento (1 Sam 28,3-25)." *Augustinianum* 3 (1963): 461-81.

Vaux, Roland de. *Ancient Israel: Its Life and Institutions.* Translated by Damian McHugh. New York: McGraw-Hill, 1961.

————. *The Bible and the Ancient Near East.* Translated by Damian McHugh. Garden City: Doubleday, 1971.

————. "Single Combat in the Old Testament." Pp. 122-35 in idem, *The Bible and the Ancient Near East.* Translated by Damian McHugh. Garden City: Doubleday, 1971.

Veijola, Timo. "David in Keïla: Tradition und Interpretation in 1 Sam 23,1-13." *RB* 91 (1984): 51-87.

————. "Deuteronomismusforschung zwischen Tradition und Innovation (III)." *TRev* (2003): 1-44.

————. *Die ewige Dynastie: David und die Entstehung seiner Dynastie nach der deuteronomistischen Darstellung.* Helsinki: Suomalainen Tiedeakatemia, 1975.

————. *Das Königtum in der Beurteilung der deuteronomistischen Historiographie: eine redaktionsgeschichtliche Untersuchungen.* Suomalaisen Tiedeakatemian Toimituksia; Annales Academiae Scientiarum Fennicae Series B 198. Helsinki: Suomalainen Tiedeakatemia, 1977.

Vermes, Geza. *Christian Beginnings: From Nazareth to Nicaea (A. D. 30–325).* London: Allen Lane, 2012.

Vette, Joachim. "Der letzte Richter? Methodische Überlegungen zur Charaktergestaltung in 1 Sam 11." *CV* 51 (2009): 184-97.

————. *Samuel und Saul: ein Beitrag zur narrativen Poetik des Samuelbuches.* BVB 13. Münster: LIT Verlag, 2005.

Viberg, Åke. "Saul Exposed by Irony: A New Understanding of 1 Samuel 15:27 Based on Two Symbolic Acts." *SEA* 70 (2005): 301-8.

Vogt, Peter T. "Centralization and Decentralization in Deuteronomy." Pp. 118-38 in *Interpreting Deuteronomy: Issues and Approaches.* Edited by David G. Firth and Philip S. Johnson. Downers Grove: IVP Academic, 2012.

————. *Deuteronomic Theology and the Significance of Torah: A Reappraisal.* Winona Lake: Eisenbrauns, 2006.

Vorländer, Hermann. *Mein Gott: die Vorstellungen vom persönlichen Gott im Alten Orient und im Alten Testament.* AOAT 23. Neukirchen–Vluyn: Neukirchener, 1975.

Wagner, David. *Geist und Tora: Studien zur göttlichen Legitimation und Delegitimation von Herrschaft im Alten Testament anhand der Erzählungen über König Saul.* ABG 15. Leipzig: Evangelische Verlagsanstalt, 2005.

Waldow, H. Eberhard von. "The Concept of War in the Old Testament." *HBT* 6 (1984): 27-48.

Wallace-Hadrill, J. M. *The Frankish Church.* Oxford: Clarendon, 1983.

Wallis, Jim. *Who Speaks for God? An Alternative to the Religious Right — A New Politics of Compassion, Community, and Civility.* New York: Delacorte, 1996.

Walsh, James. *The Mighty from Their Thrones.* OBT. Philadelphia: Fortress, 1987.

Walsh, Jerome T. *Old Testament Narrative: A Guide to Interpretation.* Louisville: Westminster John Knox, 2009.

————. *Style and Structure in Biblical Hebrew Narrative.* Collegeville: Liturgical, 2001.

Walters, Stanley D. "Hannah and Anna: The Greek and Hebrew Texts of 1 Samuel 1." *JBL* 107 (1988): 385-412.

————. "The Light and the Dark." Pp. 567-89 in *Ascribe to the Lord: Biblical and Other Essays in Memory of Peter C. Craigie*. JSOTSup 67. Edited by Lyle Eslinger and J. Glen Taylor. Sheffield: JSOT, 1988.

————. "Reading Samuel to Hear God." *CTJ* 37 (2002): 62-81.

————. "Saul of Gibeon." *JSOT* 52 (1991): 61-76.

Wansbrough, Henry. "The Jewish People and Its Holy Scripture in the Christian Bible." *ITQ* 67 (2002): 265-75.

Watson, Francis. *Text and Truth: Redefining Biblical Theology*. Grand Rapids: Eerdmans, 1997.

Watson, Nigel M. "Authorial Intention — Suspect Concept for Biblical Scholars." *ABR* 35 (1987): 6-13.

Watson, Wilfred G. E. "Hebrew Poetry." Pp. 253-85 in *Text in Context: Essays by Members of the Society for Old Testament Study*. Edited by A. D. H. Mayes. Oxford: Oxford University Press, 2000.

Weber, Stu. *Tender Warrior: Every Man's Purpose, Every Woman's Dream, Every Child's Hope*. 2nd ed. Sisters, OR: Multnomah, 2006.

Webster, John. *Domain of the Word: Scripture and Theological Reason*. London: T & T Clark, 2012.

————. *Word and Church: Essays in Dogmatics*. Edinburgh: T & T Clark, 2001.

Weeks, Noel K. *Sources and Authors: Assumptions in the Study of Hebrew Bible Narrative*. PHSC 12. Piscataway, NJ: Gorgias, 2011.

Weinfeld, Moshe. *Deuteronomy and the Deuteronomic School*. Oxford: Clarendon, 1972.

Weiser, Artur. "Die Legitimation des Königs David: zur Eigenart und Entstehung der sogenannten Geschichte von Davids Aufstieg." *VT* 16 (1966): 325-54.

Weiss, Andrea L. *Figurative Language in Biblical Prose Narrative: Metaphor in the Book of Samuel*. VTSup 107. Leiden: Brill, 2006.

Weitzman, Steven. "King David's Spin Doctors." *Prooftexts* 23 (2003): 365-75.

Welch, Adam C. *Kings and Prophets of Israel*. Edited by Norman C. Porteous. London: Lutterworth, 1952.

Welker, Michael. "Sola Scriptura? The Authority of the Bible in Pluralistic Environments." Pp. 375-91 in *A God So Near: Essays in Old Testament Theology in Honor of Patrick D. Miller*. Edited by Brent A. Strawn and N. R. Bowen. Winona Lake: Eisenbrauns, 2003.

Wellhausen, Julius. *Die Composition des Hexateuchs und der historischen Bücher des Alten Testaments*. 2nd ed. Berlin: Reimer, 1889.

————. *Prolegomena to the History of Israel*. Edinburgh: A. & C. Black, 1885. Repr. Atlanta: Scholars, 1994.

————. *Der Text der Bücher Samuelis untersucht*. Göttingen: Vandenhoeck & Ruprecht, 1871.

Wenham, Gordon J. "Were David's Sons Priests?" *ZAW* 87 (1975): 79-82.

Wénin, André. *David & Goliath: le récit de 1 Samuel 16–18*. Connaître la Bible 3. Brussels: Lumen Vitae, 1997.

————. "David roi, de Goliath à Bethsabée: la figure de David dans les livres de Samuel." Pp. 75-112 in *Figures de David à travers la Bible: XVIIᵉ Congèrs de l'ACFEB, Lille, 1ᵉʳ-5*. LD 177. Paris: Cerf, 1999.

————. "Le discours de Jonathan à David (1 Sam 20:12-16) et autres notes (2:20, 9:24, 15:9)." *Bib* 64 (1983): 1-19.

————. *Samuel et l'instauration de la monarchie (1 S 1–12): une recherché littéraire sur le personnage*. European University Studies; Series XXIII, Theology 342. Frankfurt: Lang, 1988.

Wesselius, Jan-Wim. "A New View on the Relation between Septuagint and Masoretic Text in the Story of David and Goliath." Pp. 5-26 in *Early Christian Literature and Intertextuality: Vol. 2, Exegetical Studies*. Edited by Craig A. Evans and H. Daniel Zacharias. LNTS 392. London: T & T Clark, 2009.

West, Dan C. "Beyond the Language of Monarchy." *Faith and Freedom* 65 (Spr–Sum 2012): 27-31.

Westermann, Claus. "Die Begriffe für Fragen und Suchen im Alten Testament." *KuD* 6 (1960): 2-30 = Pp. 162-90 in idem, *Forschung am Alten Testament: gesammelte Studien, Volume II*. TB 55. Gütersloh: Kaiser, 1974.

————. *Die Geschichtsbücher des Alten Testaments: gab es ein deuteronomistisches Geschichtswerk?* TB 87. Gütersloh: Kaiser, 1994.

Wevers, J. W. "1 Samuel." Pp. 155-69 in *The Interpreter's One-Volume Commentary on the Bible*. Edited by Charles M. Laymon. Nashville: Abingdon, 1971.

Whedbee, J. William. "On Divine and Human Bonds: The Tragedy of the House of David." Pp. 147-65 in *Canon, Theology, and Old Testament Interpretation: Essays in Honor of Brevard S. Childs*. Edited by Gene M. Tucker, David L. Petersen, and Robert R. Wilson. Philadelphia: Fortress, 1988.

White, Marsha C. "Saul and Jonathan in 1 Samuel 1 and 14." Pp. 119-38 in *Saul in Story and Tradition*. Edited by Carl S. Ehrlich with Marsha C. White. FAT 47. Tübingen: Mohr Siebeck, 2006.

————. "'The History of Saul's Rise': Saulide State Propaganda in 1 Samuel 1-14." Pp. 271-92 in *"A Wise and Discerning Mind": Essays in Honor of Burke O. Long*. Edited by Saul M. Olyan and Robert C. Culley. BJS 325. Providence: Society of Biblical Literature, 2000.

Whitelam, Keith W. "The Defence of David." *JSOT* 29 (1984): 61-87.

————. "Israelite Kingship: The Royal Ideology and Its Opponents." Pp. 119-39 in *The World of Ancient Israel: Sociological, Anthropological and Political Perspectives; Essays by Members of the Society for Old Testament Study*. Edited by R. E. Clements. Cambridge: Cambridge University Press, 1989.

————. "The Symbols of Power: Aspects of Royal Propaganda in the United Monarchy." *BA* (September, 1986): 166-73.

Whybray, R. N. *The Succession Narrative: A Study of II Samuel 9–20; I Kings 1 and 2*. SBT II/9. London: SCM, 1968.

Wielenga, Bill. "The Road to Endor: 1 Samuel 28." *Kerux* 20 (2005): 12-22.

Wiesel, Elie. *Five Biblical Portraits*. Notre Dame: University of Notre Dame Press, 1981.

Wilder, Amos N. "Holy Writ and Lit Crit." *The Christian Century* 107 (September 5-12, 1990): 790-91.

Willi-Plein, Ina. "1 Sam 18–19 und die Davidshausgeschichte." Pp. 138-71 in *David und Saul im Widerstreit — Diachronie und Synchronie im Wettstreit*. Edited by Walter Dietrich. OBO 206. Göttingen: Vandenhoeck & Ruprecht, 2004.

————. "Frauen um David: Beobachtungen zur Davidshausgeschichte." Pp. 349-61 in *Meilenstein: Festschrift für Herbert Donner zum 16. Februar 1995*. Edited by Manfred Weippert and Stefan Timm. AAT 30. Wiesbaden: Harrassowitz, 1995.

————. "Michal und die Anfänge des Königtums in Israel." Pp. 401-19 in *Congress Volume: Cambridge 1995*. Edited by J. A. Emerton. VTSup 66. Leiden: Brill, 1997.

————. *Opfer und Kult im alttestamentlichen Israel*. SB 153. Stuttgart: Katholisches Bibelwerk, 1993.

Williams, David M. *Receiving the Bible in Faith: Historical and Theological Exegesis*. Washington, DC: Catholic University of America Press, 2004.

Williams, Peter J. "Is God Moral? On the Saul Narratives as Tragedy." Pp. 175-89 in *The God of Israel*. Edited by Robert P. Gordon. University of Cambridge Oriental Publications 64. Cambridge: University of Cambridge Press, 2007.

Williams, R. J. "Writing and Writing Materials." Pp. 909-21 in *IDB*, vol. 4.

Willis, John T. "Cultic Elements in the Story of Samuel's Birth and Dedication." *ST* 26 (1972): 33-61.

——. "The Function of Comprehensive Anticipatory Redactional Joints in 1 Samuel 16–18." *ZAW* 85 (1973): 294-314.

——. "Samuel versus Eli, I. Sam. 1–7." *TZ* 35 (1979): 201-12.

Willis-Watkins, David. "Calvin's Prophetic Reinterpretation of Kingship." Pp. 116-34 in *Probing the Reformed Tradition: Historical Studies in Honor of Edward A. Dowey, Jr.* Edited by Elsie Anne McKee and Brian G. Armstrong. Louisville: Westminster John Knox, 1989.

Wilson, Emily R. *Mocked with Death: Tragic Overliving from Sophocles to Milton.* Baltimore: Johns Hopkins University Press, 2004.

Wilson, Ian. *Out of the Midst of the Fire: Divine Presence in Deuteronomy.* SBLDS 151. Atlanta: Scholars, 1995.

Wilson, Robert R. "Prophecy and Ecstasy: A Reexamination." *JBL* 98 (1979): 321-37.

——. *Prophecy and Society in Ancient Israel.* Philadelphia: Fortress, 1980.

——. "Who Was the Deuteronomist? (Who Was Not the Deuteronomist?): Reflections on Pan-Deuteronomism." Pp. 67-82 in *Those Elusive Deuteronomists: The Phenomenon of Pan-Deuteronomism.* Edited by Linda S. Schearing and Steven L. McKenzie. JSOTSup 268. Sheffield: Sheffield Academic, 1999.

Wilson, Stephen M. *Making Men: The Male Coming-of-Age Theme in the Hebrew Bible.* Oxford: Oxford University Press, 2015.

Witte, John, Jr. "Facts and Fictions About the History of Separation of Church and State." *Journal of Church and State* 48 (2006): 15-46.

Wojcik, Jan. "Discriminations against David's Tragedy in Ancient Jewish and Christian Literature." Pp. 12-35 in *The David Myth in Western Literature.* Edited by Raymond-Jean Frontain and Jan Wojcik. West Lafayette: Purdue University Press, 1980.

——. "Transformations of the Myth of David." Pp. 1-10 in *The David Myth in Western Literature.* Edited by Raymond-Jean Frontain and Jan Wojcik. West Lafayette: Purdue University Press, 1980.

Wolde, E. van. "A Leader Led by a Lady: David and Abigail in 1 Samuel 25." *ZAW* 114 (2002): 355-75.

Wolfe, Christopher, ed. *The Naked Public Square Reconsidered: Religion and Politics in the Twenty-First Century.* Wilmington: ISI, 2009.

Wolterstorff, Nicholas. "Reading Joshua." Pp. 236-56 in *Divine Evil? The Moral Character of the God of Abraham.* Edited by Michael Bergmann, Michael J. Murry, and Michael C. Rea. Oxford: Oxford University Press, 2011.

——. "The Unity behind the Canon." Pp. 217-32 in *One Scripture or Many? Canon from Biblical, Theological, and Philosophical Perspectives.* Edited by Christine Helmer and Christof Landmesser. Oxford: Oxford University Press, 2004.

Wong, Gregory T. K. "A Farewell to Arms: Goliath's Death as Rhetoric against Faith in Arms." *BBR* 23 (2013): 43-55.

Wootton, Janet. "The Monstrosity of David." Pp. 110-27 in *Patriarchs, Prophets and Other Villains.* Edited by Lisa Isherwood. Gender, Theology, and Spirituality. London: Equinox, 2007.

Woźniak, Jerzy. "Drei verschiedene literarische Beschreibungen des Bundes zwischen Jonathan und David." *BZ* 27 (1983): 213-18.

Wright, Jacob L. "Military Valor and Kingship: A Book-Oriented Approach to the Study of a Major War Theme." Pp. 33-56 in *Writing and Reading War: Rhetoric, Gender, and Ethics in Biblical and Modern Contexts*. Edited by Brad E. Kelle and Frank Ritchel Ames. SBLSS 42. Atlanta: Society of Biblical Literatures, 2008.

Wyatt, Nicolas. "Degrees of Divinity: Some Mythical and Ritual Aspects of West Semitic Kingship." Pp. 191-220 in *"There's such Divinity doth Hedge a King": Selected Essays of Nicolas Wyatt on Royal Ideology in Ugaritic and Old Testament Literature*. SOTSM. Burlington: Ashgate, 2005 = *UF* 31 (1999): 853-87.

———. "Royal Religion in Ancient Judah." Pp. 61-81 in *Religious Diversity in Ancient Israel and Judah*. Edited by Francesca Stavrakopoulou and John Barton. London: T & T Clark, 2010.

Wyschograd, Michael. "Judaism, the Political, and the Monarchy." Pp. 129-42 in *Covenant and Hope, Christian and Jewish Reflections: Essays in Constructive Theology from the Institute for Theological Inquiry*. Edited by Robert W. Jenson and Eugene B. Korn. Grand Rapids: Eerdmans, 2012.

———. "A King in Israel." *First Things* 203 (May, 2010): 48-50.

Yadin, Azzan. "Goliath's Armor and Israelite Collective Memory." *VT* 54 (2004): 373-95.

Yarchin, William. "Text Criticism, Text Composition, and Text Concept in 2 Samuel 23 and 24." Pp. 310-30 in *Reading the Hebrew Bible for a New Millennium: Form, Concept, and Theological Perspective; Volume 2: Exegetical and Theological Studies*. Edited by Wonil Kim et al. Harrisburg, PA: Trinity, 2000.

Yoder, John Howard. "Exodus and Exile: The Two Faces of Liberation." *Cross Currents* 23 (1973): 297-309.

———. *For the Nations: Essays Public and Evangelical*. Grand Rapids: Eerdmans, 1997.

———. *The Jewish–Christian Schism Revisted*. Edited by Michael G. Cartwright and Peter Ochs. Scottdale, PA: Herald, 2008.

———. *The Original Revolution: Essays on Christian Pacifism*. Scottdale, PA: Herald, 1977.

———. *Preface to Theology: Christology and Theological Method*. Grand Rapids: Brazos, 2002.

Yonick, Stephen. *Rejection of Saul as King of Israel According to 1 Sm 15: Stylistic Study in Theology*. Jerusalem: Franciscan, 1970.

Yoreh, Tzemah. "Van Seters' Saga of King David." *JANER* 10 (2010): 103-14.

Younger, K. Lawson. "Some Recent Discussion on the Ḥērem." Pp. 505-22 in *Far from Minimal: Celebrating the Work and Influence of Philip R. Davies*. Edited by Duncan Burns and J. W. Rogerson. LHBOTS 484. London: T & T Clark, 2012.

Zakovich, Yair. *The Concept of the Miracle in the Bible*. Translated by Shmuel Himelstein. Tel Aviv: MOD, 1990.

Zeelander, Susan. *Closure in Biblical Narrative*. BibInt 111. Leiden: Brill, 2012.

Zehnder, Markus. "Exegetische Beobachtungen zu den David-Jonathan-Geschichten." *Bib* 79 (1998): 153-79.

———. "Observations on the Relationship between David and Jonathan and the Debate on Homosexuality." *WTJ* 69 (2007): 127-74.

Zenger, Erich. *Das Erste Testament: die jüdische Bibel und die Christen*. Dusseldorf: Patmos, 1991.

———. "Was sind Essentials eines theologischen Kommentars zum Alten Testament?" Pp. 213-38 in *Theologie und Exegese des Alten Testaments/der Hebräischen Bibel: Zwischenbilanz und Zukunftsperspektiven*. SB 200. Stuttgart: Katholisches Bibelwerk, 2005.

Bibliography

Zevit, Ziony. *The Religions of Ancient Israel: A Synthesis of Parallactic Approaches.* New York: Continuum, 2001.

Ziegler, Yael. *Promises to Keep: The Oath in Biblical Narrative.* VTSup 120. Leiden: Brill, 2008.

Zorn, Jeffrey. "Reconsidering Goliath: An Iron Age I Philistine Chariot Warrior." *BASOR* 360 (2010): 1-22.

Zwickel, Wolfgang. "Dagons abgeschlagener Kopf (1 Samuel v 3-4)." *VT* 44 (1994): 239-49.

Index of Authors

322

Index of Authors

Index of Authors

Gadamer, Hans-Georg, 236n89
Galling, Kurt, 154n98
Gamble, Harry Y., 39n81
Garbini, Giovanni, 220n18
Garsiel, Moshe, 15, 28n32, 131n29, 158n115, 188n38, 224n37
Gehrig, Gail, 17n49
Genette, Gérard, 43n99
Gentile, Emilio, 17n49
Geoffrey of Monmouth, 176n17
George, Mark K., 153n97
Gerdmar, Anders, 8n25
Giercke-Ungermann, Annett, 136n46
Gilmour, Rachelle, 105n97, 220n19
Gitay, Yehoshua, 90n57
Gladwell, Malcolm, 158n115
Gnuse, Robert K., 86n47
Godman, Peter, 250n144
Goheen, Michael W., 23n10
Gordis, Robert, 2n4
Gordon, Robert P., 63n177, 190n48, 193n56, 247n132
Gorman, Michael, 2n6
Gosselin, Edward A., 246n127, 247nn130-31, 251n148
Gottlieb, Isaac B., 66n183
Grabbe, Lester L., 23n8
Gregory of Nyssa, 203n83
Green, Barbara, 188n39
Green, Joel B., 2n4, 22n6
Greenberg, Moshe, 2n4, 227n51
Greenspoon, Leonard J., 14n42
Greenwood, Kyle R., 53n138
Gros Louis, Kenneth R. R., 61n172, 156n106
Guinness, Os, 16n48
Gunn, David M., 15, 18n53, 28n32, 33n52, 42n96, 60n167, 63n177, 108n107, 138n52, 141-42, 147n78, 169n143, 219n12, 237-38, 239nn99,101, 251
Gutteridge, Richard, 8n24

Hagan, Harry, 2n4
Hahn, Scott W., 52n133
Hall, John A., 16n48
Hall, Joseph, 82, 86-87, 88n53, 148, 159n119

Hall, Sarah Lebhard, 72n7
Halliburton, John, 250n144
Hallie, Philip, 8n25
Hallo, William W., 109n109
Halpern, Baruch, 218n7, 220n16
Hamilton, Mark W., 54n142, 122n8, 147n80, 149n86, 161n126, 166n137, 211n101
Hanson, Paul D., 50n119
Haran, Menahem, 39-41, 166n138
Harden, Jamie M., 16n48
Harding, James E., 169n143, 170n144, 259n179
Hardmeier, Christof, 22n29
Harnack, Adolf von, 6, 24n12
Harrington, Daniel J., 22n6
Harrison, Timothy P., 223n34
Harvey, Graham, 201n74
Hatch, Nathan O., 17n49
Hauerwas, Stanley, 256n168
Hawk, L. Daniel, 134nn38-39
Hawkins, Ralph K., 104n94
Hays, Richard B., 2n4, 236n90
Heacock, Anthony, 169n143
Heither, Theresia, 248n135
Helfgot, Nathaniel, 145n71
Heller, Roy L., 13, 102n88, 106n102
Hendel, Ronald, 153n94
Herbst, Susan, 16n48
Heringer, Seth, 2n4
Herkommer, Hubert, 250n143
Hertzberg, Hans Wilhelm, 254n158
Herzfeld, Shmuel, 58n160, 209n95
Heym, Stefan, 218n7
Hill, Robert C., 254n159
Ho, Craig Y. S., 153n94
Hobbs, R. Gerald, 249n140
Hoffmann, H.-D., 221n23
Holcomb, Justin S., 22n6
Hollenstein, Helmut, 222n29
Holzer, Vincent, 5n14
Horner, Tom, 169n143
Housman, A. E., 2
Hoyle, James, 54n142
Hubbard, Robert L., Jr., 23n10
Hubmaier, Balthasar, 97n73
Huffmon, Herbert G., 56n151

325

Index of Authors

Index of Authors

Index of Subjects

Index of Scripture and Other Ancient Sources